This study of the Irish nationalist move-
ment has a double purpose: to examine the
social forces behind the ceaseless agitation
in Ireland from the 18th to the 20th century,
and to give an account of the remarkable
influence of the Irish question on the
political development of Great Britain.

The main body of the work is devoted
to an analysis of the forces which moulded
Irish and English history during the period
1801-1921. In particular the author shows
in what way Irish problems affected the
important developments of English history
during the last century and a half: religious
toleration, the Great Reform Bill, the
Repeal of the Corn Laws, the growth of the
modern party system, and the Parliament Act
of 1911 which crippled the House of Lords
and firmly established British democracy.

The author, an Austrian by birth, is
personally free from the emotional bias
which distorts so many books on Anglo-
Irish relations; and he is careful to bear in
mind the importance of relating the social,
political and even religious facts of Irish
history to the economic background.

IRISH NATIONALISM
AND BRITISH DEMOCRACY

IRISH NATIONALISM AND BRITISH DEMOCRACY

by
E. STRAUSS

From the divisions of Irish society,
the chief obstacles to Irish freedom arise.
T. F. Meagher[1]

METHUEN & CO., LTD., LONDON
36 Essex Street, Strand, W.C.2

First Published in 1951

CATALOGUE NO. 5367/U

PRINTED IN GREAT BRITAIN

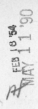

PREFACE

WHAT used to be called 'The Irish Question' has suffered the inevitable eclipse of all problems which have held the centre of the public stage for a long time. The hatreds and enthusiasms of the previous generation appear quaint and faintly ridiculous when their causes have disappeared, and nothing is less interesting than the attempt to rake up the embers of old controversies.

The following study has been written in the belief that this barren approach to a great problem threatens to obscure a story of vital importance to modern British history and, perhaps, to modern history in general. Its main purpose is a realistic interpretation of the sinister and often tragic, but always intensely interesting, chain of events which forged lasting links between two such very different nations as the English and the Irish, not to mention the Scots.

The subject of this book is, therefore, neither the history of Ireland nor that of Great Britain but the nexus between the two countries, particularly during the time of the Legislative Union of 1801–1921. It is neither a restatement of Ireland's wrongs, grievous as they have been, nor an apologia for England's historical mission. This does not imply a refusal to express opinions, nor the assumption of scientific objectivity as a cloak for moral cowardice, but judgment and criticism have been related as closely as possible to the part played by groups and individuals in the historical process in which they moved, and not to a national or a party point of view. This was, perhaps, comparatively easy for an observer who combines warm sympathy for the Irish struggle against national oppression and economic exploitation with genuine respect for the results of British political development, but who is personally free from the instinctive emotional bias which distorts so many books on Anglo-Irish relations.

If in this study the accent lies mainly on *Ireland*'s influence on *British* society, *British* politics and the *British* Constitution, this is not only due to the curious neglect of this factor in most of the abundant literature on the subject but also to the fact that the author's interest was first attracted to the problem of Ireland in the course of a study of party politics in the United States and Great Britain. Even the most superficial acquaintance with the American party structure reveals the prominent part played by Irish-Americans in the great city machines, particularly on the Democratic side, but this influence, however impressive, is in principle similar to that of other national

v

or pressure groups and falls naturally into the broad pattern of American politics.

If the Irish share in American politics strikingly illustrates the uncanny powers of assimilation of American society, Irish influence on British politics always remained not only hostile but curiously external, even when it acted on the very centre of British political life in the House of Commons. At the same time this influence was temporarily so strong that its analysis is essential for the complete understanding of the course of British history during the nineteenth century and beyond.

The interpretation of history is much more intimately connected with matters of personal philosophy than the simple narrative of events. It would, therefore, be too much to expect that this book will be generally accepted as a valid solution of the question with which it deals, and partisans on both sides of the old Anglo-Irish controversy may well object to some of its conclusions. In addition, the use of detailed economic analysis for the explanation of social and political developments stands at present definitely at a discount in English-speaking countries. There is no need to discuss in this place the general issue, but it is pertinent to observe that no realistic view of Irish history can make much headway without relating social, political and even religious facts to the economic background. Perhaps the most uncompromising version of what would commonly be called the 'Marxist' interpretation of Irish history has, indeed, been given by Mr. Ian Colvin, the biographer of the Ulster leader Lord Carson, who went so far as to insist that '"Irish Nationalism" was in reality a class-war, directed by the lower against the upper elements of society' (*Life of Lord Carson*, III, 441). Without sharing this opinion completely, and still more without accepting it as an alternative to the patient unravelling of the complex thread of events, such a statement by a writer who cannot be accused of sympathy with the rebellious 'lower elements of society' is valuable evidence of the plain language of the facts which no serious student of the problem can ignore.

Both the plan of the work and inevitable limitations on space have made it necessary to reduce quotations and notes to a minimum. Full documentation is, of course, essential in a historical mono-graph which deals with a limited subject in all its aspects. The present study attempts to cover a much wider field by concentrating on its most significant features. To this extent it is inevitably one-sided—and its justification must be sought in the exceptional importance of the special aspect which it reveals and in the (comparative) neglect of this aspect in most other books on Anglo-Irish relations. References to generally accepted facts seemed to be out of place in a work of this kind and, with few exceptions, notes refer mainly to direct quotations which illustrate salient points particularly clearly or which form a necessary part of the argument.

This method has also involved the loss of much historical detail, some merely curious, some deeply interesting at least to the author, which the historian can ill afford to miss when he tries to paint a large-scale picture of a period. The present study cannot claim to be such a picture but, at best, a cartographer's survey, and the author must be satisfied with the knowledge that people turn to the map when they want to know where a road comes from—and where it leads to.

E. STRAUSS

CONTENTS

Book V

CONTRASTS AND PARALLELS

Book 1. England's First Colony

CHAPTER I

AMERICA AND IRELAND: SETTLEMENT
AND CONQUEST

THE modern British Empire is not a uniform structure; it comprises countries of the most varied geographical and economic character, peoples of many colours, races and creeds, and political systems which have little or nothing in common with one another except voluntary or compelled allegiance to the British Crown—and even this bond will in future no longer be required in order to remain a full member of the Commonwealth. This astounding and impressive variety of results has been mainly due to the working of two fundamental, and in the long run incompatible, trends in the course of British overseas expansion—conquest and settlement.

The Commonwealth of self-governing dominions was until recently confined to Great Britain and to nations whose growth was the result of emigration from the British Isles. Force and conquest certainly played some part in the development of these modern nations: Australia was first peopled by British convicts whose real crime was often their refusal to accept the social system and the callous lack of social conscience of the rulers of eighteenth- and early nineteenth-century Britain. Canada was conquered by the sword, and the same is true of an important section of the Union of South Africa. But the subsequent development of all these dominions demonstrated their growing independence of the coercive powers of the British Government, until today they have become to all intents and purposes sovereign nations, governed by their own dominant interests which shape their destinies according to their own wishes and without enforced compliance with instructions by the government of the mother country.

The development of these self-governing members of the Commonwealth of Nations is in sharp contrast to the character and position of the dependent Empire. British colonial rule, though undergoing at present far-reaching changes, is based on the primary fact of armed acquisition and compulsory retention of the dependent territories. Some colonies were wrested by force from the native inhabitants themselves, while others were taken over by the British from other conquerors as the result of wars often fought in different quarters of the globe. The common quality of all parts of the dependent Empire is not to be found in any formal constitutional arrangement but in the decisive power of the British Government to enforce its will through the medium of the existing administration.

The foremost representatives of the two different trends of British overseas expansion are no longer within the orbit of British power. The United States of America, the greatest if somewhat involuntary product of British colonisation, has long since relinquished its association with the British Empire. India, the richest prize won by British lust for conquest, has at long last obtained formal freedom in a manner which is striking evidence of the change in the position of her erstwhile rulers, although the wounds of her unhappy history still remain to be healed.

Ireland differs from all other parts of the British Empire, past and present, by the intimate blend of conquest and settlement which distinguished her relations with Great Britain. These two factors have, indeed, produced remarkably different results within the limits of a comparatively small island. The Republic of Ireland, comprising the majority of its population and most of the modern descendants of the 'Irish enemies' of medieval times, has severed its links with the British Commonwealth, while in north-east Ulster a community governed mainly by the descendants of Scottish and English colonists remains part of the United Kingdom against the stubborn opposition of a strong nationalist minority.

A comparison between the United States and present-day Ireland would be so incongruous as to appear irrelevant, but things were very different during the earliest stages of British overseas expansion.

The beginnings of modern 'plantations' in Ireland under Queen Mary and Queen Elizabeth approximately coincided with the first voyages of exploration to North America by British seafarers, while the plantation of Ulster was contemporary with the colonisation of Virginia and the clearance of New England soil by the Pilgrim Fathers. To compare the plantation of Virginia with the plantation of Ulster appeared to Francis Bacon as absurd as a comparison between Amadis de Gaul and Caesar's Commentaries.[2] At the time of the American Revolution the population of the thirteen colonies was still substantially smaller than that of Ireland. Although the potentialities of the American colonies were bound to transform them ultimately into a much more powerful nation than the inhabitants of a small island without important natural resources, the breath-taking progress of the United States and the stagnation of Ireland reflect at least to some extent the effects of two fundamentally different social systems.

Ireland was the first substantial object in the Western world of those forces which have been vaguely but suggestively described as 'imperialist'. It was conquered by force, held by force, lost by force. Conquest and plunder are, of course, much older than Strongbow and Henry II and the peculiarity of modern imperialism lies in the combination of these age-old practices with the aims and purposes of modern capitalism. The eastern seaboard of the North American continent, on the other hand, has been the scene of a brilliantly successful movement of colonisation and settlement. In this process force played a far from negligible part, but it was not the source of its great success.

The 'undertaker' who took up Irish property in thousands or tens of thousands of acres was not a colonist in the same sense as the small farmer who left his old country together with his family in search of a livelihood—and of political and religious freedom. The adventurer or undertaker was generally a representative of the very social order from which the settler wanted to escape, and his share in a plantation was simply a money matter, a financial speculation. As far as he had any clear ideas about the government of the 'dependency' where his land happened to be, he envisaged it as a smale-scale imitation of the English system, with the King and his Privy Council represented by a Governor and Council, advised by an assembly of the most substantial landholders, and a local edition of the Established Church as its spiritual arm.

Colonies organised in this manner also flourished along a wide stretch of the American seaboard, and to the official mind they may have seemed to be the only type of colonial possession which really mattered. But behind this façade in the coastal region with its reproduction of English institutions and its domination by wealthy planters and merchants, a colonial society of an entirely different stamp was slowly reaching maturity. North America exerted a powerful pull on many of the most virile elements of the British people, not because it offered them a copy of English conditions but because of the very incompleteness of this copy. The relative weakness of the landlords and their government, temporal and spiritual, made America the land of promise for tens of thousands and induced them to leave everything behind in order to start a new life in the New World.

Behind the coastal belt, where slaveholders ruled in the South and landowners and merchants in the North, stretched an infinite expanse of unsettled free soil. This freedom was, of course, only relative because it completely disregarded the original 'owners' and inhabitants. The settlers were resolved, if not to ignore the Red Indians, which was impossible, at least to treat them simply as a pest which had to be exterminated like other pests if the land was to bear its full harvest. Instead of a life of permanent drudgery in the service of proud and exacting landowners, instead of narrow-minded persecution by the Established Church in the old country, every able-bodied and resolute immigrant could look forward, after a few years of service as a labourer, to becoming his own master on his own farm, and to worshipping God in the manner most agreeable to his conscience.

In North America colonisation in this true sense of the application of a more efficient productive technique to a country where this had not been practised before, and for the purpose of transforming the immigrants into permanent residents, was comparatively easy. The Red Indians were unable to prevent the better armed and better organised intruders from settling on the vast tracts of fertile soil and from becoming independent colonists with their own rough-and-ready scheme of social life, out of reach of the ruling powers of their old countries. By this process the American colonies received citizens of an extraordinarily good character, tough, self-reliant, independent and efficient; they were further tempered by the rigid natural selection of backwoods life, with its hard conditions and the gruesome test of incessant frontier wars against the dispossessed Red Indians.

The American colonies thus grew into countries of a new, and in many ways superior type with an exceptionally vital social organisation, though with all the surface blemishes inseparable from 'new' countries. The British plantation in Ireland, on the other hand, never outgrew its original conception and in many ways failed to fulfil even the limited expectations of its founders. This was the more surprising as Ireland seemed to present the colonists with most of the opportunities without many of the disadvantages of America. Sir William Petty, the father of modern economic science and a man with an outstanding grasp of economic matters, was not a little impatient of the unreasonable preference for North America shown by the most desirable colonists; and as he had a substantial stake in Irish land, this was only natural: 'In New England there are vast numbers of able bodyed *Englishmen*, employed chiefly in Husbandry, and in the meanest part of it (which is breeding of Cattle) whereas Ireland would have contained all those persons, and at worst would have afforded them lands on better terms than they have them in America, if not some other better Trade withal than they now can have.'[3] Froude, the literary spokesman of the English Tories in the second half of the nineteenth century, spoke of Ireland as an America at the very door of England, 'with the soil ready for the plough',[4] but in spite of this happy coincidence there was only a very small measure of genuine colonisation by the English in Ireland (although the Ulster plantation produced a thriving

Scottish settlement), while thousands of young Englishmen flocked to the American colonies.

Was the failure of English colonisation in Ireland due to the determined resistance of the natives? There is no doubt that the Irish did their best to shake off the rule of the intruders and to regain the ownership of their lands. Irish history from the middle of the sixteenth to the end of the seventeenth century is nothing but a record of these struggles. But the hostility of the Irish towards the English and Scottish usurpers in their midst, though determined, deep-rooted and at times violent, was neither more bitter, more tenacious nor more effective than that of the Red Indians towards the white settlers. Yet the Indians did not succeed in deterring the colonists from pushing deeper and deeper into their hunting grounds. After crossing the Atlantic in conditions of acute discomfort and considerable danger, after spending years of hard work in the existing settlements near the coast, the squatters went out into the wilderness in order to carve their homesteads out of the primeval forest and to defend them against the Red Indians in a war where quarter was neither asked nor given. As a matter of historical fact, a good many of these squatters were Ulster Scots who left their adoptive homelands in order to escape the excesses of their landlords and the intolerance of the Established Church. Colonisation in Ireland was not nearly so difficult or so dangerous, but it nevertheless lagged far behind the colonisation of America.

The hostility of the Irish towards the immigrants, though ever-present, remained for decades deep under the surface and cannot have been the cause of the comparative failure of colonising efforts. This was, on the contrary, due to the economic competition of the native inhabitants with the immigrants—a factor which was completely missing in the New World. Both in America and in Ireland genuine colonisation was invariably accompanied by ruthless expulsion of the previous occupiers which on the slightest provocation degenerated into naked extermination. The American backwoods men, however democratic in their dealings amongst themselves, however godfearing and pious some of them in their religious beliefs, were without exception convinced of the necessity, or even the righteousness, of destroying the Red Devils by all means, by powder, whisky or disease. Cromwell, by far the greatest of the English colonisers of Ireland, was also the most reckless and ruthless enemy of the Irish. The alternative of 'Connaught or Hell', the choice between exile into the wildest and most barren part of the country and extermination, was an apt expression of the attitude of 'civilised' colonists towards 'backward' races which dared to oppose the progress of civilisation.

Imperialism, in contrast to colonisation, is not confined to the acquisition of the soil; its main object is not the settlement of a country but the subjection of a people in the interests of the conquerors. However unscrupulous towards subject peoples who fail to recognise his superiority and the hopelessness of resistance, the imperialist conqueror is not out to kill the goose that lays the golden eggs. Ireland possessed such a subject people while America did not, and its existence ultimately frustrated the attempts to settle the whole country in a similar manner in which large parts of North America were settled. On the other hand, it proved an attractive aim for Elizabethan and Jacobean 'adventurers' eager for the tribute which could be extracted from the 'Irish enemies'.

In spite of repeated violent outbreaks which belong to the same class as peasant wars in all feudal systems, from Wat Tyler's rising in England and the French *Jacquerie* to the German *Bauernkrieg* and Pugachev's rebellion in Russia, the mass of the Irish peasants was prepared to settle down under their new rulers as they had done under the old, provided they were allowed to do so. It is a commonplace of Irish history to read of extensive grants of land on condition that only British colonists should be allowed to settle and to learn that this condition was flagrantly broken from the start because Irish tenants were willing to pay extortionate rents for the privilege of making a bare living on land which their fathers had cultivated for generations. The most spectacular case of this kind was the long-drawn-out quarrel between the City of London, as 'undertaker' of the Londonderry Plantation, and the Crown which used the violation of the city's pledge to banish all native tenants as a welcome pretext for mulcting the wealthiest corporation in the country for the benefit of Charles I's ever-empty exchequer.

Successive conquests, rebellions and reconquests took a frightful toll of suffering from the people without breaking its tenacious hold on the soil. Through periods of quick changes in the legal ownership of the land they continued their downtrodden existence as the lowest layer of the social pyramid whose full weight they had to bear. A country inhabited by a nation whose only possessions were, in Cobbett's phrase, 'potatoes and paws' was not a very attractive place for people at least used to 'oatmeal and brose and horn spoons', and still less for aristocrats with 'meat and bread and knives and forks'. English colonists who wanted to escape the rule of the landlord and parson in their own country and to build themselves new homesteads and communities had every reason to prefer the long and dangerous voyage across the Atlantic Ocean to the short journey across the Irish Sea.

In comparing the free settlements in the United States with the imperialist conquest of Ireland it should not be implied that America was completely free from the influences which made life for the Irish people hell on earth. While the backwoods men were bent on the complete extermination of the native races, the landowners in the rich coastal region strongly felt the inconvenience of the unappropriated open spaces which deprived them of their supply of labour. Their remedy was, of course, the use of African slaves who were acquired by the undisguised use of force and who came to form the basis of southern economy and society. However spectacular in its methods, the hunt for negroes in West Africa and their importation into America for the purpose of keeping their masters by the product of their labour, was an imperialist conquest. Thus the contrast between Ireland and America, between conquest and settlement, was reproduced within the United States in the contrast, and later on in the irrepressible conflict, between the slave-holding South and the free North and West. Although the ensuing war ended with the complete overthrow of the slave-owners, the negro problem still remains with the American people as a fateful legacy from its imperialist ancestors.

CHAPTER II

THE ANGLO-IRISH LAND SYSTEM

THE social structure of colonial Ireland was the result of a whole series of wars, followed by large-scale expropriations of the landed proprietors. Plantations and dispossessions played havoc with previously existing property rights and with established social relationships, until around the year 1700 the overwhelming bulk of Irish landed property was in the hands of landlords who were almost without exception Protestants and very often in no sense of the word Irishmen.

The relations between landlord and tenant under the Irish system were radically different from those prevailing in England, and the difference was grotesquely emphasised by the fact that the law was substantially the same in both countries. The law recognised all kinds of feudal limitations, like entail and primogeniture, which aimed at the maintenance of large estates in the hands of the great proprietors. On the other hand, the actual occupier was recognised by the law only when he was protected by a legal contract, mainly in the form of a lease. This legal theory was even in England as much a policy as a statement of facts, but it was particularly ill adapted for a country with a population consisting mainly of very small and poor peasants without any legal English title to the land they were occupying. The typical Irish peasant depended on his acre of potato land supplemented by the keeping of a pig and, perhaps, a cow for his year-to-year existence. The occupation of this plot of ground was for him not the subject of a commercial bargain with his landlord but a matter of life and death.

The legal fictions of the Anglo-Irish lawyers disguised and distorted the underlying social state of things. The Irish landlord was not a modern landed proprietor on the English model, but a feudal lord of the manor, minus his habitual residence. The mass of the Irish people could not be likened to free yeomen or tenants in search of suitable opportunities for the most profitable use of their labour and capital who formed the backbone of rural England; they were half-starved peasants. In eighteenth-century England, agricultural production, profit and rents bore some relationship to the state of the market and the price of agricultural produce. The relationship was far from definite and complete, but a steadily growing proportion of actual occupiers intentionally produced food and raw materials for the constantly expanding market. Although Irish agriculture was subject in an even higher degree to the vagaries of the market and to the effects of agricultural policy, the overwhelming majority of the occupiers of the soil lived on the insufficient produce of their tiny plots of land, and the possession of a small potato garden was for them a condition of survival.

Whatever the legal view of the matter, in its social reality there was much less similarity between the relation of the Irish landed proprietors and their tenants and that of their English counterparts than between Irish squires and Russian, Polish or Prussian landlords and between Irish tenants and continental serfs. The difference between Irish and continental feudalism consisted in the form of the tribute which the masses rendered their masters. In the backward agrarian states of Central and Eastern Europe the landlord's share in the produce of the ground was as a rule demanded, and frequently actually consumed, in kind. The landlord depended for his income on the possession of the largest possible number of serfs and on the surplus of their output over their own minimum requirements. This primitive feudalism was therefore invariably undermined by the growth of a money economy and the development of an internal market for foodstuffs, which in due course led to the abolition of serfdom and its replacement by a more or less modern agrarian organisation. In Ireland, on the other hand, a feudal social system was linked by the strongest possible ties, the material interests of its rulers, to a fully developed market and money economy.

From the point of view of the Irish landlords of all types, the extortion of the highest possible rental was the root problem of Irish economy. Having acquired the title deeds of Ireland by fair means or foul, and more often than not in the course of financial speculations, they wanted to make their property pay in terms of hard cash. Even if they had been willing to imitate the policy of the English landlords, who endeavoured to let large farms with all suitable improvements to wealthy tenants in actual occupation of the land, they would have found this very difficult in practice. The series of wars and revolutions during the seventeenth century eliminated most or all substantial native landholders. The new class of middlemen which sprang up during the following few decades consisted frequently of absentees and hardly ever of the actual cultivators of the soil, but represented mainly additional claimants on the surplus of the original occupiers.

The existence of these middlemen was such a crying evil during the eighteenth century, the heyday of colonial Ireland, that at times it was accepted as the true cause of Ireland's social and economic degradation. Potato gardens for which Irish peasants had to pay

£6–7 per acre may have had a head rent of a few shillings. In a
conquered country like Ireland, such a system was particularly
pernicious because it caused the growth of vested interests within
interests and made it almost impossible to gauge the real effect of
legal or administrative measures which affected the participants in
this vicious circle in almost incalculable ways. 'That system worked
like a screw-press; the increase in the rent of any farm at the close
of any half-year might be small, but the screw still went on revolving,
the pressure increasing until, at last, human nature could no longer
endure it.'[5] From an economic point of view, however, the middlemen were part and parcel of the landlord class, and their spoils
were a part of the total rental of the country.

In spite of the exorbitant rents, the average cottier might have
been satisfied with his primitive existence, provided he could have
found sufficient land for his potato garden and his cow. But these
simple demands were difficult to reconcile with the interests of the
landlords who during most of the eighteenth century regarded the
possession of a large number of cottier tenants as a doubtful asset.
The collection of rents from smallholders was troublesome in the
extreme, and it depended largely on the tenants' opportunities of
earning the necessary cash. To some extent the difficulty was met
with the help of the proverbial savings bank of the peasant, his one
and only pig, which could be sold for ready money. In districts
with flax cultivation, the women could contribute towards the
payment of the rent by spinning, but for the bulk of his rent money
the tenant depended on his labour. In a country where the great
majority of the population lived on the meagre produce of their
own work, employment was, however, scarce. It was, therefore,
almost the rule for the small cottier to pay his rent by working
directly for his landlord, who was, of course, himself somebody's
tenant. As the demand for labour was small and the demand for
land large, the cottier's labour was accepted at an incredibly low
valuation, and he often needed up to 250 working days, at an
assumed wage of from 4d. or 5d. to 8d. per day, in order to discharge
his 'contractual' debt to his immediate landlord and his legal
obligations to the tax collector and the tithe farmer.

The middleman who employed the smallholder received a large
part of his income in labour at a low rate and of very low efficiency.
But he himself was in need of a good deal of ready cash for the
payment of his own rent and for a large part of his personal expenditure. His standard of life and his tastes were governed by those of
the English squirearchy, and he wanted to import from abroad all
the luxuries and a good many of the conventional necessities of his
time and class. Apart from this, he had invariably money obligations,

either in the form of head rents or in that of mortgage interest or gaming debts, and was, therefore, always in need of ready cash. ⌈Although colonial Ireland had a fair proportion of resident landlords, absenteeism was general enough to be regarded as one of the outstanding evils of the system⌉ Like the institution of the middleman, absenteeism has frequently been singled out as the main cause of Ireland's misfortunes; in fact both were only symptoms of Ireland's position as a conquered nation, dependent on a ruling country in a more advanced stage of economic development. Nevertheless absenteeism was a very real evil. The absentee landlord usually lived in London, Bath or Tunbridge Wells, and was only concerned with the prompt receipt of his rents which he wanted to draw in English money. He was interested neither in the methods by which his tenants, or the sub-tenants of his sub-tenants, earned the rent money, nor in the transactions required for the transformation of Irish labour into a draft on his London banker or into English guinea-pieces, but he was emphatic in his insistence on the more or less punctual appearance of the finished article.

Backward agrarian Ireland was therefore compelled to find unusually large amounts of ready money and to exchange them for English currency. Although rent was not the only obligation of this kind which Ireland had to fulfil, it was by far the largest item which entered into her chronically unfavourable balance of payments. The yearly rental of the country was estimated by Sir William Petty around 1670 at £800,000, out of a total national income of £4,000,000,[6] and in 1687 at £1,200,000.[7] In 1724, Swift estimated the rents of land in Ireland, 'since they have been of late so enormously raised and screwed up', at about two million sterling, 'whereof a third part, at least, is directly transmitted to those who are perpetual absentees in England'.[8] Swift put the total net financial gain which England drew every year from Ireland at double the amount of the absentee rents, or £1,300,000–£1,400,000. Although his figures do not pretend to accuracy, they are by no means improbable. Amounts of this order of magnitude could only be found through extensive foreign trade, and an economy based on subsistence farming at near-starvation level was singularly ill-suited for exports on a large scale.

Ireland had never been a wheat-growing country, and in the general conditions of the seventeenth and earlier eighteenth centuries wheat production on a large scale was impossible: the Irish peasants lived largely on potatoes and were technically far behind their English opposite numbers, who were further aided by heavy protection and subsidies. ⌈The Irish had always regarded cattle as the embodiment of wealth, and sheep and cattle-breeding were the

characteristic features of colonial Irish agriculture. Not even the
prohibition of the thriving cattle exports to England, caused by
the alarm of the English landlords at the effect of Irish competition
on their rents, prevented the development of the cattle trade,
although it turned it into new channels. During the seventeenth
century sheep-breeding was also a very promising trade, for it
provided the raw material for the growing woollen industry, and
Irish wool commanded a ready market in England and was still
more eagerly bought in France where it was smuggled in large
quantities.

Sheep-breeding and cattle-raising were the only two branches of
Irish agriculture of real interest to the Irish landlords, but they
were completely divorced from the subsistence farming of the masses
of the Irish people and directly hostile to its vital interests. They
greatly restricted the demand for agricultural labour and even more
the supply of agricultural land for the quickly growing population.
As the best land in the fertile plains was reserved for these lucrative
branches of agriculture, the Irish peasants had to move to the hillsides in order to find land for their potato patches, and with the
increasing pressure of population during the eighteenth century the
competition for land became steadily fiercer.

The peculiar and tragic combination of a primitive feudal land
system, riveted to a modern country in the mercantilist stage of
capitalist development, enveloped Ireland in a mesh of suffering and
contradictions which determined her destinies for a very long time.
The genuine colonisation of the country by foreign settlers had been
prevented by the existence of a frugal and patient peasantry with an
infinite capacity for endurance and admirable powers of resistance
and resilience. Yet all these qualities only served as the profitable
basis for the absolute and ruthless rule of a class of greedy and
unscrupulous landlords. But the backwardness of the country and
its self-sufficiency on a near-starvation level, which had made it
comparatively easy to conquer Ireland, turned out to be serious
drawbacks for the enjoyment of the fruits of conquest. In addition,
the English business classes imposed serious economic restrictions
on the country which made it still more difficult for the landlords
to transform their rents into cash and to enjoy them where they
pleased. The partial solution of this intricate problem was found
in a policy of clearance, and the eighteenth century witnessed for
many years a long-drawn-out struggle between the landlords who
tried to clear the peasants from the land, and their victims who
fought numerous stubborn rearguard actions against their aggressive
enemies without being able to halt their advance.

The early period of English colonial rule was aptly summarised on an unusually high level by the career and the opinions of Sir William Petty. Dr. Petty was a man of many parts and of undoubted genius, one of the numerous polyhistors of the amazing seventeenth century. He accompanied the armies of the Commonwealth in his profession as a physician, but in Ireland he made his fortune as a surveyor. The famous Down survey of Ireland, an indispensable instrument of the Cromwellian settlement, was his work, and brought him £9,000. With this money he bought Irish land debentures from officers, soldiers and speculators, at four or five shillings in the pound and amassed about 70,000 acres at a price of half a crown per acre. 'Then Sir William Petty might have 70,000 acres for his work worth at two shillings the acre £7,000 per annum.'[9] (In Arthur Young's days the Shelburne estate based on the Petty inheritance had an extent of 150,000 acres.[10])

But Sir William Petty's greatness did not lie in his successful land speculation which made him the ancestor of the Marquesses of Lansdowne. Of all the great Englishmen who at different times surveyed the Irish scene, he had the most systematic and realistic head, and his *Political Anatomy of Ireland* (1672) is the outstanding source for our knowledge of the social and economic conditions of his time. An even more intimate and interesting study of colonial Ireland is his *Treatise of Ireland* (1687) which contained his own recipe for the final solution of the Irish problem. This plan amounted to no less than 'there being about 1300 Thousand People in Ireland, that to bring a Million of them into England, and to leave the other 300 Thousand for Herdsmen and Dairy-Women behind, and to quit all other Trades in Ireland but that of Cattle only. . . .'[11]

Petty's approach to the Irish problem of his day was brutally simple: the Irish landlords had a yearly income of £1,200,000; the King drew a net revenue of just under £200,000 and the Establishment produced a further £120,000 for the Irish clergy. Petty did not regard the people of Ireland either as Irishmen, Englishmen or Scotsmen, or as Catholics and Protestants, but simply '(1) as such as live upon the King's pay; (2) as owners of Lands and Freeholds; (3) as Tenants and Lessees to the Lands of others; (4) as Workmen and Labourers'.[12] He found no difficulty in proving that Ireland could maintain a cattle population of six million head minded by 300,000 dairymen and that these could produce an annual gross income of £3,600,000, of which £2,000,000 would support the herdsmen on the same level as English labourers, while a further £100,000 would provide ample payment for the small English garrison of soldiers, officials and clergymen needed for the settlement. This would leave £500,000 available for payment to England in order to satisfy the claims of King and landlords. The mass of the Irish people, 'the Cabineers of Ireland which are ten to One of all the others',[13] would be shipped to England and become 'ingrafted and incorporated into a Nation more Rich, Populous, Splendid and Renowned than themselves',[14] their pay would rise to the same level as that of the English poor, and Ireland would become a real addition to the power and wealth of England.

This plan (which also contained proposals for the acquisition of the land of recalcitrant landowners by the State and for the administration of the colony by a council of fit persons for the direction of the Irish cattle trade with a foreign trade monopoly) was clearly the work of a very powerful brain. It is distinguished by the blending of a sweeping design with supreme economic acumen and by complete indifference to the claims of existing vested interests. It was, of course, completely amoral and to the Irish nationalist it must appear deeply immoral. Petty's naïve economic optimism provokes comparison with the savage irony of Swift's *Modest Proposal*: while Petty wanted to depopulate Ireland in order to produce beef for the British owners of the country, Swift's mock ingenuity disguised an ardent protest against the policy of England which flayed the Irish people alive.

Although Petty's *Treatise* remained unpublished for more than two hundred years, its neglect was certainly not due to sentimental scruples about its callous disregard for national life in demanding the deportation of three-quarters of the Irish people as labourers to England. The mass emigration from Ireland ever since the beginning of the eighteenth century proves that he was thinking on lines parallel to actual developments. The plan for the enforced transfer of a whole people savours more of Russia than of Western Europe: it would have been the type of project which might have caught the fancy of Peter I or Catherine II. The proposal to raise the standard of the Irish poor, both in Ireland and in England, to the British level is proof of his comparative fairness and impartiality. But apart from the social and technical difficulties of the project, it was not nearly attractive enough for the great vested interests concerned. The plan offered no inducement to the landlords who were already enjoying the full revenue which Petty reserved for them—after the investment of a large amount of capital, which was never the strongest point of Irish landlords. At the same time Petty's plan aimed at the destruction of the growing number of well-connected parasites, public and private, temporal and spiritual, who found in Ireland an earthly paradise. For them a country run as a 'Kind of Factory' would have been the abomination of desolation. Last but not least, the plan depended on the closest political and economic union between England and Ireland for the marketing of the cattle and provisions, and the English market was at that period, and for a considerable time to come, hermetically sealed to Irish cattle.

Petty's plan can fairly be regarded as a small-scale model of the economic future of Ireland as an English colony. He brushed all secondary issues aside with one bold sweep and concentrated on the essential facts—the ownership of the land and the future of the people. He condemned the system of simple subsistence farming which kept the cottiers in unspeakable squalor and misery and left an insufficient surplus for the landlords. His solution had all the excellences and all the drawbacks of an unflinchingly logical approach to the facts of real life. The transformation of Ireland into a kind of factory would have solved the Irish problem after a fashion, but no government would have mustered the resolution of carrying it through except in an emergency which did not admit of half-measures.

Its neglect in practice does not lessen the theoretical importance of Petty's *Treatise*, which lies in its strong grasp of the fundamentals of the colonial nexus between conqueror and conquered. The mass of the Irish peasantry was not transported into England in the course of a single radical operation, but it was slowly driven out of its own country. In 1695, only seven years after Petty's *Treatise*, Parliament abolished all customary tenures not confirmed by formal contracts. This gave legal sanction to large-scale clearances and a new impetus to the extortion of still higher rents, leading to the adoption of the system of 'canting' farms by a kind of auction to the highest bidders, who had to promise economically unbearable rents in order to get any land at all.

During the eighteenth century the position of the tenantry was prejudiced still further by the notorious penal laws, which excluded Catholics from long leases at favourable rents and thereby proclaimed extortion as a matter of high policy. The exemption of grazing land from the payment of tithes in 1735 threw the burden of maintaining the Established Church completely on the shoulders of the Catholic peasantry and added another grievance to the list of their semi-religious and semi-economic disabilities.

One of the most important results of the social degradation of the Irish people was the virtual elimination of social conflicts between Catholics. 'In the Irish-speaking districts life was, perhaps, more homogeneous than even in the rural community of squirearchy and tenantry in England.'[15] The reverse of this process was a remarkable increase in the power of the priests over the people. The effect of the penal laws was not the suppression or even the weakening of the Catholic faith but the social and intellectual depression of the faithful which strengthened the hold of the priests over their flocks.

The proscription of Catholic education did not prevent the handful of wealthy Catholics from having their sons brought up in the manner they wanted, but it was an effective bar to the intellectual development of the common people, even within the narrow limits which the grinding poverty of the peasants would, in any case, have set to mass education. In spite of the brave efforts of the hedge-schoolmasters, the Irish remained illiterate and their fine intellectual abilities were allowed to run to waste. The inevitable result of this intentionally produced desolation was a great increase in the influence of the Catholic clergy. The priest was not only the spiritual leader but also the intellectual oracle of his parish. General popular education was just as unknown in eighteenth-century England as in Ireland, but here the result was not class education as in England, but the complete absence of education for all except the wealthiest Catholics.

But the power of the Catholic Church over the Irish people did not entirely depend on its close connection with social, national and religious grievances; at least to some extent it reflected its position as the only organised force left amongst an otherwise completely atomised subject population. The number of Church officials, though not very large in absolute figures, was considerable in relation to the total number of Catholics. Petty gave it as 24 bishops and approximately 1,000 secular and 2,500 regular priests[16] —the last figure almost certainly a gross exaggeration. In 1800, when the Catholic population was at least three times as large as in Petty's day, Lord Castlereagh's draft plan for the partial endowment of the Catholic Church, drawn up after consultation with Catholic prelates, provided for 22 bishops, 36 vicars-general and 1,200 parish priests.[17] The proposed contribution from public funds was only £40 a year for a parish priest and £300 for a bishop, altogether not more than £65,000, compared with an income of the Established Church of more than one million pounds per year and considerably less than the Irish pension list. But in spite of their poverty, the Catholic clergy were infinitely better off than most of their parishioners, who had to maintain their own priest in addition to the payment of tithes for the Protestant parson. Excessive demands by the priests on the liberality of their supporters were frequent enough for the rebellious Whiteboys to include the regulation of clerical fees amongst their reform programme.

In spite of the hostility of the authorities towards the priests, and in spite of the extra-legal position of its clergy, the Catholic Church was very far removed from the revolutionary point of view in politics. During the great convulsions of the last quarter of the eighteenth century, the Catholic prelates were resolutely on the side of the Government. In contrast to the Presbyterians, the other 'dissenting' Irish community, the official leaders of the Catholics were loyalists during the American Revolution and the French revolutionary wars. Nor was the Church even the prime mover in the agitation for the repeal of the penal laws and for Catholic emancipation. This movement was started by laymen against the wishes of the Catholic dignitaries and was, at least in its early stages, repudiated by the clergy.[18]

Even the *ecclesia militans* of Ireland was, therefore, by no means a progressive and still less a revolutionary force. Wolfe Tone, who knew priests and prelates well, and who watched them with keen interest, because he wanted to effect an alliance between Northern revolutionaries and Southern peasants, had no illusions about their conservative character. The Church did not oppose the efforts for emancipation undertaken by the more energetic middle-class Catholics, because it approved of the anti-Catholic laws and of the rulers under whom it was compelled to live, but because it had been cowed by its long persecution. In addition, the Catholic prelates were strongly influenced by the small remnants of a Catholic aristocracy which had managed to survive the expropriations. The bishops therefore at first mistrusted the middle-class agitators until the latter had proved themselves successful in practice, but in the course of time they entered into a firm alliance with these children of a new era.

The attitude of the Catholic Church towards the rebellious movements of the lower classes, on the other hand, was one of consistent and unrelenting hostility. The social and political system of colonial Ireland left no room for legal movements by the peasants, and when the pressure became intolerable their chronic discontent flared up into combinations for the redress of their grievances or for revenge on their oppressors. The succession of secret agrarian societies which disturbed the country at various times throughout the eighteenth century followed similar lines because they were produced by similar causes. The replacement of small cottiers by large herds of cattle, the screwing-up of rents and the extortion of tithes by unscrupulous tithe proctors claimed numerous victims amongst the small peasants and gave successive resistance movements their natural leaders. Nocturnal meetings, oaths of secrecy and frightful *vehme* methods against traitors, spies and informers, were their common means against the coercive powers of the law, and in a well-ordered society these methods would have been almost as intolerable as the abuses against which they were directed.

Though rarely completely successful, these organisations served their purpose for a while through the intimidation of the worst oppressors.

The secret agrarian societies were relentlessly opposed by the Catholic Church. Wherever parish priests, who depended on their parishioners for their daily bread, shut their eyes to the existence of these organisations, they probably did so more from fear than from sympathy and certainly against the wishes of the prelacy. The bitter opposition of the Church towards these societies was based as much on considerations of power as of morals. Secret organisations were anathema to the priests not only because of their illegal objects but also because they interfered with the peculiar relationship between the priests and their flocks which was the psychological basis of the power of the Church. Once the faithful began to harbour secrets, which they did not divulge even under the seal of the confessional, the hold of the priests over their souls was in danger.

The hostility of the Church towards secret societies was, of course, greatly intensified when these organisations took a political turn which the Church disliked. This was the case with the partial alliance between the Catholic Defenders and the United Irishmen, with their overwhelmingly Protestant background, during the years immediately preceding the Rebellion of 1798. In spite of the secular and anti-clerical spirit with which the United Irishmen, as ardent admirers of the French Revolution, were deeply imbued, their political appeal was strong enough to make not a few priests join the movement, not from fear but from conviction. The regulars, in particular, who did not have the same strong interest in law and order as the parish priests, seem to have been generally much more in favour of resistance to the ruling powers. The prelates, on the other hand, were almost to a man opposed to revolutionary organisations and did their best to stamp them out. Their refusal to join, or even to tolerate, the movement of protest and revolt which shook Ireland during the last years of the eighteenth century fully explains the decline in the political influence of the Church which was frequently noticed by competent observers. It was not the sceptical spirit of the age which, despite Tom Paine, rarely penetrated into the Irish village, but the conservative social and political outlook of the Church which weakened its previously unshakable hold over the peasant masses. The frequent use of threats and punishments, like interdict and excommunication, even for offences like agitating against the payment of tithes to the clergy of the Established Church, indicates both the extent of the fall in the spiritual power of the Church during this period and its most important cause.

CHAPTER III

ULSTER

ULSTER'S importance for the actual course of Irish history and for the study of colonial imperialism is out of all proportion to its size—a few counties in the north-east corner of Ireland inhabited by what is according to modern standards a mere handful of people. Yet this small group not only exerted a powerful, and at times a decisive, influence on Anglo-Irish relations, but even contributed a distinct and valuable strain to the racial, political and religious texture of the United States of America.

Ulster, though the most backward part of tribal and feudal Ireland, was not the least important of the four provinces. The rebellion of the Great O'Neill will always remain of peculiar significance to Irishmen as the last and highly memorable symbol of Ulster's part in Irish history before the final English conquest. This rebellion and the famous flight of the Earls was also the direct impulse for the plantation of Ulster, the only genuine and permanent colonisation of Irish territory from Great Britain.

The plantation of Ulster was accompanied by the abolition of the old anti-Irish laws, which dated back to the Gaelic reaction during the later Middle Ages. These laws were by then clearly out of date because they were incompatible with a social system which relied more and more on the subjection of the mere Irish to their English or Scottish masters as hewers of wood and drawers of water. A complete separation of the two groups would, therefore, have been impracticable, but the resulting relationship was not that between equals but that of masters and servants, exploiters and exploited.

The relative success of the plantation of Ulster was mainly due to the fact that it was at least partly a genuine colonising effort. To some extent it was in the hands of English country gentlemen, of speculators and of the Irish Society founded by the City of London for the exploitation of Londonderry, who left the work somewhere half-way between the completely ineffective plantations of Mary and Elizabeth and the comparatively thorough colonisation of parts of Antrim and Down by the Scottish. The English planters were first and foremost capitalists in search of lucrative investments and their undertaking was, in Bacon's words, 'rather an adventure for such as are full than a setting up of those that are low of means'.[19] The original undertakers were speculators who invested money in a financial project, and although they bound themselves to 'plant'

their plots only with Scottish or English settlers, they were as a rule
unable to resist the lure of the higher rents offered by the desperate
Irish for the privilege of not being expelled from their land and
driven into the woods.

The expulsion of the Irish population was a sore point in all
planted areas, where English undertakers had invested money and
wanted quick returns. As the highest profit could be made out of
Irish tenants, the temptation to keep the Irish and make the profits
was in practice irresistible. The most spectacular case was that of
the City of London, whose condemnation on this score in the famous
Star Chamber Trial of 1635 was of first-rate historical importance
because it helped to range the great power of the city solidly against
King Charles I. 'A depression in their economic status, not expulsion, was the usual fate of the natives on the companies' lands. . . .
Nearly all the immediate tenants, both British and Irish, had Irish
tenants under them.'[20] The English side of the Ulster plantation
thus threatened again to follow the example of the Tudor plantations: it was effective enough as an instrument for the enrichment
of the new landowners but singularly futile as a colonising effort,
and only succeeded in producing an elaborate structure of parasitic
middlemen between the head landlord and the tillers of the soil.

But the Ulster plantation also had a Scottish side, for the union
of the English and Scottish crowns in the person of James I had
the effect of opening Ulster for immigration from Scotland. Not
unlike the English settlers in North America, the Lowland Scots
who crossed the sea to Northern Ireland were not out for financial
gain, but wanted to find new homes in a new country because they
found conditions at home uncongenial or unbearable. Although
there was no lack of feudal noblemen amongst the great Scottish
grantees, a strong contingent of the immigrants consisted of urban
middle-class elements from Glasgow and Edinburgh.[21] They
wanted to escape the permanent struggle with the Highland clans
and to live their lives free from the obstacles which confronted them
at home. The many upheavals of the seventeenth century repeatedly
drove large numbers of Scottish Presbyterians from their homes to
Northern Ireland—and sometimes back again, but the net result
was a substantial Scottish settlement in Ulster.

The relations between the native Irish and the Scots were just
as bad as those between the Irish and the English. Many of the
English 'farmers' and 'tenants' were habitual absentees, and most
of the residents were middlemen with no intention of cultivating
the land themselves, while the Scottish colonists, like British settlers
on the other side of the Atlantic, actually engaged in husbandry.
Their technical methods of cultivating the land were greatly superior

to the Irish 'creaghting', a pastoral system of the most primitive
type, and the natives could not have competed with them, even if
other things had been equal.

The Scottish colonisation deprived many of the Irish peasants of
their land and forced them either to become labourers, or to take
refuge in the woods and live there as outlaws, or to move on to
barren hillsides where they were still less capable than before of
making a tolerable living. Thus it is only natural that the relations
between the settlers and the natives in Ireland were on the same
level as those between palefaces and Redskins in North America.
'Woodkernes' infested the dense forests which still covered large
tracts of the country and were ever ready to pounce on the intruders,
to steal their cattle or even to murder them. Far-sighted Englishmen
like Sir Thomas Phillips, the persistent accuser of the City of
London in its Irish adventure, prophesied as early as 1628 that the
Irish would 'Rise upon a Sudden and Cutt the Throts of the poore
dispersed Brittish'[22]—which was exactly what happened during the
Great Rebellion of 1641, when a large number of British settlers in
Ireland suffered the same fate as many American colonists and their
families who were surprised by the Red Indians suddenly raiding
outlying settlements.

Although Scottish Ulster soon surpassed the other provinces in
economic progress and prosperity, despite less favourable conditions
of climate and soil, Ulster's relative prosperity in comparison with
Southern Ireland was not so remarkable as its relative lack of
progress compared with the American colonies. Ulster's superiority
over the South of Ireland was due to the intrinsic advantages of
a colony over a conquered and ruthlessly exploited territory; its
patent inferiority to the American colonies was at that early date
not so much caused by disparity in size and resources as by the
domination of Ulster by Great Britain's narrow-minded imperialism,
and by its proximity to the rest of Ireland where the common
people were treated as serfs with results which slowly but surely
made themselves felt in Ulster as well.

Many of the early immigrants into Ulster were industrious
townsmen, artisans, traders and small business men, who imported
their superior skill and business habits into their new country.
Petty emphasised the overwhelming superiority of the 'English'
(amongst whom the Scottish played a far from negligible part) over
the Irish in all trades which required more than the most primitive
skill. He claimed even the salting and curing of meat as an English
technique, and said that butter and cheese for export could not be
produced by the 'vulgar Irish' because their goods were 'scarce a
vendible Commodity in foreign parts'. Tanning, the finer types of

woollen goods (serge, broadcloth, etc.) and linen manufacture, mining and forging were, according to Petty, all 'English' arts, and, in spite of his patent anti-Irish bias, there must have been more than a grain of truth in his assertions.[23] The obvious reason for this gulf between the standards of the settlers and of the natives was the fact that the 'wretched Beast-like habitations' of the Irish 'Cabineers' were 'unfit for making Merchantable Butter and Cheese, and the Manufacture of Wool and Linen out of the best Materials'.[24]

This difference in social and technical development was perpetuated by the working of the Irish land system which prevented the competition on even terms between the two groups and made it impossible for the natives to overcome their initial handicap. The Irish peasant could not accumulate any capital for the improvement of his farm, nor would he have dared to invest his savings in his insecure holding if he had been able to make any. The poverty of the peasants crippled the growth of an internal market for manufactures, and thereby interfered with the growth of an urban middle class, while the constant drain on the resources of the country in the interests of an alien landlord class and the English Government impoverished all classes and did not stop at the frontiers of Ulster.

The British settlers not only started on a higher level of development, but for a long time they were also to some extent protected from the hurricane of greed and oppression which broke over the conquered Irish. In the early years of the plantation, grantees found it necessary to attract British settlers by easy conditions and very long leases, which gave them a privileged position compared with the Irish cultivators. On this basis the Ulster tenants had managed to obtain the actual, though not the legal, recognition of the tenant's interest in his holding, which became known under the name of the 'Ulster custom'. At the same time the Irish masses in the South and West, prostrate after the suppression of two large-scale rebellions, were completely in the hands of their masters whose autocratic rule was only tempered by their fear of midnight murder or by their humanitarian sentiments.

Finally, Ulster was the only part of Ireland where the economic shackles of English mercantilism did not completely crush non-agricultural employment. The combination of small-scale tillage and linen manufacture, which caused Arthur Young so much disgust, enabled the small tenants in the North to pay their rents without having to work all the year round for their landlords at a nominal wage. However meagre their profits, the system encouraged them at least to exert themselves to the full, while the feudalism of the South put a premium on laziness and indifference.

While conditions in Ulster were thus incomparably more favourable to the growth of material prosperity than in Southern Ireland, they were still very unsatisfactory. On the one hand, England's mercantilist policy caused more damage to Ulster than to the more backward parts of the country, on the other hand, Ulster suffered a good deal from the backwardness of the rest of Ireland.

English rule interfered indirectly with Irish trade by restricting its home market and directly by the imposition of laws forbidding any form of Irish economic activity which seemed to prejudice English commercial interests. The embargo on Irish cattle exports to England (1666) was formally still within the recognised limits of mercantilist practice, but the restrictions on Irish shipping and the destruction of Ireland's most important industry, her woollen trade (1699), were arbitrary acts of commercial jealousy which could only be justified by the argument of superior power. As Irish trade and industry were largely in the hands of the colonists, this policy was a crippling blow to the prosperity of the British settlers, and the direct result of the legislation of 1699 was the first of several waves of emigration from Ulster to North America. The Test Act (1704), which deprived the Presbyterians of effective participation in the political life of the country, was another cause of bitter discontent amongst the middle-class colonists, who found the reactionary rule of the Irish landlords in politics and the stranglehold of British commercial interests in trade and industry incompatible with their own unfettered development.

Towards the end of the eighteenth century Ulster had become the main battlefield of powerful but contradictory political and religious tendencies. The middle class in Ulster was more interested than the rest of Ireland in the removal of the economic restrictions maintained by the English Government and in the protection of native industries against English competition. This middle class was republican in politics, sympathised warmly with the rebellious American colonies and objected to the corrupt rule of the Irish landlords through the Irish Parliament. These feelings made the people of Ulster the spearhead in the Irish Volunteer movement and the most resolute advocates of Irish 'independence' during the period of Grattan's Parliament. At the same time, however, Ulster was the seat of a bigoted and warlike Protestantism which involved deliberate hostility towards the masses of the Irish people and their religion.

The memories of the fatal year 1641, when the Irish rebels destroyed the castles and bawns of the 'undertakers', together with the farms of the British settlers, and killed them or drove them out of the country, were more alive in Ulster than elsewhere because only here did the immigrants form a large part of the population. William of Orange, the reconqueror of Ireland for British imperialism and the British colonists, was the secular patron saint of the North. The reason for the tenacity of these memories, in spite of the community of grievances of the Irish population as a whole against the Anglo-Irish landlords and the British Government, was the peculiar influence of Ireland's colonial status on the relations between the Ulster Scots and the indigenous Irish.

In the days of the Stuarts, Sir William Petty had shown in his *Treatise of Ireland* that only a fraction of the existing Irish population was required in order to produce all the cattle and provisions which Ireland could turn out. As these commodities were most profitable for landlords and rich graziers, the land devoted to cattle raising increased steadily at the expense of the land used for crops and, incidentally, for the sustenance of human beings. The pressure of a growing population and the increasing competition for the available supply of rentable land led to serious friction between the descendants of the Scottish immigrants and the Irish Catholics, who were ready to accept land at less favourable terms. The most spectacular, but not the only, instance of the replacement of Anglo-Scottish settlers by Irish tenants was the great operation carried out in and after 1772 by the Marquess of Donegal, the owner of the huge Chichester estate, who refused to renew the old leases of his Protestant tenants on terms which the latter could have accepted. His example found ready imitators and the result was a further wave of Protestant emigrants from Ulster to the United States, at least some of whom were replaced by Catholic tenants.

The Ulstermen, who still retained a good deal of the self-reliance and ruthlessness of the original settlers, retaliated against this threat to their living standards with resolute intimidation. The *Oakboys* and *Hearts of Steel* were northern counterparts of the famous southern *Whiteboys*, secret societies mainly directed against the growing exactions of the landlords. The *Peep o' Day Boys*, on the other hand, were formed for the purpose of keeping the Irish Catholics in their subordinate place; they owed their name to the practice of visiting the houses of Catholics at dawn, ostensibly for the purpose of preventing their illegal possession of arms, but mainly for their intimidation. These activities called into being a widespread Catholic counter-organisation, called the *Defenders*, and the friction between these groups produced a state of permanent tension.

The notorious result of this long and silent struggle was the formation of the *Orange Society* as a widespread and very powerful anti-Catholic organisation amongst the Protestants. It was created soon after the so-called Battle of the Diamond (1795) between the

Defenders and the Protestants in the county of Armagh, and in the tense political conditions of the day it soon assumed first-rate importance. It is significant that Armagh was the cradle of the Orange Order, as it had been that of the Oakboys a generation before. It is one of the areas in the south of Ulster, where Catholics and Protestants lived together in substantial numbers and where the competition between the two groups must have been correspondingly severe. It is, therefore, not surprising that the Protestant reaction to this threat was particularly energetic in this part of Ulster where the threat to their economic existence was greatest.

Thus the growth of the Orange movement did not take place in proportion to the strength of the Protestants but, on the contrary, as a result of their relative weakness. Antrim and Down with their solid Protestant majorities were at that time almost completely free from the infection of sectarian hatred, and the Presbyterians were in general sympathetic towards the claims of the Catholics—and the more so the greater their distance from the moving frontier between the areas of Ulster settlements and the Irish Catholics. The importance of the economic factor in the growth of the Orange Society is also reflected by the circumstance that the first victims of the expulsion policy pursued by the Armagh Orangemen were almost without exception weavers.[25] The combination of domestic industry with small-scale agriculture had been the sheet anchor of the Ulster tenants and their most valuable economic asset. The competition of the Catholics seems to have embittered the Protestants, who resolved to maintain their superior position by all means in their power in order not to be dragged down themselves to the near-starvation level of their Catholic competitors. They were confronted by the alternative of fighting the Catholic peasants on the side of the landlords, or of fighting the landlords with the help of the Catholic masses—and the political future of Ireland depended on their choice.

The dramatic climax of Irish history in the quarter-century between the American Revolution and the Union was a period of momentous decisions for Ulster and its middle class. Was the British settlement in Ireland going to take the lead in an all-Irish revolutionary movement against the British connection, or was it to remain an alien outpost in the flank of an oppressed and conquered but never quite subdued nation? Ulster, and only Ulster, could bridge the gulf of religious animosity and natioal idiosyncrasies, which condemned the Irish people to political impotence and national subjection; but Ulster could also perpetuate the rule of an imperialist government whose strength lay mainly in the internal divisions of the conquered country. The Irish Government was well aware of this crucial importance of Ulster and concentrated both on disarming the Ulster revolutionary movement and on encouraging all signs of anti-Catholic and anti-nationalist prejudice, and in particular the nascent Orange Society. The eventual success of this policy in Ulster guaranteed the survival of British rule over Ireland in the greatest crisis which had confronted it for centuries, the Napoleonic Wars.

CHAPTER IV

DUBLIN CASTLE

ON going back to sufficiently distant times, it is almost invariably possible to establish the use of force in its cruder forms as the origin of social relations which have become legally binding and even venerable by the mere effluxion of time. Force is the secret of the 'original accumulation' of power and wealth in all pre-capitalist societies, and force and fraud in varying combinations have played their part in the growth of modern capitalism. But the social system established in Ireland as the result of English conquests and re-conquests in the course of the seventeenth century was not only originally based on sheer brute and evil force, but never developed into a stable and generally accepted society. Conquest was not only the root of the title to the ownership of Ireland's soil but its very essence, force not merely the original source of the Irish colonial system, and its ultimate sanction, but the mainstay of its everyday existence.

The failure of the Anglo-Irish landlords to assume any positive economic function revealed their position as an exploiting class in its full and naked ugliness. 'Improving' landlords were so few as to be practically non-existent, and the oppression of the peasants by the agents of absentee landlords was often not much worse than their treatment by the resident squires and squireens. No ties of mutual advantage bound the tenants to their landlords, and the conflict of interests between the rulers and the ruled was so funda-mental and so near the surface that violent struggles were inevitable.

The seventeenth century with its three great rebellions was the heroic age of anti-English resistance. Neither of them was simply a peasant war, although the element of agrarian discontent was very strong in 1641, and even in 1689. But the leaders of the first two outbreaks, that of the Great O'Neill and that of 1641, were still the old semi-feudal, semi-tribal chieftains, whilst in the last the leader-ship was usurped with fatal consequences by James II and his incapable advisers. Finally, the victorious English established a system of iron rule which effectively disabled and dispersed the remnants of the old upper class and reduced the bulk of the Irish people to the position of helots.

None of the revolutionary movements during the following century achieved the nation-wide extent of the earlier outbreaks, not even the rebellion of 1798; with the partial exception of the latter these movements were mainly agrarian in character and secret in their methods, although a number of street riots in Dublin and elsewhere during the second half of the century testified to the existence of grave urban discontent.

The typical form of the Irish resistance movement during the eighteenth century was that of loose agrarian confederations, almost all of which had their origin in specific grievances. The existence of these secret societies proves the strength and the extent of mass hostility against the prevailing order, but their sporadic occurrence and their inability to change the broad features of the system demonstrate the superiority of the powers ranged against them in defence of the landlords. There was nothing subtle about the defenders of law and order, whose character was summed up by Edmund Burke in a classical passage when he wrote that 'where the hearts of the better sort of people do not go with the hands of the soldiery, you may call your constitution what you will, in effect it will consist of three parts (orders, if you please)—cavalry, infantry and artillery—and of nothing else or better'.[26]

In its external aspect, the Irish system of government was a more or less faithful copy of its English model, but the difference in spirit and conditions was so striking as to make it, in fact, its travesty. The dignitaries of the Irish Government during the colonial era included not only a Lord Lieutenant and a Lord Chancellor, but also a Lord High Treasurer (and three Vice-Treasurers), a Master of the Ordnance, a Keeper of the Signet, a Taster of Wines (at £1,000 a year), a Master of the Revels, etc.—quite apart from the numerous administrative offices created in the course of time, of which those of the Chief Secretary to the Lord Lieutenant (at £4,000 a year) and of the Commissioners of the Revenue (at £2,000 a year) were the most important.

The same impression of a wildly inflated and top-heavy system of government is conveyed by Petty's description of the administration of justice in a country of little more than a million inhabitants, most of whom were living the lives of savages in the most primitive conditions. As early as 1672, Ireland had no fewer than five central courts of law. If the English system of lawyer-made and lawyer-administered courts was a heavy burden on the classes unfortunate enough to come into contact with it, Irish law and legal administration were mockeries which the country was totally unable to afford.

The eighteenth century was even in England a time of very great power of the King's Government. The difference between British and Irish politics was, therefore, then not so striking as it became later on. But in England the centre of political gravity moved slowly but surely towards the House of Commons; in Ireland the power of the Executive was paramount and remained so throughout the period of English rule. British governments were undemocratic and not representative of the great mass of the people, but they were as a rule in tune with the interests, opinions and prejudices of the most powerful sections of the population, the landowners and the city merchants. The government of Ireland, on the other hand, fully expressed the abject subjection of the Irish people to a class of landlords, who were often strangers in the country they owned, and to Great Britain as the ultimate power on which the maintenance of Irish landlordism depended.

The oligarchic self-government of Great Britain was broadly based on the predominance of the landowning gentry which remained virtually unchallenged until the rise of new social interests in the course of the industrial revolution; no such arrangement was possible in Ireland, where a thin layer of property-owners, without economic functions or traditional claims to the allegiance of the people, was confronted by a resentful and rebellious mass of peasants. The Irish landlords failed in 1641 and 1689 to retain their position as a ruling class against the attacks of their subjects, and had to be rescued by English military power; throughout the following century they continued to owe their position as rulers of a country which they could not hold by their own exertions entirely to the support of the British Government. This fact was the root cause for the growth of a huge bureaucratic machine which remained in being up to the establishment of the Irish Free State—Dublin Castle government.

The colonial government of Ireland was a composite mechanism established for the double purpose of ensuring the maintenance of English power over the subject country, and the 'ascendancy' of the landlords over their subject classes. Neither of these purposes was compatible with the growth of a democratic society, nor even with the English system of oligarchic self-government. In addition, the friction between the economic interests of the Irish landlords and the mercantilist policy of the British Government prevented the latter from entrusting the Irish landlords, or their political agents, with the task of running the country in the common interests of England and the Irish landlords. When this experiment had to be tried after 1782 it proved an unqualified and dangerous failure and was never repeated. The conflict between the Irish landlords, both resident and absentee, and the Irish people was even less capable of democratic compromise, for the power of the landlords could only be maintained with the constant backing of an overwhelming armed force, which was freely used in order to overawe and repress the rebellious tendencies of the masses.

The executive organs of the Irish Government were, therefore, completely independent of effective outside control over their actions. They were not even responsible to the privileged groups of Irish society, but depended exclusively on the British Government. In view of the technical and political difficulties involved in ruling Ireland from Whitehall, the British Government was content with maintaining a general control, and the administrative organs of the Castle had a fair measure of independence in their day-to-day activities. Not even the Irish upper classes were in a position to shape the policies and supervise the actions of the machine of government. Apart from their share in the spoils of office, which was considerable, they were unable to determine the behaviour of the executive on whose support they relied completely for the maintenance of their position as landlords in a hostile country.

None of the powers dominating the Irish Government was primarily interested in the well-being of the Irish people. The British Government represented the oligarchy of squires and merchants who controlled the House of Commons at Westminster, while the small clique of influential Anglo-Irish families in possession of a quasi-monopoly of the more lucrative positions in the gift of the Irish Government, which were beneath the notice of English place hunters, represented only itself. The result of this combined, if at times somewhat inconsistent, pressure was the imposition of a very heavy burden on the Irish people in addition to the demands made by the landlords and the Established Church.

The exploitation of the resources of the Irish State for the purposes of the British ruling classes was effected through three main channels: the appointment of incompetent Englishmen to responsible posts in Ireland; the transformation of great offices of state into sinecures by their grant to absentees; and the burdening of the Irish establishment with pensions which had no relationship to services rendered to or in Ireland. The first of these practices was regarded in its time as the least reprehensible, although Jonathan Swift, with the acute realism of the satirist, fastened on it in his catalogue of the benefits accruing to England from her rule over Ireland: 'It has another mighty advantage by making our country a receptacle, wherein to disburthen themselves of their supernumerary pretenders to offices; persons of second-rate merit in their own country.'[27] This policy put high administrative offices and frequently also the government of Ireland into the hands of men whose incompetence made them a danger to both countries.

The granting of high Irish offices to absentee Englishmen was a public scandal throughout the eighteenth century. At one and the same time there were amongst the habitual absentees 'officers

of the Irish Post Office, whose salaries amounted to £6,000 a year;
the Master of the Ordnance; the Master of the Rolls; the Lord
Treasurer and the three Vice-Treasurers; the four Commissioners
of the Revenue; the Secretary of State; the Clerks of the Crown for
Leinster, Ulster and Munster; the Master of the Revels, and even
the Secretary of the Lord Lieutenant'.[28] Up to the time of Lord
Townshend even the Lord Lieutenant, in spite of his title, spent
only a fraction of his time and, it may be assumed, of his Irish
income of £16,000 a year, in the country where he represented the
person of the King. As early as 1702, Archbishop King complained
that all 'employments' were 'in deputation. The Government,
Chancery, Master of the Rolls, Clerk of the Council, Registrar of
the Chancery, Protonotaries, Remembrancers, etc., by which the
subject is oppressed and the money sent away.'[29] In 1729 two-thirds
of the general officers and one-fourth of the commissioned officers
in the Irish army, drawing pay amounting to £40,000 a year, were
also said to live in England.[30]

Even more notorious was the abuse of the Irish pension list by
the British Government and by the King himself. The bestowal of
large pensions on foreigners, who could have no claim whatever on
the Irish public revenue, however much reason the British Government or the royal family may have had to reward them, was a
permanent grievance: 'This polyglot of wealth, this museum of
curiosities, the pension list, embraces every link in the human chain,
every description of men, women and children, from the exalted
excellence of a Hawke or a Rodney to the debased situation of a
lady, who humbleth herself that she may be exalted' (J. P. Curran).[31]
Before its reform towards the end of the eighteenth century the
pension list of Ireland actually exceeded that of England in spite
of the discrepancy in wealth between the two countries.

The exploitation of the Irish Government and revenue by the
English aristocracy was merely the spectacular climax of the pettier
but even more thorough exploitation of their privileged position by
the men on top of the Irish administration itself. As representatives
of the paramount power which guaranteed the existing social order
they had little to fear from the Irish masses, while their distance
from London made them reasonably safe from unwelcome attention
by the English Government, provided they did not presume to
interfere in the higher direction of affairs.

The complete lack of functional responsibility and consciousness
of service in the Irish administration was the first thing to strike
Strafford at the outset of his career in Ireland as Charles I's deputy.
His judgment of the grandees in control of Ireland, nominally in
the name of the English King, but in fact as their private preserve,

could be applied to the Irish bureaucracy as a whole: 'They are a company of men the most intent upon their own ends that ever I met with.'[32] There was little glory in their rule over Ireland but much profit. The government of the country was for them one gigantic job, and their conscious hostility towards the mass of the Irish people was a complete safeguard against any moral scruples which they might have felt about their stewardship. During the seventeenth century the classical form of their exploitation of the Irish revenue was the farming of taxes, but even after the abolition of this mischievous system and the appointment of revenue officers the border between public and private money continued to be obscure.

The most obvious result of this state of things was the thorough corruption of all organs of government. Corruption was inextricably connected with Irish administration from a very early date: 'No man could imagine in what an inconceivably short time the scriveners in the courts of Justice in Dublin have scraped together enormous properties. It is not by inches but by cubits, to use a common phrase, that they ascend to wealth.'[33] Ireland was no India, and the scope for the amassing of fortunes was more restricted, but on the more modest insular scale of the sixteenth and seventeenth centuries these 'scriveners' were the genuine predecessors of the 'writers' of the East India Company, who left home without a penny, received pitiable salaries and returned as nabobs. King George III's instructions to the new Lord Lieutenant of 1765, Lord Hertford, observed as a matter of common knowledge that 'every public department in Ireland was saturated with dishonesty. There were frauds in the revenue, frauds in the muster reports, frauds in the ordnance and the victualling stores; evasion, jobbery and peculation, where there was any public property to be stolen and official hand to steal it.'[34]

Lord Buckingham spoiled his career at the start of his second Viceroyalty in 1787 by an untimely show of puritanism: 'He instituted an immediate enquiry into the departmental frauds. The clerks were called on suddenly to surrender their books and keys and produce the outstanding balances. The result was a tragicomedy. It was as if the police had come unexpectedly upon a gang of forgers.'[35] More than thirty years afterwards, Robert Peel, the foremost administrator of his generation, served his political apprenticeship as Irish Chief Secretary and did his best to refute Burke's famous dictum: '*Non regnum sed magnum latrocinium*—the motto ought to be put under the harp.'[36] After five years of painstaking efforts he summed up his reactions to Irish official life in one sentence of disgust: 'I am quite tired of the shameful corruption which every Irish enquiry brings to light.'[37]

Quite apart from the shameless corruption which was practised unofficially, though with little attempt at decorous disguise, the official cost of collecting the revenue was extremely high; in 1781 it was given as 17⅛ per cent of the gross revenue, compared with 7½ per cent in England, which at that time was itself no model of correct and economical administration.[38] Grattan quoted for 1783 a figure of £157,000 or 16 per cent of the revenue, and in 1790 he complained that the cost had increased since 1784 by no less than £105,000.

The cumulative effect of these influences was an additional heavy burden on the Irish people. Nowhere was the contrast between settlement and conquest easier to assess in terms of money than in the cost of the systems of public administration established on these radically different foundations: 'All the different civil establishments in North America, in short,' said Adam Smith, 'exclusive of those of Maryland and North Carolina, of which no exact account has been got, did not, before the commencement of the present disturbances, cost the inhabitants above £64,700 a year; an ever-memorable example at how small an expense three millions of people may not only be governed, but well governed.'[39] At the same time the Irish Government demonstrated how badly a country with a somewhat larger but incomparably poorer population could be governed at the then formidable cost of one million pounds per annum.[40]

The dependence of the Irish colonial system on a frequent show of armed force found its expression in the prominence of the army in the government of the country. During the eighteenth and early nineteenth centuries Ireland's military establishment was nearly as large as that of Great Britain, and even in times of peace the Irish army could not complain of lack of work. Quite apart from its frequent intervention in riots and other disturbances of the peace, it was the mainstay of the administration in its day-to-day relations with the subject population. 'The king's troops', wrote General T. A. Pitt, 'have been fully employed in assisting to collect the revenue, and to carry into execution the common and statute law, in supporting the king's writ and suppressing tumultuous risings,' and it was nothing but the stark truth when he added 'that but for the military there would be no government at all in this country'.[41] In many places there was, indeed, little difference between army and government, and officers were freely employed as magistrates. 'Our civil power is a sinecure,' Peel declared in 1815, 'not because there is no occasion for its exertions, but because it makes the military power perform its duties whenever it can.'[42]

The reliance of the civil authorities on the armed forces lasted as long as English rule, although the army could stay more in the background after the police reforms of Peel and Drummond. The excessive use of force by the authorities was an indication of the popular opposition to 'common and statute law' and the other activities of Dublin Castle. The dictatorship of the army in Ireland was in striking contrast to its studied subordination to the civil power in England. 'The guards on horseback,' observed a highly placed onlooker of an official procession in 1772, 'the principal officers of the household with their wards, and the pages in their livery paddling on foot through the mud, with grooms of the chambers and footmen, through the streets lined with soldiers, had an air of absolute monarchy and of military force to support it, that, had I been an Irishman, I am certain I could not have endured the sight of.'[43] The annual Mutiny Act, in England for centuries a jealously guarded symbol and instrument of parliamentary supremacy, remained unknown in Ireland.

The inevitable reverse of this privileged position of the armed forces was a complete lack of discipline and a degree of corruption far in excess of the unpleasantly high norm of the period. 'The captains', wrote Strafford in the early days of his Irish career, 'begin to fear they may be called upon to do their duties, which will be to their loss.'[44] The ease with which Irish rebellions overcame the resistance of purely Irish forces and had to be quelled by British arms is sufficient evidence of the weakness and unreliability of the leadership of the Irish army, for Irish regiments acquired at the same time the highest reputation for bravery on numerous battlefields outside Ireland. Absenteeism in the army was just as widespread as in the administration and amongst the gentry, while the cost of the army establishment was excessive even by contemporary English standards—sometimes double that of comparable English institutions.

The demoralisation of the Irish army reached its climax at the time of the 1798 rebellion. Just before this event an absurdly paradoxical conflict developed between the Commander-in-Chief, the Scotsman Sir Ralph Abercromby, who tried to apply British legal principles to Ireland and censured the excesses of the army, and Dublin Castle which insisted on making the military absolute master of the country against the wishes of its Commander. Abercromby's classical description of his army as being 'in a state of licentiousness which must render it formidable to everyone but the enemy',[45] was completely borne out by its treatment of real or alleged rebels and ordinary citizens, as well as by the ignominious Castlebar Races, when a handful of French soldiers set a greatly superior force scurrying over the Irish countryside.

The growth of a truly bureaucratic government in Ireland dates back to the middle of the eighteenth century. The Irish grandees whom Strafford found in full possession of the machine of Irish administration were not bureaucrats in the true sense of the term, but adventurers whom the reconquest of Ireland under the Tudors had transformed into the rulers of the country, just as the Norman conquest of Ireland transformed the riff-raff followers of Strongbow into the Irish territorial aristocracy under the new régime. A big capitalist like Richard Boyle, first Earl of Cork, a financier like Lord Mountnorris, a sharp lawyer like the Lord Chancellor, Lord Loftus, all used the Irish Government as a tool for their private purposes, but their power was only to a small extent due to their functional administrative capacity as Privy Councillors or Lords Justices.

The gradual separation of administrative and social power must have been favoured by the practice of granting high Irish offices of State as sinecures to Englishmen of rank and influence. In the administrative hierarchy only the law offices remained available for Irishmen, and for this reason these offices assumed a political importance which their opposite numbers in England never possessed. Up to the last third of the eighteenth century, most administrative posts were at the disposal of a handful of powerful magnates who ran the country almost without control, though within the political limits laid down by Britain, and clerical and administrative offices were filled, as a matter of course, with their retainers in the same manner in which American bosses divide the spoils of office amongst their henchmen.

During the administration of Lord Townshend (1767–71) the British Government made use of the growing internal opposition to the oligarchy in order to break the stranglehold of the great 'undertakers' on the machinery of government, while the limitation of Parliaments to a maximum of eight years weakened the political monopoly of the great aristocrats. As every one of the 'undertakers' had surrounded himself in his official capacity with a staff of his own creatures, who filled all posts down to the lowest ranks, the administrative revolution implied a more or less complete change in the staff of large departments like the Ordnance Board and the Revenue Board.[46] Although the process may have been less sweeping in practice than in theory, its outlines are familiar to every student of modern American politics.

The most prominent members of the clique which ruled Ireland during the period of Grattan's Parliament were John Beresford, the Chief Commissioner of the Revenue, John Fitzgibbon, Earl of Clare, the Lord Chancellor, and Edward Cooke, the senior Under-Secretary.

Its power was not due to the social position of its leading members, which was by no means exceptionally high, but to their administrative functions and to their influence as the most reliable confidential agents of the British Government. They were the backbone of the opposition to parliamentary reform, they were the only resolute enemies of concessions to the Roman Catholics, they were personally responsible for the recall of Lord Fitzwilliam (1795) and the resignation of Sir Ralph Abercromby (1798), and they were the indispensable instrument for the perpetration of the legislative Union. Two other prominent Irishmen, John Foster, at first Chancellor of the Exchequer and later on Speaker of the Irish House of Commons, and Sir John Parnell, his successor as Chancellor of the Exchequer, were closely connected with this group until after the rebellion of 1798, when they quarrelled with its permanent members on the question of the Union.

The position of this clique illustrates both extent and limits of the power of the Irish colonial bureaucracy. Its most prominent members, Beresford and Fitzgibbon, had earned the political gratitude of the English Government and of Pitt personally by their valuable help in critical situations. Beresford was Pitt's adviser and agent during the crucial commercial negotiations of 1785; Fitzgibbon was the outstanding exponent of Pitt's policy during the grave Regency Crisis (1789). Both opposed concessions to the Catholics tooth and nail in 1792, only to pocket their pride and their convictions a year later, when the British Government made up its mind on the matter. The heroic but futile remedy of resigning their positions apparently never even entered their heads, and Fitzgibbon was the main Government spokesman in favour of the Bill which he had tried in vain to strangle.

Both managers of the Irish bureaucracy reaped the reward for their reliable services during the Fitzwilliam crisis. In 1794 the needs of English party politics forced Pitt to come to terms with the Portland faction of the Whigs whose close political allies in Ireland were Grattan and Ponsonby, the deadly enemies of Fitzgibbon and Beresford. Although Pitt had to hand over the general management of Irish affairs to the Whigs, he insisted from the start on Fitzgibbon's retention in office, and Beresford's dismissal by Lord Fitzwilliam was the occasion for a showdown in which the Viceroy and the Irish Whigs were completely worsted. But it was not on Irish soil that the struggle of Beresford and his faction was waged and won: his dismissal was accepted with singular calm in Ireland, and it was in London that he regained his power. Fitzgibbon's backstairs approach to the King on the question of conscience involved in full Catholic Emancipation and Beresford's appeal to Pitt were completely successful: Fitzwilliam had to go, and his successor, Lord Camden, was the mouthpiece of the ascendancy party and of its exponents, Fitzgibbon, Beresford and Cooke.

The subordination of all other interests but their own to their duty as servants of the British Government made the leaders of the bureaucracy the absolute masters of Ireland. It was, as Henry Grattan bitterly called it, 'a monarchy of clerks, a government carried on by post and under the dominion of spies'.[47] This it was destined to remain for a full century after Grattan's death.

CHAPTER V

IRISH RENTS AND BRITISH COMMERCE

THE economic and financial counterpart of Ireland's position as a conquered territory was her debtor relationship towards England. The amount of Ireland's current payments to England, in addition to the payments for imports of goods, depended on the share of absentee landlords in Irish rents, on the number and emoluments of absentee clergymen of the Church of Ireland, on the amounts paid to Englishmen through the Irish pension list, and on the Irish public debt held by English capitalists. The total figure was undoubtedly large enough to cripple the accumulation of capital in Ireland and thereby to perpetuate the dependent position of the country. Towards the end of the seventeenth century the total sum was probably less than one and a half million pounds sterling, which Petty—and one generation later Swift—regarded as the probable annual profit of England from her rule over Ireland. Early in the nineteenth century the remittance for absentee rents alone was estimated at more than two millions.[48]

However backward the methods by which British rule had been established and was being maintained, the economic result of the process was a modern creditor-debtor relationship comparable to that made familiar by large-scale foreign investments during the last hundred years. To-day it has become a commonplace of theoretical economics and of practical economic policy that such a relationship is in the long run unworkable, unless the debtor nation can discharge its obligations through the export of goods and services, either directly to the creditor nation or in a roundabout manner through trade with other nations. Conversely, a creditor nation may either re-invest its income abroad or consume it at home, in which case the excess of consumption over production will find expression in a passive balance of trade.

As capital investments in the modern sense are closely connected with the export of capital goods, they were comparatively small before the growth of large-scale industry. International trade during the mercantilist era was confined to raw materials and foodstuffs, including wines and spirits, on the one hand, and to finished consumption goods, on the other, offering little room for genuine investments. The mercantilist policy of every nation wanted to make foreign trade as profitable as possible for its own business men by enforcing an ample and cheap supply of raw materials and ensuring wide and lucrative markets for its manufactures. Conversely, it wanted to prevent its foreign competitors from buying their raw materials either cheaply, or at any price, and from selling their manufactures in any market from which they could be excluded. Although mercantilism was not quite so subservient to the active balance of trade as its enemies tried to make out, it certainly regarded an excess of exports over imports as *prima facie* evidence for its success and the opposite as unwelcome and potentially dangerous.

The resolute mercantilist system enacted by the English Parliament was applied as far as possible to all English colonies, including the North American dependencies as well as Ireland, but its consequences were far more serious in the latter case than in the former. The interference with the development of native industries was just as ruthless in the American colonies as in Ireland, but it did not cause them such grievous injury: 'Unjust, however, as such prohibitions may be,' Adam Smith remarked about the prohibition of steel furnaces and of inter-colonial trade in woollen goods in America, 'they have not hitherto been very hurtful to the colonies. Land is still so cheap and, consequently, labour so dear among them, that they can import from the mother country all the more refined or more advanced manufactures cheaper than they could make them for themselves. . . . In their present state of improvement those prohibitions, perhaps, without cramping their industry, or restraining it from any employment to which it would have gone of its own accord, are only impertinent badges of slavery imposed upon them, without any sufficient reason, by the groundless jealousy of the merchants and manufacturers of the mother country. In a more advanced state they might be really oppressive and insupportable.'[49]

None of the circumstances which, according to Adam Smith, lessened the impact of mercantilist restrictions on the economy of the American colonies, were present in Ireland. No endless reserve of free soil waited for cultivation by the active and industrious poor; a severely limited quantity of good land was progressively being cleared of the inhabitants in order to make room for cattle and sheep. When the people tried to cultivate the barren hillside, the landlords followed them, appropriated their commons and demanded rent for the use of ground, which would have been completely worthless but for the labour of the occupiers. Labour was not dearer in Ireland than in England, but very much cheaper; although the Irish poor were generally denounced as lazy and stupid, these qualities were only foisted on an active and intelligent people by the double burden of an oppressive land system and a restrictive code of industrial legislation. Far from presenting

England with a natural market for her industrial output, Ireland was, on the contrary, an actual or potential rival in certain branches of English trade, which were very near to the hearts of the controllers of England's commercial policy.

This rivalry was most real in agriculture, but even in the field of trade and industry the gap between England and Ireland was then by no means so great as it became after the industrial revolution and the legislative Union. On Ireland's pastures grazed sheep of similar type as those which supplied the English manufacturer with his raw material for a highly prized export article of the greatest economic importance. Ireland's geographical position was not unfavourable for direct trade with the continent of Europe, particularly with France, Spain and Portugal, and excellent in relation to the New World with its swiftly growing economic importance. Before the creation of an iron and coal technology, England's industrial superiority over Ireland was not so much due to her natural resources as to certain social factors the monopoly of which was regarded as precarious without stringent measures for their perpetuation. The low standard of life of the Irish masses itself seemed to be a threat to English prosperity, because it might have created a reservoir of cheap labour for an energetic class of Irish manufacturers, who could have undersold their English competitors abroad or even in the English market.

Though a strong and healthy industrial system could not have been based on the social structure of colonial Ireland, the same objection would not have applied to certain parts of Ulster, which were inhabited by business-like Lowland Scots who did not suffer from the same disabilities as the mass of the Southern Irish. However this may have been, the measures taken for the prevention of Ireland's industrial development were only too successful. With the exception of the tolerated linen industry, Irish industry almost ceased to exist during the eighteenth century before the great impetus imparted by the abolition of trade restrictions, the effects of the industrial revolution, and economic protection under Grattan's Parliament.

Ireland could only pay her annual tribute to England by exporting more than she imported. An active balance of trade, wrongly regarded by mercantilist opinion as a boon in itself and under all circumstances, was obviously vital for Ireland—not as a means of accumulating wealth, but as the only possible method of paying her most pressing debts. But most Irish exports were either in direct competition with English trade, like those of woollen cloth, or threatened to provide England's rivals with the means of competing more effectively with English goods, like the export of Irish raw wool to France; other Irish staple commodities, like cattle and provisions, directly competed with English goods in the home market itself and were, therefore, still more obnoxious to powerful British interests. The prohibition of cattle imports into England, the prohibition of the export of Irish woollen goods to all destinations and the restriction of Irish wool exports to the English market were as many obstacles to the remittance of absentee rents, salaries and pensions to the tune of well over a million pound a year.

Apart from direct interference, as in the classical case of the woollen industry, British policy attacked the growth of Irish industries by the use of differential taxation: Restoration England adopted high protective duties on manufactured imports, but Ireland had to admit English manufactures at low rates of duty.[50] Thus Ireland was put into the position of a free-trader against her own will in a protectionist world, and this development completed the reversal of the economic relations between the two countries demanded by the facts of the situation. England, the creditor country which according to Jonathan Swift got more out of Ireland than of all the world besides, tried to export as much as possible into Ireland without permitting her unwilling customer to discharge her financial liabilities, or even to pay for her imports. Ireland, saddled with debts far beyond her economic capacity, was forbidden to sell her most valuable raw materials in the best markets and prevented from building up the industries which might have enabled the people to pay their tribute to the conquerors in acceptable forms.

The only important industries left in the country after the strangulation of the woollen manufacture were the linen trade, the provision industry and, at a great distance behind, the distilling industry. The encouragement of linen manufacture had been the *quid pro quo* offered by the British Government for the destruction of the Irish woollen trade. This engagement was not carried out in a generous spirit, for only the coarser and therefore less profitable linens received preferential treatment in England, but the linen manufacture developed nevertheless into the staple export from Northern Ireland to Great Britain and North America. The value of linen sales abroad had been insignificant at the time of Petty's catalogue of Irish exports in 1687; twenty years later they amounted to £150,000, and by 1771 they almost reached the two-million-pound mark.[51] Between 1710 and 1770 exports of linen yarn rose from 7,975 cwt. to 33,417 cwt. and of linen cloth from 1,700,000 yards to 20,560,000 yards.[52] During the economic discussions before the Union Ireland's dependence on the English market for linen exports of more than £2,500,000 played a considerable part.

In contrast to the linen trade, the provision industry owed less than nothing to England. Its mainstay was the provisioning of ships, which entered the harbours of Cork, Waterford or Wexford for the express purpose of taking cheap Irish provisions on board, and it also exported large quantities to foreign countries. But these exports and the proceeds of Irish linen abroad were quite insufficient to pay for Irish imports and in addition to discharge Ireland's tribute to England.

Ireland's economy was therefore in a state of perpetual coma. The incubus of a parasitical landlord class kept the peasants in grinding poverty, while the mercantilist policy of the British Government prevented the people from earning a living in any way except on the land. The steep rise in agricultural prices during the second half of the eighteenth century benefited almost exclusively the landlords, because the pressure of an increasing population on an inelastic supply of land permitted them to appropriate any increase in the value of agricultural produce by raising their rents. The country found itself on the horns of a dilemma, which was insoluble on the premises of the *status quo*, and which remained intractable by all methods which the rulers were able and willing to apply.

'Ireland has paid to Great Britain for eleven years past double the sum she collects from the whole world in all the trade which Great Britain allows her; a fact not to be paralleled in the history of mankind. Whence did all this money come? Our very existence is dependent on our illicit commerce.'[53] Smuggling was, indeed, for decades an essential part of Ireland's economic life. The most important object of eighteenth-century smuggling was wool, which was exported in large quantities to France, where it helped the most dangerous rivals of the English manufacturers to undersell English exports abroad. Although the exchange of Irish wool against French wine and money seems to have been very extensive, smuggling must also have been the explanation of the curious fact that in 1785, at the time of the Commercial Propositions, 'the Irish accounts showed a far larger export of goods to Great Britain than of imports from Great Britain; while, on the contrary, the British Custom House returns gave the balance of trade as largely against Ireland'.[54] It is a safe guess that a large part of Irish exports to Britain never reached the British Custom House.

These makeshifts and subterfuges indicate the straits to which the Irish economic system was reduced by the combination of an intolerably heavy burden in the interests of a parasitic aristocracy with artificial obstacles against Irish trade. If it was impossible to live within the framework of British mercantilist policy, this obstacle had either to be circumvented by smuggling or broken by open defiance. In times of England's strength, defiance was hopeless, but with the outbreak of the American Revolution the power of Britain received a shock which was felt nowhere outside America stronger than in Ireland.

The strategic point for all serious attempts to defy the mercantilist system was an attack on Irish imports from England which, according to the dominant theory and in stark truth, were a drain on the currency of the country and prevented the growth of flourishing Irish industries. It was only one step from Swift's question, 'Am I a freeman in England, and do I become a slave in six hours by crossing the Channel?' to his classical advice to burn everything English except their coals.

In his advocacy of voluntary non-importation, Swift was the precursor of movements which assumed great practical importance at the beginning of the American Revolution and in the nationalist struggle of modern India. But in spite of its soundness there was little chance for such a policy in eighteenth-century Ireland. The Anglo-Irish colony, which dominated the country and consumed most of its non-essential imports, was English in culture and habits and, like all such colonies, inclined to stress its kinship with the mother country by a meticulous and exaggerated imitation of 'home fashions': 'Nobility and people of quality *in* or rather *of* this Kingdom are to all interests and purposes almost very Londoners.'[55] The craze for English cloth, which the patriotic Dublin weavers denounced so bitterly, expressed the fact that its ultimate consumers consisted mainly of Anglo-Irish landlords and officials and their satellites.

Serious men of business and politicians were convinced of the need for more effective and less idealistic methods in order to break the stranglehold which Britain had acquired over the Irish economy by the time of the American Revolution. The twin demands of the Irish middle classes and of the more progressive landlords were at that time of imperial emergency 'free trade' and protective duties against English competition. This seemingly ill-assorted combination of battle-cries did not imply the demand for foreign trade free from import and export duties. To demand the right of admission to the trade of another country on equal terms with native producers and merchants would at that time have been regarded as absurd, and in these days of neo-mercantilism such an attitude does not appear quite so old-fashioned as it would have seemed to the classical economists.

The Irish supporters of 'free trade' simply demanded the repeal of the high-handed restrictions imposed by English interests on Ireland's foreign trade, and thereby on her industrial development.

Free trade in this sense of the term was well compatible with protection in the Irish home market, and the weakness of Irish industry would not have made it very desirable on other terms. But the political difficulties of a resolute protectionist policy remained insuperable, even after the repeal of the artificial shackles on Irish trade. The Irish Volunteers achieved free trade by the pointed language of their guns in an hour of English weakness, but they represented a coalition of the landlords and the urban middle classes, in which the commercial and industrial interests were by far the weaker partners in every respect with the exception of numbers. The landlords shared the resentment of the commercial classes at the arbitrary restrictions on Irish foreign trade which was at that time voiced even by the Irish absentee landowners in the British House of Lords. They had every reason to be concerned about the position, for the American Revolution caused the loss of the American markets for Irish linen, while the British Government put an embargo on provision exports from Ireland, thereby acutely endangering their rent receipts. 'Free trade' was won, not without the help of a first-rate upheaval which shook the British Empire to its foundations, and not without the bitter opposition of English commercial interests. The momentum of this success and the weakness of the British Government enabled the Volunteers to add political victory to economic concessions—Grattan's premature and incomplete triumph in May 1782 which re-established the legislative independence of the Irish landlord Parliament.

This success raised middle-class hopes of a resolute protectionist policy for the purpose of strengthening Ireland's backward economy. What, indeed, was the use of legislative independence for the Irish middle classes, if the Irish Parliament refused to legislate for the revival of trade and industry which had languished so long under English injustice? But the union of landlords and middle classes, which had been one of the decisive causes of success, did not continue unimpaired in the new era. The clash came in the political field over the question of parliamentary reform, and in the economic field over that of anti-British protection.

The strong protectionist agitation which swept the Irish towns in the early years of Grattan's Parliament had, therefore, comparatively little practical success. The first important protectionist measure was, ironically enough, an unalloyed landlords' Bill— Foster's Corn Law of 1784. This law put a substantial premium on grain exports and thereby helped to cure the landlords' permanent headache at the public expense, by assisting the transformation of their Irish rents into English cash. The ultimate basis for the success of the scheme was the lifting of English objections to Irish tillage. England had become an importer of wheat, and this change in her grain production balance made Ireland a desirable source of necessary foodstuffs instead of a potential rival in foreign grain markets. Amongst Irish manufactures, the most important case of effective protection was that of the cotton industry, and at the time of the Union a respectable industry had developed behind this protective wall—very much to the disgust of the British cotton masters.

Although the Irish Parliament was generally unwilling to antagonise England by provocative measures of protection, it was by no means indifferent to the growth of Irish trade and commerce. The encouragement of industries by bounties was not always effective, but, under the impulse of the developing industrial revolution, its actions were sufficiently successful for the unstinted praise of generations of nationalist historians.[56]

However little the masses may have benefited from this partial prosperity, the economic dilemma from which Irish economy had been suffering for a century was well on its way towards solution. The poverty of the peasants was bound to continue while all the surplus of their labour above the subsistence minimum was confiscated by their landlords, lessees, middlemen, parsons and other parasites with vested interests in their exploitation; but the absurd situation had come to an end, which had forced a poor country to pay year by year large sums to its rich neighbour without being allowed to use the labour of its people or the produce of its soil in such a way as to make these payments possible. In the conflict between English mercantile interests and Irish landlords, the latter seemed at last to have gained the day.

The causes of this surprising and, as it turned out to be, temporary triumph were complicated. Internally, it had been due to the formation of a coalition between the progressive wing of the landlords and the urban middle class which had been successful beyond hope, and on the maintenance of which the consolidation of the initial success was entirely dependent. In the international sphere, the English business interests had been forced to abandon their rigid mercantilism—not through an intellectual conversion to a saner view of economic facts and laws, but through sheer necessity. But in spite of the persistence of old prejudices amongst many 'practical men of business', the economic doctrines of Adam Smith were making rapid headway amongst statesmen like the younger Pitt and the more go-ahead manufacturers in the growing textile industries. In the economic relations between England and Ireland it was no longer a question of English commercial jealousy against a potential rival, for Great Britain had advanced so far in the race that its influence and proximity completely overshadowed the development of the smaller island. Instead of letting Irish economy rot in an economic slum, English statesmanship was soon endeavouring to swallow Ireland whole, because it had become convinced of England's ability to digest the morsel. In this change of attitude, economic motives may have played a smaller part than economic facts, but they were by no means completely absent.

On a different plane, Ireland's destinies had become involved in the great crisis of British power which began with the American Revolution and ended with Napoleon's overthrow. England's defeat in the former had presented Ireland with the opportunity of reasserting herself as a nation. But England remained engaged, with only a few years' interruption, in a drawn-out struggle against a formidable continental power, which strained all her resources and which made it impossible to permit Ireland to leave the orbit of British power, because this would have weakened Britain and given a dangerous access of strength to France. In the unfolding drama of the French Revolutionary Wars Ireland was destined to play a crucial part, in which the grand strategy of a world conflict was interwoven with the play of powerful material interests and with the revolutionary struggle for freedom of a small subject nation.

CHAPTER VI

'GRATTAN'S' PARLIAMENT AND THE UNITED IRISHMEN

REGARDED as a national revolution, the arrangement of 1782 fully deserved Wolfe Tone's contemptuous description as a most bungling, imperfect business whose main effect was the doubling in value of the numerous Irish pocket boroughs. In fact, it was not a revolution at all but the political by-product of an economic readjustment demanded by the absurdity of a debtor country being compelled to pay its debts, while at the same time the creditor prevented it from doing so. The promoters of the settlement of 1782 on both sides of the Irish Sea were Whigs, landed gentlemen who were very much concerned about the welfare of their class and of the social system on which this welfare depended. English Whigs whose material interests were not so closely concerned in the matter as to blur their political vision, had considerable misgivings about the ultimate results of Irish legislative independence, but for the time being there was little reason for their anxiety, for not even the most enthusiastic followers of Henry Grattan were ready to turn their newly achieved independence into an instrument of separation.

Grattan himself always combined his advocacy of Irish national claims with unqualified insistence on Ireland's duty to follow Britain without questioning in all matters of Imperial policy, and particularly in all decisions on war and peace. This was the inevitable result of his social outlook, which was just as conservative as that of the English Whigs; as the social order of colonial Ireland depended entirely on English power, the necessity of the English connection for a 'free' Ireland was a fundamental article of faith for Grattan and for all Irish Whigs. But in the political field, Grattan involved himself in hopeless difficulties. He wanted to maintain the English connection, while abolishing English interference in the internal affairs of Ireland. He demanded parliamentary reform and responsible government, coupled with a clean-up in the Augean stable of Castle administration, although the fulfilment of these demands would have destroyed the very basis of England's power over Ireland. His policy would have been reasonable only if the basic interests of the two countries had been identical or at least compatible, instead of being radically opposed to one another, thereby necessitating the repeated use of force by the stronger nation.

Grattan's liberalism was the expression of his desire to put the

Irish political system on English foundations. He rightly regarded the representation of property as the basic principle of eighteenth-century parliamentarism, and he was in advance of the semi-feudal ideas of his times and his class by wishing to extend its privileges to personal property, i.e. to the middle classes. He was, therefore, a formidable critic of the unreformed Irish House of Commons with its large majority of placemen and pocket-borough members, who falsified the representation of genuine property interests, and a warm friend of the Catholic claim for 'full emancipation'. His political master plan was the union of all Irish property owners irrespective of religion; his method was an alliance between the progressive landlords and the middle classes on the lines of the Irish Volunteers.

The radical defect of Grattan's political programme was the incompatibility of the 'English connection' with the interests of the growing urban bourgeoisie which formed the left wing of his alliance. The settlement of 1782, which removed an artificial obstacle to the enjoyment by the Irish landlords of the fruits of their conquest, completely satisfied even the most progressive land-owners. Their and Grattan's pro-British attitude was not entirely a matter of sentiment, for the Irish land system would have broken down after the withdrawal of British armed support, particularly after the outbreak of the French Revolution. The urban bour-geoisie, on the other hand, saw in the 'revolution' of 1782 only an earnest of greater things to come—above all the establishment of a protectionist Irish government which would allow the develop-ment of Irish trade and industry unhampered by superior British competition. The business interests of the North never completely agreed with Grattan's policy, and even in the Dublin Whig Club, the plebeian elements tried to raise their voices, and demanded a more democratic programme than appeared suitable to the aristo-cratic leaders who retorted with the ominous words 'that if the people of Ireland were dissatisfied with the share of liberty they enjoyed under the wisest of constitutions, the people of property would have to consider a Union with England'.[57]

The fragile alliance between the progressive wing of the country gentlemen and the middle class had little prospect of wresting the government of the country from the reactionary majority of the landlords, who regarded themselves first and foremost as England's garrison in hostile territory and who had no illusions about their chances of staying in power without British support in the shape of soldiers and ships of the line. They had none of Grattan's scruples about national honour and independence and were willing to pay the price of subordination to England in exchange for the maintenance of their privileged position by British force of arms. On the other hand, they found it necessary to give the more solid mercantile interests a share in the administration, and the spokesmen of this group, Speaker Foster and Sir John Parnell, played a considerable part in the economic policy of the Government.

The impotence of the progressive landlord party under Grattan and the unassailable power of the 'ascendancy' reactionaries resulted in a complete polarisation of Irish politics during Grattan's Parliament. The leadership of the opposition moved from the moderates to the extremists until the practical alternative before the country was narrowed down to the choice between revolution and a régime of terror by the vested interests, leading to the legislative Union. The individual stages of this process are reflected in the gradual transformation of the United Irishmen from a radical reform organisation into a revolutionary secret society.

Wolfe Tone, the ablest political strategist amongst the Irish revolutionaries, made his political *début* as a 'Northern Whig', but he did not remain for long in the Whig camp. The hopelessness of achieving real political progress on the lines advocated by Grattan was too easy to see for a mind not befogged by social interests which were incompatible with a realistic approach to the problems of colonial Ireland. The Society of United Irishmen, founded by Tone and his associates as a practical alternative to Whiggism, was essentially modern in its aims and methods. It was created by professional and business men of the Protestant minority, almost all of whom were Ulstermen, and it was in Ulster that it had the greatest immediate success. Nevertheless it was neither sectarian nor provincial, but a movement of national and social regeneration.

The United Irishmen were originally a radical reform party with legal aims whose work began where that of the Whigs and the Volunteers had come to an end. They shared with both their support of parliamentary reform which they combined with a new emphasis on the Catholic question, but by asking for political self-expression for the subjected masses of Catholic Ireland, the United Irishmen turned away from the privileged actors in the foreground of the political scene and appealed to the authentic people.

The first step in the radicalisation of the United Irishmen was their alliance with the Catholic agitation. Tone sponsored the Catholic claims effectively as a Northern Whig and served as agent to the political committee of the Catholics, which had turned to the left when it became clear that the Whigs were too weak to persuade a majority of the pensioned Irish Parliament to grant Catholic emancipation in the usual parliamentary way. The leadership of the Catholic Committee passed from the handful of landowners who had managed to keep their estates through the period of persecution and expropriation to the Catholic middle class. Byrne and Keogh, two wealthy Dublin merchants, were responsible for Tone's appointment, although their personal radicalism was by no means of sterling quality, as Tone himself ruefully observed. Keogh lived long enough to be the leader of the moderates on the Catholic Board in opposition to the 'radical' Daniel O'Connell, but in 1792 he was largely responsible for the daring manœuvre which turned the Catholics away from the highly respectable Grattans and Burkes to Wolfe Tone and Richard McCormick, who were at the same time prominent United Irishmen and agents for the Catholic Committee which they led to a great, though incomplete victory.

While Burke, the son of the foremost opponent of the French Revolution, had seemed a living guarantee for the loyalty of the Catholics, Tone and the new Catholic Committee soon embarked on a policy which was clearly modelled on French revolutionary methods. Without the help, and frequently against the opposition, of the Catholic clergy, the Committee organised a Convention, followed by a delegation to London which impressed Pitt so strongly with the seriousness of the situation that he broke the resistance of the Dublin Government to the enfranchisement of the Catholics. Up to this point the alliance between the United Irishmen and the Catholic middle class had been triumphantly successful, but its very success was fatal to its continuation. The Catholic merchants were not just 'bad revolutionaries', as Tone had discovered, but no revolutionaries at all. They were frightened by the very size of their victory: the entry of 30,000 Catholic smallholders into politics threatened to open the doors of the political underworld, and the respectable Catholics began to shrink from the consequences of their own agitation. In order to overthrow the ascendancy party, the Catholic middle class had to appeal to the masses, which did not want to carve out a niche for the respectable Catholics within the existing system, but to abolish the system as a whole. Hardpressed by the Government, which demanded the dissolution of the Catholic Committee as the price of the Relief Bill of 1793, and faced by the alternative of a serious revolutionary struggle, the Committee dissolved itself, to the great comfort of the gentry and the hierarchy. The United Irishmen, who had been largely responsible for its success, were left out in the cold—in Tone's case with a handsome testimonial. Their strategy had proved its potential value, but it left them bitterly disappointed with their respectable allies and in search of an auxiliary capable of supplying the driving force behind their plans.

Meanwhile the Irish Government was teaching their leaders an object-lesson about the limitations of constitutional methods. The great Catholic Convention of 1792 had frightened the authorities, and the Anti-Convention Act of 1793 made its repetition impossible and remained for generations a shackle on all popular organisations. At the same time the possession of arms was made illegal, except for the upper classes, and the Government began open warfare against the potential revolutionaries.

The absence of organised competition for the loyalty of the Catholic masses gave the United Irishmen their greatest chance. Particularly in south Ulster, where friction between Protestants and Catholics was most severe, the Catholic Defenders had a considerable following. An alliance with the United Irishmen promised to transform the Defenders from isolated and therefore ineffective groups of rebellious peasants into a well-knit movement with central leadership and a policy of its own. This process was greatly assisted by the creation of a military *cadre* within the framework of the Society of United Irishmen: towards the end of 1796, the civil society had been practically duplicated by a military organisation which tried to combine administrative and military functions under strict central leadership with democratic control over policy.[58]

Most of the United Irish leaders were aware at an early date that their approach to the problems of Irish society made them *de facto* revolutionaries, although their political methods remained during the first few years of the Society's existence perfectly constitutional. The logic of their position made them at the same time separatists, or from the English point of view traitors. Ulster, the birthplace and the stronghold of the United Irish movement, had a long record of disloyalty, from the time of the Glorious Revolution of 1688 to that of the American Revolution in which so many Ulstermen played a distinguished part. Ulster's enthusiasm for America was due to a feeling of solidarity with the colonists who successfully challenged the power which was an incubus for Ulster as well, and the Ulster people were proud of their kinship with many of the finest fighters in the Revolutionary army. The shock administered by America to the British Empire made it possible to achieve Free Trade and legislative independence for Ireland. The resumption of trade with the United States on a steadily increasing scale after the cessation of hostilities was of special benefit to Ulster and particularly to Belfast, which became a first-rate port as a result of its position in transatlantic trade.

Ulster welcomed with similar enthusiasm the French Revolution of 1789. Important as was the influence of the United States, America was too far away and too preoccupied with the problems of its own growth to exert a substantial influence on Anglo-Irish relations. France, on the other hand, was near, and England's leadership of the anti-revolutionary coalition made the French Government vitally interested in any real chance of inflicting damage on its most dangerous enemy. Royalist France had struck the British Empire a body blow through the encouragement of the American Revolution; Republican France might strike at England just as effectively, and far more conveniently, through supporting an Irish revolution. It was to France, therefore, that the United Irishmen turned in their search for an ally whose power could balance the overwhelming superiority of England over their own unaided efforts.

Informed Irish opinion differed very little about the probable effect of a French descent in force on Ireland. Nobody doubted that such an event would have meant at least the temporary eclipse of British rule. The failure of Hoche's powerful expedition during the winter of 1796 did not reassure the friends and dependants of the English connection, who were deeply disturbed by the ease with which the French Fleet had reached Bantry Bay and had got home again without being even contacted by the English Navy. Competent observers were well aware of the inferiority of the troops stationed in Ireland compared with the French army, even before the Castlebar Races and Sir Ralph Abercromby exposed them in their different ways.

In view of the crucial importance of Ireland in the struggle between England and France, it must appear strange that the French leaders did not redouble their efforts after the failure at Bantry Bay. The French Government and High Command, and especially the French Ministry of Marine, were singularly inept in their Irish policy and strategy. This may have been partly due to the acknowledged superiority of the British Navy, but the main cause may well have been the rapid decline of the revolutionary impetus in French policy in favour of militarist and imperialist tendencies. Wolfe Tone's comparative success in Paris was not exclusively due to his powers of persuasion but to the obvious promise of the situation. Nobody was, indeed, better aware than he himself of the limitations of his success and of the decline of the French revolutionary forces who were the most reliable allies of the Irish rebels and conspirators.

Tone's personal hero and the leading advocate of a resolute attack on Ireland was Lazare Hoche, whose strategic gifts made him Bonaparte's main rival for military fame, while his attachment to the principles of the revolution made him the exponent of a way of life which at that time belonged already to history. With Hoche's early death, Tone lost his most powerful friend and Bonaparte his most dangerous antagonist. The future emperor regarded the Irish revolutionaries with little sympathy, and with not a little of the scornful suspicion which he reserved for their allies, the French Jacobins. Bonaparte's anti-English policy was never revolutionary but strictly imperialist. His attack on Egypt was a striking expression of the gulf between his ideas and the conceptions which had dominated Hoche in his Irish policy. Bonaparte wanted to wrest the most precious part of her colonial wealth from Britain, while Hoche aimed a decisive blow against English imperialism by supporting the subject Irish people. Bonaparte's rejection of an alliance with the Irish revolutionary forces was the logical result of his subordination of society to strategy and of his revulsion from the principles of the French Revolution. This decision may well have been the turning-point of the whole war, as Napoleon himself regretfully thought on St. Helena, and it certainly meant the salvation of the governing Irish class.

While the Irish Government could do little to prevent a French invasion, it strained every nerve to destroy the revolutionary body which endangered its very existence. The United Irish movement was strongest in Ulster, and Dublin Castle was more afraid of a revolution in Northern Ireland than of peasant risings in other provinces. The measures employed by the authorities against the revolutionaries were effective but very ruthless, and are a matter of historical notoriety.

In southern Ulster the Government's policy of unrelieved ferocity was supplemented by the official and semi-official exploitation of the religious feud between Protestants and Catholics. It seems that the Orange Order originated amongst the Episcopalians, who formed the large majority of the English settlers in County Armagh. On the other hand, many Presbyterians, in spite of their strong aversion to the Catholic religion, even offered their hospitality to the victims of the expulsions in Armagh, while areas with a large majority of Presbyterian dissenters were usually known as hotbeds of sedition. The Government was at first afraid of the effects which the rabid anti-Catholicism of the Orange Order might have on the army and militia, both of which consisted predominantly of Roman Catholics. But its scruples dwindled during the months preceding the rebellion, and many Yeomanry formations simply consisted of Orange clubs, which had been taken over almost in their entirety by the military authorities.

The reverse of this development was the quick growth of the United Irish movement amongst the Catholics: 'Wherever the Orange system was introduced, particularly in Catholic Counties, it was uniformly observed that the numbers of the United Irishmen increased most astonishingly. The alarm which an Orange Lodge excited among the Catholics made them look for refuge by joining together in the United system, and, as their number was always greater than that of bigoted Protestants, our harvest was tenfold' (Memoir of the State Prisoners).[59]

Hunted by the Government and abandoned by their respectable Catholic allies of yesteryear, the United Irishmen became steadily more radical. In the year before the rebellion, the authorities believed they noticed that the leaders were losing control and that 'a set of lower mechanics' had assumed the direction of affairs.[60] At the same time the reign of terror unleashed in Ulster by General Lake seems to have made a profound impression on potential rebels with substantial property at stake, particularly in Belfast. Whether the Ulstermen were really 'cowards and braggarts', as Wolfe Tone asserted as early as 1793, or whether the concentrated frightfulness of the army, militia and yeomanry had achieved its purpose, the rebellion never really got under way in Ulster.

Apart from force, espionage was probably the most effective weapon of the authorities for the decapitation of the conspiracy. Spies and informers always played an important part in the system of Irish government, but during the period before the rebellion of 1798 they were just as necessary and important an instrument of Government policy as the armed forces. One valuable source of information which frequently had a bearing on events in Ireland was Pitt's spy service in France, which comprised a good many Irish priests in English pay.[61] The Irish Government itself was being kept informed by spies within the highest circles of the United Irishmen, and almost all successful measures against the leaders of the conspiracy were based on information from these sources.

In the final convulsion of 1798, remnants of the middle-class Catholic element in the United Irish organisation played a remarkable and sinister part. Richard McCormick, the ex-secretary of the Catholic Committee, fled from Ireland in March 1798 more in fear of his comrades than of the Government. Thomas Reynolds, the man who delivered the Leinster Committee of the United Irishmen into the hands of the authorities, was a Catholic of considerable property, though this did not prevent him from demanding money for his revelations. Magan, a Catholic barrister, betrayed Lord Edward Fitzgerald. The ship was sinking, and the rats left while the going was good. The organisation of revolt was destroyed, but the rebellion could not be prevented, even if this was the intention of the Government. But when it came, it was not an organised war of the Irish people against its conquerors but an elemental rising of the peasantry of a few counties with a definitely anti-Protestant bias. The Wexford rebellion, though aimless and leaderless, was nevertheless a very impressive popular movement. In Castlereagh's words, the rebels consisted of 'the entire male inhabitants of Wexford, and the greatest proportion of those of Wicklow, Kildare, Carlow and Kilkenny'; and though he exaggerated the importance of the rebellion when he said that 'there never was in any country so formidable an effort on the part of the people',[62] it certainly was a movement of elemental force with outstanding potentialities. But in the absence of effective nation-wide organisation, and unsupported by the French, even the most determined local rebellion was doomed to failure.

The suppression of the rebels was organised and supervised by the Irish upper classes as a whole, both Protestant and Catholic, but its immediate result was the strengthening of the ascendancy party, which had consistently opposed any concessions to the masses and which now pointed out the fatal results of a policy, that, thanks to its opposition, had never been really tried in practice. The 'loyalty' of the wealthy Catholics and of the prelacy was brushed aside and the Government exploited the patent disaffection of the Catholic masses and a good many members of the lower clergy as justification for a strictly Orange terror régime. The new Lord Lieutenant, Lord Cornwallis, who was moved by humanity and policy alike to abridge the horrors of retaliation inflicted on the population of the disturbed areas, found strong opposition amongst his closest subordinates to a policy which he regarded as essential for the success of the Union, the main purpose of his mission.

CHAPTER VII

TOWARDS THE UNION

IRELAND's legislative independence during the period of Grattan's Parliament was a mere by-product of the American Revolution. Great Britain had been so dangerously weakened by the long and humiliating struggle against the alliance between France and the rebellious American colonies that it could not face the threat of another amputation of the Empire near to its most vital parts. The British Government bowed to the facts, and Parliament formally renounced its disputed power of legislating for the Kingdom of Ireland. Yet the recognition of the independence of the Irish Parliament in no way reduced the dependence of the Irish Government on that of Great Britain: St. Stephen's Green was declared to be independent of Westminster, but Dublin Castle remained a subordinate branch of Whitehall. If Ireland's new-born legislative independence was to be more than an empty word, it had to be crowned by the exclusive responsibility of the Irish executive to its local Parliament; if Dublin Castle was to remain the servant of every British ministry, the independence of the Irish Parliament was an intolerable nuisance and complication of the process of government. The settlement of 1782 was 'an experiment to accomplish impossibilities; to reconcile the ancient government of jobbers and dependents with the new spirit of the people who had recovered their constitution by a victory over that government' (Grattan).[63]

The Irish House of Commons comprised some representatives of the country gentry, but in its overwhelming majority it was not an elective body at all. Out of its 300 members, only the 64 county representatives were elected on a more or less open franchise which enabled the resident landlords to influence the results in proportion to their land and position. Of the rest, '124 were nominated absolutely by 53 peers, while 91 others were chosen by 52 commoners'.[64] In addition, the Government disposed of a large number of members who were 'placemen' of one kind or another; in 1790 no fewer than 108 members received Government salaries or pensions.[65] This direct hold of the administration over a large block of votes, coupled with its ability to secure the support of powerful borough owners, was essential in order to make the system work at all, through the factual subordination of the sovereign and independent Parliament of Ireland to the 'British Minister'.

Although the English defeat in the War of Independence had

been final and conclusive as far as the American nation was concerned, it was no more than an episode in the imperialist struggle between Great Britain and France. During the American Revolution the continental monarchy helped the struggling republic to maintain itself against the forces of its legitimate king, because such a policy promised to weaken its most powerful rival. But Britain, although seriously weakened by defeat, was by no means permanently disabled. After a few years of peace she made a remarkable recovery, while France became in turn involved in an internal upheaval which led to her temporary eclipse as a great power but to her final emergence as *la grande nation*.

The home policy of the younger Pitt centred on the resolute encouragement of the economic development which confirmed England's position as the foremost industrial and mercantile nation. In this policy Ireland played a peculiar and important part which differed characteristically from her Cinderella role during the mercantilist century just drawing to its close.

When the French plenipotentiaries demanded in the Peace Treaty of 1783 the conclusion of an Anglo-French Commercial Treaty within a specified period, they intended to clinch England's military defeat by a hard economic bargain. Instead of this, the Commercial Treaty of 1786 became the first triumph of the new economic policy which furthered Great Britain's true economic interests through the practical application of free trade principles. In the framework of this policy Pitt's famous Commercial Propositions of 1785 for the settlement of Anglo-Irish economic relations were cast for a first-class role.

In the heyday of *laissez faire* it may have been sufficient to explain this fateful episode by Pitt's admiration for Adam Smith and the gospel of the *Wealth of Nations*. In fact it was a complex measure conditioned by very practical considerations. In the international sphere Pitt was greatly in need of a stronger bargaining position with France over the impending Commercial Treaty, and in 1785 the entry of Ireland on England's side into the negotiations was a far from negligible factor. In Anglo-Irish relations proper, the clamour for protection against England was raised so loudly by the Irish middle class, that it was obviously necessary to forestall this danger by an arrangement which would make protection impossible for the independent Irish Parliament. The growing importance of the Ulster middle-class element amongst the Irish Volunteers, aided by acute distress during the hard winter of 1784, gave a strong impetus to the protectionist agitation in Ireland, which culminated in an Address by the Irish House of Commons in May 1784 asking for a review of the commercial relations between the two kingdoms. Pitt's Commercial Propositions were, amongst other things, an

attempt to allay this clamour for protection in England's nearest
and one of her best markets.

Ireland's population was almost one-half of that of Great Britain,
although in wealth and economic importance its weight was considerably less. Even more important than the simple quantitative
aspect was the possibility of using the Irish trade question as a lever
for freeing England's economic life from the traditions of protection
which had become a shackle to its further growth, although the
bulk of the trading classes clung to them with all the tenacity of
unreasoning habit. The only serious obstacle to an unprecedented
increase in England's wealth through the use of new mechanical
methods of production seemed to be the crippling burden of taxation,
due to the ruinous war expenditure and the corresponding increase
in the public debt. Pitt's Commercial Propositions were admirably
contrived to further his ends in all these directions: they would have
unified Great Britain and Ireland for all purposes of trade, both
internal and external; they would have reduced the general level
of protective duties in both countries; and they would have assured
England of a substantial and permanent Irish contribution towards
English Imperial expenditure.[66]

Historians are agreed that the failure of the Commercial Propositions contained the germ of the Legislative Union. This was not due
to any personal resentment or animosity on the part of Pitt. The
English Prime Minister knew very well how to accept a rebuff, as
is shown by his inglorious career as a parliamentary reformer, and
by his still more compromising attitude on Catholic Emancipation.
His very different reaction to the failure of his Irish commercial
policy was due to weightier and less personal reasons.

An independent Irish Parliament which would not agree to the
only terms of economic union acceptable to the British business
interests was not the asset in England's international balance which
Pitt sorely needed but a definite liability. In spite of the outcry
amongst English manufacturers about the dangers of Irish competition, Pitt believed with the best economic opinion of his time
in the advantages of open competition, which could not fail to benefit
the more advanced country more than its backward competitor,
but free trade was incompatible with a political system which
permitted Ireland to build up her own industries behind protective
tariffs. The more enlightened leaders of British industry wished for
nothing better than competition on formally even terms with foreign
industries, both in Britain and abroad. The admission of British
goods into the home markets of their rivals was, however, essential
because it prevented the use of non-economic weapons by other
countries as a counterweight to Britain's economic superiority.

English foreign trade found its most serious obstacles not in the economic but in the political field, in the exclusion of its goods from foreign markets by prohibitions or prohibitive duties. An Anglo-Irish Union at the end of the eighteenth century differed, therefore, in its economic consequences from the Union which had been so warmly desired by a good many patriotic Irishmen at its beginning —and the difference was all in favour of Great Britain. Instead of admitting a dangerous rival to a jealously guarded trade preserve, which nobody could enter without damage to the monopolist, the Union would now create equal rights without equal opportunities for the weaker partner. Instead of opening the door of a mercantilist paradise to the hungry traders of Ireland, the Union threatened to expose the emaciated economy of the less advanced partner to the competition of the most highly developed industrial nation on earth, while its very definition would exclude the use of non-economic measures like bounties, import duties and trade regulations by the weaker country.

The French Commercial Treaty of 1786 occupies a curious intermediary position between domestic economy and international power politics. In this treaty the English plenipotentiary, Lord Auckland, triumphed through astuteness and corruption, for the degeneration of the French Government was such as to allow the betrayal of the French textile industry for hard English cash. This triumph of British trade and diplomacy was, however, paid dearly by the bitter anti-English feeling on the other side of the Channel: the French urban middle class saw in England its great, and for the time being its superior, competitor, and England's leadership of the anti-revolutionary coalition fanned the embers of industrial rivalry into a nation-wide flame of hatred, which was a much more intense and dangerous feeling than the contempt of revolutionary France for her decaying feudal enemies in the East.

The dangers of this new international conflagration, and the unexpected success of the revolutionary armies, gave a new urgency to the problem of Ireland's position within the British Empire. The economic disadvantage of an unco-operative, and even a protectionist, Ireland would have been substantial but not at all fatal to the growth of British trade, but the possible strategic results of a hostile Ireland overshadowed economic and political considerations. An independent Ireland would have been automatically an ally of France, for Irish independence could be maintained against British opposition only in alliance with another Great Power. The sweeping success of the French revolutionary armies and their appeal to all subject peoples transformed this possibility into a pressing and at times almost overwhelming danger.

England's rule of the seas was at that time not yet so firmly
established that the attempt of a French invasion of Ireland could
be safely ignored. When this attempt was undertaken in force, it
was not prevented by the British Navy but frustrated by a series of
accidents. The strategic implications of a successful descent of the
French on Ireland would have been very serious and might have
decided the war. If Antwerp was a pistol aimed at England's heart,
Ireland under French occupation would have produced an obstruction in the British system of communications, which might have
choked England altogether. Free access to the Atlantic was the
absolute condition of England's life as it had been the source of her
historic greatness. With Cork, Waterford, Wexford, Dublin and
Belfast in enemy hands, the British Navy and British commerce
would have been exposed to an unbearable strain. The flaring-up
of the French Revolutionary War made English rule over Ireland
a necessary condition for Britain's survival in her as yet greatest
struggle against a continental Great Power.

The recognition of Ireland's legislative independence in May 1782
made the maintenance of this rule much more difficult than before.
The plan of a mutually advantageous economic union had failed,
partly owing to Pitt's inept management and his subsequent surrender to the clamour of backward English opinion. The rejection
of the revised proposals by the Irish Parliament had been due to
its abhorrence of a measure which, though economically still
favourable, was stigmatised by Grattan as 'an incipient and creeping
Union'.[67] The prevailing government by corruption was expensive
and, even according to the far from squeamish standards of the
time, somewhat repulsive, but above all cumbersome and in times
of crisis dangerously inefficient. The conception of replacing this
outgrowth of colonial times by a complete remodelling of Anglo-
Irish relations through a Union was, therefore, irresistibly attractive
to the British Government.

In the second half of the century, the idea of a Union with
England had become thoroughly unpopular in Ireland, as Arthur
Young noticed even before the era of Grattan's Parliament and the
liberation of Irish trade. This opposition had greatly increased in
strength after 1782, and for the next ten or fifteen years the accomplishment of the Union had to be ruled out as a practical measure.
The most the British Government could do was the gradual assimilation of Irish to English conditions, wherever this was possible.
In the course of time this policy degenerated into a kind of government by blackmail which prevented the redress of patent grievances
for the duration of Irish legislative independence, in order to discredit
the Irish Parliament by making reforms dependent on the Union.

The first great subject where progress in Ireland was prevented by the lack of progress in Great Britain had little or no connection with the prospective Union. Parliamentary reform was still more urgent in Ireland than it was in England, and the demand for a clean-up of the Parliamentary Augean Stable on St. Stephen's Green followed immediately on Grattan's 'revolution'. This demand was happily voiced at the very moment when an avowed, if moderate, reformer was taking the helm of the British Government. But Pitt not only dropped parliamentary reform in England when he found the resistance of vested interests too strong for his taste, but made Government approval of Irish reform dependent on the adoption of a similar measure in Great Britain.

From the very start of his active career, Pitt regarded the unification of Great Britain and Ireland as a foremost object of his statesmanship. As he expressed it in a letter to the Duke of Rutland, the Irish Lord Lieutenant of the day, he wanted to use free trade as a vehicle for making the two nations 'one country in effect, though for local concerns under distinct legislatures' (6th January 1785).[68] Parliamentary reform in Ireland would have increased the differences between the two countries, quite apart from causing domestic difficulties for the British Government, and it had therefore to be dropped, although it was absolutely vital for the growth of a healthy political life in Ireland.

The first occasion when Pitt confessed that the idea of a Union had long been in his mind occurred in 1792 in connection with the question of admitting the Irish Catholics to full political rights. 'I hardly dare flatter myself with the hope of this taking place, but I believe it, though it is not easy to be accomplished, to be the only solution for other and greater difficulties. The admission of Catholics to a share in the suffrage could not then be dangerous' (18th November 1792).[69] The overriding need for a phalanx of all anti-revolutionary forces against the onslaught of the French Revolution induced him in 1793 to give the Irish Catholics the vote, however much such a concession went against the grain of the masters of Dublin Castle, but the admission of Catholics to Parliament remained as an attractive bait for upper-class Catholics during the Union crisis.

The partial emancipation of the Catholics in 1793 illustrates by its extent, as well as by its limitations, how completely the idea of assimilating Irish to English conditions dominated the thoughts of the British Government. The Whigs, who had always prided themselves on their championship of the Catholic claims, were taken aback when Pitt told them that he had decided to enfranchise all Irish forty-shilling freeholders, and tried in vain to enlighten him about the dangerous consequences of this excessive political generosity: the admission of 30,000 Irish peasants to the vote seemed to throw open the flood-gates of revolution, instead of transforming the wealthy Catholics into pillars of the existing order. The reason for Pitt's insistence on this jacobinical franchise was revealed many years afterwards by Lord Donoughmore, one of the Protestant supporters of Catholic emancipation who accompanied the Catholic delegation and was a witness of its embarrassing success: 'We found that Pitt and Dundas, after two or three interviews with these delegates, said they would advise the prayer of their petition being granted, and that the qualification should be forty shillings. Upon this, Grattan and I asked to see Dundas, and we had different interviews with him, in which we stated that the Catholics in Ireland, in asking for a *qualified* franchise, had never thought of less than £20 a year and that they would be content even with £50. We urged again and again the impolicy of so low a franchise; and all we could get from Dundas was that it must be the same as it was in England.'[70] This consideration, and not the alleged impossibility of differentiating between Protestant and Catholic franchises, of which much was made in the Irish House of Commons, seems to have been the true reason for this important decision.

After the outbreak of the French War, the need for a legislative Union appeared more and more urgent to Pitt, and the system of Irish government by blackmail reached fantastic proportions. Its result was a complete political stalemate in Ireland. The refusal to reopen Anglo-Irish commercial negotiations did not prevent Ireland's economic advance, though it may have delayed it, but the veto on parliamentary reform, coupled with the admission of a substantial number of Catholic peasants to the vote, made Grattan's Parliament a hotbed of corruption and destroyed its reputation amongst the Irish people. The most effective use of this policy of blackmail was made by the authorities in the highly delicate negotiations with the Catholics during the Union crisis. The British Government did not make a direct promise of Catholic emancipation under the new United Parliament, but it authorised the Lord Lieutenant to give the Catholics thoroughly misleading assurances on the subject, while Pitt made it clear that he would oppose Catholic emancipation as long as the Dublin Parliament remained in being.

The abortive rebellion allowed the Government to deal piecemeal with the opposition against the Legislative Union. Most landlords were frightened into acquiescence or support by the conviction that their position depended, in the last resort, on English arms; others were impressed by the resolute action taken against prominent anti-Unionists in high places, such as the Marquis of Downshire or Sir John Parnell; while some were bought outright by Lord Castlereagh, particularly if they disposed of the eminently marketable commodity of a seat in the House of Commons.

But there still remained even among the Anglo-Irish gentry a recalcitrant minority which opposed the Union to the bitter end. It consisted in the main of two sections with little in common except their loyalty to a separate Irish legislature. A very small number, whose most influential spokesman remained Henry Grattan, still believed in the principles of 1782, the ideal of a coalition between the landlords and the middle class, including its Catholic section. A larger body opposed the Union from fear for their monopoly of power. (Their fears proved groundless and they became the staunchest supporters of the new régime when they found that it actually strengthened their position.) These anti-Unionists of a kind were the most extreme advocates of the ascendancy system, the wire-pullers behind the Orange lodges and the most resolute enemies of Catholic emancipation, which they expected as the inevitable result of the Union. Their leaders were Sir John Parnell, the Chancellor of the Exchequer, and Speaker Foster, both of whom were prominent members of the ruling clique who particularly distinguished themselves by their hostility to any show of mercy after the Rebellion.

Foster and Parnell were closely connected with important business interests; they had managed the financial affairs of the Government during the period of prosperity after 1785, and they now voiced the fears of all business men, who found the prospect of cut-throat competition by the far superior English industry not at all to their liking. They were familiar with the financial position of the country, and their criticism of the economic clauses of the Union was proved to the hilt by the course of events. But although their opposition was a serious nuisance, the weight of the Irish business interests could not affect the issue. They would only have been formidable as leaders of the masses in a life-and-death struggle against the landlords and British rule. But this course was closed for them, for the masses would in all probability have turned against them, as well as against the landlords. At the time of the Rebellion they had ranged themselves solidly behind the Government, and in the struggle against the Union they could not even create a united front of the whole Irish middle class: an alliance with the Catholics would have been essential for the success of their resistance, but Foster and Parnell were rabid opponents of the Catholic claim for full political rights.

Castlereagh's cool and competent brain grasped and exploited

this fatal weakness of the opposition. The purchase of a parliamentary majority could not have carried the Union against a
determined popular mass movement, and the Government had to
prevent at all costs a junction between the Catholics and the
Protestant anti-Unionists. Castlereagh's unscrupulous dealings with
the Catholics were aimed at this very end, and they proved highly
successful. The anti-Protestant character of the rebellion, and the
share of Catholic priests in the actual warfare, gave him a lever
which he was not slow to use. By hardly veiled threats he black-
mailed prominent Catholic prelates into the acceptance of the royal
veto on clerical appointments and of the endowment of the priests;[71]
by a judicious mixture of three-quarters promises for the future and
iron refusal for the present he got their agreement to the Union
without prior enactment of Catholic emancipation, and this success
sufficed to offset the anti-Unionist propaganda amongst the lower
classes, which were in any case too dazed to count for much after the
recent catastrophe of the rebellion and the ensuing reign of terror.

The political achievement of carrying the Union was greater than
the simple, if sordid, transaction of buying a parliamentary majority.
It involved the delicate task of browbeating recalcitrant Protestants
without hurting them and coaxing suspicious Catholics without
coming down decisively on their side, although the Government
had to pledge its honour so far that its failure to grant full emancipation after the Union was a plain breach of faith. The treatment
of the Catholics was a piece of sharp practice, equalling in its dishonesty and the polish of its execution the finest diplomatic
manœuvres of the classical era of Cabinet diplomacy, which fitted
its hero for his future distinguished tenure of the British Foreign
Office.

The legislative Union was in a very real sense the most complete
expression of Ireland's subjection and England's supremacy. It was
the categorical denial of the existence of an independent Irish nation
with interests of its own. By limiting the parliamentary representation of Ireland to less than one-sixth of the new House of Commons
(although at that time Ireland's population was one-third of that
of the United Kingdom as a whole), it transferred the control over
Irish legislation to a body where Irish influence was screwed down
to a minimum. By maintaining the exclusion of the Catholics from
Parliament, Irish influence was further restricted to members of the
'English Garrison', and the mere Irish were effectively kept outside
the pale of the constitution.

The Union was conceived entirely in the interests of Great
Britain, and hardly a voice of protest against its enactment was
raised on the English side of St. George's Channel. The reduction,

and later on the abolition, of the customs barrier between the two countries deprived Ireland's struggling industries of protection and encouragement and freed British industry from a prospective competitor; while stunting Irish industrial development, the Union preserved Ireland as a source of cheap food and cheap labour for Great Britain and strangled her direct intercourse with the outside world. By creating the conditions for assimilating Irish taxation to that of England, the Union mobilised Ireland's financial resources for the support of a system designed to perpetuate Irish subjection and the sacrifice of Ireland's vital interests.

Most or all of these consequences of the Union which the future was to reveal were foreseen at the time by its opponents, whose judgment was almost invariably more correct than that of its supporters. However, the Union affected not only the weaker partner but also the stronger. The union of the two legislatures was the final resource of English power for the maintenance of its slipping hold over Ireland. The English Government decided on the Union not in order to change the existing relationship between the two countries but in order to prevent a threatening change. The Government of Ireland had been dependent for a long time on the British legislature, if not always in name, at least in fact. But in order to maintain this state of things it now became necessary to give to the representatives of Ireland a voice in the government of England, if not in fact, at least in name.

This new departure may have appeared harmless enough in the days of Pitt and Castlereagh and the rotten House of Commons, where the only likely result of the addition of one hundred Irish members meant a new phalanx to the ministerial hosts in a 'pensioned parliament'; but the organic political connection between a colonial subject people and the world's largest empire was bound to have momentous results. The steady progress of capitalist industrialisation produced formidable complications in the English political system during the nineteenth century: they were further increased by the echo within the British House of Commons of the clash between a semi-feudal land system and a starving subject population. For one hundred and twenty years from the Union to the Irish Revolution Ireland exerted a powerful influence on British politics and contributed far more than its proportionate share to the transformation of the British political system from the land- and money-owning oligarchy of 1800 to the near-democracy of the present day.

Book II. The 'United' Kingdom, 1801-1846

CHAPTER VIII

IRISH NATIONALISM AND BRITISH DEMOCRACY

THE régime established by the Act of Union of 1800 lasted exactly one hundred and twenty years—from the Napoleonic Wars to the end of the First World War. It coincided with the period of England's industrial and political supremacy, and its end marks, though it did not cause, the end of England's expansionist imperialism. From an Irish point of view, the milestones of this era are, however, very different: they are formed, not by two great wars for English world power, but by two great rebellions for Ireland's independence. The Union was occasioned by the Rebellion of 1798 and destroyed by the Anglo-Irish War of 1920.

The story of Anglo-Irish relations during the nineteenth century is in keeping with this strangely un-Victorian setting. It differs completely from that gradual and ordered progress towards material abundance and higher mass standards of living which followed the onrush of British capitalism in its homeland; it contains few examples of the political sagacity shown by the English aristocracy in its dealings with the English middle classes, in the course of which the old rulers gradually surrendered the trappings, and even the reality, of political power without a resort to armed struggle. In Ireland, the material exploitation of the masses was pushed to extremes far surpassing the horrors of the industrial revolution which were reached in no other country of Western Europe, and which can stand comparison with the condition of the people in Tsarist Russia or Imperial Turkey. The political relations between rulers and ruled were complicated by the existence of an unbridgeable gulf between privileged and disinherited. Ireland's political history during the nineteenth century was shaped by elemental forces of an intensity and complexity which makes it a fascinating model of modern imperialism and colonial nationalism.

A generation for which the certainties of the Victorians have ceased to be even prejudices may yet recognise in nineteenth-century Ireland the contemporary of its own colonial world. If this is true of the grim realities of economic exploitation, it applies with still greater force to the unfolding of Ireland's political struggle against British domination. Under this double pressure from outside, the Irish people were forced on to a path of political activity which made Irishmen all the world over supreme experts in the technique of founding and marshalling mass organisations, and at least respectable amateurs in the more dangerous art of conspiring against the law, which they came to regard as nothing better than an instrument of foreign domination. As conspirators they had to cede the place of honour to the Russian and Polish revolutionaries, but as organisers of political mass movements they were in a class by themselves, and their mastery of this art has made them the most formidable machine politicians in the United States and elsewhere.

The Irish nationalist agitation is particularly remarkable through the intimate intermingling of national, religious and social aspirations which is such an outstanding feature of most colonial movements. Close observation will show that, contrary to all appearances, social factors were the determining influence throughout the stormy history of Irish nationalism. It was sheer necessity which forced the respectable political leaders of the Irish middle class into an alliance with the sporadic and inarticulate, but infinitely more dynamic, movement of the peasant masses. In spite of their contemptuous repugnance towards these dangerous allies, they had to establish at least a temporary understanding with them, because the British Government and the Anglo-Irish aristocracy were completely indifferent to the pious wishes, exhortations and protests of the middle-class politicians, while they were backed by nothing more substantial than appeals to fair play and the spirit of the British constitution. Only when it was threatened by a united front between the Irish middle classes and the labouring poor did the Government take their demands seriously and offer substantial concessions as the price of the dissolution of this dangerous union. Conversely, the prevention of such an alliance between the different classes of the Irish people was the constant preoccupation of the most intelligent English statesmen in their dealings with Ireland, and the breakdown of English rule was largely due to their failure to convince the dominant powers of British society of the merits of such an enlightened policy.

National oppression and struggles of national emancipation have been for centuries a commonplace of European history. From the early days of the Habsburg monarchy, both in its Spanish and in its Austrian branches, the growth of small peoples to full economic stature and independent nationhood was accomplished by tenacious struggles against powerful empires which tried to reduce them to the position of mere provinces. Russia endeavoured for centuries to impose its iron rule on Poland without being able to crush her independent national character. The Turkish Empire was based on the stupid and cruel oppression of many nationalities which nevertheless survived generations of grim and barbarous misrule. The long history of the British conquest of Ireland and of the age-old struggle of the Irish against their conquerors differs in one important respect from these classical examples of imperialist domination. The Dutch, the Poles and the Greeks were on a higher level of material civilisation than their Spanish, Russian and Turkish rulers; but in spite of the mythical grandeurs of early Irish history, the English were a more civilised and materially progressive nation than the Irish. To this extent, Ireland's position can be more properly compared with that of the Slav countries under Teuton and Austrian rule, but such comparison would still ignore the most characteristic feature of Anglo-Irish relations.

Ireland was not only a backward subject nation in the grip of a more powerful country, like the Czechs under Austrian domination, it was at the same time the first important colony of the country which blazed the trail for modern capitalism. Irish history reflects the forces which transformed Great Britain from a feudal into a capitalist country, and the Anglo-Irish nexus affected the political development of the ruling nation almost as deeply as that of its unwilling victim. This connection, however painful and tragic for generations of Irishmen, raises Irish history from the respectable but limited level of the chronicle of a brave and unfortunate small nation to the sphere of world history.

The vicissitudes of what was then known as the Irish Question have attracted considerable attention both from Irish and from English historians, although no work comparable to Lecky's *Irish History in the Eighteenth Century* has yet been produced for later periods. The main reason for this omission may well have been the difficulty, or impossibility, of separating Ireland's history during the nineteenth century from that of Great Britain. However this may be, the effect of English rule on Irish destinies has always been in the forefront of the discussion, for the use and abuse of English power has been the *leitmotiv* of Irish history since the Middle Ages. The interest of most investigators was, therefore, absorbed by the question whether this influence was good or bad, or rather whether its undeniably evil effects were due to necessity or to wanton malice; and their conclusions were almost in all cases determined by their political beliefs or prejudices.

But the bond of Anglo-Irish relations was not quite so one-sided as the preoccupation of the historians with Irish wrongs or Irish failings would seem to indicate. The proximity of a smaller island and of a people on a lower material level which made it inferior in armed combat to the English, whatever its physical courage and intellectual gifts, affected the outlook of influential sections of the

English people from the days of Strongbow, and particularly since the times of the Tudors when English expansion began in earnest. Ireland figured largely in the Great Rebellion and in the Glorious Revolution, just as it played an important part in the formulation of English mercantilist policy, which was nowhere pursued with greater zeal and more pernicious results than towards Ireland. In England's mortal struggle with revolutionary France, Ireland was the Achilles heel of the British Empire, although good luck and French irresolution saved England from the danger of a powerful army across St. George's Channel.

From the time of the Union, Ireland's influence on Great Britain became so much more intimate that it changed its character: it was, in fact, the most powerful influence ever exerted by a colony on an imperial power since the cultural penetration of the Roman Empire by Greece. But Ireland's influence on England had nothing to do with its culture. Although a large number of Irishmen achieved fame in England, they did so by a successful assimilation of English culture, for which Ireland supplied merely the gifted and receptive human raw material. Ireland's economic importance for England, which was far from negligible in the early years after the Union, greatly declined from the middle of the nineteenth century onwards, and it had really never been paramount. It was mainly as a result of the political settlement made at the time of the Union that Irish problems and the Irish people became one of the most powerful factors in British public life, from Parliament down to the inarticulate and politically semi-conscious movement of the submerged masses. This political development was deeply rooted in the social conditions of the Irish people, and its analysis provides an important clue to the understanding of British democracy.

Even on the most superficial view, the extent of Irish influence on British politics between Waterloo and Versailles is astounding. The fall of British ministries on Irish questions or through the use of the Irish vote was for many years more the rule than the exception. The number of famous English politicians of the first rank who started their career in the office of Chief Secretary for Ireland, as the best school for the more responsible job of English government, makes impressive reading. Names like that of Lord Castlereagh, the Duke of Wellington, Sir Robert Peel, Lord Melbourne, Lord Derby, the Duke of Devonshire, Sir Henry Campbell-Bannerman and Lord Balfour appear in the list, and Irish problems were amongst the main preoccupations of statesmen like Lord John Russell, Gladstone and Joseph Chamberlain, although none of them was ever directly concerned with the day-by-day government of Ireland.

On a less personal plane, Ireland's influence on the growth of modern British institutions is a subject worth more detailed consideration than it has so far received. At a time when English local government still remained the happy hunting-ground of local squires and parsons, the necessities of the situation compelled the Irish Government to work out the principles of a more effective system of administration. The institution of the stipendiary magistrate and the modern police of Sir Robert Peel owe a great debt to Irish examples. Competitive examination as a method of appointment, at least to some technical government offices, had to be tried out in Ireland long before its more general application in India, not to mention in Great Britain. The first attempts of grappling with the denominational stranglehold on popular education were not made in England but in Ireland, on lines which later on were followed in England. Above all, at a time when *laissez faire* was still the economic gospel of Great Britain, it had to be abandoned in Ireland under the impact of the famine and later on under the pressure of a radical political and agrarian movement. The large-scale expropriation, albeit against ample compensation, of the class which for so long had ruled Ireland with a rod of iron, was a curious experiment for a Victorian and Edwardian House of Commons, and it was Ireland which compelled the proudest oligarchy in the world to surrender to a plebeian democracy.

The part played by the Irish, both in Ireland and in Great Britain, in the growth of British democracy is, perhaps, their most remarkable contribution to modern political development. The Irish Question gave the first and most difficult impetus to the chain of circumstances which culminated in the Reform Bill of 1832, the first body-blow to the rule of the previously all-powerful aristocracy; the Irish party in the British House of Commons, irrevocably committed to this course by the logic of its position, was ultimately responsible for the Parliament Act of 1911 which formally recognised the near-sovereignty of the democratically elected House of Commons. Ireland's influence on the modernisation of the relations between Great Britain and the Dominions, though less obvious, has also been considerable.

The course of British party politics during the nineteenth century and until after the war of 1914–18 is almost unintelligible without consideration of the Irish influence, both as an irritant and as a catalyst. Long before the formation of a genuine Irish party, the question of Catholic Emancipation, which was a first-rate political question only owing to its peculiar effect on Ireland, undermined the unity of the old Tory party which finally broke to pieces on this issue. Soon afterwards a future leader of the Tories left the

Whigs because he disagreed with them on an Irish question, and towards the middle of the century the Irish Famine was the occasion for the irreparable split between Sir Robert Peel and the landed gentlemen of England. Forty years later it was the turn of the Liberals to experience the explosive effect of Irish disagreements on British politics. Chamberlain and Hartington, like Graham and Stanley before them, abandoned the Liberals on the issue of Irish government and coalesced with the Conservatives. This time the ultimate effect was not a temporary realignment of party forces but a break within the classical British party system which led to its transformation into something radically different from the nineteenth-century pattern. The Irish party was the first large-scale model of an extra-parliamentary body acting through a parliamentary mouthpiece, and its example contributed a good deal to the growth of a Labour party on lines which were just as incompatible with the see-saw of Tories and Whigs as the Irish party of the early eighteen-eighties.

Irish organisational methods had long before that time been accepted as a model for working-class organisations. The success of Daniel O'Connell's political *levée en masse* can be traced as an important influence in popular British mass movements, from the Reform Bill Unions and the early Trades Union Federations to the Anti-Corn Law League. In the Chartist agitation Irish models were probably less important than direct Irish participation which was responsible for some of its most characteristic features, and not a little also for its obvious inconsistencies and internal disagreements.

This bare recital of facts, some of which are matters of fairly general knowledge while others are buried in the records of nineteenth-century public life, in newspapers, political biographies and parliamentary reports, suggests the depth and width of Irish influences on British politics during the last century. In the following chapters some of these facts will be examined in greater detail owing to their importance for the main theme of this study, which is not a description of these influences but the analysis of their place in the history of the English and Irish peoples during their involuntary and uneasy political partnership.

The peculiar character of the whole era endows the problem with an interest beyond its purely historical importance, considerable though this may have been. In the economic field, it was a period of advancing and triumphant industrial capitalism; in the political arena it witnessed the gradual and comparatively peaceful replacement of one dominant class by another, and the change-over from oligarchic to democratic methods of government. The economic system of Ireland, with the partial exception of Ulster, did not benefit from the rapid progress of modern industry in Great Britain; on the contrary, the process only added to its exhaustion and to the exploitation of the Irish people. But Ireland's political reaction to this economic degradation assumed first-rate importance because it added an element of fierce explosive energy to the forces ranged against the British landowning oligarchy.

Whether this addition was an inconvenient complication of the political game for the cliques in control of the British party machines is another matter. It may even be asked whether this alliance between colonial nationalism and indigenous British radicalism was the most effective combination for the achievement of its aims; it certainly furnished the enemies of democracy in their difficult defensive struggle with an effective means for political counter-attacks by permitting them to play off one of their opponents against the other. But for better or worse, the growth of British democracy took place in conditions which included as an important element the fact of British domination over a dependent Empire in addition to the classical conflict between the old and the new ruling classes and the unprivileged masses. In this connection, Ireland alone amongst British dependent territories was in a position to exert direct political pressure on British public life, and in the course of time the weight of this pressure outgrew Ireland's intrinsic importance within the developing system of British world power.

CHAPTER IX

THE ECONOMIC CONSEQUENCES OF THE UNION

ALTHOUGH economic motives were not completely absent from the minds of the English and Irish statesmen responsible for the legislative Union, they played a very subordinate part in their grim resolution to achieve it by fair means or foul. Pitt and Castlereagh were thinking in terms of strategy, of empire and security, and their interest in economic problems was almost completely confined to the fiscal side of the matter. But the tremendous problems which they hoped to solve or alleviate with the help of the Union were, in the last resort, due to social and economic causes.

The 'disaffection' of the common people of Ireland, both in the North and in the South, expressed the clash of interests between the masses and their rulers. The 'disloyalty' of large sections of the Irish middle class, particularly in Ulster, reflected its discontent with the predominance of English interests, and the perpetuation by force of arms of an unclean and incompetent system of government. The friction between the semi-independent Irish Parliament and the subordinate Irish executive simply brought this underground conflict into the open, and the dangers inherent in this clash of interests had to be averted by the lavish use of corruption and intimidation in the 'management' of the Irish legislature. It was by the notorious use of these methods that the Union was carried, and it is, therefore, not surprising that in this transaction all Irish interests, with the exception of the private advantage of the parties to the bargain, were ruthlessly disregarded.

The most obvious material injury to Irish interests, because it could be measured in pounds, shillings and pence, was the clause according to which Ireland had to contribute two-seventeenths of the cost of all imperial expenditure until such time when the two exchequers could be amalgamated without unfairness to Ireland. From a somewhat wider point of view, an even more damaging result was the injury done by the Union to Ireland's industrial development.

That the necessarily protectionist economic policy of a truly independent Irish Parliament would have led to a collision with England is undeniable; but it is no less certain that the abolition of the very moderate Irish protective duties at the time, or as a result, of the Union destroyed Ireland's slender chances of establishing a healthy and balanced economic system. The English cotton manufacturers had done their utmost during the negotiations before the Union to prevent the maintenance of Irish duties on textile imports from across the Channel. At that time Lord Castlereagh estimated the number of workers in the Irish cotton industry at 30,000–40,000,[1] and during the first few years after the Union the industry continued to flourish. Its first great setback came during the Anglo-American War of 1812–14, when the British manufacturers dumped their coarse stuffs on the Irish market, because the war interrupted their exports to the United States. In 1822, the total number of workers in the Irish cotton-spinning trade was estimated, perhaps unduly low, at 3,000–5,000 hands,[2] and owing to the superior British competition the industry was in a state of decline. The premature termination of the so-called Union duties under pressure from Manchester completed the process of its destruction not only in Leinster and around Cork, but also in Belfast; there cotton spinning employed 13,500 people at the time of the Union,[3] while the total number of hands employed in the Belfast district in the cotton trade as a whole was twice as high.[4] The effects of the new free trade régime appeared in their fullest rigour during the crisis of 1825, the first great modern industrial depression on record, when English manufacturers swamped the Irish market with a minimum of inconvenience to themselves and drove their Irish rivals completely out of business.[5]

It was generally expected before the Union that Dublin would be the chief sufferer from the measure, and this forecast proved correct. The distress in the Dublin luxury trades was acute and almost instantaneous. One of the first recorded speeches by Daniel O'Connell was delivered in Dublin in September 1810, when he complained that since the Union 'Ireland saw her artificers starved, her tradesmen begging, her merchants become bankrupt',[6] and even the staid members of the Dublin Corporation were shaken by the 'numerous bankruptcies almost unparalleled in this city'. But the industrial decay of Southern Ireland, after its vigorous development during the period of Grattan's Parliament, was not confined to the capital nor to the textile trades. Only Ulster managed, after a period of doubt and uncertainty following the destruction of its cotton-spinning industry, to reorganise its old-established linen trade on a new basis and to develop new industries, like shipbuilding in Belfast and shirt-making in and around Derry, while continuing to act as a sweated-labour shop for British textile manufacturers, who had their yarn cheaply woven into cloth by some 10,000 Belfast handloom weavers.[7]

Despite the unlimited confidence of most Irish nationalists in the natural resources of their country, it is unlikely that Ireland could have become a serious industrial rival of nineteenth-century England. On the other hand, it is inconceivable that the influence of the industrial revolution would have completely by-passed Ireland and that the vigorous economic progress noticeable during the short period of Grattan's Parliament would have prematurely exhausted itself for internal reasons. It was the unfettered competition by English manufacturers, superimposed on the continuing drain of absentee rents, which completely crushed Irish industry outside Ulster.

The social and economic results of the destruction of mining and industry in the south of Ireland cannot easily be exaggerated. It prevented the development of a modern urban middle class capable of playing a part comparable with that of the British business classes. It created an industrial surplus population in every country town where previously a colliery or a cotton mill had employed a few hundred hands. It closed the Irish towns for the 'surplus population' of the countryside at a time when the clearance policy of the land-lords increased this redundant population from year to year. The competition of British mechanical industry, particularly the inven-tion of cotton- and linen-spinning machines, further increased the economic troubles of the peasant masses by depriving them of their small but vital income from domestic industries.[8]

Ulster's partial escape from this general economic blight widened the existing gulf between North and South. From that time onwards the economic contrast between these parts of Ireland was no less pronounced than their religious disagreement, and considerably more so than their racial difference. The Ulster tenant farmers, though in better circumstances than the mass of the Southern cottiers and small farmers, had a good deal in common with them, but the industrial population of the north-east belonged to a different world altogether. The new industrial middle class of the North looked to Great Britain, because its economy formed part and parcel of the system of British trade and industry. And this orientation was not confined to the employers. Thus a Belfast hand-loom weaver actually pleaded with a Parliamentary Select Committee in 1835 to maintain the lower wage rates then existing in Ireland, which kept Irish cotton weaving alive and at the same time afforded 'protection and encouragement' to capital.[9] Industrial Ulster was linked to Great Britain by vital material interests which made any idea of repealing the Union, with the chance of customs barriers between the two countries always in the background, anathema to the Ulsterman, while in the South the need for protection from superior British competition assumed in the course of time the dignity of an indisputable axiom.

The virtual absence of modern trade and industry confined Ireland's social life within the rigid framework of the semi-feudal land system which had grown up during the previous centuries, and which the accomplishment of the Union made virtually indestructible from within. The ownership of the soil continued to be the title to almost the whole surplus product of the country beyond the scanty subsistence needs of the inhabitants, although the archaic methods of production and the wasteful treatment of natural resources kept this surplus very much below its possible maximum. According to Arthur Young, the average rent per acre in Ireland was less than half the English figure.[10] On Irish soil this contrast was maintained on a lower level between Ulster and the South. The natural fertility of the soil in Ulster was lower than in many parts of the other provinces, but Ulster rents after the middle of the nineteenth century were on an average five shillings per acre higher than in the rest of the country.[11] It was the wastefulness of the Irish system, as much as its injustice, which made its maintenance by force of British arms a permanent, and finally an intolerable, grievance for the Irish people, and which found its terrifying climax in the Great Famine of 1846.

The dependence of Irish agriculture on foreign markets, which contrasted so strangely with the crude subsistence farming of the mass of the people, was the necessary result of Ireland's colonial status. In the early eighteenth century, when the all-powerful English landlords jealously protected their home market from outside supplies which might have lowered the profits and rents of English land, Irish agricultural exports found their way to other countries—France, Spain, the West Indies—and into the holds of sea-going vessels, which thought it worth their while to enter Cork or Waterford for the special purpose of getting their provisions in the cheapest market. After the Seven Years War and the American Revolution many of these outlets were temporarily blocked, but a nearer and seemingly inexhaustible market for Irish produce was opened by the growing import needs of Great Britain. The removal of the ban on Irish cattle imports and the change in the balance of British grain supplies, followed by the amendment of the Corn Laws, acted as a strong stimulus to Irish exports. After the middle of the eighteenth century cattle and grain prices advanced steadily, and rents kept fully abreast of prices. During the American Revolution, Young commented on the 'rise in the prosperity of Ireland, about the year 1749, owing to the high price of provisions, which raised rents and enforced industry'.[12]

The pace of this development quickened during the French Revolutionary Wars under the influence of scarcity and inflation.

From an economic point of view, the Rebellion of 1798 was merely a local interlude, although it caused acute distress to tens of thousands, and the years between the Union and the Battle of Waterloo were the golden age for Irish landlords. The cutting-off of continental supplies during the Napoleonic Wars made grain prices go up by leaps and bounds. During the twenty years 1792–1812, foreign grain imports into Great Britain fell from 642,598 quarters to 243,833 quarters, or by 62 per cent. In these circumstances, grain and flour imports from Ireland became a factor of first-rate economic and even military importance. When Irish grain exports to Great Britain reached 875,000 barrels (or approximately 540,000 quarters) in 1808, this achievement was hailed with glowing praise by the prim *Edinburgh Review*: 'It is impossible to contemplate the immense supplies of the very first importance, which we receive from this fruitful island, and their prodigious capability of increase, without feeling the conviction that it should ever be prized and cherished by us as our richest mine of wealth as well as our strongest pillar of defence.'[13]

Ireland thus helped to feed the British people with bread, and Wellington's armies, and particularly their horses, with oats. But the great rise in war-time rents for the Irish landlords, and in profits for the Irish farmers, was mainly due to the exorbitant prices which grain fetched in the famished British market. The value of Britain's grain and flour imports from Ireland increased from £598,370 in 1792 to £1,641,583 in 1812,[14] partly due to the substitution of wheat for oats but largely as a result of the steep increase in market values.

This dependence on scarcity prices caused considerable misgivings to the Irish landlords, the chief beneficiaries of the high price of corn. With the French defeat in Russia the spectre of peace loomed on the horizon, and the market broke with a bang even before Napoleon's final overthrow. The harvest of 1813 produced a bumper crop, and the allied entry into Paris was hardly sufficient compensation to the landlords for the entry of foreign grain into British ports. During 1814, no less than 800,000 quarters of wheat and the same quantity of oats was imported from abroad,[15] and the war boom collapsed. During the following thirty years wheat prices fluctuated wildly with the vagaries of the seasons and the Corn Laws, but, except for short periods of stringency, they were rarely higher, and often considerably lower, than half their top price in the halcyon days of 1812 and early 1813.

This change in the terms of the grain trade had dramatic results in Ireland. Irish agriculture was tied to the British market by the most powerful bonds, the material interests of the Irish landlords.

The internal market for wheat and even for oats rested on a narrow basis, for the mass of the people outside Ulster were too poor to buy flour, or, indeed, any food and lived almost exclusively on home-produced potatoes. The small Irish farmer now found it very difficult to economise on the two most important elements of his costs—labour and rent. He rarely paid his labourers in money, but usually in land, and he had always driven the hardest possible bargain with them. The landlords, on the other hand, insisted on extracting the highest possible rent from him. Even where they were ready after the collapse of the war boom to accept lower payments than those reserved in most war-time leases, they rarely cancelled the difference and preferred to hold the accumulated arrears as a constant threat over the head of the tenant.

As grain prices fell much more radically than cattle prices, the weight of economic considerations, represented by the constant pressure of the landlords on their tenants, was all in favour of the radical abandonment of tillage and the return to grazing. The small tenant was, however, rarely able to take and stock a grazing farm, and the years following the return of peace in 1815 were, therefore, especially unfavourable for him. Particularly in Leinster, which was geographically in the best position for the British market in livestock, the dispossession of small farmers and the laying down of their land for cattle ranches was widely practised.[16] At the same time, the demand for land by the steadily increasing population was so pressing that the mass of the peasants clung to their holdings on any terms, however extortionate, and sold their produce at any price, however low, in order to pay their inflated rents, which were often fixed on the basis of the number of cattle which the land might support under grass.

The dislocation in the Irish economic system after the downfall of Napoleon marks the end of Ireland's immediate post-Union history. From this time onwards the trend of events can be easily followed on the social surface without the help of economic analysis. The period between Waterloo and the Famine was a true Thirty Years War for the Irish people—a war between their vital needs and the interests of the landlords and their moneylenders; a war which wasted more lives than the costliest campaign, and which drove ever-growing numbers of the conquered out of their native country, while it made the position of the victors more precarious than ever before.

CHAPTER X

IRELAND'S SOCIAL DISINTEGRATION

IGNORANCE of the facts was not one of the causes of Irish misery during the nineteenth century. The average number of parliamentary committees or commissions of inquiry into the state of Ireland was in the neighbourhood of five every year, at least during the first half of the nineteenth century, and although many of them were mainly concerned with outrages and disturbances, their records contain a wealth of detail about the conditions of life of the Irish people after the Union.

The twin problems which invariably pushed themselves into the centre of every inquiry were those of the land and the population. They were, indeed, only different facets of the same problem. Of the stupendous increase in the numbers of the Irish people since the middle of the eighteenth century there can be no doubt. Up to the famine of 1740, Ireland was generally regarded as under-populated; but in the half-century between the peace of Aix la Chapelle and the Union its population more than doubled and exceeded five millions in the early years of the new century. The first census, held in 1821, surprised even the experts by the unexpectedly high figure of 6,800,000, and at the time of the Great Famine in 1846 Ireland's population substantially exceeded 8,000,000.

The Irish population problem was the inevitable result of the Irish land system which subordinated the lives of the peasants to the demands of their landlords. Even at a time when experts regarded the number of people as insufficient for the requirements of the country, Ireland suffered from a 'redundant' population, although it was, in fact, the population which suffered from a pernicious land system. During the greater part of the eighteenth century, grazing farms for sheep and cattle were the most lucrative ventures for the landlords and their large tenants, and the inhabitants had to crowd into barren and mountainous districts, because the most fertile land was needed for the raising of beasts.

The industrial revolution on the other side of the Irish Sea indirectly alleviated the pressure of this growing surplus population by encouraging tillage in addition to the traditional types of Irish agriculture. With the increase in population, Great Britain ceased to be self-supporting in grain and began to import growing quantities for its industrial population. Although the revolution in Irish agriculture due to the export of wheat to Great Britain can easily be exaggerated, it had an important, if temporary, effect on the attitude of the landlords towards the common people. The sharp rise in corn prices enabled the landlords to push their rents to fabulous heights, and they were not likely to be inquisitive about the character of their sub-tenants' cottiers, provided their inflated rents were paid on time. Farmers big and small wanted to increase their output in order to pay their rents and to reap the golden harvest of war profits, and this could not be done without an increase in the numbers of their labourers.

In these somewhat less unfavourable conditions of life in Ireland, emigration mainly took the form of service in the British army and navy. The number of Irishmen in the armed forces of the Crown was a very controversial subject, but there is no doubt that it was very substantial. The radical 'axing' of the army and navy after the victory over Napoleon inundated Ireland with a flood of discharged soldiers and sailors at a time when there was less chance than ever before of absorbing them. For with the return of peace in 1815 the economic idyll of the war years came to a sudden end, and a systematic hunt of the 'redundant' population was organised by the landlords. To make things worse, the potato crop of 1816 was a failure, as if to bring home to the landlords the disadvantages of a large pauper population dependent for life on a single crop. The landowners and their agents were quick to learn their lesson and to take measures for clearing the land of undesirable tenants. 'The landlords of Ireland', said a well-known Irish Tory in 1825, 'are at length deeply convinced that, though a stock of cattle or sheep will afford profit, a stock of mere human creatures, unemployed, will afford none.'[17]

From the point of view of the Irish landlords as a whole, the success of the eviction policy depended on preventing the paupers of one estate from finding a refuge on another. In 1826 Sir Henry Parnell, the most determined parliamentary spokesman of the Irish landlords, sponsored a Bill which prohibited sub-letting root and branch, except with the clear consent of the landlord. This happened at a moment when the consolidation of farms on the English model was regarded as the patent cure for Ireland's agrarian troubles, and large numbers of tenants found themselves evicted at the end of their leases or through non-payment of rent without hope of ever again obtaining holdings of their own.

The economic revolution set on foot by the landlords received a final fillip through the political revolt of the forty-shilling freeholders and their ensuing extinction. The disfranchisement of these nominal freeholders in 1829 'broke the last link of connexion between the landlord and the pauper tenant',[18] and was followed

6

by mass evictions of these pitiful 'freeholders', whose number fell from 191,000 in 1828 to 14,200 in 1830.[19] Not all the others were actually thrown out of their holdings, but their pseudo-security of tenure, based on their political servility towards the landlords, was at an end.

The population problem of pre-Famine Ireland was thus not simply due to the natural growth of the population but to the social conditions in which this growth took place: it was the Irish land system and nothing else which made the majority of the population in an under-developed and unimproved country economically useless. In a country where the landless poor were the vast majority, they found themselves hemmed in on all sides by new laws and regulations made by a landlord government, driven out of their hovels and prevented from settling down again by the distaste of their masters for a turbulent pauper population—a huge mass of moving misery. There were still gradations among them. The recently dispossessed small farmers and cottiers tried desperately to maintain at any price, however extortionate, a precarious hold on the land, and their land hunger was the basis of the conacre system which became characteristic of the pre-Famine period. This was an agreement between a farmer, acting as landlord, and a labourer for the use of a small patch of land for a single crop of potatoes. The conditions were usually so harsh that the labourer had to work most of his time for the farmer in order to pay the rent, without even the relative security of the cottier who was settled more or less permanently on his little plot.

With the growing competition for land there was a further fall in the unbelievably low standards of living of the poor. In Arthur Young's day, a regular cottier economy normally included the possession of a cow or pigs; two generations later this had become the exception. Young stressed the abundance of potatoes, of which even the poorest Irishman always had 'a bellyful'; two generations later actual hunger had become a regular occurrence for the mass of Irishmen. 'I confess that the annually recurring starvation in Ireland for a period, differing according to the goodness or badness of the season, from one week to three months, gives me more uneasiness than any other evil existing in the United Kingdom,'[20] wrote the Duke of Wellington, least sentimental of statesmen.

The foodless period during the early summer was marked by a wave of seasonal migration from the barren districts of Connaught into the fertile counties of Eastern Ireland. 'At the ripening of the harvest the family breaks up; the man comes to England to look for labour and the woman and children beg through Leinster and other parts where they think they can obtain a livelihood.'[21] This periodical begging excursion of the semi-nomadic Connaught peasants was superimposed on a permanent stream of beggars, who moved through the country at all times of the year and who were maintained by the charity of the not-yet-destitute poor. The human by-products of the process of farm consolidation and agrarian de-population remained for some time near the place of their previous existence as cottiers or tenants, just as the ghosts of Irish folklore continued to hover round the neighbourhood in which they had spent their real lives; when the hope of reinstatement into their former homesteads faded for good, they went elsewhere—in the beginning, perhaps, in the vain hope of land and work, but sooner or later as mere vagrants and beggars.

Thus it was inevitable that more and more Irishmen looked for their livelihood abroad, at first temporarily as harvest workers in Great Britain, but later on permanently. In the early part of the century, the main stream of emigration from Ireland was directed into England and Scotland, but in spite of the presumable attraction of a more highly civilised neighbouring country, migration into Great Britain was not regarded as a boon by most Irishmen. Industrial England, it was said at the time, 'is far from being their Mecca, and is indeed the last place they would willingly approach'.[22] Their settlement in the industrial towns of Great Britain was the result of irresistible economic pressure applied by the eviction policy of the landlords and by the severe, though partial, crop failures of 1817 and 1821 which greatly quickened the pace of emigration. Soon afterwards the introduction of a steamboat service between Great Britain and Ireland (1824) increased the opportunities and reduced the fares. Sometimes the crossing in cattle boats could be made for sixpence per head,[23] while charges from one shilling to half a crown were not unusual.[24] From the time of Waterloo to the middle of the century, Irish mass immigration had an important influence on British industrial development. In 1841, no fewer than 419,256 inhabitants of Great Britain had been born in Ireland,[25] and in the summer of that year 57,651 deck passengers crossed from Ireland into England,[26] though this number must have included many seasonal migrants.

The emigration from Ireland after the Union differed in many important respects from the mass emigration from Ulster to the United States in the eighteenth century. Immediately after Waterloo, the number of Protestant emigrants was still large, and amongst them there may have been a good many industrial workers; later on the large majority were Catholic peasants. Before the hungry 'forties the number of overseas emigrants averaged less than 20,000 a year,[27] and in many years it was probably less than that of emigrants to Great Britain. From 1842 onwards, overseas emigration increased by leaps and bounds, even before the onset of the Great Famine. This may have been partly due to the rising dissatisfaction of the small farmers with their conditions, including a series of bad harvests; but it also reflected one of the most remarkable social achievements of the Irish peasantry in that period of misery and degradation, the solidarity of the emigrants with their people at home. It was the general custom for the strongest of the younger members of a family to emigrate first, and to accumulate by hard work enough money to enable the rest of the family to follow them. Nassau Senior estimated that the annual total of remittances amounted to one or two million pound sterling, and the bulk of this money was not intended for maintenance in Ireland but for travelling expenses. The movement of overseas emigration thus gathered strength with its duration, until during the time of the Famine it reached the dimensions of a mass exodus. The means by which it was made possible might well form the raw material of a great saga of humanity.

The Great Famine is the chasm separating Ireland's past from its historical present. Its horrors, which have left an indelible imprint on the memories and the character of the Irish people, and its external results are matters of common knowledge, and it is only necessary to recall the decisive fact that it was not a natural but a social catastrophe. At least until a very late stage it was not due to an absolute insufficiency of food, and this stage could have been completely avoided by timely imports from abroad. In December 1845, when the situation began to be critical, the Duke of Wellington did not believe that even in Ireland there was 'scarcity of food, between potatoes and oats, to feed the people for the year. . . . The harvest of 1844 was excellent and abundant beyond example and the produce of 1844 has not yet been all consumed. . . . Then the harvest of 1845 has been good in England, Ireland and Scotland, and the price is moderate, even provokingly so.'[28] All through the famine, just as in 1822, foodstuffs continued to be exported from Ireland to Great Britain. It was not the lack of food as such, but the destruction of the subsistence of the poor, who had no money to buy other food, which produced all the effects of a total famine.

In the early part of 1846, the younger O'Connell could still praise the British Government for wisely stepping into the breach 'to supply food to the starving millions of Ireland, and prevent the depopulation of the land by the cruel death of starvation'.[29] Sir Robert Peel was forced by his own prejudices, by the clamour of the British public for safe food supplies and by the powerful vested interests of the grain trade, to import large quantities of maize into a country which exported large quantities of food into Great Britain, but his preoccupation with the problem of food supplies at least prevented mass starvation in the early summer of 1846. In his great speech on 27 March 1846, on the Repeal of the Corn Laws, Peel found it necessary to defend himself against the reproach of having taken the Irish potato failure of 1845 too seriously. He rightly gloried in this accusation and refuted it with words which were only too well justified by the event: 'No reproach will attach to me even if it be proved that our precautions were superfluous. Before the month of July it will be established to the conviction of every man that the precautions we took were not superfluous and that our motives were not impure.'[30]

At that moment it could not be foreseen that the potato crop of 1846 would again be destroyed by the blight, and when this awful fact became known Peel was no longer in office. The policy of the Whig Government which succeeded him was, perhaps, the most tragic misfortune which befell Ireland as a result of her involuntary connection with England. Lord John Russell was with all his palpable defects, his weakness and his stubbornness, if one of the most unimaginative, at least one of the most unbiased of the English Whigs. But he was the advocate of free enterprise against paternalism, and he represented the City of London in the House of Commons. As the leader of the protectionist party put it, he 'had pledged himself to the mercantile interest—that is to the corn speculators and corn merchants of the City of London—"that the supply of the people of Ireland should be left to private enterprise" and "that private enterprise and free trade should not be interfered with" '.[31]

In October 1846 Lord George Bentinck demanded the use of the fleet for the transport of grain from America to Ireland, but the Government only suspended the Navigation Laws (which were soon afterwards completely repealed) and trusted to the normal processes of trade. The sequel is best related in Lord George's own words with their curious air of Cobbett's style and outlook: 'But the famine had come on so suddenly, private enterprise was taken by surprise, and was quite unprepared. The Irish people were like an army on a desert island, like the Israelites in the wilderness, only, happily for them, the God of Israel was not a Whig, or a Free Trader, or a political economist, or a Scotch philosopher; and thus I really believe a well-counted million of Irish perished of famine and fever, before assistance reached them. The Irish starved all December, January, February and March; in April they began to be glutted; in May there were 34,000 tons of shipping in New York unable to obtain freights. . . . Such was the improvidence of the Whig Government that for three months they allowed the opportunity to pass of laying in stores at two-fifths of the price at which the great mass of food was eventually purchased; they allowed a million to perish, and the Irish people to draw the odious comparison and contrast between the English Government which preferred keeping 17 ships idle in the Tagus nursing a Coburg, and the Congress of the United States which sent two ships of war . . . with 1,000 tons of breadstuffs. And I verily believe there is not an Irishman in Ireland who has not marked the contrast.'[32]

Meanwhile the system of public works, by which the Government gave the masses the purchasing power necessary to buy the imported maize, came under attack by the vested interests. The Irish peasants desired nothing better than the chance of earning steady wages; it took a crop failure and famine to give them this opportunity, and the effort exacted by the organisers of the relief works was naturally not very great. Landlords and farmers watched with dismay their labourers flocking to the public works and abandoning the farms where they had to do more work for lower pay. This threatened to cause a complete breakdown of the system under which the actual tillers of the soil worked for farmers in exchange for small potato gardens, and such a calamity would have wiped out Irish rents. The landlords were alive to this danger and to the still deadlier threat to their incomes implied in the wholesale relief granted to the pauperised Irish people. They argued that the proprietors of Ireland would be 'irretrievably ruined' if the able-bodied poor were given a distinct claim for relief,[33] and they were effectively represented in both Houses of Parliament and, indeed, in the Cabinet, where Palmerston had their interests (including his own) very much at heart.

Lord John Russell was too weak to resist this pressure, and after some fine and brave words he agreed to a complete reversal of policy, the abandonment of public works and their replacement by relief in kind, mainly through the agency of soup kitchens. In order to speed up the depopulation of Ireland, Parliament enacted the notorious Gregory clause which forbade the Poor Law Guardians to relieve persons possessing more than one-quarter of an acre of land. The smallest occupiers were thus given the choice of starving on their land or of leaving it in exchange for their daily soup, and the landlords got rid of some of their most inconvenient tenants. The Lord Lieutenant, Lord Clarendon, a Whig of the Whigs, and therefore no friend of the peasants and no enemy of the landlords, could not help saying that many of them contemplated 'in the most cold-blooded way the relief from a starving and redundant population by the operation of famine'.[34] The inability of many thousands of tenants to pay their rents led to a huge rise in evictions in the famine years, reaching 25,700 during 1847-9 and no less than 58,423 (affecting 306,120 persons) in the following four years.

The spectacle was so heartrending that even the cynical and detached Charles Greville was hurt to the quick: 'Here is a country,' he wrote in his diary, 'part and parcel of England, a few hours removed from the richest and most civilised community in the world, in a state so savage, barbarous and destitute that we must go back to the Middle Ages or to the most inhospitable regions of the globe to look for a parallel. Nobody knows what to do; everybody hints at some scheme or plan to which his next neighbour objects. Most people are inclined to consider the case as hopeless, to rest on that conviction, and let the evil work itself out, like a consuming fire, which dies away when there is nothing left to destroy. All call on the Government for a plan and a remedy, but the Government have no plan and no remedy; there is nothing but disagreement among them; and while they are discussing and disputing, the masses are dying.'[35]

Lord John Russell's polished definition of the catastrophe as 'a famine of the thirteenth century acting upon a population of the nineteenth'[36] shows only the irresistible tendency of the Victorian mind to regard the social conditions of the nineteenth century as natural and immutable. But, except in remote mountain districts, the famine was not due to the insufficiency of food production and the impossibility of making good the deficit by imports, nor to the absolute numbers of the population. It was the colonial position of Ireland, the combination of the archaic semi-feudal Irish land system and the market economy and *laissez faire* principles of Great Britain which produced in the famine a gigantic scourge for the Irish people and an indelible symbol of the extreme results of British rule in Ireland.

CHAPTER XI

CATHOLIC EMANCIPATION

EVER since the rebellion of 1798, the ground trembled beneath the feet of the Irish upper classes. Isolated insurrections were stamped out easily enough by the forces of the Crown, but they were merely the outward symptoms of a deep-rooted social disease which obtained with every passing decade a stronger hold on the life of the country. Immediately after the Union, a Parliamentary Select Committee asserted the existence of a secret and extensive conspiracy in Ireland. In 1803, the workers of Dublin responded to Emmet's call, and serious fighting broke out in the Liberties of Dublin. In 1807, Sir Arthur Wellesley, the later Duke of Wellington, employed his short tenure of office as Chief Secretary not only for the compilation of a guide through the jungle of private interests and public jobs, which made up the civil side of Irish government, but also for the drafting of a severe and comprehensive Insurrection Act which had the blessing of Henry Grattan. This was occasioned by the outrages of the *Thrashers* in answer to the increased rents and tithes of the war years.

When Peel came to Ireland in 1812, the country was disturbed by *Orangemen* and *Ribbonmen* in the North, and by *Caravats* and *Carders* in the South. His main task as Chief Secretary was the reorganisation of the police. Before he left the country in 1817, Peel thought that he could not remember it to have been so tranquil for five years past,[37] but in the same year the Insurrection Act was still regarded as an indispensable instrument of government. The potato failure of 1821–2 was accompanied by a wave of disturbances throughout Munster and parts of Leinster and Connaught: the *Michael Coffeys* were abroad, and in the next few years they were followed by other members of the same family—*Terry Alts* and *Rockites*, *Whitefeet* and *Blackfeet*, and later still by the formidable *Molly Maguires*.

These secret agrarian organisations were afterwards described by the general name of the Ribbonmen, who were at first a continuation of the Defenders, founded for the purpose of protection against Peep o' Day Boys and Orangemen, whose organisation they tried to imitate. At the same time they were already closely identified with rural insurrection. Although they included both agricultural labourers and dwarf tenants, they can best be described as rural Trade Unions. They lacked leadership, organisation and a common ideology, their methods were crude, barbarous and more effective as a relief for the pent-up emotions of their members than as remedies against the evils of the Irish land system. Their attempt to enforce by terrorism solidarity amongst the disinherited remained largely unsuccessful in a society where a poor man's economic salvation depended on his skill in getting a foothold on the necks of his fellow-sufferers, but with all their obvious limitations they were formidable opponents for a government machine completely out of touch with the sentiments of the people and for landlords whose bad conscience was a strong brake on their ambition to control the local life of the country.

The Ribbonmen were by no means conscious revolutionaries either in their motives or in their 'policy', but they constituted a serious threat to the established social order, and their existence was the most important underlying fact of Irish internal history up to the days of the Fenians and the Land League. The policy of the 'respectable' Nationalists makes sense only by reference to their activities. They survived all attempts at forcible extermination, for they were the direct product of the Irish land system, particularly in the form which it assumed after the Union. The disintegration of the Irish people supplied them with countless recruits, and even when they were driven overseas they took with them their memories of intolerable wrong and their undying hostility towards England, which they had learnt to hate as the power behind landlords and police in their native country.

The position of the agrarian movements in Irish politics was exactly the reverse of the role of the Chorus in Greek tragedy. Instead of commenting on an action in which they took no part, their silent existence determined the speeches and actions of the personages in the forefront of the political stage. In the last resort their influence was due to the dependence of the Catholic middle class on the support of the ragged masses which it feared and despised. The development of this middle class dated back to the penal era, when Catholics began to make fortunes as traders, merchants and usurers, and to train their children for the learned professions. With the abolition of the Penal Laws and the boom of the Napoleonic Wars these groups made quick progress. While the large mass of their countrymen and fellow Catholics sank deeper and deeper into the morass of misery, they succeeded in keeping on dry land and in carving out a niche for themselves in the rock of Irish 'society'. As priests, farmers and gombeen men in the villages, as traders, lawyers, doctors and even officials in the towns, they slowly acquired a vested interest in the existing order, and their new status was further endeared to them by the memory of the recent efforts which its acquisition had cost them or their parents.

This Catholic middle class was entirely unsympathetic towards the agrarian rebels; it detested their aims no less than their methods, and keenly felt the threat to its own position implied in their activities. It was inclined to join with the authorities in the struggle against these fanatics, provided it was allowed to do so on reasonable terms. But its advances were stubbornly repelled by Dublin Castle and the British Parliament which refused to accept these respectable Catholics as equal citizens. Their political *credo* was well put by Bishop Doyle, the famous J. K. L. of Irish literature, who told a Committee of the House of Commons in 1825: 'If we were freed from the disabilities under which we labour, we have no mind, and no thought, and no will but that which would lead us to incorporate ourselves most fully and essentially with this great kingdom; for it would be our greatest pride to share in the glories and riches of England.'[38]

Nothing would have been easier for a British Government enlightened enough to know its own interests, than to reinforce the legal framework of the Union with the solid props of an identity of interests between the imperial power and the Irish middle class. But in spite of strong pressure by the Whigs and a sensible minority amongst the Tories, notably Canning and Castlereagh, this policy was repeatedly defeated by the combined powers of Dublin Castle and the Protestant ascendancy party in Ireland, backed by the English High Tories and the King. In trying to rule Ireland by eighteenth-century methods, when the upper classes had been identical with the 'Protestant interest' and all Catholics could be disregarded as 'rabble', the Tory Government lagged sadly behind the times, for the accumulation of wealth by the Catholics was making such progress, that they were even starting to buy land. The pathetic solicitude of these respectable Catholics for permission to enter within the pale of the British Constitution remained un-rewarded, and the wanton stupidity of the Tories in rejecting these submissive advances and in failing to conciliate the Catholic Church can only be explained by a combination of bigoted ignorance with the exigencies of the British party system.

For the first thirty years of the nineteenth century the respectable section of Irish politics was dominated by the question of Catholic Emancipation. Pitt, Castlereagh and Cornwallis were agreed that this measure was an essential part of a Union settlement, but the ardour of their convictions abated somewhat after they had carried through this measure, largely through the co-operation of the Catholic Prelacy. The sequel of Pitt's betrayal of the Irish Catholics is more a part of English than of Irish history. The farce of his resignation, the accession of Addington as his man-of-straw, the dramatic promise to spare the King and to drop Emancipation during his lifetime, the cat-and-mouse play with his incompetent successor and his return to office as a theoretical friend but practical opponent of Catholic emancipation: this whole ritual of a bad conscience has been frequently described and almost as frequently excused. But quite apart from the moral aspect of such blatant deception and dishonesty, the refusal to solve the Catholic question at the time of the Union and to endow the Catholic clergy was the greatest political blunder ever committed by a British Government in its dealings with the Irish people.

The Irish middle class was the driving force behind the demand for Catholic Relief, because it wanted a share in political power and thought to achieve it by this means. For this reason, support of this claim was not confined to Catholics, but was given by all 'progressive' Protestants who regarded it as the way of getting rid of the absolute domination of the landlords over Irish affairs. Even a large majority of the Irish members in the House of Commons, particularly the county members who were to some extent exposed to popular influence, shared this view. That it was in the last resort a matter of social weight and political power and not a question of conscience and religion was shown by the Veto Controversy, the opening move in the game which ended in 1829 with the surrender of the King's conscience in exchange for O'Connell's political principles.

Castlereagh and the other pro-Catholics in the Tory camp knew that the Catholic Church was conservative by its very nature, and that its political radicalism in Ireland had been forced on it by centuries of persecution. By identifying its material interests with the ruling system, they hoped to make it independent of popular influences and to transform it into the strongest pillar of English rule. O'Connell won the first and greatest political victory of his career when he convinced the Catholic bishops that such a policy would lose them too much support in Ireland to be practicable. By frustrating the plans of the English 'friends' of Catholic Emancipation (including the leaders of the small English Catholic community), he kept the Irish middle-class agitation in a strategic position, where he still remained on the firm ground of the existing social order without, however, losing his ability to establish contact with the rebellious masses, should the recalcitrance of his opponents force him to take such a step.

To stir the Government out of their lethargy, the spur of immediate inconvenience or danger was wanted, and after a good deal of indecision O'Connell decided to apply it. The famine of 1821–2 stung the Irish peasant masses into greater activity, and instead of trying to prevent them by pious words from committing outrages, O'Connell resolved to organise them in support of his political agitation. It may well be that this resolution was not the result of political foresight but was forced on him by the danger that the elemental movement of the masses might sweep him and his respectable followers off their feet. In the speech which foreshadowed the foundation of the famous Catholic Association (25th April 1823) O'Connell declared that 'it was dangerous to leave the people without some body of recognised friends of theirs to whom they could at least give vent to their complaints . . .'[39] and this suggests that in his opinion the movement might have shown tendencies of getting out of hand. 'When the Catholic Association existed,' O'Connell said shortly afterwards, 'were they not enabled, by addressing the suffering peasantry, to quell three different attempts at insurrection? If the Catholic Association had existed, would they not have been able to warn the unsuspecting peasantry against the villainy of persons who had an actual interest in promoting disaffection?'[40]

The Catholic Association which O'Connell then proceeded to form is famous as the New Model of modern political mass organisation which had a powerful influence far beyond the limits of Irish politics. However, it was not a democratic movement of equals but a complicated mechanism designed to transform the elemental power of mass discontent into political pressure on the British Government in the interests of the Irish middle class. It consisted of two tiers—a middle-class club of the traditional type with members subscribing their guinea a year, and an army of humble sympathisers who contributed one penny per month and who gave the organisation its mass basis and its regular income. O'Connell had to surmount great objections before persuading his respectable friends to approve of this venture, and the factor which helped him to overcome them successfully was his appeal to the co-operation of the Catholic Church.

The first suggestion for this arrangement, which became the foundation-stone of the new mass organisation, came from the London Irish, who formed an Association on the Dublin model to which all Catholic priests were admitted as *ex-officio* members without payment of subscription fees. This idea was adopted by O'Connell for the parent body and became the starting-point for the great career of the Catholic Association. The accession of the clergy gave the movement a higher standing in the eyes of most Catholics, it prevented clerical jealousy of a rival organisation under

lay leadership, it was an important safeguard for the efficient
collection of funds—and it was the strongest possible guarantee of
the submission of the masses to middle-class leadership. The participation of the priests in the new mass movement was eminently
practicable, and it made such a movement safe for the middle class
whose outlook was shared and whose policy was approved by the
Church. Clericalism was the inevitable form of a nationalist
movement combining middle-class purposes with lower-class
support.

Friends and foes alike soon recognised that this time O'Connell
had played a winning card. The Government and the landlords
saw with grave misgivings, and perhaps with some regret, that
outrages were falling off, while a mood of growing resolution and
expectancy was gaining ground. The 'agitators', priests and laymen
alike, tried to convince the people that Emancipation would mean
an end of oppression and the dawn of a new era for all Catholics,
rich and poor.[41] Their propaganda was overwhelmingly successful
in men and money. The payments of the poor, collected at every
church door and passed on to Dublin, far surpassed the larger
contributions of the few wealthy patrons of the movement, and
without any of the burdensome political stipulations which the latter
were wont to make. By the end of 1823 the figure reached £1,000
a week, and two years later double that amount. The unimaginative
stubbornness of the High Church Tories and Dublin Castle had
produced the junction between the hesitating middle class and the
masses of the Irish people, which England's cleverest politicians had
tried to prevent because of their knowledge that it would make
Ireland completely ungovernable.

The political dangers of the new departure for the rulers of the
country were fairly obvious. In recent years, election contests in
Leitrim, Sligo and Dublin had raised doubts about the reliability
of the freeholders as electoral cannon fodder for their landlords.
In 1793, 30,000 Irish forty-shilling freeholders had been given
the vote as a first step of assimilating Irish to English conditions.
The political usefulness of these dependent voters had induced their
landlords to increase the number of so-called freeholds most
extravagantly, in order to increase their political influence. Shortly
before the passing of Catholic Emancipation their number was
191,000[42] out of a total Irish county electorate of 216,000.[43] These
freeholders were driven to the poll like cattle to market, and their
incipient revolt against the landlords was not only a portent for
the future but an immediate threat to the political power of the
aristocracy. The Catholic Question could no longer be shelved
without grave consequences, and both Houses of Parliament

inquired into the state of Ireland in order to help the Government to make up their minds on an acceptable measure of relief.

The *leitmotiv* of these searching investigations was the connection between emancipation of the wealthy Catholics and the disfranchisement of the poor, with the endowment of the clergy in the background. These so-called 'wings' of the Emancipation Bill now assumed the same importance which the Veto Question had possessed ten years earlier—but the champion of the Irish middle class was no longer the tribune of the people. O'Connell now took pains to stress the essentially conservative character of the Catholic Church, which was eager to a fault in upholding the Government of the day, but he nevertheless advocated the payment of the priests by the State as a 'golden link' which would give the Government 'proper influence over them'.[44] He looked forward full of complacency to a future when 'the Catholic clergy would become in the nature of officers belonging to the Crown', although this development would have clearly destroyed the usefulness of the Church in a movement which made the clergy the main link between the middle class and the people. The vexed question of disfranchising the forty-shilling freeholders was more troublesome for O'Connell, for this had been his strongest bargaining counter, and in using it he was playing with the political future of the Irish nation; his evidence on this point was inconsistent and insincere, although he made it clear that he would accept an increase in the qualification to £5. The moral of this elaborate shadow-boxing was driven home by his more moderate associate Richard Sheil, who told the Committee that O'Connell's great influence could easily overcome any opposition to the disfranchisement of the masses as the price for the enactment of Catholic Emancipation.

However, for the time being O'Connell's enemies saved him from the consequences of this betrayal of his best supporters. Of the two Irish Bills before Parliament, the one providing for the dissolution of the Catholic Association was passed with alacrity, but the Relief Bill, with its 'wings' duly attached, was thrown out by the House of Lords on the personal initiative of the Duke of York, the heir presumptive to the throne. It is at least possible that the spinelessness of the Catholic negotiators, far from conciliating the House of Lords, may have encouraged it to flout the Irish Catholics and to reject the measure.[45]

O'Connell, whose prestige suffered a grave setback after the intended betrayal of the forty-shilling freeholders, recovered the lost ground when the Government returned to their policy of repression. The anxiety of the landlords about the attitude of the voters confirmed O'Connell in his original intention to use the elections as his foremost political weapon, and the following three years witnessed a good deal of hard work in preparation for the struggle at the polls. The elections of Waterford and Clare, which proved the success of his efforts, hold their place in English political history: they convinced the Tory Government that the rigid policy of refusing concessions had turned into a danger to themselves, and Wellington and Peel forced Emancipation on the digusted King and carried it through Parliament with the support of their enemies and against the Church Tories.

The reason for the sudden *volte face* of the Wellington Government was summed up by Robert Peel, the 'Orange Peel' of 1812, and in 1828 still the staunchest defender of Protestant supremacy, on the occasion of the Clare election in words of impressive power: '. . . the instrument on which the Protestant proprietor had hitherto mainly relied for the maintenance of his political influence had completely failed him. . . . In such an exercise of that franchise, not merely permitted but encouraged and approved by constitutional law, was involved a revolution in the electoral system of Ireland, the transfer of political power, so far as it was connected with representation, from one party to another.'[46] While O'Connell exploited the political enthusiasm of the small tenants for the simple purpose of embarrassing the Government, Peel realised the social dangers of further resistance which outweighed any political advantages on the other side. For him and his friends, Catholic Emancipation had itself become a bargaining counter for the disfranchisement of the Irish masses; thus he was ready to do business with O'Connell who arrived at the same result from the opposite point of view. The suddenness of the 'surrender' was due to the fact that the Irish masses could not be disfranchised before a Dissolution, except with the approval of the middle-class Catholics in exchange for the grant of Emancipation. This was the great mystery which, in Croker's words, 'burst like a *bubble* and not like a *shell*',[47] because it did not represent an act of superior statesmanship or even a genuine change of conviction, but the sullen evacuation by the garrison of a fortress which had become untenable.

From a tactical point of view, O'Connell had gained a spectacular triumph, the most resplendent of his career; the combination of a middle-class pressure group and a genuine mass organisation of the under-privileged had been his personal policy, and it had gained all that he could have hoped from it. Henceforth he was for his followers, and remains for succeeding generations of Irishmen, the *Liberator* pure and simple. But his victory had been purchased at the expense of Ireland's political future. The alliance between the middle class and the peasants had proved its irresistible power only to be sacrificed on the altar of Catholic Emancipation for the wealthy. If this sacrifice was to be justified even from the narrowest point of view, Catholic Emancipation should have implied such a transfer of power from the landlords to the middle class as that which Peel expected as the possible result of the freeholders' revolt. But the Act of Emancipation with the concurrent disfranchisement of the Irish people, instead of being the instrument of such a transfer, was the Tory method of preventing it, and O'Connell had gained the shadow while sacrificing the substance.

The struggle for Catholic Emancipation was not only the zenith of O'Connell's political career and an epoch in British political history but a model for later generations of Irish moderate nationalists. The history of the Irish nationalist movement from then onwards to the Treaty of 1921 was dominated by the gulf between the aspirations of the Irish middle class, with its radical political claims on England and its fear of social upheaval in Ireland, and the volcanic forces of mass suffering and mass discontent, which provided the motive power behind the demands of the middle-class leaders during the period of agitation, only to be disappointed at the time of reckoning, when their betters compromised their claims at their expense. The comparative ease with which this policy could be repeated suggests that it was due more to general conditions than to the political astuteness and unscrupulousness of individuals, whether O'Connell or Parnell. The unfolding development of the nationalist movement may show that it was an almost inevitable result of Ireland's colonial position.

CHAPTER XII

REPEAL AND YOUNG IRELAND

CATHOLIC emancipation was 'a famous victory' with momentous parliamentary results, but for the Irish people it was a great disappointment. The pessimists who feared that the reconciliation of the wealthy Catholics would be accompanied by growing discontent on the part of the Irish masses, showed better judgment than the Catholic leaders, who protested that the removal of religious disabilities would transform all Irishmen into loyal and contented subjects of His Majesty King George IV and his heirs and successors. So did Sir Robert Peel, who doubted 'whether there could be that identity of interest and feeling which would permit the practical application of the principle of perfect civil equality in the administration of Irish affairs, and whether, if the equality were nominal and not practical, there would be satisfaction and contentment on the part of the Catholics'.[48]

That the reactionary critics of Catholic Relief were so much more accurate in their forecasts than its liberal supporters was largely due to the fact that the prophets were in an excellent position to justify their forebodings by their actions. The policy of emancipation was forced on a hostile Government by the threat of civil war, and it was unaccompanied by the endowment of the Catholic Church, which all experts, from Daniel O'Connell downwards, had urged upon Parliament as an essential part of a lasting settlement. Furthermore, the equality of the Catholics remained, as Peel correctly prophesied, purely nominal. 'It is too bad,' sighed Lord Melbourne, 'that when the right thing was done it was done so tardily and insincerely as to falsify every reasonable anticipation and to realise every evil augury. What all the wise men promised has not happened; and what all the damned fools said would happen has come to pass.'[49]

The bewilderment of the Catholic middle class increased with the advent to power of Lord Grey's Whig Government. Although the new Lord Lieutenant was the popular Marquess of Anglesey, whose earlier support of the Catholics had led to his dismissal by the Duke of Wellington, the Whigs added in Mr. Stanley a Chief Secretary known as an ardent supporter of the Protestant Establishment and opponent of O'Connell. The precedents of the long series of Tory Governments were fully maintained in the appointment of lower officials, and the key position of Irish Attorney-General was

7   97

filled with an undisguised and unrepentant Tory and enemy of the Catholics.

Stanley was an avowed and venomous enemy of the Nationalists who was destined to leave the Whigs only a few years later on Irish policy. Meanwhile he was strong enough to commit the Government to a policy of ruthless coercion, and his measures could be described by a Tory as 'of a character and rigour that no Tory minister would have ever dared to hint at'.[50] It was this policy of coercion at a time when a thorough change of system was needed which made Tom Moore, himself a moderate Whig but an Irishman, sadly exclaim that

> Your Whigs, when in office a short year or two
> By a *lusus naturae* are turned into Tories.

Stanley actually prided himself on his contemptuous hostility towards the 'Repealers', although the partial reform of the Irish borough franchise greatly increased the strength of O'Connell's 'tail' in the House of Commons: in the first election to a reformed Parliament, out of 105 Irish members 40 were Repealers, another 32 were Whigs and only 33 were Tories, the majority of them from Ulster.

However, the parliamentary importance of the Repealers in the House of Commons and the aversion of the majority of the Whigs to coercive measures led to Stanley's retirement from the Irish Government, and soon afterwards from the Whig party. The resignation of Lord Grey removed the other most important obstacle to the co-operation between the Irish followers of O'Connell and the British Whigs, and the interlude of the first Peel administration lent strength to the arguments of the sensible Whigs who regarded a durable understanding with O'Connell as indispensable in the interests of both England and Ireland.

This understanding, known in English history as the Lichfield House Compact, satisfied the Irish Catholics at least in the field of Irish administration. Although Lord Melbourne could not override the unreasoning opposition to O'Connell himself for high judicial office, the Lord Lieutenant consulted him on all matters of importance, the anti-Catholic tradition in the administration of justice was broken and the central bureaucracy was compelled by the Government to change its attitude towards both Nationalists and Orangemen, though in opposite directions. The dismissal of Orange magistrates, the refusal to employ army and constabulary for civil purposes and the appointment of prominent Catholics to public offices, all formed part of an integrated policy, which found an exceptionally able representative in the person of the new Under-Secretary.

Thomas Drummond was a Scottish Radical with a good knowledge of Ireland, and it is a historical injustice that his only lasting achievement should have been the reform of the Irish police. The Royal Irish Constabulary, which he created, completed the work begun more than twenty years earlier by Robert Peel; it became a formidable and powerful machine, ruled directly from Dublin Castle by an Inspector-General who was less subject to local influences than the provincial authorities of earlier days. The need for such an organisation demonstrated the weakness of the Irish middle class which could not be relied on to guarantee the good behaviour of the masses. The Royal Irish Constabulary was less a police force in the conventional sense than an army of occupation with police functions.

The years immediately following the Catholic Emancipation Act of 1829 were, indeed, a period of acute crisis in the relations between the middle class and the unprivileged masses, which were completely indifferent to the admission of a few wealthy Catholics to Parliament and to the plums of the professions and the bureaucracy. For them 'emancipation' had a wider and more fundamental meaning than for the middle-class Catholics. When the speakers of the Catholic Association told them in glowing terms of the great aims for which they were to brave their landlords at the polls and risk their economic existence, when the priests exhorted them from the pulpits to contribute towards the common victory by paying the Catholic rent, they responded in the hope and expectation that victory would mean the end of their servitude: 'When the Bill passed,' an eye-witness related many years later, 'there were bonfires lit all about the village, and on the top of the hill, and the greatest excitement that ever was. The people did not know exactly what it was about. They thought O'Connell and Sheil would stream gold in their pockets, and I know some that wouldn't sow a crop in those years because they had been told the millennium was coming.'[51] They soon found out by bitter experience that victory at Westminster had been purchased at the expense of almost two hundred thousand freeholders and that they were, if possible, worse off than before.

The extent of this revulsion of the masses from the merely political agitation of the middle class brought the country to the brink of civil war. Early in 1832 the Lord Lieutenant, Lord Anglesey, described the position as alarming: 'The country is at this moment all but in a state of rebellion. . . . I tremble at every day's post. I cannot cover the whole country, and can only subdue two or three counties at a time and then fall upon others.'[52] (The writer

was one of Wellington's most distinguished generals.) Soon afterwards a Queen's County magistrate stated that the condition of his
district differed very little from open rebellion.[53] Although 20,000
troops were stationed in the country, the Viceroy asked for twice
that number if he was to keep Ireland in submission.

The danger of a country-wide peasant rising was a challenge not
only to the Government, which never doubted its ability to crush
armed rebellion by force, but to the middle class and, above all, to
the Church. For O'Connell and his friends emancipation was
merely a stepping-stone towards political power. From their point
of view, the demand for repeal of the Union was the logical answer
to the frustration of their hopes in the immediate effects of the
Emancipation Act which remained a dead letter until 1835. Repeal
would appear and disappear as a political slogan as their chances
of success within the existing system grew dimmer or brighter: when
the Whigs were in power and promised concessions, the repeal
agitation died down, only to come up again under a Tory administration.

The immediate raising of the Repeal question after the Emancipation Act was undoubtedly a grave tactical error on the part of
O'Connell. However logical from the point of view of the middle
class, this agitation did not appeal to the peasants and was positively
distasteful to the Church. After the ruthless betrayal of his peasant
allies in the struggle for the Emancipation Act, O'Connell was
ill-advised to pass on to Repeal without giving the masses tangible
proof of his sincerity and of the advantages or the new agitation
for themselves. The peasants had been induced once before to delay
the fight for their own economic interests for a different and sup-
posedly greater purpose, and the results did not justify a repetition
of the process. Above all, their economic condition was steadily
deteriorating until it reached a point where an explosion seemed
difficult to avoid.

While O'Connell's tactical triumph in the matter of Catholic
Emancipation blinded him to this stark reality, the clergy were in
a better position to judge the facts of the situation. They had been
body and soul with O'Connell in the campaign against the archaic
religious disabilities, and used their full power over their flocks for
a purpose which was of supreme importance to the Church. But
their intimacy with the lives and thoughts of the peasant masses
made them acutely aware of the dangers of a destructive revolutionary outbreak which threatened the very fabric of Irish society.
In these conditions Repeal of the Union, if successful, would have
meant something very different from the middle-class Utopia of
the respectable Repealers, and, with the events of the French

Revolution still fresh in their minds, the priests were chary of supporting an agitation which might have led to similar results. Furthermore, Rome was unalterably opposed to the separation of Ireland from England. From the point of view of papal world policy, Ireland was much more important as a part of the United Kingdom than as an independent nation. A strong Catholic party in the British House of Commons was infinitely more valuable as an auxiliary of the Court of Rome than the largest imaginable majority of Catholics in an Irish Parliament.

The political leader of the Church, Bishop Doyle, disagreed violently with his good friend Daniel O'Connell on Repeal. He wanted to direct the elemental movement of popular discontent into channels of solid advantage to his Church and, if possible, to the tenants themselves. He insisted that the Tithe Question, much more than that of Repeal, contained the material for such a controlled movement, and for the next few years the Tithe Question occupied Parliament for many a weary month, splitting British parties and overthrowing British Governments.

The scandal of the Irish tithe system had been crying out for more than a century. Not only had the small Catholic tenants to pay for the maintenance of an alien Church, but the rich graziers, many of whom were Protestants, were actually exempt from the payment of tithes. The absentee clergyman treated his Irish living merely as a source of income, just like the absentee landlord treated his Irish estate: the result was the growth of a class of tithe proctors and tithe farmers, as rapacious as, and still more objectionable than, the agents and middlemen of the landlords. Due to the chronic poverty of the masses, any periodic claim on part of their miserable output, however moderate its original amount, was bound to involve them in endless exploitation. Being never able to pay on time, the peasants were the predestined victims of usurers, who naturally flocked into positions like those of rent agents and tithe farmers which promised them a rich harvest. The palpable injustice of the case and the combination of religious and economic grievances made the tithe question one of the most popular grounds for complaint. An 'emancipation' which did not even free them from this burden was bound to be regarded by them as a fraud. The priests could safely encourage the peasants in their resistance to tithe collection, not only because they justly condemned the system as unfair in itself and a badge of slavery for Catholics, but also because the anti-tithe agitation permitted them to keep control of the popular forces.

The Catholics were not alone in their opposition to tithes, which were just as obnoxious to the Presbyterians of Ulster. Even a large section of the landlords, particularly the Whigs, objected to the palpable wastefulness of the Church Establishment which was out of all proportion to the number of Protestants in the country and to the actual duties performed by the Protestant clergy. This combination of interests determined the final solution of the problem by a compromise which did not abolish tithes in the interests of the peasants, but transformed them into a rent charge, with substantial benefits for the landlords. The occupiers of the soil were freed from the double pressure of two separate sets of middlemen by the abolition of tithe proctors and tithe farmers. The scaling down of the tithes themselves benefited mainly the landlords, for the competition by the peasants for land was greater than ever before and led to an increase in rents which absorbed the reduction in the amount of tithe.

The settlement of the tithe question seemed to remove another specific grievance by merging it into the great general grievance of the Irish people, the land system which was the root cause of Irish poverty and exploitation. Thus it was not a question whether the 'agitation' should continue or cease, but whether it should continue under the leadership of the clergy and the middle class, or in opposition to them.

The weakness of the Whig Government and the likelihood of the return to power of the Tories compelled Daniel O'Connell at last to prepare again for active warfare against England. For this purpose he founded first the Society of Precursors as a hardly veiled threat to the Whigs and in due course the Repeal Association. In the original programme of this his last venture, the demand for Repeal of the Union was smothered by a host of other points likely to gain the adherence of the masses—amongst them fixity of tenure, abolition of tithes and a radical democratisation of politics on Chartist lines. These demands were, however, too extreme for O'Connell's middle-class followers and the Catholic clergy, and the election of 1841 was a severe rebuff to his party which was reduced to complete impotence in a House of Commons dominated by Sir Robert Peel at the head of a large Tory majority. Even amongst the masses the agitation did not make much progress during the first year or two, partly no doubt due to the hostility of the Church and to repeated disappointments in the past, but to some extent also as the result of the dangerous competition by the secret agrarian societies for the loyalty of the most active elements of the peasantry.

O'Connell thus found himself in the most paradoxical position of his whole career: his appeal to the masses estranged the middle class, but at the same time the masses were in no mood to listen to historical and constitutional dissertations. In order to escape from this dilemma, O'Connell turned simultaneously into opposite directions. He gained the ear of the middle classes by a striking oratorical effort which induced Dublin Corporation to back a Repeal petition, purged his programme of all demands unpalatable to the middle class and confined it strictly to the simple issue of Repeal pure and simple, without agrarian or democratic demands: almost immediately the new Repeal Rent soared to levels far beyond those of the Catholic rent of glorious memory.

But while O'Connell gave such convincing proof of the moderation of his aims, the opposition of the British Government and the silent competition of the revolutionary underground movement of the secret societies pushed him to the use of desperate words, and to actions which were senseless or worse except in preparation for an armed struggle against Great Britain. He entered on a speech-making campaign of unprecedented violence and his utterances, particularly those at Mallow and Cashel, were remarkably free from his usual legalistic reservations. The creation of the arbitration courts in competition with the official Courts of Law was a practical measure which went beyond a mere battle of words. It would have been an excellent tactical device for a movement with the aims of the Sinn Fein movement of 1920; otherwise it was an even more criminal provocation than O'Connell's hints at physical resistance to the Coercion Act which the Tories were pushing through Parliament. The truth was, of course, that O'Connell was playing a gigantic game of bluff, and that he tried to bully the Tories into concessions to the Irish middle class, just as he had intimidated them into granting Catholic Emancipation. When his bluff was called at Clontarf, the hollowness of his fighting speeches revealed itself just as clearly as the insincerity of his fight for the small freeholders had been shown up by his behaviour during the earlier crisis.

O'Connell's surrender increased his popularity with the Irish middle class and even with English Radicals like Joseph Sturge of Birmingham, who told the Repealers that 'the peaceful and constitutional manner in which the people of Ireland are seeking to obtain justice has justly excited great admiration'.[54] At the same time it killed the strategy of a nationalist movement on the grand scale— a mass organisation of the Irish people directed by the middle class and in its interests.

In Ireland the 'hungry forties' began as early as 1838 with the first of five calamitous harvests, both for grain and potatoes. The sheer impossibility of making ends meet in a year of bad potato yields produced a staggering increase in emigration figures. Overseas emigration from Irish ports, which had fallen from 33,007 in 1832 to only 4,424 in 1838, jumped to 28,148 in 1840, 29,554 in 1841, and reached the astonishing total of 89,686 in 1842. In the five years 1840–44 almost a quarter of a million people left Ireland for the New World,[55] quite apart from the many thousands who could not afford the luxury of an emigrant boat and who crowded into the Irish slum quarters of the industrial towns of Great Britain. The end of the tithe war thus coincided with a further deterioration in the position of the peasants which destroyed the slender hope that the settlement of the tithe question would end the unrest of rural Ireland. Ribbonism received a powerful impetus during the tithe struggle when it enjoyed the toleration of the clergy, but not even the renewed hostility of the priests could prevent its further growth during the ensuing lean years. By that time it had completely outgrown its original purpose as a Catholic defence organisation and, after absorbing numerous local agrarian societies, assumed the character of a widespread, if loosely knit, conspiracy of the poor peasants.

The years of the Repeal Agitation were thus a time of violent agrarian unrest and upheaval: while the middle class became more conservative, the masses became more rebellious. This divergence of trends sealed the fate of O'Connell's agitation, for his attempt to throw overboard the agrarian and radical planks of his pro- gramme, while compensating for this betrayal of the masses by exaggerated appeals to their anti-English emotions, led him straight to the *débâcle* of Clontarf and the State Trial which terminated his career as a leader of the Irish people.

The State Trial cowed O'Connell so thoroughly that he aban- doned the most important measures of his previous agitation and dropped the conciliation courts. When he went to prison, there were no outrages and an unusual calm reigned at the assizes throughout the country. The Repealers, incapable of leading the people, were acutely conscious of the chance with which their failure presented the Ribbonmen, and wasted their breath on denouncing the criminal absurdity of secret societies. O'Connell himself implored the Irish nation 'to preserve tranquillity and to avoid ribbonism and all secret societies whatever and to prove themselves worthy of the moment they had arrived at'.[56] From the day of his release from prison O'Connell strove to replace the combination of mass organisation and middle-class leadership by a coalition of the Protestant and Catholic middle and upper classes. He appointed a Protestant Whig, W. Smith O'Brien, as his deputy during his imprisonment and wanted to set up a caricature of the old Irish Parliament in the shape of a Preservative Society, which 'would comprise so many of the wealthy and influential of Ireland that it would be an effectual check to any rash revolutionary outbreak'.[57] In addition, he tried his best to arrive at a compromise platform with the progressive wing of the Ulster middle class, led by the land reformer Sharman Crawford, who advocated a modified form of Home Rule under the title of federalism.

The direct result of O'Connell's flirtation with federalism was serious friction within the Repeal ranks between the O'Connell machine and a small but important group of middle-class intellectuals known as *Young Ireland* and grouped round *The Nation*, which was by far the most important literary expression of middle-class nationalism in Ireland. Young Ireland was no more radical in its social programme than O'Connell himself; its leaders were not even ready to attack the Irish landowners as a class, and their appeal was almost exclusively directed to the urban middle class, in particular to the Protestants to whom most of them belonged.

The talents of Thomas Davis, Blake Dillon, Gaffan Duffy, etc., and O'Connell's need for Protestant middle-class allies made the Young Irelanders in a certain way a power behind the throne of the leader, but their ability to influence events depended entirely on their membership of the Repeal movement, because they had no independent link with the masses. This weakness became apparent as soon as they clashed with the O'Connell machine and wanted to follow an independent policy of their own. The Young Irelanders were reduced to the ridiculous position of having to protest in private against O'Connell's disastrous moves, without being in the least able to prevent them. All they could hope to do was to drive the leader for the moment into their own direction and to contribute their share to the pathetic mixture of confusion and blustering which mars the last period of O'Connell's public career.

The claim of the Irish Catholic middle class to political leadership perished thus ignominiously even before the shadow of the Great Famine had descended on Ireland. The subsequent history of Young Ireland is a further illustration of the weakness of the Irish middle class as an independent political force. O'Connell's sickness and death seemed to remove the greatest stumbling-block in the path of that resolute anti-British nationalist policy which the leaders of Young Ireland demanded with such incisive force of style. This development coincided with the supreme crisis of the Great Famine which threw social Ireland into the melting-pot and made the acceptance of the most radical policies the most natural course, because it reduced the manifold problems of Ireland's position to their simplest and most fundamental form—whether the food produced within the country should be used for the sustenance of the Irish people or for the payment of rents to the Irish landlords.

Yet it was this crisis which revealed the complete break between the middle class and the people.

It is untrue that the peasants submitted everywhere to their fate without resistance. Particularly after the stopping of the public works programme by the Whig Government, serious rioting took place in the autumn of 1847 in Clare, Limerick, Tipperary and King's County. Many tenants withheld 'both rent and produce from the landlord, living in a state of unwholesome expectancy of some great social or political change'.[58] The Government flooded Ireland with troops to such an extent that the Viceroy, Lord Clarendon, felt 'at the head of a provisional Government in a half-conquered country'.[59] Yet the leaders of Young Ireland never managed to establish contact with the elemental rebellious forces of the peasantry. This was partly due to the differences between moderates (Smith O'Brien, Duffy, Dillon, etc.) and extremists (Mitchel, Martin, Fintan Lalor) which paralysed Young Ireland as a political force and caused the pitiable failure of the organised risings of 1848. But above all, the failure of the Repeal movement had the effect of permanently discrediting the respectable leaders in the eyes of the militant elements of the peasantry.

In the absence of organised and efficient leadership, the policy of the Whig Government met only sporadic and ineffectual resistance. The authorities regarded the Famine as a regrettably expensive but none the less extremely potent engine for the reshaping of Ireland along the lines prescribed by the fashionable economics of the time. Hunger and death loosened the hold of the stubborn peasants on their miserable homesteads, and with the help of the notorious Gregory clause (which refused relief to persons in possession of more than one-quarter acre of land) large numbers were compelled to give up their holdings and emigrate to Great Britain or the United States. At the same time, and in hardly more intolerable conditions, the leaders of Young Ireland left the country as convicts, condemned to long terms of transportation, or as fugitives; and it was amongst these Irish emigrants that the nationalist movement of the next generation found some of its most effective leaders and masses of eager supporters at a time when it had well-nigh expired in the 'old country'.

CHAPTER XIII

IRELAND IN THE IMPERIAL PARLIAMENT

ALTHOUGH the entry of an Irish party into the British House of Commons was delayed for thirty years after the Union, Ireland exerted from the beginning of the nineteenth century a strong, and at times dominant, influence on Government and parties in Great Britain. Catholic emancipation was for many years the outstanding issue in British politics, and its controversial character was entirely due to its Irish aspect.

The first Cabinet crisis of the new century was the resignation of the younger Pitt, after seventeen years of uninterrupted rule, on the question of Catholic emancipation. Although Pitt abandoned office primarily as a pretext in order to wriggle out of his obligations to the Catholics, and although the change of government did not imply a change in policy, it was remarkable as showing the acceptance of unalloyed Tory principles by the King's ministers, and soon afterwards by Pitt himself. Thus the Irish problem effected the final metamorphosis of the Reform minister of 1783 into the idol of the Tories.

The political usefulness of the Catholic question was demonstrated in a very different fashion a few years later in the break-up of the Ministry of All the Talents. It had been hateful to the King from the start, although he could not resist its formation in the emergency after the Battle of Austerlitz and the death of Pitt. When C. J. Fox entered the Cabinet, the Irish Catholics naturally believed that he would actively sponsor their cause, but in view of the delicate position of the Whigs in the Government he advised them not to press their full claims and to be satisfied with substantial concessions. When the Catholics grew restless after Fox's sudden death, the Government took up the paltriest of all Fox's promises, the admission of Catholics to commissions in the army, and it was over this miserable 'reform' that the Whigs were dismissed by the half-mad King.

Ever since the establishment of Grattan's Parliament in 1782, the English Whigs had been closely connected with the Irish reformers, and the advocacy of full Catholic Emancipation was the traditional symbol of this alliance. Complete religious toleration was one of the most important tenets common to the progressive Irish landlords and the new Irish middle class; the Whigs shared this outlook and were, therefore, in favour of admitting Catholics to Parliament and to all public offices. Yet the matter was not strictly a party question, for Pitt, Castlereagh and Canning, as well as some of the 'Portland Whigs' who were then coalescing with the Tories, were also convinced of the need for Catholic emancipation in order to make the Union a success. Catholic relief soon became the only important plank in the thin platform of the Whig party. The ill-assorted combination of Foxites and Grenvillites was badly in need of a few common aims, and Catholic emancipation was the only first-rate question on which they managed to agree. Even more valuable from a practical angle was the fact that it was at the same time the main question on which the Tories disagreed. Thus it became a recognised part of the Whig programme, and votes on Catholic emancipation gave the Whigs their rare chances of mustering widespread parliamentary support against the Tory Government.

In these circumstances the Whig championship of the Catholics became as much a matter of necessity as of choice. Not only was emancipation the single question 'on which Whig opinion was united while Tory opinion was divided',[60] but the emancipated Catholics were bound to be the enemies of their enemies and the friends of the Whigs. The prediction of a great increase in Government influence over the House of Commons through Irish votes, which had been freely made by the opponents of the Union, was borne out by the facts during the first generation after the Union, and the only way of altering the balance in favour of the Whigs was the admission of Catholics to seats for Irish constituencies. Although the Whigs were ultimately too weak to carry Catholic Emancipation by their own unaided efforts, they were indispensable for the parliamentary success of the agitation. The Catholic Association under Daniel O'Connell supplied the necessary driving power behind the speeches and resolutions of the Whig parliamentarians and strengthened the conviction of the progressive Tories that relief could not be safely denied much longer.

With the agitation in Ireland nearing its climax, Lord Liverpool broke down and his Government broke up. The accession of the pro-Catholic Canning to power was the sign for an open split in both parties on the Catholic question: an influential section of the Whigs under Lord Lansdowne agreed to join the Government, while the unbending High Tories, Peel, Wellington, Eldon, refused to take part in the new administration. The history of Canning's government was in many respects similar to that of the Ministry of All the Talents twenty years earlier: although consisting of declared supporters of Catholic emancipation, it was too weak to tackle the matter boldly, and the sudden death of its guiding spirit

put an end to its existence. It was followed, after the short and
farcical interlude of the Goderich administration, by a Tory
ministry of the old type under the Duke of Wellington, who tried
in vain to maintain the balance between High Tories, like Peel and
Eldon, and progressive Canningites, like Huskisson, Palmerston and
the later Lord Melbourne. This Government, which after the
departure of the Canningites was pledged to the hilt to the maintenance of Protestant supremacy in all its rigorous exclusiveness,
found itself compelled after a few months to capitulate to the
Catholics. The combination of Irish agitation and parliamentary
strains and stresses was too much for the conqueror of Napoleon,
who had to throw overboard his declared policy and his most
reliable supporters and to bribe the Catholic leaders by the offer
of full emancipation into acquiescence in the disfranchisement of
the Irish peasantry.

As far as Ireland was concerned, the intrinsic importance of this
long-delayed concession was comparatively small, but British
political history was deeply influenced by the admission of genuine
representatives of the Irish Catholic middle class. In spite of the
reactionary change in the Irish county franchise, the Catholic Relief
Act of 1829 heralded the end of the long era of Tory rule and the
reappearance of the Whigs as the prominent political party.

The immediate result of Peel's and Wellington's change of front
was the disgust and bewilderment of the Tory party with the
faithless upholders of Protestant ascendancy. Peel had clearly foreseen that Catholic relief could only be carried with the help of the
Whigs against the stubborn opposition of the High Tories, and he
suffered from deep misgivings, personal and political, about the
whole transaction. He doubted whether the Whigs would be willing
to pay the price of disfranchising the forty-shilling freeholders
which, from his point of view, alone made the whole bargain worth
while. But on this point the Whigs proved no less conservative than
the Tories: although four years previously the same problem had
almost led to an open break between the Radical Lambton and the
'trimmer' Brougham,[61] the Whigs voted for the Relief Bill and for
both its 'wings', whose dovelike office it was, in the poetic language
of the Edinburgh Review, to waft home the messenger of peace[62]—by
emasculating the democratic Irish movement.

Perhaps the most curious detail in which Catholic Relief prepared
the way for the great Reform Bill of 1832 was its effect on the
attitude of the High Church party towards the unreformed House
of Commons. The Standard, the organ of the ultra-Tories, inveighed
against the 'scandalous composition of a House of Commons which
could pass Catholic Relief by an act of sheer despotism over the

heads of a Protestant nation'.[63] Lord Eldon, the High Priest of reaction, wrote to his brother during the Reform Bill struggle that many of the persons whose petitions against Catholic Relief he had presented now petitioned for a reform, 'for, say they, a House of Commons which could vote for that Emancipation Bill cannot be such a House of Commons as ought any longer to exist'.[64]

If the Irish question thus conditioned the minds of otherwise unalterable opponents of Reform in favour of a change, Irish votes had a much more direct influence on the parliamentary balance of power during the struggle. The decisive trial of strength in the House of Commons occurred at the very beginning of the campaign when the second reading of the first Reform Bill was carried by the majority of a single vote. This decisive vote must have been cast by Daniel O'Connell or one of his handful of supporters who managed to get into Parliament on the very restricted Irish franchise at the general election of 1830, for this Irish party or 'tail' was the only new element in the parliamentary arena. The Bill was opposed by a majority of the British 'representatives' and of the totally corrupt Irish boroughs, and the issue was decided by the Irish counties.[65] The situation was the more dramatic because at that moment the Whig Government were prosecuting O'Connell himself, but they could not afford to send the man to prison whose absence from the critical division would have endangered their parliamentary existence.

The terms of the Reform Bill, particularly as amended, were by no means favourable to Ireland, and still less to the mass of the Irish people. The number of Irish seats remained practically unchanged, while the total membership of the House rose from 596 to 658, thus reducing Ireland's relative importance. The forty-shilling freeholders who had been swept away in Ireland three years previously, were retained in Great Britain. The £10 qualification in the boroughs restricted the franchise to a much narrower class in a poor country like Ireland than in Great Britain. Under the new régime England and Wales had one member of Parliament for 27,800 inhabitants, Scotland for 44,624 and Ireland for 73,975; in the counties of Great Britain one man in twenty-five had the vote, in the Irish counties only one man in one hundred and fifteen;[66] of the 60,607 voters in Irish counties, over one-third (or 20,546) lived in the nine counties of Ulster which returned fourteen out of twenty Tories for Irish counties in the first reformed Parliament.[67]

The struggle for the Great Reform Bill was the first occasion on which Irish representatives as such played a decisive role in British parliamentary politics. The elections of 1830, which turned against the Tories in Great Britain, favoured them in Ireland owing to the influence of Dublin Castle and the restriction of the franchise, but during the following election in 1831, when a Whig administration was in power for the first time since the Union, the pressure of Dublin Castle was not used in favour of the Tories, who became a small minority everywhere except in Ulster. In the first reformed House of Commons, the representation of Ireland was almost exactly the reverse of that customary before the Emancipation Act: 33 Tories, the majority of them from Ulster, had been returned as against 72 Whigs and supporters of O'Connell, and during the next twenty years the 'Irish brigade' made and unmade Governments.

The Whig Government of Lord Grey was almost identical in its Irish policy with that of the Duke of Wellington, and O'Connell opposed it as much from necessity as from choice, until it resigned on the question of Irish coercion after a complicated intrigue. At the General Election of 1835 the Tories gained so much ground that they achieved a small British majority, and it was only the two to one Liberal majority in Ireland that turned the scales against the Government. Thus it was only fitting that Sir Robert Peel was turned out of office on an Irish question, which was supplied by Lord John Russell's resolution on Irish tithes.

Lord Melbourne's long second Government owed its existence to the famous Lichfield House Compact between O'Connell and the coy Whig leaders, and its duration to Irish support. But although the new Government was little better than O'Connell's creature, he was nevertheless its prisoner, and for the next five years he learned a bitter lesson in British politics, and particularly in the power of the House of Lords over a hostile Government. Since the Reform Bill of 1832, 'the Lords had rejected not merely the Irish Tithe Bill, but also a Constabulary Bill, a Marriage Bill, a Dublin Police Bill, and a Voters' Registration Bill, all interesting Ireland',[68] and O'Connell answered this brutal challenge with a great speech-making campaign through the industrial North of England and through Scotland in which he denounced the power of the Peers and appealed to British Radicalism as Ireland's only ally in its struggle against feudal privilege. This tour made him for the moment the darling of the advanced section of the Liberal party, but it could not shift the House of Lords. The Peers remained contemptuously hostile to the second Melbourne Government which had no effective means of hitting back at its privileged enemies. The reform of English local government escaped unshorn by the second chamber, but the Lords unhesitatingly rejected the Irish Municipal Reform Bill, in spite or because of its importance for the Government and for Ireland. For the next few years the two Houses were at loggerheads on almost all Irish questions, and in the end the Lords invariably enforced solutions which were unacceptable to the Irish middle class.

The Irish party was not by any means extremely radical, even according to the lax standards of the time: the property qualification for members of Parliament would have been alone enough to prevent this. The Irish middle class was, however, forced to side with the British Radicals by the obstinate resistance of the Tories to even the most moderate reforms—just as the refusal to grant Catholic Emancipation with a good grace and at an early date had pushed it into the arms of the English parliamentary reformers. The obstruction of all progressive Irish measures by the Tory-dominated House of Lords compelled a fundamentally conservative politician like O'Connell to attack the privileges and the legislative power of the Lords from every angle, and particularly by opposing the feudal claims of the hereditary lawmakers with the democratic title of the popular representatives. The bitterness against the Lords, which had reached a climax before their surrender on Reform, gradually subsided in England, but the Irish question, and the contemptuous indifference of the Lords to the opinions of the Irish middle class, perpetuated the political issue of the House of Lords and of the narrow limits of British democracy.

The first English statesman to sense the constitutional importance of the Irish issue for the balance of power between Lords and Commons was the great Conservative, Sir Robert Peel. He was the dominant parliamentary personality of the first half of the nineteenth century, and one of those rare politicians who outgrow the limitations of their youth. As far as Ireland was concerned, the system of government by King, Lords and Commons had always been a sham, and the legislative Union, which made Ireland simply a province of the United Kingdom, brought it even formally to a close. Before the passing of the Catholic Relief Bill in 1829 the Irish people were to all intents and purposes outside the constitution: King, Lords and Commons were equally alien and hostile to the large majority of Irishmen. The emancipation of the Catholics made at least the middle class eligible for participation in British politics, and the House of Commons was the only place where genuine Irish representatives could share in decisions on Ireland. For this reason it was the only constitutional power whose pronouncements on Irish affairs had even a semblance of moral authority.

The first inkling of this important fact which was to be of crucial constitutional importance for the next generations, appeared in Sir Robert Peel's announcement of the resignation of his first government in a letter to King William IV (29th March 1835). His explanation made it clear that a defeat on an Irish measure was something fundamentally different from other adverse votes in the House of Commons: 'There are many cases in which public opinion, or the opinion of the House of Lords, might counterbalance a vote of the House of Commons carried by a considerable majority; but the Tithe question in Ireland is one upon which, as opposed to such a majority, neither public opinion in England, nor that of the House of Lords would have a material effect.'[69] Eleven years later, similar considerations were to decide Peel, after one of the most impressive and successful administrations in modern British history, to abandon power without a struggle rather than to violate what he had come to regard as the spirit of the British constitution.

In 1841, Melbourne's long-expected resignation could no longer be delayed, and at the general election the Catholic bogy played a prominent part in Tory propaganda and made its contribution to the large Tory majority. Even in Ireland the Tories made substantial progress, nowhere more conspicuously than in Dublin, where for the first time since the Reform Bill the Liberal members, including O'Connell himself, were thrown out. The Repealers in the new House of Commons were almost reduced to an O'Connell family party, and the centre of political gravity in Irish affairs moved back from Westminster to Ireland. During the next four years the Whig and Irish opposition was powerless in the face of a large and well-led Tory majority in the House of Commons and of a docile House of Lords under Wellington's command. Yet it was again on Ireland that the strongest Tory administration since the days of Pitt suffered its first major rebuff, before it was wrecked by the Corn Laws in a crisis for which Ireland furnished at least the occasion.

The Government answered the dangerous progress of the Repeal movement by yet another commission on the eternal subject of Irish land. The Devon Commission, whose political bias did not lie by any means on the side of Irish nationalism, reported in 1845 that the tenants should be given security of tenure, although such a step was deeply distasteful to the High Priests of private enterprise and *laissez faire* on both sides of the House of Commons. Peel's cautious and inadequate Bill in partial implementation of the Report was buried by the House of Lords in a Select Committee: by trying to interfere with the material interests of the Irish landlords Peel reached the limits of his power, 'though in both Houses he had a majority for all ordinary purposes'.[70] Even the politically futile proposal to increase the grant to Maynooth College, the seminary for Catholic priests, led to the resignation for religious reasons of W. E. Gladstone, at that time the rising hope of the High Church Tories.

8

Peel's Irish troubles were, however, insignificant compared with the storm which broke over his head when he decided to outrage the English landlords by striking his colours to the Anti-Corn Law League. This was basically a quarrel between the most powerful classes in Great Britain, the landlords and the commercial interests, but Ireland had its peculiar share in its development. Peel's conversion to free trade principles had been in progress for years before the Irish potato failure of 1845 created the sudden emergency which crystallised his opinions and induced him to act on the larger issue. Ireland was neither the pretext for Peel's conversion, as his slanderous opponents asserted,[71] nor its cause, as he may have believed himself, but the occasion which transformed his general ideas into concrete political action, thereby demonstrating the peculiar role of the Irish problem in British politics between the Union and the First World War. That his action was quite irrelevant to the Irish situation does not invalidate this interpretation, though it shows Ireland's plight from a revealing angle. In Peel's important memoir on the whole crisis, the Irish famine dominates the narrative until the controversy reaches Cabinet level; then Ireland and the failure of the potato crop drop completely out of the picture, and Peel's mind is wholly preoccupied with the problem of parliamentary support for the repeal of the Corn Laws. The practical side of the Irish situation had no bearing on the question of free trade, for it consisted simply in the feeding of a huge population, left utterly destitute by the disappearance of its essential foodstuff and by its inability to afford any other. The Duke of Wellington expressed the difficulty perfectly clearly when he said that 'the evil in Ireland is not a deficiency of food for the year, or even of a particular description of food, potatoes; but the great and supposed general deficiency of that description of food operating upon the social condition of Ireland; the habits of the great body of the people . . . who have not the pecuniary means, and if they had the pecuniary means, are not in the habit of purchasing their food in the markets'.[72]

The legal side of the Irish crisis, however, led straight into the Corn Law controversy: Ireland was in a state of free grain trade with Great Britain, and the suspension of the Corn Laws in Ireland would either have meant their suspension in Great Britain, or the prohibition of corn exports from Ireland, which had been resorted to in earlier emergencies. Peel has been severely blamed by Irish historians for his failure to take this step, but in the circumstances it would have made very little difference: nothing short of a social revolution would have enabled the starving Irish peasants to appropriate their crops without payment, and otherwise they were not in a position to afford wheat or oats instead of potatoes, however plentiful the supply. At the same time the measure would have been politically impossible, because the Irish landlords would have prevented it by all the formidable means in their power and because, in a year of mediocre crops in Great Britain, they would have been fully supported by the English public.

This dilemma, serious as it was, would not have produced a complete change of front on the part of the Government, if Peel and Graham had not been converted to the policy of free trade, and if Cobden and Bright had not rallied behind them the whole British middle class and a substantial section of the workers. The Anti-Corn Law League owed much to O'Connell's Catholic Association as a model for its organisation and propaganda, and this similarity in technique reflected a remarkable similarity in social structure and purpose: both were middle-class bodies pursuing middle-class aims with the support of the masses which had become convinced by persistent propaganda that these aims were essential to their own well-being. In both cases, the ruling classes finally made large concessions in the hope and for the purpose of breaking up this dangerous alliance—and in both cases their hopes were realised and the democratisation of public life was delayed for a considerable time. In Ireland their success was transitory, in spite of the ruthless disfranchisement of the masses, because the two anti-Irish interests, the landlords and the Castle bureaucracy, prevented the application of the policy which had been promised in principle after the removal of Catholic disabilities. In Great Britain the surrender was final and complete, and there the Repeal of the Corn Laws justified the political hopes of its conservative sponsors. 'One of the great benefits and blessings which I anticipate from the Repeal of the Corn Laws,' wrote Sir James Graham, Home Secretary and second-in-command in the Peel Government, 'is, that at last there is some hope of surviving the din of this odious and endless topic of democratic agitation.'[73] The Anti-Corn Law League dissolved, to the great relief of Tories and Whigs, British radicalism lost the greater part of its middle-class backing, and the further reform of the Constitution was shelved for more than twenty years.

With the split between free traders and protectionists in the Tory camp, the Irish party had at last a chance of reasserting its parliamentary position. In spite of Peel's belated attempts to curb the anti-Catholic bias of Dublin Castle and of his Irish supporters, Tory rule in Ireland was synonymous with Protestant ascendancy, and Repealers and Whigs alike bent their powers to the destruction of the Tory Government. The opportunity came on Peel's decision to deal with the growing unrest of the famine-stricken country by means of a new and drastic Coercion Law, the only apparent alternative to the policy of agrarian reform which had been turned down decisively by the landlords in the House of Lords. The coincidence of the passing of the Repeal of the Corn Laws and the defeat of Peel's Government on the Irish Coercion Bill was one of the most dramatic events in British parliamentary history; less known, though remarkable in itself and fraught with significance for the future, was the reasoning which induced Sir Robert Peel to end his ministerial career without a struggle instead of dissolving Parliament and appealing to the middle classes of Great Britain, whose idol he could have become. Apart from a surprisingly accurate forecast of the future obstructionist tactics of the Irish party in the House of Commons, Peel flatly refused to make a dissolution of Parliament 'turn on a question between Great Britain and Ireland'. He was convinced that in such a question the House of Commons was the highest constitutional forum, and he developed this theme in words curiously reminiscent of the attitude of his greatest pupil at a moment of similarly critical importance forty years later: 'Shall Ireland be subject to a severe and unconstitutional law which is not to be applied, and never was applied, to Great Britain? It will be vain to say that our object is to protect life in Ireland. The answer will be that there are scarcely 20 out of the 105 Irish members who agree with us in the necessity or probable efficacy of the measure. The Irish representative body is against us—is against an unconstitutional law intended separately for Ireland. . . . "No Popery" was a dangerous watchword for a General Election. I firmly believe that the more dangerous watchword "Coercion for Ireland" would shake the foundations of the Legislative Union.'[74]

Reduced to a bare outline of events, the record of the Irish Question in the Imperial Parliament during the first half of the nineteenth century was as follows: it directly overturned Pitt's long administration in 1801, the Ministry of All the Talents in 1807, Lord Grey's Government in 1834, Sir Robert Peel's first administration in 1835 and his second administration in 1846. In the shape of the Catholic Question it provided, in the words of the *Edinburgh Review*, 'the most important branch of our national policy by far, since the conclusion of the war in Europe—indeed the branch which alone required either vigour or talent to conduct it'.[75] It set in motion the train of events which culminated in the Great Reform Bill of 1832, and it was the proximate cause of the crisis which ended in the Repeal of the Corn Laws—the two outstanding social and political measures of British history during the first half of the century. It formed the rallying cry for the forces within each of the two great parties, which produced in turn the split within the Tory ranks on Catholic Emancipation and the secession of the Conservative High Church men from the Whigs, and through its influence on the Repeal of the Corn Laws it contributed to the final break between free traders and protectionists inside the Tory party. It kept alive the dormant issue of the House of Lords and its constitutional position within a community which gradually accepted democratic standards of public life and it gave unsuspected strength to the forces which prepared for the inevitable battle between democracy and aristocracy. Its influence on the evolution of the modern British party system far exceeded that of any other merely political factor and was second in importance only to the political effects of the industrial revolution which provided the general framework for the slow growth of British democracy during the nineteenth century.

CHAPTER XIV

THE IRISH IN GREAT BRITAIN

BEFORE the onset of the industrial revolution the movement of population between Great Britain and Ireland flowed almost exclusively westwards from England, and particularly from Scotland, into Ireland. Emigration from Ireland was largely confined to the Dissenters of north-east Ulster and continued the westward trend over the Atlantic into North America. During the later part of the eighteenth century, this movement showed the first signs of a reversal. The clash between the Irish land system and the needs of an expanding population drove a good many Irish peasants into the wealthy neighbouring island in search of work. 'Spalpeens', or seasonal harvest workers, had been in the habit of coming from Ireland into Great Britain for a long time, though the movement was a mere trickle. This was, indeed, almost inevitable owing to the high cost of the sea passage. Since the beginning of the nineteenth century more and more Irishmen emigrated in order to escape starvation, and a steady stream of hungry and homeless men, women and children crossed the Irish Sea, in order to make a new start in a country where human labour was not an embarrassment but an asset which found ready buyers at terms which, though inhumanly bad for the workers, the Irish were ready to accept.

The most important goal of the sporadic Irish immigration during the eighteenth century had been London, and the first immigrants were reapers who remained behind when their comrades went back to Ireland after the harvest. Irish sedan-chair carriers in the respectable parts of London were just as common by the middle of the century as Irish dock labourers in Wapping. There a Catholic congregation of about four thousand people existed at the time of the Gordon riots. London, and especially its East End, remained a magnet for Irish immigrants, and the parishes of St. Giles and St. Luke, Middlesex, were overrun by thousands of Irish 'vagrants'. In view of the small number of English Catholics, the strength of the Irish influx into London may be measured by the increase in the number of London Catholics from 20,000 in the time of Queen Anne to 71,422 in 1819 and almost 120,000 seven years later. Of the total, 30,000–40,000 were Irish immigrants, and a large part of the remainder must have been the descendants of Irish settlers.

But by that time London had ceased to be the main centre of Irish settlement in Great Britain. The growth of modern industry

in Scotland and the north of England, and to a lesser extent in the
Midlands, absorbed the large majority of the recent Irish arrivals.
The great reception centres for the Irish influx were Glasgow for
Ulster, Liverpool for the centre and Bristol for the South of Ireland.
Glasgow with its surroundings was itself the industrial centre of
Scotland, while the great port of Liverpool was the front door to
industrial Lancashire and the back door to the West Riding of
Yorkshire, the home counties of the modern English cotton and
woollen industries. Lanarkshire, Ayrshire, Kirkcudbrightshire and
Wigtonshire in Scotland, London, Lancashire and the industrial
parts of Yorkshire, Staffordshire and Warwickshire in England
contained the bulk of the Irish population in Great Britain one
hundred years ago.

From the point of view of the British authorities, and even from
that of the British working classes, there was precious little difference
between the various types of Irishmen who inundated the country,
undermined the standards of pay and life of the native workers,
raised the poor rates by the cost of their relief and transportation
from one parish to another, and increased the squalor of industrial
Britain by their poverty and their poverty-bred habits. Yet such
differences existed, and their effects can be traced in the behaviour of the immigrants and in their influence on their new
surroundings.

The first great wave of Irish immigration reached the shores of
Great Britain just before the Union. It was occasioned by the
hurricane of terror which broke over Ulster before the Rebellion
of 1798. General Lake's army and the yeomanry destroyed the
power of the United Irishmen by hangings and half-hangings,
flogging and torture, and their chosen victims were the most intelligent, and therefore the most dangerous, elements of the lower
classes. Large numbers of these did not wait for compulsory transportation or the naval tender and anticipated the inevitable by
voluntary emigration. These settlers were mostly artisans, and they
found work in Glasgow and Manchester, the centres of the British
cotton industry. In Scotland their arrival coincided with acute
labour difficulties in the newly established cotton-spinning mills
which were desperately short of hands owing to the refusal of the
native artisans to work in factories and thereby forfeit their independence. In Manchester, where cotton spinning on a large scale
had started earlier than in Scotland, Irish handloom weavers flocked
in, because the mechanisation of the spinning process had caused
an insatiable demand for weavers.

Although the art of weaving was not completely restricted to
Ulster, it was practised there much more generally than elsewhere

in Ireland. A substantial part of the early Irish immigrants were Ulstermen, though not exclusively, or even predominantly, Protestants. Their most important feature was not their racial or religious character but their previous industrial training and experience which enabled them to settle down comparatively quickly in their new circumstances. The war years interrupted this movement of population which was, however, followed in the early 'twenties by a large wave of immigrants who were driven out of Ireland by the abolition of the protective Union duties.

The Irish textile industry came for the time being practically to a standstill: the abolition of protection completely destroyed the modest remnants of the silk and woollen industries, and cotton spinning which at the time of the Union employed many thousands of hands, though with very backward methods, practically disappeared: in 1838 Belfast had only four cotton mills, with a further six or eight in the neighbourhood, employing altogether fewer than a thousand hands, many of them children. Cotton weaving, on the other hand, actually increased after the abolition of the duties, for the starvation wages of the Irish weavers attracted some Scottish and English manufacturers who found Irish workmen more pliable and frugal than their own artisans. At the same time Ulster's traditional industry, the linen trade, went through a serious crisis due to the competition by Scottish manufacturers who outpaced their old-fashioned Irish rivals in the application of both capital and of modern methods of production. Apart from this, the linen trade could not compete with the cheaper cotton goods, and its survival was made possible only by the reduction of the meagre earnings of the handloom weavers below starvation level.

The quickening pace of Irish immigration into industrial England and Scotland during these years seems to have been due at least to some extent to the final destruction of almost the whole Irish textile industry. During this period several hundred Dublin silk weavers moved to Coventry, Manchester and Macclesfield. A colony of 400–500 Irish wool combers from County Cork settled in Bradford. The linen trade of Drogheda, which had been one of the main Irish exporting centres for plain linens, rapidly declined in the same period, and as a result of the growing pressure on men's wages many weavers emigrated to England.

Ireland sent a large proportion of its skilled textile workers to England, because it had no use for them at home. The bulk of the Irish immigrants, however, did not consist of artisans but of uprooted peasants without any particular skill or experience which they could have used in their new surroundings. The harvesters who came to Great Britain on seasonal work during the summer were usually mountaineers from the barren hills of Connaught—small and feeble-looking men whose main endeavour was to earn sufficient ready cash for their rent while their families were begging their livelihood in the more prosperous counties of eastern Ireland. These poorest of the poor were despised by the other Irish immigrants who often refused to work with them and who made life unbearable for them when they were lucky enough to find employment in the industrial towns. But even the prouder beggars from Munster, Leinster or Ulster had to be satisfied with very humble positions in their land of involuntary adoption. The means by which they established themselves in Great Britain were 'willingness, alacrity and per-severance in the severest, the most irksome and most disagreeable kinds of coarse labour, such for instance as attending on masons, bricklayers and plasterers, excavating earth for harbours, docks, canals and roads, carrying heavy goods, loading and unloading vessels'.[76] They provided a good deal of the human raw material for the growth of industrial Great Britain, and their share in this process was much greater than their numerical strength would suggest.

Although in Britain the enclosure movement made rapid progress, and although the position of the agricultural labourers got worse and worse, the disappearance of the 'redundant' population and its absorption by the quickly growing industrial towns did not make so much progress as the landlords and the manufacturers desired. This was largely due to the operation of the Old Poor Law which supported the country people of southern England in their natural reluctance to leave their homes for an uncertain and uninviting future in the squalid towns of the industrial north. The alteration of the Poor Law, and still more its effect on the behaviour of the English poor, took many years, and meanwhile English and Scottish industrialists cried out for a supply of cheap and docile labour. Soon they learned to look to Ireland for an answer to their prayers.

The Irish parallel to the English enclosure system was the consolidation of farms involving the eviction of small tenants who were unable to pay the high rents fixed during the years of the war boom. No Poor Law, nor even prudential or humanitarian con-siderations, prevented the Irish landlords from clearing their land from its 'redundant population' which was thrown out of its hovels and left completely destitute on the roadside. The proximity of Ireland to the industrial North-West of England, and the cheapness and ease of sea communication with the west coast of Great Britain after the introduction of a steamboat service, encouraged the use of Irish labour in British industry in preference to the employment of English ex-agricultural workers.

The evicted peasants who flocked in their thousands towards the growing industrial centres willingly took their place at the bottom of the social scale. In Ireland they had been starved of employment, and although the squalid surroundings of industrial Britain could not evoke any enthusiasm in the minds of people who had been used to fresh air and the irregular pace of seasonal agricultural work with its rhythm of slackness and great efforts, they found at least steady work at wages sufficient to eat their fill of potatoes and to drink more whisky than they had ever been able to afford. English overseers of the poor who made the mistake of regarding them as workshy because they roamed the countryside without means of support, soon discovered to their disgust that work, far from keeping them off, acted as a magnet for them: 'If we find them employment,' complained the Vestry Clerk of St. Luke, Middlesex, 'they would work for ever, they do not mind work; they would be glad to be employed breaking stones on the roads, but that does not answer our purpose; we furnish that employment as a test against idleness.'[77] When they found employment, they were tragically content with the most repulsive conditions of existence, and the dirt of their lives made 'Little Irelands' of the vast slums in most great industrial cities. Any money they earned beyond their food and rent they spent on drink, and their competition, much more than their example, made them a terror to British labourers.

In mere physical strength these immigrants had, moreover, a great initial advantage over the native workers who had been subjected from childhood to the crippling experience of work in mills or mines, and who had grown up as stunted and prematurely aged human wrecks. It is, indeed, questionable whether the reckless exploitation of British children could have taken place on the same scale without the existence of a huge reservoir of Irish muscle at a convenient distance from the industrial areas of Great Britain. Most of the Irish immigrants, with the exception of the Connaught men who bore all the marks of permanent semi-starvation, were at first distinguished by a splendid physique, attributed by competent observers to the absence of heavy work in their childhood, although the excessive toil to which they were subjected in Britain soon made them bend and break under the misery of their condition.

The inundation of industrial Britain by hordes of Irishmen was quickly recognised as one of the most important social facts of the time. In the beginning public opinion reacted very unfavourably and was seriously alarmed. However, in the course of time the substantial material advantages of Irish immigration for the employers of labour were reflected in a significant change of tune in the opinion of representative Englishmen. Sir Robert Peel, the consistent advocate of moderate progress and a man in close touch with the big business interests of Lancashire, advised the Irish Chief Secretary in 1829 not to 'condemn too precipitately the incursion of Irish labourers into England. We must bear in mind the growing increase of manufacturers in other parts of the world, and consider well the advantages as well as disadvantages of cheap labour'.[78] The *Edinburgh Review*, which in 1826 estimated that Irishmen formed almost one-third of the labourers in the west of Scotland and England and which at that time felt seriously alarmed at this development,[79] asked itself eight years later 'whether the labour of the Irish immigrant was in all cases a source of evil in Britain',[80] and came to the comforting conclusion that a surplus population in Ireland encouraged the use of Malthusian principles in England and tended to diminish the burden of the English poor rates. Three years later, G. Cornewall Lewis, a future Chancellor of the Exchequer, reviewed all the arguments against the employment of Irish labour in British industry and refuted them one by one to his own satisfaction. He went so far as to deny that Irish competition had lowered wages anywhere except in handloom weaving, and he was particularly impressed by the usefulness of Irish labour as a check on the combination of English and Scottish workmen.[81]

Still more illuminating than the opinions of statesmen, officials and journalists, are those of the employers of Manchester, Liverpool and Glasgow, who were almost unanimous in their assertions that it would be impossible to carry on the trade of their towns without the assistance of the Irish—at least not at the same rate of wages. A large number of witnesses declared that Irish brawn was, indeed, physically indispensable for the volume of manual work in British trade and industry. Business men in Birmingham, Liverpool and Manchester gave it as their opinion that the Irish were employed, not because they were preferred to the British, but because there were not enough English workers available to supply the demand.[82] Some occupations, like those of bricklayers' mates or hod-carriers, were almost entirely in the hands of the Irish, because Englishmen refused to do the work.[83] A Manchester magistrate stated it as a well-known fact that 'the manufactures of Manchester could not have increased as they did, had it not been for the labours of the Irish workmen'.[84] In particular, the spectacular expansion of the Manchester cotton trade depended to a large extent on the use of Irish labour. Friedrich Engels, a keen and unbiased observer of the English industrial scene, accepted the fact that 'the rapid extension of English industry could not have taken place if England had not possessed in the numerous and impoverished population of Ireland a reserve at command'.[85]

Yet the main advantage of the employment of Irish labour was not its physical strength but its economic influence on wages and conditions. It may well be doubted whether the absence of Irish labourers would have set unsurmountable physical limits to the progress of British industry, but the cheapness of Irish labour was regarded by the English and Scottish employers as an essential element in their prosperity. Most of them accepted the depressing effect of Irish competition on British wages as self-evident, and not unnaturally regarded it as highly desirable.

British employers, therefore, stimulated the immigration of Irish workers, particularly in the textile industries. Handbills distributed amongst Ulster weavers, recruiting agents in Ireland or the encouragement of Irish workers who wanted to bring their friends and relatives, were all resorted to. From the importation of Irish labourers for the purpose of getting or keeping wages down it was only one step to their use as strike-breakers. Even before the beginning of the century the masters at Stalybridge tried to break the strike of their spinners by importing Irish workmen who thus founded a large and tumultuous Irish colony.[86] In the strike of Liverpool bootmakers in 1803 some Dublin workmen figured amongst the scabs.[87] A Manchester silk manufacturer used to send to Connaught for ten or fifteen families at a time, whenever he was 'fast for hands' as the result of a turnout. 'The whole family comes; father, mother and children. I provide them with no money. I suppose they sell up what they have, walk to Dublin, pay their own passage to Liverpool and come to Manchester by the railway, or walk it.'[88]

A variant of this device was the policy of Glasgow manufacturers who broke a strike amongst their weavers by sending cotton yarn to Ulster for weaving. This practice became possible only after the abolition of the Union duties and was continued afterwards for many years; cotton weaving was kept alive in County Antrim exclusively as a result of the lower rate of wages in Ireland.[89] The abuse of Irish labour as blacklegs against British workers was not confined to the industrial west coast nor to the textile trades: the great strike in the Tyneside collieries in July 1844 was defeated, at least in Durham, by the mass importation of Irishmen, and this experience remained unforgotten by the native pitmen for many years.[90]

The resentment of the British workers at this type of competition was naturally keen, but this need not have been due to racial or religious animosities. When the introduction of the New Poor Law was followed by the experiment of transplanting some four thousand East Anglian paupers into Lancashire and Cheshire, their reception was equally unfavourable, and the resident Irish were, indeed, prominent in their opposition to this scheme. It was not the bare fact of the Irish influx but the strong, and soon overwhelming, contingent of half-starved peasants amongst the newcomers which created the powerful anti-Irish prejudice of the election campaign of 1841, where it assisted the Tories a good deal. Irish industrial workers, on the other hand, even if they had come to Britain in the first place as strike-breakers or as cheap labour, soon assumed a similar attitude towards their employers and towards society in general as their British comrades. When the Dublin silk weavers first settled in Coventry, they were regarded with suspicion by the native workmen, but ten years later these feelings had been forgotten. At the same time an official investigation in Scotland found 'a great repugnance, and in some cases evident fear, on the part of Scotsmen to give any evidence to the inferior, mental and moral, grade held by the Irish'.[91]

While the mass immigration of uprooted Irish peasants formed a grave danger to the material standard of life of the British workers, the immigration of Irish spinners and weavers had very different results. Even this cream of the immigrants owed their comparative success to their willingness to work for lower wages than Englishmen and Scotsmen, and thereby they contributed to the steady deterioration in working-class conditions during the first half of the century. But for the same reason the Irish workers were always the first to feel each turn of the screw and they were also amongst the first to organise working-class resistance to the steadily increasing encroachments on the meagre rights of the workers by their employers.

In the cotton districts of Lancashire and Lanarkshire, which were centres of Irish immigration, strikes and combinations were naturally most numerous. Although the Catholic priests generally minimised the part played by their Irish flocks in industrial disturbances, in Manchester even a Catholic priest agreed that the Irish were 'more prone to take part in trades' unions, combinations and secret societies than the English'.[92] The employers, particularly the textile manufacturers, were unanimously of the opinion that the Irish took a leading part in most movements of discontent, and did not refrain from intimidation and violence in order to enforce solidarity among the workers. Most strikes occurred in the small hand-weaving sheds which employed most Irishmen, and in the occasional firing of mills and the destruction of power looms the Irish were recognised leaders.

John Doherty, the Ulsterman who organised the cotton spinners' union of 1829 and led the great, though unsuccessful, general strike of the cotton spinners, retains a permanent place in the history of the British labour movement. Perhaps more important than this

personal connection is the strong resemblance between the organisation of this union and that of the United Irishmen: '. . . every five
representative spinners elected one amongst them to hold a certain
office, who communicated from that five to another officer; that
man was called a constable; when elected, every five constables
appointed one out of themselves, to be called a warden, and every
five wardens appointed a councilman. The committee consisted of
councilmen chosen in that way.'[93] This scheme was in all essentials
identical with the military organisation of the United Irishmen,
although there is no evidence linking it with this pattern. On the
other hand, it was probably more than a compliment when Doherty
said that his National Association for the Protection of Labour
(1829) 'took a good deal of example from Mr. O'Connell's proceedings in Ireland; I thought as he had been successful in Ireland,
we might be successful in England'.[94]

Five years later a Manchester builder expressed the general view
of the employers of his town when he said that the Irish were 'more
disposed to combination than any other men; they are the talkers
and ringleaders on all occasions. The chairman and secretary of
the present general trades' union is an Irishman.'[95]

Irish influence was just as prominent in the Lanarkshire labour
movement. There Irishmen had actually preceded the native
workers in the cotton-spinning mills which the Scotsmen boycotted
at first, and thirty years later Irishmen still formed a large proportion
of the factory population. The formidable consolidated union of
the Lanarkshire cotton spinners seems to have been mainly the work
of Irishmen 'who scrupled at little in accomplishing their ends, even
to the destruction of life and property'.[96] In the trial of Glasgow
cotton spinners in 1837 two out of five convicted men were Irish.[97]

In a curious, pre-Marxist, passage of his classic on *The Condition
of the Working Class in England in 1844*, Friedrich Engels speculated
on the advantages of mixing the 'more facile, excitable, fiery Irish
temperament with the stable, reasoning, persevering English', and
concluded that 'the rough egotism of the English bourgeoisie would
have kept its hold upon the working class much more firmly, if the
Irish nature, generous to a fault, and ruled primarily by sentiment,
had not intervened and softened the cold, rational English character
in part by a mixture of the races, and in part by the ordinary
contact of life'.[98] In 1844, with the human and political drama of
Chartism before his eyes, this may have seemed a pertinent explanation, but the later history of the British labour movement does not
justify this attractive approach. In fact, Chartism was not a start
but a finish, and the peculiar and characteristic part played in it
by the Irish element must be explained by social and not by racial

factors. It was not a question of Irish nature in British politics but the result of sudden economic changes which produced memorable political effects.

The three forces which contributed most to the making of Chartism were the London Working Men's Association under the leadership of Lovett, the Birmingham Political Union under Attwood, and the mass movement of the industrial North which soon fell under the sway of Feargus O'Connor. 'Fully developed Chartism derives its programme from London, its organisation from Birmingham, its personnel and vehemence from Lancashire and Yorkshire.'[99] Although Irish influence was most prominent in the North, it was not completely confined to any one part of the country. The London Working Men's Association, the stronghold of the level-headed English artisans, traced its origin through the National Union of the Working Classes (1830) to the Society for Radical Reform (1829), and ultimately to the Association for Civil and Political Liberty (1828), which had been organised by the democratic London Irish in protest against the policy of the Catholic leaders who were prepared to purchase Catholic Emancipation at the price of a reactionary change in the Irish county franchise. The first split within the new Chartist body was caused by the clash between Daniel O'Connell, at that time one of its parliamentary supporters, and Julian Harney, who founded the more radical Democratic Association with a following of a few hundred Spitalfields weavers whose misery made them impatient of the cautious manœuvres of the London Working Men's Association—and it is well known that a large proportion of these weavers were recruited from Irish immigrants. Thus even on the extreme left wing of British politics Ireland served as the touchstone which distinguished middle-class radicals from working-class democrats, with all the implications which this dreaded word had a hundred years ago.

The Irish workers in Great Britain helped to shape the development of Chartism for good or ill through their weight in the industrial North. The disproportionate importance of the handloom weavers in the Chartist movement has been noted by all its historians, and the prevalence of the Irish amongst the handloom weavers of that period is a well-established fact. But in the years after the industrial depression of 1836 the main body of Irish immigrants, the half-savage peasants turned industrial labourers, were in a no less dangerous mood.

The handloom weavers had watched for years the steady deterioration in their position. This constant pressure engendered a mood of hopelessness which could easily change into outbreaks of violent discontent where factories were burnt to the ground and power looms smashed into scrap iron. The Irish unskilled labourers, who had tried to escape from the slow death of starvation through unemployment at home, had been docile enough as long as they had reasonably steady employment. But now they were caught in the toils of an industrial depression which sharply reduced the demand for labour, while thousands of Irishmen continued to pour into Great Britain year after year. The series of bad harvests from 1837 to 1842 increased the cost of living at a time when earnings had dropped and intensified the competition for jobs between English and Irish labourers. Irish navvies who had been prominent in the construction of roads and canals, were almost excluded from the next great feat of British transport engineering, the building of the railway system. Thus the large majority of the Irish in Great Britain were predisposed for a radical policy, more or less on the lines of the Catholic Association with which many of them must have been familiar from their own experience in Ireland. In the Chartist movement they found the ideal opportunity for expressing their radical discontent with their conditions of existence, and in Feargus O'Connor the ideal spokesman for their inarticulate yearnings and confused hopes.

The Chartism of the industrial working class of the North and West was mainly a social reflex movement, conditioned in outlook and intensity by the material pressure on the masses which were the raw material of Great Britain's industrial progress. For them the Charter was not a move in a political game of chess but a symbol of social revolution. This attitude was, indeed, far more realistic than the illusion of the enlightened and sensible London artisans and the middle-class Birmingham Radicals that the oligarchic Parliament of 1839 could be induced by peaceful means to hand over the seat of political power to the masses. The moderates, on their part, were on safe ground in rejecting the 'physical force' policy of the extremists: an armed rising might have brought relief to the pent-up feelings of the miners, weavers and factory workers of the North, but it had no chance of success and would have involved the movement in total ruin. The social dilemma of Chartism found its ideological expression in an unattainable minimum programme which reflected the mixture of incompatible elements within its organisation. The characteristic contribution of the Irish element to this dilemma was its keen opposition to all counsels of moderation, through which it accelerated the inevitable dissolution of the coalition between the middle-class Radicals and the workers.

The importance of the Irish contingent finds its clearest symbol in the personalities of the leading agitator and the leading theoretician

THE IRISH IN GREAT BRITAIN

of the Chartist movement, and its deepest expression in the
programmes which Feargus O'Connor and Bronterre O'Brien
developed for the solution of the social problems of their time.
O'Brien, the famous and impressive schoolmaster of Chartism, disagreed with Feargus O'Connor on most important points of principle and tactics, but he was at one with him in seeking the key to
social reconstruction in a thorough solution of the land question.
His fundamental measure of social reorganisation was the resumption by the State (against equitable compensation) of its ancient
dominion over all land. The State was then to let land on fair
terms to anybody who wanted it, and the establishment of a comprehensive system of national credit would enable everybody 'to
rent and cultivate land on his own account, instead of being
subjected, as now, to the injustice and tyranny of wages slavery'.[100]

In Bronterre O'Brien's conception of society, modern industry
played the purely negative part of an evil to be avoided. Although
a modern realist in his insistence on the need for organised political
action, O'Brien was clearly Utopian in his assumptions and conclusions. The worker of his time was in his eyes not a representative,
however unwilling, unfortunate and degraded, of a new social
system but simply an ex-peasant whose best interest, just as his
heart's greatest desire, was the return to the land from which he
had been driven through the iniquitous powers of the landlord and
the moneylender. It is impossible to ignore the close agreement
between O'Brien's basic attitude and the social problem confronting
the Irish workers in Great Britain; their plight seems to have determined the content of O'Brien's political philosophy, while the
condition and the needs of the poor in industrial Britain may have
provided the basis for his political realism in the means which he
suggested for the execution of his programme.

Feargus O'Connor was greatly inferior to Bronterre O'Brien in
his choice of methods. Like O'Brien, he advocated the return to the
land as the true solution of the social question, but he differed from
him in his propaganda for self-help through co-operative land
purchase as the best way to the common end. After the failure of
the ill-starred convention and the ebbing away of the first great
wave of extra-constitutional agitation, O'Connor abandoned the
purely political approach of the early years in favour of a constructive policy which shows him as an ideological spokesman of the
uprooted Irish peasants. Perhaps the most illuminating expression
of this attitude is his attack on the system of large farms and free
trade, because 'large farms and grazing throw the agricultural
labourers out of employment, and drive them into their slave market
as competitors with the already surplus pauper population'.[101] The

9

key to his attack on the large farm, and his crusade in favour of the spade, was his attitude towards the Irish land system. 'The curse of Ireland', he explained, 'has been, not the small farm, but the large farm system, while the requirement for a provision for the poor has arisen out of the abrogation of small allotments . . . every advance in the large farm system has led to increased pauperism in Ireland, while it has contributed to the increased glut of Irish labourers in the English market. . . . Irish pauperism, Irish crime, Irish slavery and Irish murders are consequences of oppression and misrule and (that) the want of the small farm system, and not its existence, is the immediate cause of Irish distress. . . . To correct the several evils of which all now complain, to reconcile the people of both countries in a bond of union and brotherhood, to destroy the social inequality so destructive of peace, prosperity and harmony, I see no remedy but an abandonment of our present artificial position, and a nearer approximation to the laws of nature. . . .'[102]

The two outstanding personalities amongst the leaders of Northern Chartism were thus not only Irishmen by birth but to a large extent the spokesmen of Irish ideas and illusions amongst the British workers. They did not accept the modern industrial system as a reality which had come to stay, but regarded it as an aberration which had to be overcome by a return to the life of the small peasant farmer, the ideal of the Irish ex-peasant in the British slums. O'Connor's appeal to the masses was not that of the rabble-rouser without any impersonal objective but that of a genuine leader whose sincerity was none the less complete for all the defects of his theoretical understanding and the inadequacy or ineptitude of his practical measures.

The peculiar contribution of the Irish contingent to the Chartist movement was a radicalism, a readiness for revolutionary change, which was out of all proportion to the real social power it could muster for the practical achievement of such a change—not to mention the complete lack of any practicable policy. Dissatisfaction verging on despair is in all cases the necessary condition of successful revolutionary action, but it is not by itself a sufficient basis for a movement of fundamental social reconstruction. The handloom weavers, crushed out of existence by the competition of the modern power loom and the marginal labourers thrown out of work in their thousands by the first breath of industrial depression, contributed to the Chartist movement all their honest yearning for a radical change; but their ideas of the nature of this change were quite as inadequate as their power to bring it about, not least because their outlook was still firmly fashioned by their agrarian past.

From a practical point of view, the Irish contribution to the

Chartist movement was, therefore, of doubtful value. The turbu-
lence and determination of the extremists probably delayed the
extension of the franchise and frightened many middle-class sympathisers with radical democratic slogans into indifference, if not
into actual hostility. But the historical place of Chartism is not due
to its effects on constitutional law or party politics, but to its
influence on the British working class; and in this respect its practical
failure is amply compensated by its emotional triumph. Chartism
bore witness to an unquenchable spirit amongst the downtrodden
British working class in a time of economic depression, misery and
almost unlimited exploitation. It raised the standard of independent
working-class principles and action at a time when the monopoly
of power maintained by the governing classes was unshaken and
may have appeared unshakable; and the share of the Irish in
loosening the hold of the 'rough egotism of the English bourgoisie'
on the masses was a powerful contribution to the Chartist tradition
which may have remained ineffectual in the days of Peel and
Palmerston, but which became a living force long after the death
of its victorious antagonists.

Book III. Revolt and Reform

CHAPTER XV

IRELAND IN THE HEYDAY OF BRITISH CAPITALISM

THE year 1846 forms the great watershed in Anglo-Irish relations. The Repeal of the Corn Laws, carried by Sir Robert Peel in the interests of the British business classes at the cost of his commanding political position, was a final defeat for the landowners and the starting-point for a realignment of political forces. In economic policy, the Anti-Corn Law League abandoned at an early date the crude conception of using free food imports for the purpose of cutting wages. On the contrary, its propaganda gained its prophetic fervour, and finally its irresistible impetus, from the conviction that Great Britain was predestined to the proud role of the workshop of the world and that the workers would also reap some benefit from the victory of Free Trade. Cobden and Bright did not want cheap food as a lever for depressing the piteously low wages of the working class, but as a key for opening the trade of the food-producing countries to British manufactures. Their expectations proved reasonably correct, and the years following the abolition of the Corn Laws were an era of expanding foreign trade based on the exchange of British manufactures for abundant and cheap foodstuffs and raw materials.

In this conception there was no longer any room for a separate treatment of Ireland and her problems: she had to take her place with other countries as a market for British manufactured products and as a supplier of food for the British market. With the growth of English industry and the almost complete decay of Irish manufactures, the potential threat of Irish competition vanished into thin air, and for this very reason the Irish market for British mass consumption goods, though restricted by the poverty of the people, was far from negligible. The monopoly of supply for a population of eight million people, however poor, was well worth having, and any threat to this market was sure to provoke violent resentment and opposition amongst the British business classes.

The policy of *laissez faire* thus implied the maintenance of the British monopoly of manufactures in the Irish market, but it was incompatible with Ireland's '*monopoly* to supply England with grain in average years',[1] which had lasted until the Repeal of the Corn Laws. The greater the success of the new economic policy, the larger became the radius of the area from which England could draw her food in competition with Irish produce. After the withdrawal of the economic monopoly implied in the Corn Laws, the only protection for Irish producers was their physical proximity to the great British centres of consumption. This was of little use in the case of grain, which could even then be shipped easily and cheaply from Eastern Europe and North America, but it remained an important factor in the case of meat and butter until the development of modern transport and mechanical refrigeration left Ireland face to face with superior overseas competition against its most important produce and inaugurated the final economic crisis in Anglo-Irish relations.

The transition from grain growing to cattle raising had been going on long before the Repeal of the Corn Laws, but it was vastly accelerated by this measure. Complaints about the abandonment of tillage by the more prosperous Irish farmers were voiced in most inquiries into the state of Ireland after the Battle of Waterloo, and the sharp fall in wheat imports from Ireland into Great Britain was engaging Sir Robert Peel's anxious attention in 1841.[2] Between 1827 and 1847 the population of Ireland rose by more than two million people, or by fully one-third; the area under crops fell in the same period from 5,450,000 to 5,239,000 acres,[3] and it is probable that the area sown to grain crops actually declined, while that under green crops rose correspondingly. The fall in grain acreage during the following generation was, however, much more spectacular and can be proved by accurate figures. In 1876 the total area under crops was practically the same as in 1847 (when, however, the potato acreage was unusually small owing to the blight); but the area under wheat, oats, barley, etc., had been reduced from 3,278,000 to 1,849,000 acres, while that under clover, etc., had increased from 1,140,000 to 1,860,000 acres.[4] Wheat production on an economically significant scale had to all intents and purposes ceased.

This process took place in a period of declining population, but it was not caused by emigration and a shrinkage in the home demand; the great majority of the famine victims and the emigrants had never been grain consumers, except in Ulster where oatmeal was a common staple food; most of them lived on potatoes and, in later years, on imported maize, because they were unable to afford wheaten bread. The main reason for the sharp fall in grain acreage was the rapid growth of a lucrative British market for animal products which was the direct result of Britain's growing prosperity. Before the great agricultural depression of the late 1870s grain prices were only a little higher than in 1840, while the prices of most animal products exported from Ireland had risen to fabulous heights:

IRISH FARMERS' PRICES (IN s.d. PER CWT.)[5]

	1826	1840	1870
Wheat	10/–	10/– to 14/6	10/4
Oats	6/–	5/8 ,, 6/10	7/11½
Barley	7/–	6/– ,, 7/9	8/1½
Butter	69/–	80/– ,, 90/–	110/– to 130/–
Beef .	33/–	40/– ,, 56/–	70/– ,, 72/6
Mutton	34/–	37/4 ,, 56/–	74/8 ,, 77/–
Pork.	25/5	36/– ,, 42/–	52/– ,, 60/–

Such a change in the agricultural price list was the infallible sign of an economic revolution. Comparing 1870 with the golden age of Irish agriculture, the famine period of the Napoleonic Wars, wheat prices had fallen to half their level, while butter and beef fetched as much as during the earlier peak period. After two centuries, Sir William Petty's bleak vision of Ireland as England's cattle ranch seemed almost completely realised.

The wholesale abandonment of tillage in favour of cattle rearing reflected the complete economic dependence of Irish agriculture on the British market to the exclusion of all other considerations. In the expanding system of British economy, agriculture, whether in Ireland or in England, had no claim to special treatment, and its interests were sacrificed without hesitation when they clashed with those of Britain's growing foreign trade. The social changes in the structure and personnel of the Irish countryside were accompanied by a social policy on the part of the British Parliament designed to carry them out with a maximum of ruthlessness and a minimum of consideration for the amount of human suffering involved.

Ireland was an important bulwark in the position of the British landowning aristocracy which still contested every inch of ground against the encroachments on its position by the middle classes, and Ireland had, therefore, a powerful attraction for English Radical reformers. The existence of a feudal agricultural slum in the immediate neighbourhood of modern middle-class England had grave disadvantages which in the long run outweighed the convenience of a cheap and plentiful labour supply. The reformers naturally viewed Irish agrarian conditions in the light of their British experience, although the English system was without parallel anywhere in the world, based as it was on the application of capitalist business principles to the land. The reformers tried to transform Ireland into a smaller agricultural England, and, although they utterly failed in this purpose, they effected important social and economic changes in the structure of the subject country. These changes were, however, almost completely one-sided: the English middle-class Radicals had equally little use for Irish landlords and for Irish cottiers. But while their attacks on the latter were easily successful, the Irish landlords withstood all onslaughts until the catastrophe of the famine years completed their moral bankruptcy and weakened their material position to such an extent that their enemies were able to make some progress against them.

The battle against the cottiers was opened by the landlords themselves with a series of ejectment laws enacted soon after the Napoleonic Wars. Its next and most important stage was the application of the English workhouse system to Ireland by the reformers against the opposition of the Irish landlords who were afraid of the expense of the new system. The Irish Poor Law was authoritatively described as an attempt 'by offering to the poor man a sure prospect of a maintenance in case of absolute need, to loosen his hold upon the land, and thus to relieve the landlord from the incubus which now presses upon him'.[6] The landlords' opposition to the scheme was based entirely on their fear of the financial burdens involved, and their anticipations came true during the famine, when poor rates soared and rents dropped. The virtual bankruptcy of many Irish landlords whose estates were mortgaged to the hilt was thereby thrown into sharp relief. The Government had to intervene and passed the Encumbered Estates Act (1849) which was, to all intents and purposes, a special bankruptcy law for Irish landlords. It was preceded by a bitter struggle within the Whig Cabinet between Irish landlords and London City financial interests whose main concern was the safety of the loans made on the security of Irish land.[7] This Act cut right across the tangle of legal technicalities enmeshing the ownership of Irish land. It gave the purchaser a valid title and the seller, or his creditors, the ready cash he lacked. During the following thirty years the Encumbered Estates Court sold 4,930,000 acres, one-fourth of the land of Ireland, for £52,700,000[8]—often with scant consideration for the nominal owners. This legislation was fully successful in its extent but quite barren in its true purpose, which had been the replacement of feudal rent-consumers by capitalist profit-producers.

The British reformers, Whigs and Radicals, set out to free Ireland from the traditional hard-drinking, hard-swearing and swashbuckling squireen by making him bankrupt, and in this they succeeded tolerably well. They wanted to put into his place the hard-headed business man for whom land was simply an investment or, still better, the thrifty owner-occupier. The last solution was quite impossible with the means adopted at that time, and the introduction of the modern speculating landlord was an unmixed evil.

Many estates were naturally bought by neighbouring proprietors wanting to round off their possessions, and in these cases the only change was the replacement of bankrupt by solvent landlords. The majority of the 12,400 lots sold by the Court were, indeed, bought by Irish business men—land agents, solicitors and large shopkeepers—who regarded land simply as an investment; but very few of them made improvements or used modern methods of management in their dealings with their new properties. They left things pretty well as they found them, except for the raising of rents, which they did with a ruthlessness rare even for Irish landlords.

Almost a whole generation after the famine and the establishment of the Landed Estates Court the ownership of Irish land was still completely divorced from the people, and even the middle class had only a very modest share in it. Of 32,610 landed proprietors, just over one-half (18,100) held a mere 474,000 acres or 2.3 per cent, a further quarter (8,010) held 1,956,000 acres (9.7 per cent), and the remaining 6,500 landowners held 17,720,000 acres (88 per cent) with estates averaging as much as 2,726 acres each.[9] This handful of landlords dominated the Irish policy of the British Government. This extreme concentration of ownership co-existed with a no less extreme prevalence of uneconomic dwarf-holdings amongst the actual occupiers of the soil, which only recently had begun to give way to consolidation on a substantial scale.

The consolidation of holdings was an inevitable consequence of the abandonment of tillage which was mainly carried out by small tenants. But the combination of this factor with the Poor Law and, above all, with the Great Famine rapidly reduced the holdings of small tenants and cottiers whose numbers fell through death, eviction and assisted emigration:

NUMBER OF AGRICULTURAL HOLDINGS IN IRELAND[10]

	1841	1851	1871
Up to 1 acre .	135,314	37,728	48,448
1–15 acres .	563,235	279,937	246,192
15–30 acres .	79,342	141,311	138,647
Over 30 acres	48,625	149,090	159,303
Total .	826,516	608,066	592,590

The influence of the famine is shown by the fact that the process was almost completed by 1851. In 1841, after twenty-five years of eviction and consolidation, only one tenant in seven had a holding of more than fifteen acres; thirty years later fully one-half of all tenants were in that category. Thus the famine was the most powerful influence in the benevolent scheme of reform designed by the middle-class Radicals, but the effects of the Poor Law did not go for nothing: it proved 'the great instrument which was clearing Ireland. It was passed in order to keep the Irish paupers at home; it has expatriated them by the thousand.'[11]

Total figures cannot give an adequate idea of the extent of this revolution in social conditions. A large proportion of the remaining small tenants were concentrated in parts of Connaught and Ulster, although the decay of handloom weaving undermined their economic basis even in that part of the country. Many of the richest counties of Leinster and Munster were depopulated to a striking extent. In 1852 William Nassau Senior, one of the apostles of the workhouse system, found in Queen's County large enclosures, well drained and cultivated land but no cabins and scarcely a single person. 'There seems to be neither poverty nor over-population.'[12] In 1869 Friedrich Engels toured the countryside, found it practically clear of people and was immediately struck by the thought that there were far too few people about.[13] Some parts of the west presented much worse scenes of desolation. As late as 1886 Wilfrid Scawen Blunt, the English poet and anti-Imperialist, still observed in Galway 'the traces of old evictions everywhere in the little potato plots, with their marked ridges and furrows, now under grass, and here and there the site of a house long swept away'.[14]

This transformation of the Irish countryside, effected by the unholy trinity of starvation, eviction and emigration, was an important social development. After the climax of the famine years, emigration continued in a steady stream and between 1841 and 1880 nearly four million people left Ireland, mainly for the United States but also for Australasia and Canada, and the movement constitutes in volume and importance one of the great migrations of history. The emigrants were mainly recruited from the ranks of the smallest tenants, farm labourers and farmers' sons who saw no prospect of getting land of their own in their native country. The knowledge of an alternative livelihood in the United States reduced the tenacity of the peasantry in holding on to their plots in hopeless conditions, and the Golden West powerfully attracted the strongest elements of Irish youth. As a result of this steady drain on her human resources, Ireland presented all the features of a rapidly ageing population which depended on its livelihood to some extent on alms from the other side of the Atlantic. The proportion of old men over 65 years of age in the working population showed an alarming increase, not so much due to a sudden drop in the birth rate as to the mass emigration of the young and strong manhood of the Irish people. As late as 1861, only 78,000 or 7·3 per cent of a total of 1,072,000 Irishmen engaged in agriculture were over 65 years of age; twenty years later their number had increased to 107,000 or 12 per cent of the much smaller total of 890,000.[15]

Poor Law, mass emigration and the disappearance of the majority of dwarf holdings over large parts of Ireland radically altered the position of the agricultural labourers and their relations to the tenant farmers. The typical labourer of the pre-famine era had been a small cottier who was still an occupier of land, although on a tiny scale. The Poor Law did not induce him to part voluntarily with his holding in exchange for the doubtful blessing of a pauper's existence in a 'bastille', but it convinced the landlord and farmer of the drawbacks of having him on their land. The landlords did not like to pay poor rates on the hovels of the poor; they started organised campaigns for the wholesale eviction of these undesirables, followed by the destruction of their dwellings and stringent estate regulations against the erection of labourers' cottages and even against the harbouring of strangers by their approved tenants. As a result of this policy, labourers ceased to live in comparative isolation on farms all over the country under the close control of the farmers. They were compelled to huddle together in villages, more often than not in conditions of indescribable filth and poverty.

The money wages of labour necessarily increased, because the labourers had to keep themselves and their families on their wages after they had been deprived of their small plots of land. This increase in the money cost of labour was not without influence on the switch-over from tillage to cattle rearing which needed less labour and brought better returns, but it was quite insufficient to improve the living standards of the poor. Although opinions varied widely, it is probable that the rise in money wages was actually too small to compensate for the increase in the prices of all the necessaries of life. The price of potatoes more than doubled in the thirty years after the famine, and labourers were often too poor to afford even potatoes and had to live on Indian meal which had been unknown before the famine when it made its appearance as 'Peel's brimstone'.

This change in the position of the rural labourer could be observed in most parts of Ireland, but it was least complete in Ulster and most advanced in Leinster and Munster. In view of the abandonment of tillage, the economic importance of the process was not so great as its social and political implications. It was an integral part of the differentiation in the Irish village, which involved at one end of the social scale the dispossession of a large number of small tenants and their disappearance through emigration or their change-over into paid labourers without any right in the soil, and at the other end the consolidation of holdings into larger units, cultivated by more substantial tenant farmers.

This social revolution in the Irish village during the generation after the famine promised to fulfil in a certain measure the reform programme of the British middle-class Radicals. A fair number of the old happy-go-lucky squires had been disposed of by the opera- tion of the Encumbered Estates Act, and energetic and solvent busi- ness men, who regarded the ownership of land as a simple commer- cial proposition, had taken their place. The large majority of the dwarf tenants had been swept away as if by magic, most of them through emigration, but a good many by famine and typhus fever; the remainder were well on the way towards becoming paid day- labourers, dependent for their livelihood on their money wages, without the demoralising influence of food supplies from their tiny holdings. The land from which they had been driven by the force of circumstances or by their landlords, formed part of a smaller number of medium-sized farms cultivated by substantial tenants who employed hired labour and paid economic rents to their land- lords.

However, such an optimistic view of the Irish land system after the famine would ignore the crucial fact that this revolution was taking place within the framework of a social order based on con- quest and exploitation. Most Irish landlords, old or new, cared for nothing but their rent rolls and left the 'improvement' of their estates completely to their tenants who continued to be at the mercy of the landlords or their agents. The new purchasers under the Encumbered Estates Act were, indeed, more business-like than their predecessors, but in practice this amounted only to disregard of the few traditional restraints on the exploitation of the tenantry. Rents which before the famine had been estimated at fifteen million pounds sterling rose ten years later to eighteen millions. The relentless screwing up of rents encroached on the value of the tenant right owned by many tenants under the Ulster custom, and endangered the position, and with it the conservatism, of the Ulster farmers. Throughout the country the accumulation of capital was delayed, if not completely prevented, by the payment of excessive rents, and the investment of capital in agriculture, the main remaining industry, was made practically impossible by the land system which involved the periodical confiscation in the interests of the landlords of all improvements made by the tenants. The social stability predicted by the economists as the result of the social changes which were introduced at such speed and with such complete disregard for the sufferings of their victims, was not achieved.

The economic system of the country remained as precarious as ever: before the famine it rested on the avoidance of serious potato failures; now it depended completely on the maintenance of the lucrative English market for cattle, meat and dairy produce without which the farmers could not pay their rents. Serious industrial depression in Great Britain might reduce the purchasing power of the English masses; overseas competition might destroy Ireland's practical monopoly of supplying the English market with meat and dairy produce. Either of these events would be enough to close the period of relative prosperity enjoyed by the Irish farmers which enabled them to pay the inflated rents asked by their landlords. As it happened, both events tended to coincide in the later eighteen-seventies, and their effects were powerfully reinforced by a series of potato failures which revolutionised the Irish poor at the very time when the impoverishment of the rural middle class prepared the ground for a formidable political agitation. This was the signal for a serious crisis in the relations between the two countries which was never really solved within the framework of the existing political and social régime.

CHAPTER XVI

THE FENIANS

THE deep changes in the social structure of the Irish people as a result of the Great Famine were duly reflected in the course of political events. The Catholic middle class, which had dominated Irish internal politics from the days of Grattan's Parliament, lost its leading political role with the floundering of Repeal. Its political position was further weakened by the economic results of the famine period. The impoverishment of the peasantry and the decline in population restricted the means of livelihood for merchants and shopkeepers, lawyers and doctors, whilst by the middle of the century the remnants of Irish industry outside a small area in Ulster had completely succumbed to English competition. The contraction in the economic basis of the country led to complete stagnation, and the most gifted sons of the Irish middle class joined in the general movement of emigration. They found rewarding positions in the service of the British Empire as soldiers and administrators, or on their own account as business men or journalists in Great Britain, not to mention the chance of successful colonial careers or the lure of the United States.

At the same time the wealthier members of the Catholic middle class were given their first opportunity to join as principals in the exploitation of the Irish peasants. Formerly they had participated in this process as land agents, solicitors and moneylenders on behalf of the old gentry, but the Encumbered Estates Act opened the doors to the coveted positions of landlords to a large number of wealthy Catholics. Irish attorneys or land agents, like the father of the notorious Captain O'Shea who was to play such a sinister part in the great Parnell drama, merchants and shopkeepers eagerly bought the land which slipped from the grasp of the spendthrift squires of pre-famine days. The records of the time abound in tales of the ruthless and unscrupulous methods used by these new landlords in their dealings with the peasantry. They had managed to scrape together a few thousand pounds by the petty trading and trickery of a decaying country, and now they eagerly took the opportunity of living like real gentlemen on the income from their capital. This was only possible by employing on their tenants all those methods which had already proved their efficacy in the acquisition of their treasures.

The metamorphosis of the leading characters of the old Catholic middle class into small landlords decapitated the middle class as a social and political power and completely severed the precarious alliance between its leaders and the peasant masses. The relations between town and countryside had grown very loose even at the beginning of the post-famine period. This was demonstrated by the failure of the short-lived League of North and South which was a brave effort by a few middle-class intellectuals led by Charles Gavan Duffy and Frederick Lucas, to resurrect the alliance of the 1840s with the demand for universal tenant right as its social basis. This tender plant was destroyed, after an initial success at the General Election of 1852, by the refusal of the Catholic hierarchy to permit the use of the Church organisation as an organising medium, and by the notorious betrayal of the Pope's Brass Band—a clique of Catholic middle-class adventurers under the leadership of a fraudulent financier and a demagogic lawyer. Their part in this disreputable episode has made the names of Sadleir and Keogh a byword in Irish politics ever since, but in their day they found little difficulty in making their fortune by buying parliamentary seats in the cheap market of bigoted clericalism and selling parliamentary votes where they would count most. Their sincere, if unimaginative opponents had to watch helplessly the wreck of their last hopes before throwing up the sponge in disgust, like Duffy, or dying of discouragement, like Lucas.

For the next fifteen or twenty years, 'the season was the most pleasant and profitable that the political adventurer has ever known in Ireland. The country had fallen from rage to despair, and from despair to cynicism. The electoral contests of the time were conducted on a principle well understood though not publicly avowed. The political aspirant was to make profession of strong patriotic purpose, which the elector professed on his side to believe, and as the candidate used Parliament solely for the purpose of personal advancement, the elector pocketed the bribe.'[16] The Irish middle class had been reduced to impotence by the failure of its political leadership during O'Connell's Repeal agitation and during the famine, by the admission of its wealthier members to the landlord class and by the industrial and commercial stagnation of the country. It became reconciled to its inglorious position as a hanger-on of the landowners and tried to capitalise its modest advantages—economically through whole-hearted participation in the exploitation of the peasants, politically through the use of the still very limited franchise for private profit.

At the same time the explosive power of agrarian discontent, which had always been the driving force behind the respectable politics of the middle class, was greatly reduced by the differentiation of the peasantry. The number of medium and large farmers increased by leaps and bounds at the expense of the smallest tenants whose ranks were being rapidly thinned, at first by starvation and afterwards by emigration. The substantial tenants were not without their grievances: their interests as tenants were still unprotected by the law and very little regarded in their practical dealings with the landlords. Their support of the tenant right agitation, or the demand for the 'Three Fs' (fixity of tenure, fair rents and freedom of sale), never ceased even when times were good, but they had acquired a certain stake in the country and did not share the elemental and ferocious hostility towards the whole social fabric which distinguished the secret agrarian societies of the pre-famine era.

Not the least important factor which blunted the fervour of the most influential section of the peasantry was the growing friction between farmers and labourers. Widespread destruction of labourers' cottages, refusal to give them potato land in conacre, or on any any other terms, and the general replacement of a domestic economy by a money economy in the dealings between farmers and labourers put an end to the old social solidarity of the Irish countryside. The village was no longer an agglomeration of tenants holding 'farms' of varying but mostly very small extent, but a society with two classes which still had a good many interests in common, but which were opposed to one another in many ways.

This process of social disintegration and differentiation in town and country is the background for the growth of the Fenians. Their programme of 'Ireland a Nation', completely independent of Great Britain, was open to the same criticism which J. Finton Lalor levelled against the Repeal agitation of O'Connell's last days: it was exclusively 'the question of the town population', and therefore not a suitable lever to move the mass of the Irish people, who were country-dwellers, to participation in the struggle for the aim of national independence which Lalor, of course, accepted. The same criticism applies with even greater force to the Fenians' conception of a secret Irish Republican Army at war with Great Britain, to their subordination of all social purposes to the overriding aim of freeing Ireland by force of arms and to the whole of their military ideology. This conception was not even common ground for all Irish townspeople, but it was highly characteristic of the attitude of many emigrated Irishmen who retained their hatred of England at white heat but who had come to look at both Ireland and England from outside; it reflected, above all, the predominant part played by the Irish-Americans not only in financing the activities but also in shaping the policy of the whole movement.

The importance of Fenianism for Irish history and for the course

of Anglo-Irish relations lies in its treatment of the whole existing
fabric of English rule in Ireland as a hostile external force. In the
conscious policy pursued by the Fenian leaders this attitude was
confined to the political sphere: the Fenian swore allegiance 'to the
Irish Republic now virtually established' and confirmed his willingness 'to defend its independence and integrity'. This intentionally
provocative phrasing stressed the attitude of mind which determined
to treat Great Britain not as the *de facto* ruling power but merely as
an external enemy of Ireland in temporary occupation of the
country, and to brand all the results of British rule in Ireland as
illegal.

There was nothing in the contents of the Fenian programme to
mark it out as the expression of a social movement; the special
interests of the oppressed classes of Irish society were not even
mentioned in it. But the radicalism of the Fenians, although
entirely confined to the political sphere, cut them off from the
respectable classes of Irish society. All those who had managed to
establish themselves within the existing system and who had a stake
in the country were repelled by the wholesale negation of the existing
social order inherent in the idea of the Fenian as a soldier in the war
against England; the Fenian appeal was mainly effective to those
who felt themselves as pariahs within society, like the most active
elements among the Irish poor, or who were still smarting under the
blow of their expulsion from Ireland, like the Irish emigrants in the
towns of Great Britain and the United States of America.

The leaders of the movement were intellectuals, but the rank and
file were recruited almost entirely from amongst the most active
young men of the lower classes in town and country. The early
American Fenians were manual workers almost to a man; the Dublin
organisation consisted in its early stages mostly of skilled workmen,
of the same type and class of intelligent artisans who had joined
Finton Lalor's revolutionary circle in 1848 which Devoy regarded
as the fountain-head of all later Fenian groups.[17] After 1860 the
Fenians began to organise the shop assistants who played an increasingly important part in the spread of the movement over the
smaller towns of Ireland. 'If I were to judge from my own experience, and from what I could ever gather', said John O'Leary, Editor
of the *Irish People* and one of the leading men in the movement, 'I
should say that we had a great proportion of shopmen . . . from the
country shebeen to the monster houses of Dublin, Cork and other
large cities. In these last we had from the beginning and all along
some of our best workers, and in the end seem to have absorbed
nearly the whole *personnel* of many of these big houses. . . . I should
say that the men in the shops, as compared with the men in the

10

workshops, were relatively more important in '65 than in '48. But of course these last were also most numerous in our movement. . . . Shopkeepers we had, too, but chiefly in the smaller towns and of the smaller sort.'[18] In the absence of an industrial working class, shop assistants formed the most radical element in the town population and were, therefore, most susceptible to the radical Fenian gospel of separation. The only specifically working-class agitation of that period was the movement of the journeymen bakers against night work, and this may well have contributed to the growth of Fenianism in the towns where this agitation had been most active, as there seems to have been a close co-operation between the Unions and the Fenians.

In the countryside, Fenianism flourished mainly amongst the agricultural labourers, whose growth as a class was one of the most significant social facts of the post-famine era. 'Servant boys, farm labourers and the like' formed from the start a large part of the active strength of the Fenian body, and counties like Kilkenny, where the condition of the labourers was described as particularly bad,[19] were amongst the best organised districts in the country. The *Irish People*, the short-lived organ of the Fenians, was very critical of the tenant right agitation which was at that time revived with the express approval of the Catholic hierarchy: 'Why so much should be said about tenant right, and so little about anybody else's right, is what agitators alone may understand, but what we are sure no one else can. 'Tisn't that the tenant farmer is in a more wretched condition than the farm labourer or the mechanic. There are comparatively few tenant farmers, we are sure, who are obliged to live on a meal a day of the worse kind of food, yet there are thousands of labourers and mechanics, who couldn't probably recollect when they ate one full meal in the 24 hours. . . . Cruel landlords and ambitious tenants have blotted out every trace of our once numerous cottiers.'[20]

In their propaganda amongst the rural workers, the Fenians were greatly aided by the remnants of the old ribbon conspiracy which had survived the famine. Their existence can be gathered from a number of repressive statutes—the Habeas Corpus Suspension Acts of 1849 and 1850, the Crime and Outrage Acts of 1851, 1856, 1858 and 1860, and the Unlawful Oaths Acts of 1853, 1854 and 1855 which bridge the gap between the rebellion of 1848 and the Fenian conspiracy. The ribbon society had been the residuary legatee of the numerous secret agrarian bodies of the pre-famine era, and although it suffered a good deal from the mass exodus of these years, it never ceased to exist. The series of bad harvests which began in 1859 gave new strength to the expression of discontent and

enabled the Fenians to make substantial progress in the countryside.

The contrast between the abstract and rather nebulous nationalism of the Fenian programme and the social composition of the
Fenian body is curious and reflects important characteristics
of the colonial position which Ireland continued to hold as a part of
the United Kingdom. The Fenian *ideology* was simply nationalist as
such; its aim was independence without any specific ideas about
the social contents of the virtually established Irish Republic. The
Fenian *body* was an organisation where the lower classes of Irish
society, supported and financed by the Irish workers abroad, tried
to assert themselves independently of, and frequently in opposition
to, the traditional nationalist agitation under the leadership of the
middle class. The gulf between social realities and political aims
may well be typical of a colonial attitude: the radicalism of the
unprivileged masses did not express itself in their concrete social
and economic demands but in their intransigent and self-sacrificing
nationalism. Their fervour was a very different thing from the
calculating cant of the middle-class politicians of whom Ireland had
more than her fair share: 'your average bourgeois may make a very
good sort of agitator, for here he can be shown, or at least convinced,
that his mere material interests are concerned, and that he may
serve them with little or no material risk. A rebel, however, you
can rarely make of him, for here the risk is certain and immediate,
and the advantage, if material advantage there should be, doubtful
and distant.'[21]

The most interesting and politically significant expression of the
social nature of Fenianism was its attitude towards the Catholic
Church to which the large majority of the Fenians belonged. The
omnipresent and all-pervading organisation of the Church had
played a crucial part in all previous nationalist movements. The
Irish middle class was too weak and too much identified with the
towns to have ever succeeded in building up a nation-wide organisation of its own in support of its political aspirations. The support
of the clergy was, therefore, essential to the success and even to the
existence of a large-scale 'agitation', and the clergy transmitted
middle-class aims and slogans to the people under its direction, and
thereby helped to provide the punch behind the mainly vocal claims
of the Catholic middle class.

The support of the Church was, of course, withheld unless the
prelates felt that the agitation would be in the interests of the Church
as well as in that of the secular leaders. The clergy therefore backed
and even led the movement for Catholic Emancipation and the
Tithe War, while hanging back from the Repeal agitation until its

'safe' character had been sufficiently proved. For the same reason the Church opposed the Young Irelanders when they tried to use the Repeal organisation for their own purposes which included an alliance between middle-class Protestants and Catholics. This would have given dangerous power to the Protestant bourgeoisie of Ulster and might have led to a violent clash with the power of the British Government which was at that time doing its utmost to conciliate the Catholic Church. Opposition to inter-denominational policies and to revolutionary tendencies was and remains one of the cardinal political principles followed by the Church in its relations with secular organisations.

For the same reason the Church kept aloof from the ill-starred Tenant League of 1850–4, although its aim was nothing more revolutionary than the enactment of 'tenant right', while its method was the strictly constitutional use of Irish parliamentary representation for such a policy instead of for the personal advantage of members of Parliament. The Tenant League tried to combine the Presbyterian tenants of Ulster and the Catholic tenants of the South under the leadership of the moderate remnants of the Young Ireland party. Its local mainstays were the Presbyterian ministers in the North and the younger Catholic priests, mainly curates, in the South. Their removal from the organisation was followed by its collapse in a matter of months.

The political impotence of the Tenant League was painfully shown by the unavailing struggle of its leaders against the withdrawal of the priests from 'politics'. Archbishop Cullen, as Apostolic Delegate, tightened the hold of the prelacy over the priests for reasons of stricter ecclesiastical discipline, and one of the first victims of this procedure was the Tenant League which lost its all-important local leaders when the hierarchy ordered all priests to withdraw from active work in its branches because priests should not become involved in politics.

'Exclude priests from politics!', Gavan Duffy cried in disgust. 'It was for this object that English intrigue laboured for the last half-century . . . if the policy succeeded, the people, hopeless of agitation would fly to secret societies and violence. "No priests in politics" would set up the Ribbon lodges again. . . .'[22]

It was one of the frequent ironies of Irish history that the newly proclaimed political aloofness of the Catholic Church should have been put to a practical test only a few years afterwards by the Fenians. Its main purpose had been itself political, i.e. the prevention of any nation-wide movement which might have injured the special interests of the Church which the bishops regarded in the political field as inseparable from the Palmerston régime. The removal of all priests from 'politics' was simply intended to block the access of the middle-class leaders to the peasants, because it might have interfered with the peace and stability required for the success of the social reorganisation of the Irish village. But the replacement of middle-class agitators by lower middle-class and working-class conspirators was the last thing the bishops wanted. It was, therefore, speedily discovered by the Fenians that the Catholic clergy everywhere was their determined enemy, which did not even shrink from denouncing them to the authorities, and a large part of Fenian political warfare consisted in a running fight against the political power of the priests.

The Church backed the business-politicians who were in the saddle throughout Ireland, and it was closely allied with the 'ambitious tenants' who were hopefully participating in the hunt for smallholders and cottiers organised by the landlords. The educated writers of the Fenian *Irish People*—Charles Kickham, John O'Leary and Dr. T. C. Luby—could well afford to sneer at the 'aristocratic shopkeepers, attorneys, parish priests, and others of the *haute monde*',[23] who despised the rabble in the Irish Revolutionary Brotherhood, but this alliance, made formidable by the all-pervading influence of the Church, set narrow limits to the growth of Fenianism in the Irish countryside. It was only after the onset of depression in the late 1870s that the radical counsels of the rebels were heeded by large numbers of ordinary people.

For in spite of the complete and unrelieved failure of the so-called Fenian rising of 1867, the underground influence of Fenian ideas continued to increase with hardly an interruption. The Fenian amnesty movement was the first revelation of the breadth of silent mass sympathy with the uncompromising and self-sacrificing handful of Fenian activists. Apart from its intrinsic importance, this movement was an interesting link between the extreme left of the Irish nationalist movement, the radical movement in Great Britain and the First International, where Karl Marx took the lead in support of the national claims of the Irish people.

The political contribution of the Fenians to Irish nationalism was made as much on British soil as in Ireland. Fenianism developed on something approaching a mass scale only in the larger Irish colonies of British industrial towns, and the Fenians aroused the attention of the world—and that of the Irish masses in their own country— mainly through their actions in Great Britain. The most famous of their exploits was the rescue of the Fenian Head Centre from a prison van in Manchester which involved the accidental shooting of a policeman and the execution of three of his assailants as murderers. The political results of this indefensible act of revenge were truly momentous. Engels compared the deed with the execution of John Brown after his attack on Harper's Ferry and regarded it as 'the definite Deed of Separation between England and Ireland'.[24] Charles Stuart Parnell, at that time a young Irish squire with no political interests, was for the first time thrown out of his indolence by an event which crystallised his hatred of England. Nine years afterwards he advanced towards the political leadership of the extreme wing of the legal Irish movement by his passionate denial in the House of Commons that any murder had been committed at Manchester. The Fenian outrages which exasperated respectable Englishmen and fanned all the anti-Irish prejudices of the English workers had a very different effect on the Irish immigrants, and Fenian 'cells' developed in most industrial centres with numerous Irish families.

That the Fenians were the cream of the Irish people is proved not only by their selfless, if generally misdirected, devotion to their aims and by the qualities of the leaders which they gave to the nationalist movement but also by the grudging praise of their political opponents. Isaac Butt was much impressed by the personalities of the men whom he defended in the State Trials and by their movement which exerted an important indirect influence on his Home Rule League. One of Butt's followers, a virulent enemy of Fenianism who had first-rate opportunities of knowing the Irish masses in Great Britain, testified that 'Fenianism tended to sobriety, to solid reading, to self-respect and general improvement of conduct and appearance'.[25] The finest representative of this ex-Fenian working man was Michael Davitt, the son of an evicted smallholder from County Mayo, the Lancashire mill hand who had to sacrifice one arm to the Moloch of capitalist industry when he ought to have been still at school, and who underwent years of penal servitude for his participation in the dangerous but futile dynamiting activities of the Fenians.

Although the Fenian movement was not stopped by the failure of its insurrection and the imprisonment of its leaders, its survival could not disguise the fact that its policy had not been a whit more successful than that of the Repealers, the Young Irelanders or the Tenant Leaguers. The Irish Republic may have been virtually established in the imagination of the Fenian Head Centres and Supreme Councils, but for its actual establishment it would have to wait for the dim and distant hour of England's military defeat, preferably by the United States. Plotting and scheming for this event, combined with the inevitable internal quarrels of secret societies, may have sufficed for the political needs of a handful of conspirators, but it was not enough to keep the loyalty of the best elements amongst the

Irish workers abroad and of the smallholders and labourers in Ireland. These classes found themselves in sympathy with the Fenians' clear-cut and uncompromising hatred of England and the beneficiaries of English rule in Ireland and with their hostility towards the political priests who made their Church a mere adjunct of a pernicious system, but they wanted more practical forms of activity than a conspiracy which was fed entirely on hopes of a remote future and of events completely outside their own sphere of influence.

The keystone of the Fenian edifice was the conception of force as the only effective weapon for the overthrow of English rule and the establishment of the Irish Republic. But this insistence on violent action in the full ripeness of time involved, after a few costly failures, practically complete inactivity in the meantime. This paradoxical state of things endangered the survival of Fenianism as a political power. For this reason the Fenian leaders were in practice not always so hostile to legal mass movements as their theory implied. Their worship of physical force was, in the last resort, an attempt to maintain their independence in the face of the bribery, corruption and selfishness of Irish middle-class politics; for this reason it was liable to temporary modifications when the Fenians thought they saw the growth of popular movements untainted by the blemishes of official politics. In particular, the predominance of workers and labourers in the Fenian ranks made them sympathetic to every serious attempt to oppose the Irish landlords and their satellites, however different it might be in aims and methods from the Fenian programme.

If Ireland had been an independent nation, the process of social differentiation, which was such a distinctive feature of this era, would have almost certainly led to an open struggle for political power between movements representative of the conflicting social interests, but in colonial Ireland this issue was interwoven with the problem of national self-assertion against English rule. To the Fenians and their opponents alike, nationalism and hostility towards England was the acid test of political sincerity; social interests they regarded as secondary matters which were unimportant except in so far as they affected the main issue, the attitude of the group or individual in the anti-English struggle. They did not know, and probably would not have cared to understand, that this attitude was in the last resort determined by social interests and reflexes, and their inability to grasp this intricate but decisive connection enveloped the Fenians in an ideological fog which most of them found quite impenetrable. Internal dissensions, quarrels, expulsions and the more or less permanent impotence of the movement as such were the inevitable consequences of this failure.

The oscillation of the Fenians between complete rejection of any method except that of armed warfare against Great Britain, and a more or less grudging support of other groups with a nationalist, anti-English tendency, was represented by different groups and personalities within the Fenian camp. Most of the middle-class intellectuals—Kickham, Luby, Patrick Ford, O'Leary and many others—adhered to the rigorous tenets of Fenianism and viewed any abandonment of the straight and narrow path of chivalrous warfare with great distrust or downright hostility. Others, amongst whom John Barry, Joseph Biggar, Patrick Egan, Michael Davitt and John Devoy were the most prominent, abandoned the original Fenian standpoint for ever or for a time in favour of an attempt to revolutionise the constitutional movement which entered into a new phase with the onset of economic depression in 1876–7.

Although the surface effect of the Fenian movement on respectable politics seemed to be negligible, appearances were as usual very deceptive. The Fenians had the most profound influence on the Irish policy of the British Government and on the Irish middle class. When they started to attack the political power and the political line of the Catholic hierarchy in 1862–3, the moderate *Freeman's Journal* initiated a campaign against the Protestant Established Church as a diversionary move. It set up a commission of inquiry into the problem which unearthed a good deal of damning evidence concerning the Irish Church which had been readily available to anyone who cared to look for it, for the Irish Church Establishment was utterly indefensible on every ground of reason and justice. This somewhat half-hearted agitation was then taken up by Archbishop Manning, the most powerful personality amongst the English Catholics. Manning devoted in 1867 a whole Pastoral to an attack on the Fenians and presented both Gladstone and Disraeli with copies of this document. When the Fenian outrages in Manchester and London convinced Gladstone at last of the reality of Irish discontent, Manning was the channel of communication between his old college friend Gladstone and Cardinal Cullen of Dublin who advocated the disestablishment of the Irish Protestant Church as the proper antidote to Fenianism.[26] In contrast to the Irish prelate who had lost every sense of social realities in his preoccupation with the interests of his Church, Manning's own frank exposition of the situation to Gladstone showed the clear-headed realism which made him one of the most influential men in the Church of Rome. His argument was bound to appeal to his lifelong friend who was at that time responsible for the destinies of the British Empire for which Manning cared just as much as Gladstone: 'The only hope of restoring Ireland to social order and peace is to give free course to the only powers of Christianity which control it. Weaken these in the upper classes as they have been by various causes weakened in the lower, and you will have to deal with '98 over again.'[27]

The disestablishment of the Protestant Church of Ireland probably did not strengthen the hands of the Catholic clergy against the Fenians, but it was certainly intended to do so. At the same time the measure served as a kind of lightning conductor for the hostility of the newly enfranchised English nonconformists against the Church of England. The abolition of the Irish Establishment by a sincere and devout Churchman like Gladstone was the strategic withdrawal from an untenable outpost in order to defend the main position with the utmost tenacity—a connection which was insufficiently appreciated by the English dissenters who applauded the Irish Church Bill of 1869 only to find themselves outwitted and out-manœuvred by the Education Act of 1870.

Whatever the abstract merits of his Disestablishment measure, Gladstone soon discovered that it had done very little to strengthen the allegiance of the lower classes to their betters. The sensational election of the Fenian convict, Jeremiah O'Donovan Rossa, in November 1869 by the farmers of Tipperary was, perhaps, the most striking expression of rising tension amongst the Irish tenants which had been witnessed for many years, and Gladstone resolved at last to tackle the Irish land question, made one of the most prickly parliamentary hardy annuals of the century by the resistance of the Irish landlords in both Houses of Parliament.

The significance of the Land Act of 1870 consisted in the reversal of the traditional policy of the British Government, which for the first time interfered in the struggle between landlords and tenants on the side of the weaker party. The measure itself was more important as a step in Gladstone's Irish education than as a solution of the land question. This was largely due to the tenacious opposition of the landlords of England, Scotland and Ireland to a measure which, apart from other drawbacks, might some day 'cross the water'—a fear which was not confined to the Tories but affected many Whigs and even a few Radicals.[28] The practical value of the Land Act was further reduced by an amendment of the Peers which restricted its application to cases of 'exorbitant' (instead of merely 'excessive') rent, and the Bill as a whole fully deserved Engels' scathing comment 'that it was very funny indeed if good Mr. Gladstone thought to have eliminated the Irish land question by this newly-opened vista of interminable litigation'.[29]

The defects of Gladstone's first Land Act were not due to any lack of information on the facts. Quite apart from a dreary series of select committees and royal commissions on Irish land, the subject had been frequently discussed in Parliament, and as late as 1865 or 1866 Gladstone refused even to listen to a proposal which anticipated some of the clauses of his own Act because it involved interference with the management of a man's property.[30] Shortly before the Land Bill of 1870 was passed into law, the Irish bishops told Gladstone that security of tenure and judicially fixed rents, the twin pillars of the Land Act of 1881, were essential, but these measures were not regarded as practicable in the political climate of 1870.

The reason for Gladstone's failure at this attempt was the existing balance of parties and social interests in Parliament which made a lasting settlement of the Irish land question impossible. His farseeing attempt to strengthen the political position of the Irish middle class by wringing substantial concessions from the landlords was scotched by the resistance of the landed interest in both Houses of Parliament. The enactment of fully-fledged tenant right legislation would have outraged the landlords so greatly that it was impossible 'even for Mr. Gladstone, in all the plenitude of his power, to persuade either cabinet or parliament to adopt such invasions of prevailing doctrine'.[31]

Gladstone's next important Irish measure, the reform of higher education, came to grief owing to the opposition of the other great vested interest of Irish society, the Catholic Church. The Roman hierarchy in England opposed the Education Act of 1870 because it regarded this cautious measure as unfavourable to the claim for completely denominational Catholic schools—the Irish bishops preferred stagnation to any reform which would not make them complete masters of the whole educational system. Instead of setting the Irish middle class on its legs, as Gladstone intended to do, the Irish Universities Bill almost wrecked his first Government.

The close alliance between the Irish middle class and the English Liberals, which dominated Irish politics for twenty years after the fall of the Tenant League, did not long survive the Reform Bill of 1867. The unexpected popular response to the Fenian amnesty movement and the Tipperary election were serious warnings of the risks of open collaboration between Irish 'representatives' and the British Government. At the other end of the scale, the Irish landlords began almost for the first time to doubt whether the English connection really was a reliable guarantee of their privileges. Their doubts were most vocally expressed by the militant Tories who trusted in the House of Lords for the rejection of the Irish Church Bill and who were grievously disappointed by the acquiescence of the Peers in that measure.

The more serious fears of the Irish landlords found a characteristic expression in the politics of Isaac Butt who was not only the foremost Irish lawyer of his day but an impressive politician. He began his political career as an Irish Tory, but the experiences of a lifetime convinced him that Irish Toryism was incompatible with the conservative principles which he never abandoned. Butt raised the alarm when the progress of democracy in Great Britain persuaded him that the privileged classes of Irish society could no longer rely on the assistance of England for the maintenance of their position. The Irish Home Rule League which Butt founded in 1870, the year of Gladstone's first Land Act, was an attempt to secure Irish political leadership to the landlords and the upper middle class, and to keep the dangers of English democracy away from the shores of Ireland. 'There is no people on earth less disposed to democracy than the Irish,' Butt explained. 'The real danger of revolutionary violence is far more with the English people. The time may not be far distant when a separate Irish Parliament might be, in the best sense of the word, a Conservative element in the British Constitution.'[32] And still more clearly: 'A time may come when every Irishman would wish that we had in Ireland a Parliament and a Government which an English revolution could not touch, to guide the people and control the fortunes of our country.'[33]

The Irish Home Rule League appealed to a section of Irish landlords with definite Tory sympathies. This factor was so much in evidence that Cardinal Cullen, the leader of the Irish hierarchy, and in his political opinions the head of the Irish Whigs, regarded the whole organisation as an attempt by the Orangemen to put Gladstone out and get Disraeli into power. From the progressive landlord point of view, Home Rule was essentially a way of maintaining the political power of the squirearchy in spite of the threatening victory of democracy in Great Britain, and the immediate victim of the Home Rule agitation were the Irish Whigs who formed the political link between the Irish middle class and the English Liberal party.

For the landlords the need for a new and stream lined vote-getting movement was greatly increased by the Ballot Act of 1872 which curtailed their power of political blackmail and increased the chances of a popular movement dangerous to their privileges. The Home Rule League seemed to satisfy these requirements, not least owing to the personality of its leader who combined the basic aims of the Conservative with the modern outlook in points of detail and, above all, with a vivid sympathy for the Irish people and its sufferings. Butt was the foremost advocate of moderate tenant right and had been the leading counsel for the defence in the Fenian trials. This record gave him a strong claim on the gratitude of the Left

wing of Irish politics, as well as a true appreciation of the importance of securing the good will of the men who to many of his
political associates were simply dangerous criminals. In his Home
Rule propaganda, warnings of the effects of English revolution
always went hand in hand with appeals for the prevention of revolution in Ireland: 'An Irish Parliament', he predicted, 'would most
assuredly be able to guard Ireland from revolutionary perils which,
I believe in my conscience, nothing but an Irish Parliament can
very long avert.'[32]

In trying to gain the confidence of the Fenians Butt was, therefore, not simply a naïve humanitarian but a shrewd politician: one
of the avowed aims of the Home Rule movement was the neutralisa-
tion of the revolutionary energies of the extreme Left. The willingness of the Fenians to co-operate in their own political emasculation
was much more remarkable, but their cordial co-operation with the
Home Rule League is a fact. Arrests and trials had deprived them
of all their prominent leaders, and the remainder were naturally
influenced by their gratitude towards a great national figure who
had stood by them in their hour of greatest need. Above all, the
collapse of their insurrectionary plans and the unbroken peace
which England continued to enjoy for the time being weakened
their confidence in the gospel of armed struggle based on secret
organisation and made them susceptible to the advantages of open
propaganda.

The Tipperary election of November 1869 was the first step in
the new direction. In the opinion of Friedrich Engels, than whom
there was no better judge of such a matter, it was an event which
roused the Fenians 'from their tedious conspiracies and small outrages on to a road of action which, although legal in appearance, was
nevertheless much more revolutionary than anything they had undertaken since the failure of their insurrection'.[34] One year later they
put up a candidate in County Longford who was defeated by the
joint efforts of the Whigs and the Catholic clergy, although he had
been a close personal associate of John Mitchel. From then onwards they co-operated very closely with the Irish Home Rule League,
although Butt's policy, and still more that of his landlord supporters,
was directly opposed to their ultimate objectives. They may have
been attracted by the principles which the Home Rule League professed in public, or they may have hoped to exploit the League for
their own purposes. The most important Fenians who participated
in the movement were certainly not willing to follow Butt in his
attempt to make the Tory majority of the House of Commons
converts to Justice for Ireland. On the other hand, in the process
of criticising the official policy of the Home Rule League they

changed their own standpoint and abandoned sooner or later the distinctive Fenian traits of their political faith.

The two most important Fenians who actively co-operated with the Home Rule party from an early date, Joseph Biggar and John Barry, were both wealthy business men. Both of them belonged at one time to the Supreme Council of the Irish Revolutionary Brotherhood, and both used the Home Rule League for much more radical policies than those of Butt and his associates. Biggar, a Belfast provision merchant and convert to Catholicism, was one of the inventors of Irish obstruction in the House of Commons. Barry was a prosperous linoleum manufacturer long resident in Great Britain whose most important work was the creation of the Home Rule Confederation of Great Britain. Its membership consisted almost entirely of workmen, because the vast majority of Irishmen in England and Scotland belonged to the working class. It was, therefore, particularly open to Fenian influence and little more than a legal subsidiary of the Fenian secret society, although many of the old Fenian leaders did not want to have anything to do with it. Fenians were strongly entrenched in the governing body of the Home Rule Confederation of Great Britain and occupied most of the key positions, although they kept in the background and left the front of the stage to well-known national figureheads, chief among them Isaac Butt who acted as President of the Confederation.

For a number of years the Fenians and ex-Fenians had very little to show for their enthusiasm and hard work in the service of the Home Rule League, while the dangers of the new policy for the secret Brotherhood were obvious enough. Cardinal Manning observed in 1873 that 'Home Rule has divided the Irishmen and reclaimed many Fenians. Without in any way committing myself to it I have been very tolerant about it, believing it to be "like vaccination to small-pox".'[35] This was exactly what men like Butt and King Harman wanted it to be, and what the intransigent old Fenians like Luby, Kickham and O'Leary feared when they deprecated any such attempt to sully the bright shield of the conspiracy. The forces which prevented the consummation of this development were the stubborn refusal of the Irish and British Tories to arrive at a tolerable compromise and the social effects of the great economic crisis which hit British industry in 1874 and which a few years later widened into a chronic agricultural depression.

CHAPTER XVII

HOME RULE *VERSUS* AGRARIAN REVOLUTION

TO the Irish privileged groups, Home Rule, as preached by Isaac Butt and his supporters, held out a promise of at least partial immunity from the results of democratic progress in Great Britain, while at the same time diverting the hostility of the lower classes from the Irish landlords and their satellites to the common struggle against England. At the election of 1874 which overthrew Gladstone's first Government, the Irish Whigs were badly mauled and a majority of all Irish members of Parliament described themselves as Home Rulers.

This resounding success was, however, the prelude to complete failure. Genuine conservatives like Butt himself had no illusions about the dangers to their cause inherent in the Irish land system, and, despite the strength of the landlord element in the Home Rule party, Butt and his followers were sincere, if not ardent, supporters of agrarian reform. The minimum conditions of a satisfactory settlement of the land question were still the 'three Fs'—security of tenure at fair, i.e. judicially fixed, rents and recognition of the tenant's alienable interest in his holding. Gladstone's Land Act of 1870 fell short of this objective, and the Home Rulers tried to amend it in order to make all Irish tenants as 'contented' and therefore conservative as the Ulster smallholders. In this truly conservative policy Butt and his party received, however, less than no support from the Tory House of Commons. Irish landlords had been very strong in the period of Gladstone's first administration, but they were paramount during the years 1874–80, with the Tories firmly in the saddle. The stupid landlord majority blocked the path for the only policy which might have given their class a new lease of life. Their excessive power in the House of Commons and their predominance in the House of Lords frustrated the good intentions of the Home Rulers, and the combination of social exploitation and national oppression without the hope of redress by peaceful means intensified the force of nationalist anti-English propaganda in Ireland.

The final blow to the efforts of the moderate Home Rulers was the catastrophic change in the Irish economic climate in the late 1870s. During the fifteen years up to 1876, large and medium farmers enjoyed a period of considerable prosperity, based on the high prices of meat and dairy products in the British market.

From then onwards industrial depression in Great Britain and over-seas competition with Irish produce screwed prices down until the farmers were left without profits—and without the money needed to pay high rents to their English and Irish landlords. In 1870, butter fetched 110s. per cwt.; in 1879 it was sold for 61s.; during the same period the minimum price of beef dropped from 70s. to 50s., of mutton from 74s. 8d. to 56s. and of pork from 52s. to 46s.[5] The land-lords who used their parliamentary strength in order to vote down all amendments to the Land Act of 1870 stubbornly refused to lower their rents in step with the fall in prices, and the clash of interests between them and all classes of tenants became more violent than at any time since the famine. To cap it all, the depres-sion coincided with a series of bad potato harvests culminating in the dangerous crop failure of 1879. Potatoes, alone of all agricul-tural produce, rose in price. The small tenant-labourers in the west of Ireland, who were already badly hit by the lower demand for their labour in England and Scotland, were thus faced with economic annihilation.

In an agricultural country like Ireland, the sudden threat of bankruptcy all over the countryside immediately reacted on the position of the urban middle class. High livestock prices and a hopeful interpretation of the 'tenant right' created by Gladstone's first Land Act had greatly increased the volume of credit. This inflation burst like a bubble when the onset of depression with its train of eviction and bankruptcy proved that tenant right was only a hollow pretence. Without ever having participated in the pros-perity of the British business classes, their atrophied Irish cousins suffered severely from the slump which came to them from the other side of the Irish Sea.

While Ireland had seemed to develop more or less according to British models through the dispossession of the smallholders and the growth of a class of 'substantial' tenants, the leadership of the landlords in the 'national' movement, though based on a very slender foundation, was not obviously impossible. The sudden reversal of previous economic trends brought proprietors and tenants into sharper conflict than ever, and threatened to discredit every politician who continued to accept the leadership of the landlords. The middle-class element in the Home Rule party which had long chafed under the ineptitude of Butt's tactics, now rebelled in earnest and challenged the official leadership of the movement all along the line. Its methods consisted of parliamentary obstruc-tion combined with an alliance between middle-class parliamen-tarians and lower-class Fenians or ex-Fenians.

The first practical exponent of Irish obstructionism was Joseph

Biggar, a successful Ulster business man and a living negation of the gentlemanly Home Rulers of the day. He was joined, amongst others, by Parnell, who was a landlord by position and a gentleman by breeding, but who soon took the lead in the reorientation of respectable Irish politics. Parnell's aim was the detachment of the Home Rule movement from the landlords in order to prevent its falling into disrepute amongst the masses of the Irish people, and he relied for this purpose mainly on the Fenians.

Biggar was at that time still a leading member of the I.R.B., and although Parnell never joined the Fenian society he established his position by an informal yet fruitful alliance with the revolutionaries, cemented by frequent appeals to their nationalist sentiments. He first attracted their attention by an effective parliamentary defence of the Manchester Martyrs, consolidated his position by his spectacular performance as an obstructionist and gained prominence by ousting Isaac Butt from the leadership of the Home Rule Confederation of Great Britain, in close alliance with the Fenian leaders of that body. In 1878, Parnell met the official representatives of orthodox Fenianism, John O'Leary and Dr. Carroll of Philadelphia, and although the interview was inconclusive, his aggressive policy secured Parnell at least the neutrality of the ruling Fenian caucus and the whole-hearted support of the Fenian rank and file.

The economic crisis radicalised the middle class, the tenant-farmers and the labourers of Southern Ireland and threatened to move the Protestant Ulster tenants out of their political lethargy. This change in the political temper of the Irish people induced an important section of the Fenians, led by Michael Davitt in Ireland and John Devoy in America, to reconsider the strategy of their movement in the light of the new situation. The New Departure connected with their names consisted in the use of the secret Fenian organisation as the skeleton for an open semi-revolutionary movement of the masses whose economic conditions had sufficiently deteriorated in recent years to make them ripe for such an alliance. The natural starting-point for the practical execution of the new policy was the West, and particularly Davitt's home county, Mayo, where the impoverishment of the tenants was more complete, and the influence of the Fenians more effective, than anywhere else in Ireland. The Fenian Davitt thus founded the Land League with the prominent support of the local Fenians,[36] and it was to the Fenian-led American Irish that he successfully appealed for political and financial support of the new venture.

The question of participation in the new movement split the Fenian organisation. The traditional leaders, at their head O'Leary and Kickham, refused to sanction such a complete break with the methods of the past; the advocates of the New Departure were not all social revolutionists like Michael Davitt, but they were all agreed on the need for closer contact with the masses. Davitt's plan of solving the social problem of rural Ireland through the nationalisation of the land and not through its transfer to private peasant proprietors, however truly revolutionary, was in the best Irish tradition. Hugh Doherty, the Irish editor of the *Phalanx* of 1841, tried to persuade the French Provisional Government during the revolution of 1848 'to buy up all the land and redistribute it according to socialist principles'.[37] Land nationalisation had been the cornerstone of Bronterre O'Brien's socialism, and in taking up the same policy at a time of acute social crisis, Davitt followed a line which, if successful, would have inevitably led to the complete severance of a socialist and revolutionary Ireland from Victorian England. Although the orthodox Fenian leaders ought to have enthusiastically supported a policy leading to such a consummation, their aversion to the methods of social revolution proved insuperable.

Although the practical contributions of the Fenians to the revolutionary agitation of the Land League were very great, they were perhaps less important than the mere existence of the Fenian movement as the framework for an alternative leadership. Since the days of the Chartists, British politics had seen no parallel to such an openly rebellious movement which offered steady and consistent opposition to the official leaders of political life. The most dangerous weakness of earlier Irish mass movements had been their reliance for leadership on the urban middle class which was always ready to make compromises with the landlords and the English Government at the expense of the peasant masses. Fenianism supplied a much-needed corrective to this fatal tendency, though not in the healthiest manner, and the steady progress of political democracy made it probable that the I.R.B. would in due course overcome its impracticable and sometimes positively dangerous features. In Davitt, Egan and Devoy the 'Ribbon Fenians' found leaders of great ability who strained every nerve towards the creation of a powerful revolutionary movement of the Irish people.

While the stalwarts of the Fenian Supreme Council refused to have anything to do with such a purpose, the rising leader of the Irish parliamentary party could not afford such a negative policy. Although Parnell stood at the extreme left of the Irish members in Disraeli's last parliament, he was a conservative in his social ideas and tried to direct the growing movement into channels which would benefit the Irish middle class. Parnell had every reason to dislike and suspect the Land League with its revolutionary possibilities, but he could not simply oppose it. After some initial

hesitation he even decided to become its nominal leader. A movement which within little more than a year from its foundation in
a remote corner of the country numbered one thousand branches
with two hundred thousand members in Ireland alone,[38] and which
gained the immediate support of the Fenian-led Irish communities
in England, America and even Australasia, could be ignored by the
Irish middle class and the parliamentarians only at their peril.

But the President of the Land League cordially hated the semi-
revolutionary movement which had been forced on him; he was
deeply convinced of its intrinsic weakness and falseness, and his own
policy did not a little to justify this diagnosis. 'At least I am very
glad', he wrote from Kilmainham Prison to Mrs. O'Shea, 'that the
days of platform speeches have gone by and are not likely to return.
I cannot describe to you the disgust I always felt with these meetings
knowing as I did how hollow and wanting in solidity everything
connected with the movement was.'[39] T. M. Healy, at that time
Parnell's devoted follower and later on his most venomous enemy,
was on safe ground when he said that 'the enemies of the alleged
agrarian *Jacquerie* in Ireland little supposed that at its head was a
moderate, almost a conservative, leader, averse, except when driven
to it by the "stokers" of the movement, to lend his approval to
extreme demands'.[40]

The struggle for the soul of the Land League continued unceas-
ingly through its short and stormy career. The left wing under
Davitt and Egan advocated from the start a policy of steadily increasing semi-revolutionary demands, culminating in a nation-wide
'rent strike'. Such a policy would have almost certainly led to
bloodshed and civil war,[41] but in its course Irish landlordism
might have disappeared, thus leaving room for a complete settlement with England on a new social basis. Parnell's genius as a
political tactician never shone more brightly than in his handling of
this extremely delicate situation. Far from openly resisting the
demands of the extremists in the hour of their strength and his
weakness, he seemed to agree with them in principle, while opposing
the application of their policy in practice. At the same time he
used the strength of the extremists as a lever for the extortion of
substantial concessions from the British Government. Thus he
delayed the use of the measures for which his left wing clamoured,
and tried at the same time to detach the following of the radicals
by dangling in front of the peasant masses the concessions obtained
from the Government.

The success of this daring policy depended to a large extent on
the attitude of the English Government towards the Irish movement.
At the time of the crop failure in 1879 Ireland stood on the brink of

revolution. The balance of power had shifted in a manner ominous for the maintenance of English rule. The economic nexus between England and Ireland had been loosened, first by the abolition of the Corn Laws and more recently by the appearance of competitive supplies for the British market from overseas countries which were free from the rule of oppressive landlords. At the same time the political power of the landlords had suffered from the progress of democracy, both in Ireland and in Great Britain.

Under the Tory Government of Lord Beaconsfield, with one of England's great territorial magnates as Viceroy and the government of the country completely in the hands of the landlords, the Land League would have inevitably come into head-on collision with the forces of law and order, and not even Parnell's consummate tactics could have spared him the trouble of making his choice between these extremes. But the Tories went out at the right moment, and from the early days of the Land League the Irish revolutionists were not confronted by the 'stupid party' in power but by the most versatile and imaginative statesman ever produced by the British parliamentary system, who was just then at the age of seventy, entering on the most amazing metamorphosis of his political existence. In 1880 Gladstone was, according to his own confession, quite unaware of the severity of the Irish crisis, although Disraeli's election manifesto had consisted almost entirely of a denunciation of the Irish Home Rulers. This is the more remarkable because Gladstone had always shown an extremely vivid appreciation of Irish problems and difficulties. As early as 1845, when it seemed to be only a question of a money grant to Maynooth College, Gladstone described Ireland as 'that cloud in the West, that coming storm, the minister of God's retribution upon cruel and inveterate and but half-atoned injustice'.[42] In 1868 he regarded Ireland as 'the imperious and overpowering subject'[43] of his first administration, although the Disestablishment of the Irish Church and the Land Act of 1870 merely touched the fringe of the problem. In 1880, on the other hand, when he was about to revolutionise the relations between the two countries, and the British political system as a whole, Gladstone was unaware of the urgency of the crisis that was already swelling upon the horizon and that shortly afterwards rushed upon him and his Government 'like a flood'.[44]

The time-honoured English policy of disciplining the Irish people by detaching the middle class from the masses was not completely abandoned but considerably modified by Gladstone. The clue to his Irish policy from the beginning of his first government to the end of his great career is contained in a letter to Queen Victoria, written during the very crisis of the struggle, on 13th February 1882:

'. . . There is a very real danger which may come above the horizon, and which Mr. Gladstone humbly desires to avert. That danger will have arisen, should a decisive majority of the representatives of Ireland unitedly demand on behalf of their country the adoption of some scheme of Home Rule which Parliament should be compelled to refuse. To prevent the formation of such an Irish majority is, in Mr. Gladstone's view, a great object of Imperial policy. There was much risk of it at the beginning of the session of 1880, when between 60 and 70 Home Rulers had been returned at the election. This majority, Your Majesty's Government have done their best to break up; and they have succeeded.'[45] Like Peel before him, Gladstone aimed chiefly at the disintegration of the all-Irish coalition confronting him. Even in his policy the element of coercion, involving State Trials and a drastic Protection Act, was very much in evidence, but his remedial legislation was bolder and more effective than that of his old Chief. Peel had not been strong enough to persuade the Irish landlords to concessions involving the partial abandonment of their rights; Gladstone grappled resolutely with the land problem—on lines which promised to split the ranks of his opponents from top to bottom.

The Land Bill of 1880, a simple extension of the compensation clauses of the Land Act of 1870, was frustrated by the Lords in open alliance with the landlord wing of the Liberal Party. Gladstone showed his peculiar greatness in his reaction to this rebuff: instead of becoming more cautious he grew more resolute. In 1880 the landlords had refused to pay the moderate ransom of the Compensation for Disturbance Bill; in 1881 Gladstone forced the famous Land Act down their throats, legalised the system of double ownership and reduced rents to a less intolerable level.

The Land Act of 1881 had two almost instantaneous results in Ireland. It prevented the threatened alliance between the tenants of Ulster and the rest of Ireland, and it brought the dissensions within the Land League to a head. In December 1880 the Ulster supporters of the Government warned the Chief Secretary that only the acceptance of the 'three Fs' would keep their constituents from joining the Land League.[46] The behaviour of the Ulster tenant, who rushed into the Land Courts at the first possible moment in order to obtain rent reductions straight away, was entirely in accordance with Gladstone's intentions and proved an acute embarrassment for the moderate Land Leaguers under Parnell.

The Irish leaders, revolutionaries and parliamentarians, were caught unawares by the boldness of the new law which went far enough to remove the grievances of the larger tenants and thereby endangered the unity of the movement. At a convention of the

League, called in order to consider its attitude towards the Bill, the extremists tried to commit the movement against the measure which was clearly going to kill their favourite rent-strike policy. Parnell had to use all his power to prevent such a decision and to leave the matter to the parliamentary party. In the following months he skilfully veered through a sea abounding with dangerous rocks and shallows: he wanted the Bill to become law, not only because he regarded it as a great step towards the settlement of the land question, but also because it promised to reduce mass support for his extremist opponents. At the same time he had to avoid appearing to be in favour of the Bill in order not to forfeit the confidence of his followers. 'In fact it was Parnell who got the Land Act, and it was Parnell who administered it in the South, though he refused to make himself responsible for it and even appeared to be hostile to it. He played a deep game, and he played it with great ability. He kept his whole party together by not cordially accepting the Land Act, and he took pains at the same time to secure the best administration of it in the interests of the tenants.'[47]

The struggle for the Land Bill did not end with its enactment. On the contrary, at a second Land League Conference in September 1881 the extremists proved even stronger than in the spring. They wanted a complete boycott of the new law, and Parnell had to use all his influence to get his own policy of 'testing the Land Act' adopted. But this success did not delude him about the uncertainty of his hold on the movement; he seems to have felt clearly the approach of a crisis, and his main concern was a solution of the conflict which would shatter the power of the revolutionaries without compromising himself by open co-operation with the authorities. Parnell's words and actions clearly betray his intention to provoke the Government into arresting him just before the Land Act came into operation in the autumn of 1881 and when, in his opinion, the movement was breaking fast and all would be quiet in a few months.[48] As soon as he was safely behind lock and key, he had no further scruples to agree to a 'No Rent' manifesto which proved his own radicalism and in the success of which he did not believe for a moment. Then he had only to watch W. E. Forster, the Liberal Chief Secretary for Ireland in Gladstone's Cabinet, putting the revolutionists down by force and making him the undisputed ruler of the nationalist movement.

The first victim of the struggle between the authorities and the extremists was the Land League itself. It had been seriously weakened by the arrest or flight of its prominent leaders, and after the issue of the 'No Rent' manifesto Forster declared it, with doubtful authority, an illegal organisation. During the following winter the conflict between the Government and the left wing of the peasant movement assumed the character of a civil war and completely belied Parnell's complaints of the lack of 'solidity' of the organisation. Deprived of its national leaders and of any comprehensive policy, the local Land League groups, frequently led by ex-Fenians, kept up a campaign which was none the less formidable for being blind and frequently criminal in its methods. 'The very foundations of the social fabric were rocking,' a high Irish official told Lord Morley about this period. 'The demoralisation, the terror, the rage, the fierce hatred had grown to such a pitch that we were in sight of general resort to knife and pistol.'[49]

While the Government waged unrelenting war on the local representatives of the revolutionary movement, Parnell watched from his cell with benevolent interest the defeat of the extremists and of their 'No Rent' policy. He had reached the moral nadir of his career as an agitator and was contemplating a complete change of tactics by negotiating with the Government on a compromise policy. Gladstone, from his different but by no means opposite angle, summed up the decisive features of the period in a letter to his discouraged Chief Secretary shortly before Parnell's release: 'In the main point, namely the deadly fight with the social revolution, you have not failed, but are succeeding. Your failure, were it true, is our failure; and outrage, though a grave fact, is not the main one.'[50]

The famous Kilmainham Treaty, in which Parnell agreed to 'slow down' the agitation and to co-operate with the Liberal party not only in the suppression of outrage in Ireland but also in its general policy, while the Government promised to strengthen the hands of the moderates by a new Arrears Bill, was thus only the culmination of a policy which Parnell had been secretly, though perhaps not always consciously, pursuing ever since the start of the Land League. Nevertheless, this open compact was a crass blunder on Parnell's part, due to his hatred of the revolutionists in Ireland and to the pressure of Mrs. O'Shea in England. The Kilmainham Treaty might, indeed, have been fatal to his political career if he had not been saved from its consequences by the Phoenix Park murders. The slaughter of the newly arrived successor to W. E. Forster and his Under-Secretary was the work of a small gang of fanatics, but the weight of the left wing of the movement was still much greater than Parnell expected, and open co-operation with the Government would have greatly reduced his influence in Ireland. The drastic new Crimes Bill passed after the murders, and its relentless enforcement by the Viceroy Lord Spencer, the 'Red Earl', enabled Parnell to continue in his old role of open opposition to the

Government, coupled with secret but very effective hostility to the revolutionary section of the nationalist movement.

The Land League had been semi-revolutionary in its methods and democratic in its structure. Experience quickly showed that neither of these features was compatible with the domination of the movement by the Irish middle class. Parnell was, therefore, no more than consistent when he set his face against the resurrection of the old League under a new name, as Michael Davitt and the extremists wanted. The result was a sham compromise in the shape of the Irish National League. In contrast to the democratic Land League, the new body was ruled by a Council of 48 members, 16 of whom were members of Parliament, while 32 represented the local branches. As Parnell was the undisputed leader of the parliamentarians, he needed only nine out of the popularly elected 32 members for a majority on the Council which was, therefore, his obedient tool. Nevertheless he distrusted the popular element in the League constitution to such an extent that he revived the plan used sixty years earlier by O'Connell for the regimentation of his unprivileged supporters. By a small-scale *coup d'état* in 1884, Parnell 'packed' the League conventions from top to bottom by appointing all priests *ex-officio* delegates. His fear of the extremists threw him into the arms of the Catholic Church which thus became through his agency the dominant power within the official nationalist organisation, and thereby the arbiter of Parnell's own fate when it hung in the balance after the O'Shea divorce in 1889.

While driving the revolutionaries out of the official movement, Parnell used all his influence to secure the elimination of the Land Question from Irish and Anglo-Irish politics. His suggestions of further agrarian legislation were invariably constructive, i.e. intended to improve the relations between the tenants and their landlords, while he resolutely opposed any attempts to use the agrarian problem again for revolutionary purposes. He openly opposed Davitt's scheme of land nationalisation with arguments typical of the difference between revolutionists and constitutionalists, extremists and moderates: 'I said in New York in 1879, when I landed there, what I say to you to-night, that you must either pay for the land or fight for it. . . . Constitutional agitation and organisation can do a great deal to whittle down the price that the landlord asks for his land, but it must be paid unless you adopt the other alternative which I say nothing about.'[51] Davitt even retired for some time from Irish politics, and when he returned he was very critical of the direction which they had received in the meantime. Brennan and Egan, the other leaders of the Land League, were also eliminated.

Thus Parnell limited himself to constitutional and parliamentary action and left 'the Government and the Fenians to fight it out in Ireland'.[52] This move to the right brought him into sharp conflict with the extreme wing of the nationalist movement, with results which were equally fatal to moderates and to extremists. Parnell, in order to keep in power on his own terms, had to hand over his organisation to the Catholic clergy, the only force strong enough to balance that of the extremists. The revolutionists, on the other hand, degenerated from a political movement with an intelligible programme and a promising strategy into a gang of outrage mongers, whose motives might be perfectly sincere, but whose actions could only be understood as pathological reactions to a course of events beyond their political grasp. By their insensate dynamite propaganda and the series of explosions in British towns which followed one another during these years, they wasted their energies and proclaimed their bankruptcy as an alternative leadership of the nationalist movement.

Ever since the Kilmainham Treaty, Gladstone regarded Parnell as a moderating influence in Irish politics and became increasingly reconciled to the idea of a scheme of Home Rule which would put the trouble of dealing with the revolutionary elements in Irish politics on the moderates. In this change of attitude he was assisted by Parnell's advocacy of Home Rule as the only practical alternative to the land agitation of the extremists. Gladstone was as determined as any Tory or Orangeman to prevent Ireland's separation from the British Empire through violent social revolution in Ireland, but he came to the conviction that in the long run Ireland could only be saved for the British Empire by full and free co-operation between the British Government and the privileged minority of the Irish people. He differed from the Tories in looking for such co-operation farther than to the Ulster 'loyalists'—to the middle class of the rest of Ireland under Parnell's leadership. Abortive plans for provincial councils in Ireland, each more radical than the last, engaged the attention of the British Cabinet throughout 1883 and 1884, although the delicate balance of power between Whigs and Radicals, Peers and Commoners, prevented any real progress. Thus it happened that Parnell, his hands strengthened by the Reform Bill of 1884 which greatly increased his potential parliamentary power, succumbed to the wooing of Lord Randolph Churchill and Lord Carnarvon, and joined the Tories in an effort to oust Mr. Gladstone and to put Lord Salisbury into office, with the Home Rule question still undecided.

The gigantic political double-cross by which the Tories gained Parnell's support for their bid for power and for the General Election of 1885 did all honour to their tactical skill, if not to their political morality. From the Irish point of view, this episode was a political catastrophe which showed Parnell in the most unfavourable light. The man who had played a consummate game of cat-and-mouse with his own left wing, and who had proved himself the most cautious and sceptical negotiator in his dealings with the 'Grand Old Spider', was easily bamboozled by an unscrupulous demagogue like Lord Randolph Churchill and deceived himself in a singularly sanguine manner about his true relations with the Tory Viceroy, Lord Carnarvon.

The key to this curious and fateful error of judgment, and to the ensuing realignment of British politics on the question of Irish Home Rule, may well be found in the field of economic interests. It will be seen that the importance attributed to protective tariffs both by Parnell and by the Radical wing of the Liberal party blinded the Irish leader to the most elemental political truths and drove the British business classes into the Tory camp.

CHAPTER XVIII

THE ECONOMIC ROOTS OF THE HOME RULE CRISIS

FROM an era like the present which is studded with the traces of great political and economic upheavals, the second half of the nineteenth century looks like a period of steady and uninterrupted economic advance. Nevertheless, it had its industrial slumps as well as its booms, and, as far as Great Britain was concerned, its later part was in many ways a very critical and by no means universally successful time. The great depression of the eighteen-seventies and early eighteen-eighties was, indeed, a milestone in the development of the capitalist system throughout the modern world. This crisis was more prolonged than most and more extended than all earlier trade depressions, it affected agriculture at least as severely as industry, it was followed in all countries by a great wave of political radicalism—and it was the occasion for the rise of protectionist principles on an international scale.

For British capitalism in particular this depression was the end of an era. The thirty years between the Repeal of the Corn Laws and collapse of the boom after the Franco-German War of 1870–1 were a period of undisputed and hardly challenged British industrial supremacy. During the following ten or fifteen years British industry marked time, and although it shared in all the good things of the ensuing era of prosperity, its domination of the economic life of the modern world had vanished for ever.

Industrial development in other countries, particularly in the United States and Germany, could not simply ignore the fact of British industrial supremacy which was a definite threat to the growth of profitable native industries. British competition was a dangerous enemy, and sooner or later economic hostility found expression in the rise of customs barriers. Protective tariffs might be regarded at first simply as the best means for sheltering struggling home industries from the full blast of foreign competition, but they soon grew into powerful levers for prizing open the doors of the world market for the products of 'protected' industries. Tariffs raised the level of prices and profits in the home market to such an extent that business men were enabled to sell their goods abroad without profit, or even at a loss, and still grow rich and powerful in the process. The conquest of the world market was, indeed, in most cases—except in the United States—essential for the full utilisation of the technical advantages of large-scale production which could not be fully employed by the needs of the 'protected' and thereby impoverished home consumers.

The political leverage of the business classes might not have been strong enough to force such a policy on their governments, except for the coincidence of industrial and agricultural depression. Partly as a result of the improvement of land and sea communications, partly in consequence of the industrial depression in the United States which interfered with the marketing of their crops at home by the American farmers, overseas food producers began to export food to Europe in substantial quantities at approximately the same time. Protection for agriculture went hand in hand with protection for industry, either as the result of a bargain between industrialists and landlords, as in Germany, or between manufacturers and farmers, as in France. The price of such a policy was invariably intensified exploitation of the home market, both through low wages and a high cost of living, but this price was not paid by the business classes which flourished under the new system.

As far as Great Britain was affected by this process, every departure by its competitors from the principles of *laissez faire* was felt to be an unnatural and unfair obstacle to the predominance of British trade. Protection in all its forms was just as suspect to the British manufacturers as free trade was to their struggling foreign rivals. Far from appreciating the beauties of a system which enabled their backward customers of yesterday to become their competitors, and often their unfair competitors, of to-morrow, British industrialists had every reason to hate it with all their hearts. British economists denounced the new tendency as an unwarrantable interference with the immutable laws of economics which in the long run would infallibly ruin its advocates, but which meanwhile had serious effects on British prosperity. The bargain between industrialists and landlords or farmers at the expense of the consumers had no attraction for a country like England, with its large food imports and its extensive trade relations with overseas producers of cheap food. It was only many years later that one section of the British business classes tried to oppose the manufacturer-agriculturalist alliance of French and German economy with a similar conception on a much larger scale, in which Great Britain was cut out for the role of the industrial partner and the colonies represented the agricultural interest. This attempt was undertaken by Joseph Chamberlain early in the twentieth century, but it split the Tory party from top to bottom and failed completely. Not even the economic dislocation after the First World War convinced the British public of the expediency of protective tariffs, and the first

Baldwin Government fell on this very question. Only the impact of the Great Depression of 1931 overcame the ingrained aversion of the British public to the abandonment of the well-tried, and in its time highly successful, free trade policy.

Britain's economic *malaise* during the years 1875–86 was one of the most potent causes of the critical and at times almost catastrophic turn in Anglo-Irish relations during that period. While British industry felt the effects of the economic crisis, intensified by those of protection in other countries, agriculture suffered from the refusal of government and public opinion to protect the home producer against foreign competition. Agricultural Ireland felt the first effect of growing overseas competition for the British market. The coincidence of this incipient change in the trade relations between Ireland and England and of three years of unusually bad harvests, the last of which included a widespread failure of the potato crop, formed the basis for the semi-revolutionary agitation of the Land League and Parnell's meteoric rise to power.

The immediate crisis passed with the return of normal climatic conditions and the passing of the Land Act of 1881; but neither this important concession to the interests of the tenants nor the *entente* between Parnell and the Liberal leaders could alter the fact that Ireland's position within the British economic system had suffered further deterioration. With the exception of north-east Ulster, Ireland had been reduced to the position of an agricultural province, and the Repeal of the Corn Laws followed by the rise in livestock and butter prices, had led to the abandonment of tillage on a large scale. With the industrial depression of the eighteen-seventies and the growth in agricultural imports from overseas the last stronghold of Irish farming was seriously menaced. In 1876 Ireland exported to Great Britain 666,328 head of cattle, 668,808 sheep and 513,316 pigs; in 1885 these exports had dropped to 640,470 head of cattle, 629,090 sheep and 397,564 pigs.[53] The quantitative decline was not so serious as the fall in cash returns, for during the same period livestock prices fell by as much as one-third or even one-half. The value of Ireland's agricultural output declined from £72 million in 1866–70 to only £54 million in 1884–8, or by almost exactly one quarter[54], and the bulk of this loss fell on the tenant farmers who had to force even modest rent reductions on the landlords through long and bitter struggles. The old conflict between landlords and tenants, never quite at rest, flared up with renewed fierceness; compromise, though frequently tried, became more and more difficult and a radical solution appeared more and more inevitable. The need for buying out the landlords became increasingly accepted by politicians of all parties, and by the landlords themselves. A leading Whig like the Marquess of Lansdowne hoped that the transfer of all landed property 'upon terms stopping short of confiscation' would be the 'ultimate solution'[55] of his and the other landlords' troubles. Nevertheless it was many years before this policy was practically applied on the grand scale necessary in the circumstances.

The impoverishment of the Irish producers through the change in the terms of trade affected not only the relations between Irish landlords and Irish tenants but also those between England and Ireland. It undermined the economic foundations of the Union which insisted on treating Ireland as 'nothing more than an agricultural district of England, separated by a wide arm of the sea from the country to which it yields grain, wool, horses and cattle, and industrial and military recruits'.[56] If England was not prepared to make substantial concessions to rent-ridden Irish farmers and preferred to buy her food in the cheapest market, the last link of mutual economic interest between the two nations was in danger of snapping asunder. If Ireland could not prosper even if she degraded herself to the position of England's cattle ranch, with all the implied results in loss of population and industrial growth, the social forces of revolt against such a position were greatly strengthened while their opponents lost the last plausible argument in defence of the *status quo*. In particular, the Irish middle class whose scope and prospects under the Union had never been very bright, began to clamour for a change in the economic relations between Ireland and England and for a change in the system of government which maintained them by force.

This class found a leader of formidable fighting qualities in Charles Stuart Parnell. Although a landowner by social position, Parnell was remarkably like a modern industrial man of affairs in his personal tastes, with a natural bent for technical problems. Mechanical engineering, mining and chemistry, particularly the assaying of gold and silver, were more than mere hobbies to him, and he engaged in commercial quarrying on a fairly substantial scale. His quest for gold in his native Wicklow mountains may well be regarded as symbolical of the economic side of his policy. But his interest in Irish industrial development was not entirely a matter of personal choice. The main internal problem for Parnell as a political leader, and for the middle class which followed his lead, was the reimposition of middle-class control on the movement of the masses which had been lost after the *débâcle* of the Repeal agitation. In the political sphere, Parnell found a reasonably effective counter-slogan to social revolution in Home Rule which had proved its value for this purpose in the period following the abortive Fenian rising. But in spite of his narrow social outlook Parnell realised that a policy of Home Rule under middle-class leadership could not hope to retain the support of the masses unless it could be matched by an economic renascence of the Irish middle class.

The abject dependence of Ireland's economy on the British market for meat and dairy products would have been in any case incompatible with a policy of national independence, even within the framework of the British Empire, and at that very moment the British market proved to be entirely unreliable as a sheet anchor for the economy of the country. The need for industrial development appeared more obvious than ever, but industrial development was out of the question if Irish industry had to face the overwhelming competition of British industry. In this dilemma Parnell withdrew to the position which had been occupied by the middle-class representatives in Grattan's Parliament and, later on, by Daniel O'Connell and proclaimed the need for protective tariffs against England.

The slogan of protective tariffs was the necessary economic supplement to Home Rule as a policy, and the more Parnell veered away from the left wing of the nationalist movement with its insistence on agrarian social revolution, the more essential was the provision of an alternative social policy which centred on the need for protecting Irish industries against British competition. This new line of argument was thus in the first place a necessary consequence of the social cleavage in the nationalist movement, but it became almost immediately the real crux of the Home Rule struggle which dominated English politics for more than a decade and remained a factor of first-rate importance right up to the First World War.

Protection against British competition may well have been essential for the encouragement of the Irish urban middle class outside Ulster if it was to hold its own against the radical section of the nationalist movement which had just been given new opportunities by the extension of the franchise to the rural working class; at the same time it was bound to be regarded and resented as an intolerable provocation by British business men who were at the very moment bitterly complaining about a trade depression caused, in their opinion, by the protectionist policy of their German, French and American rivals. The raising of this issue as a major part of the Home Rule programme was, therefore, bound to meet with uncompromising refusal on the British side.

English fear and suspicion of the protectionist tendencies of Irish nationalism was much older than the Home Rule crisis of 1885-6. Daniel O'Connell's Repeal agitation had been connected with a half-hearted campaign in favour of Irish industries, and one of the first political pronouncements of the newly founded London *Economist* was a determined attack on the Repealers for this very reason: 'We hold it to be inevitable that the first popular movement in Ireland if a Repeal of the Union were obtained, would be a movement in favour of Irish manufactures. And this could only be effected by a hostile tariff against England. The operation of this would be defeated by the superior skill and capital of England, through the agency of the smuggler. Meantime the regular trade between the two countries, instead of vastly enlarging, as it would do under the Repeal of the Corn Laws, would be interrupted, if not broken up, under a Repeal of the Union. It would end in injury to England and in ruin to Ireland.'[57]

The same suspicion seems always to have lurked at the back of the minds of English middle-class Radicals in their attitude towards Ireland, although it was rarely expressed so explicitly and brutally. Sympathies with Irish demands for democratic self-government were usually tempered by uneasy watchfulness about the uses to which such self-government might be put by the Irish. This was true of Joseph Sturge, the famous Birmingham Radical and advocate of 'complete suffrage' in O'Connell's day, and of Joseph Chamberlain, his still more famous successor, in Parnell's generation. Hostility towards Ireland's economic independence which he regarded as a serious threat to British interests is the key to Chamberlain's puzzling attitude to the Irish problem which otherwise seems to have been a mass of contradictions. From the beginning of his career, Joseph Chamberlain tried to find his way through the maze of Anglo-Irish relations with the help of recent American history: 'I say to Ireland what the Liberals or Republicans of the North said to the Southern States of America: "The Union must be preserved." Within these limits there is nothing which you may not ask and hope to obtain. Equal laws, equal justice, equal opportunities, equal prosperity—these shall be freely accorded to you. Your wishes shall be our guide, your prejudices shall be by us respected, your interests shall be our interests, but nature and your position have forged indissoluble links which cannot be sundered without being fraught with consequences of misery and ruin to both our countries, and which therefore we shall use all the resources of the Empire to keep intact.'[58]

This was the attitude to which Chamberlain clung throughout his career, at least as far as the use of the resources of the Empire was concerned; his deference to Irish wishes, prejudices and interests did not last very long. His conflict with Gladstone centred on the question whether Home Rule would mean Irish local self-government in the widest sense of the term, or disruption of the Union.

Gladstone was vividly impressed by the great potential dangers of a revolutionary development in Ireland; he was ready to back the moderates against the extremists to the extent of handing the administration of Ireland over to them. Chamberlain was convinced that Home Rule would only be the stepping-stone to separation, and the factor which seems to have determined him in his opposition towards the measure was Parnell's rashly avowed intention to use Home Rule in the first place for the protection of Irish industries against British competition.

Parnell was, of course, well aware that no Liberal Government would allow him the power to exclude British business men from the Irish market. Apart from the tactical consideration of the Tory majority in the House of Lords, he seems to have been attracted towards the Tories mainly by the quite illusory hope that they would not only grant Home Rule, if pressed sufficiently by the balance of power in the House of Commons, but that they would not object to a protectionist policy on the part of Home Rule Ireland. This will-o'-the-wisp may well have influenced Parnell's fateful decision before the General Election of 1885 to throw the Irish vote in Great Britain to the side of the Tories, although his only substantial reason for doing so was the well-known, if vague, sympathy of the Tory Viceroy, Lord Carnarvon, with the political aspirations of the British colonies in general. On the concrete issue of Irish protection, Parnell tried to impress the Viceroy with its absolute necessity, but received the memorable answer, 'I entirely agree with you, but what a row there will be about it in England.'[59]

Far from noticing the ominous ring of these words, Parnell did not take them as a warning but as the official endorsement of Irish protection by the Tory party—a concession which he could never have wrung from Gladstone with the latter's absolute belief in free trade and powerful middle-class backing. Parnell's first important pronouncement in the ensuing election campaign was, therefore, an uncompromising demand for protective tariffs against British competition. On 20th August 1885, in his first pre-election speech, he went out of his way to emphasise that 'without a Parliament with full powers for Ireland we can do nothing in the way of reviving her industries. . . . We are met face to face with this fact that we find ourselves at the commencement of our industry confronted by the competition of England, with her perfect system of manufactures, with her trained population and her vast possession of capital and wealth, and we know well that the English manufacturers and the English traders are so unscrupulous that they will compete against and trample underfoot any struggling Irish industry in order that they may thereby earn more for their own industries.'[60] Five days later Parnell enlarged on this theme in a still more outspoken declaration of policy in Dublin which named national independence as the aim of the next struggles and which again included the fostering of Irish industries amongst the most urgent tasks of the Home Rule Parliament.

The English Press was immediately on Parnell's trail. The programme outlined in these speeches provoked the tart rejoinder from *The Times* that, if this was to be 'the first and most valuable boon' which a native Parliament was to confer on Ireland, 'we may well wish, in the interest of the country, that no such power to do mischief may be placed in hands which would be so forward to use it'.[61] The hue and cry was also raised by *The Economist* which developed the argument in terms almost identical with those used by it against O'Connell forty years before: 'The Irish Parliament which he (Parnell) would create, . . . is, he says, to protect Irish industries. It cannot do so otherwise than by establishing a protective tariff against English and Scottish goods. In other words, the Irish Parliament is to have complete control not only of the finance of Ireland, but of financial relations between Ireland and England. The possession of such a power is perfectly incompatible with the unity of the Empire, which vests the final and absolute control of finance in the Imperial Parliament.'[62]

Even more important than these damaging newspaper comments was the public reply to Parnell's programme by the recognised leader of British radicalism. Joseph Chamberlain had recently had sufficient reasons, both public and personal, for disliking Parnell and his works. Not only had Parnell succumbed to the advances of the Tory democrats but he had also wantonly insulted Chamberlain and Sir Charles Dilke in the Press and in the matter of their projected tour of Ireland. Now the protectionist war-cry became the occasion for a final rupture which was destined to have grave consequences for all concerned, and for the future of British politics. In his speech at Warrington, Chamberlain brusquely refused to accept Parnell's terms which implied the establishment of a foreign country within thirty miles of the English shores, governed by a Parliament 'whose first object it will be to put a protective duty against all British manufactures'.[63]

In his refusal to accept these conditions, Chamberlain spoke for the overwhelming majority of British business men. The determined opposition of the landowning aristocracy to the Home Rule idea could be taken for granted, but the violent, and even more hysterical hostility of the British middle class would be almost incomprehensible but for this intermingling of political and economic factors. Imperialism had not yet gained the same hold on the minds of the English middle class which it possessed at the time of the Boer War, but it was even then strongly in the ascendant. Home Rule clashed not only with the ideology of Empire unity but also with the underlying economic interests and motives of a strong section of the Imperialists: the endeavour to use the special position of the Empire as a means for overcoming the stubborn economic depression which afflicted British industry. An Irish Home Rule Parliament with the power of making anti-English trade laws would have been regarded as an intolerable provocation by practically the whole of the British business classes.

The classical reflexion of this attitude was a speech made by Lord Randolph Churchill early in 1886, which expressed both the thin ideological opposition and the real material hostility of British business to Irish Home Rule: 'Let us go in for a party of Union', the Tory leader told his public; 'and it is not only to be a party of union of the United Kingdom . . . it is only by the union of all the subjects of the Queen in all parts of the world and by the rein-vigorated co-operation, cohesion and consolidation of all parts of the widely separated British Empire that you can hope to restore to your commerce and to your industries their lost prosperity.'[64] The struggle for and against Irish Home Rule formed the central link of the chain which led from the progressive Radicalism of 1870 to the aggressive imperialism of the Boer War and to the tariff dispute within the Tory party. This development was in a certain way personified by the powerful and sinister figure of Joseph Chamberlain.

The clash between the economic implications of Home Rule and the interests of the British business classes was the ultimate reason why even land purchase failed to reconcile the dominant classes of Great Britain to Home Rule. The acceptance of the transfer of land ownership from Anglo-Irish landlords to Irish peasants involved the withdrawal of the landlords as a social power from Ireland. According to the time-honoured slogans of Irish nationalism, they had been England's true garrison which governed Ireland in its own interests and those of the mother country. But their involuntary withdrawal was not the signal for the complete abandonment of the now untenable Irish fortress by the English Government. Although the transfer of land from the Irish landlords to their tenants made rapid progress before the First World War, not even the key position of the Irish party after the elections of 1910 could induce even a Liberal Government to evacuate Dublin Castle. The Liberal industrialists were, at best, unfriendly neutral to the progress of the Home Rule Bill, while the more important Tory business men, headed by Bonar Law, opposed Home Rule tooth and nail in an intimate and highly effective alliance with the Ulster Protestants under the leadership of rich Belfast business men.

The complete alienation of the British business classes was the most fatal result of Parnell's hasty and ill-considered proclamation of industrial protection as an integral part of the Home Rule programme; its influence on the attitude of Ulster was, however, far from unimportant. Lord Randolph Churchill's gambler's resolution 'to play the Orange card' against Gladstone would in all probability have proved much less successful than was actually the case if religious fear and bigotry had not been backed by the widespread expectation of a first-rate economic calamity threatening the existence of the Ulster business community.

A protectionist Home Rule Ireland would not have been more than a nuisance for British business, and its true danger was that of a precedent which would prevent for all time the establishment of Empire economic unity; for Belfast, the 'Orange Manchester', on the other hand, it would have been a mortal blow. Thus the hostility of the Protestant section of Ulster was by no means confined to the middle classes. The contrast between the industrial Belfast area and the purely agricultural South and West of Ireland grew steadily throughout the century, until in the question of free trade versus protection it assumed all the force of an irreconcilable conflict, as long as the South and West acknowledged the leadership of its own middle class. Belfast's shipyards and textile mills were integral parts of the British industrial system, and no amount of protection in the Irish market could have indemnified them for the loss of their British trade. No declamations against northern bigotry, intolerance and arrogance, however justified in themselves, could remove the hard fact that on the decisive economic question of the future, as seen through the eyes of the leader of the Southern middle class, the interests of Belfast were diametrically opposed to those of Dublin and Cork. Within the social framework of the time there was no escape from this dilemma.

Although the mysticism of round figures is rarely rewarded in the study of history, it is worth recalling to mind that Parnell's advocacy of protection as an essential part of Home Rule was separated by exactly one century from the fateful wrangle over Pitt's Commercial Propositions of 1785. At that time the alliance between the progressive Anglo-Irish landlords and the growing Irish middle class broke down on the resistance of the English commercial interests which refused to admit their Irish rivals to a full share in their own privileges. Instead of a union of interests between all classes with a stake in the country against the masses, a legislative Union was carried through which left the Irish middle class deeply dissatisfied.

As a result of this failure, the Union had to be maintained by military and administrative force, and its voluntary acceptance by the majority of the people was limited to the Protestant parts of Ulster, most of which benefited greatly by the development of Belfast as an industrial auxiliary to the British economic system. Elsewhere the growth of the Irish middle class was arrested, it became deeply dissatisfied with its position and was always ready to improve it by blackmailing the English rulers of the country, chiefly through alliances with the rebellious peasants whose misery and resentment made them eager to join in any movement with an anti-English programme.

After many abortive attempts, the Irish middle class under Parnell was again leading a powerful nationalist movement dominated by the magnetism of its leader who for the time being overbore all opposition, though the flaws in his character vitiated even his most brilliant successes. Amongst his many blunders, the advocacy of protection, and his consequent support of the Tories at the decisive General Election of 1885, stands out for dramatic suddenness and long-term results. Well might the revolutionist Michael Davitt warn Parnell that protection tacked on to Home Rule would do more to alarm 'the shopkeeping instincts of the English nation than a demand for an Irish Republic on a free-trade basis would do';[65] Parnell was too deeply committed to the policy of maintaining and strengthening the position of the Irish middle class to listen to such counsel. Although the defeat of the first Home Rule Bill in 1886 was due to many causes, the revelation of an irreconcilable conflict of interests between the Irish middle class outside Ulster and the dominant business groups of Great Britain must be regarded as the root-cause of the catastrophe.

CHAPTER XIX

IRELAND AND THE BRITISH PARTY SYSTEM

DURING the twenty years of Whig rule between the Repeal of the Corn Laws and the death of Lord Palmerston radicalism suffered an almost total eclipse in official politics both in England and in Ireland. Beneath the smooth political surface of these years important developments took place in both countries, but their trends diverged more and more.

While in Ireland the political centre of gravity moved away from the strictly constitutional vote-getting organisations of the middle class to the secret revolutionary society of the Irish Revolutionary Brotherhood, in England the radical movement was temporarily stunned by the failure of the radical, and potentially revolutionary, Chartist agitation. In Ireland, the supreme crisis of the famine years intensified the social disintegration of the countryside and thereby destroyed the basis of political co-operation between the middle class and the masses for a long period; the former was busily engaged in exploiting the opportunities offered by the social changes, while the latter were inevitably driven into opposition to the ruling system as a whole, or driven out of their native country altogether. In England, the far less serious crisis of the hungry 'forties was followed by an era of spectacular economic expansion during which Great Britain really played the part of workshop (and warehouse) of the world and reached the climax of her position as the dominant world power. This miraculous change not only reduced the aggregate pressure of working-class discontent, which had risen to such dangerous heights during the Chartist agitation, but it also deepened the gap between the different sections of the working class which even in the days of the Chartists had contributed not a little to the ultimate downfall of the movement. The period was so patently favourable to the improvement in the material position of the skilled and educated workmen that most of them abandoned the stony paths of political agitation and the uncongenial fellowship of unscrupulous rabble-rousers and semi-starved Irish labourers, in order to concentrate on the energetic pursuit of their economic interests, mainly through the building-up of large and financially sound craft unions, but also through steadily increasing, though studiously moderate, claims for a certain share in political representation.

Their claims were ultimately successful owing to the growing friction between the still predominant landowning aristocracy and the industrial middle class. The business classes remained in Parlia ment, and in both political parties, very much the junior partners, and their economic power contrasted strangely with the subordina-tion of their political representatives to old-established cliques, which retained their monopoly of Government almost unbroken. A rearrangement of the political system was overdue, and the twenty years' gap between the Repeal of the Corn Laws and the Reform Bill of 1867 was mainly due to the difficulty of admitting just enough working-class voters to oust the landowners from power, while preventing the new electorate from using the vote in the interests of the class of which it was mainly composed.

The gradual abatement of social discontent and the exemplary moderation of the skilled working men convinced the more enlight-ened leaders of the middle class that democracy could be made safe for their own rule. The guiding principle of this 'progressive policy' was clearly expressed by Gladstone, its greatest representative, in a letter to one of his aristocratic relatives who protested against the increasingly radical turn of Gladstone's public speeches: 'Please to recollect that we have got to govern millions of hard hands; that it must be done by force, fraud or good will; that the latter has been tried and is answering; that none have profited more by this change of system since the Six Acts and the Corn Laws than those who complain of it.'[66] This statement was not only characteristic of its author but it may also be regarded as the *leitmotiv* of the policy pursued by the Liberal party as a whole, and even by an influential section of the Tories.

The succession of abortive reform bills with their varying rating qualifications and fancy franchises came to an abrupt and startling end with the granting of household franchise to all urban voters in 1867. The difference between Sir Robert Peel, who found the Whigs bathing and stole their clothes by adopting free trade as his own policy, and Disraeli who made his reputation as Peel's most venomous critic only to 'dish the Whigs' in 1867, may appear on the surface to have been very small; actually it was profound, both in respect of the personal motives and the political effects involved. Disraeli's bold and clever move in 1867 was infinitely less honest and sincere than Peel's painful and conscientious conversion to a new principle; politically, on the other hand, the wide sweep of Disraeli's franchise reform was not a surrender to the principles of his Whig opponents but the overthrow of an era to which the old Whigs belonged just as much as the old Tories, and the beginning of modern British politics.

By opening the flood-gates of democracy instead of admitting a mere trickle of working-class electors, Disraeli transformed a carefully guarded mill pond into a turbulent sea. A House of Commons based on an eight-pounds or six-pounds qualification could have been relied on to return moderate but secure Whig majorities at one election after another, at least in the boroughs: parliaments based on urban household franchise might—and, in fact, did—return huge majorities for either party, neither of which might be able to survive the admission of the urban working class to the vote without far-reaching changes in structure and policy. Whigs and Tories were doomed by this violent change in their political environment, even though they did not know it, and they were destined to be replaced in due course by Liberals and Conservatives.

After 1867 the internal relations between the two governing classes of Victorian England, the landlords and the business men, became gradually less critical and the real crux of British political life became the relationship between them and the unprivileged masses. Although it would be too simple to say that the Tories were the party of the landlords and the Whigs the party of the capitalists, the two classical parties were backed by these great vested interests in very unequal proportions. The political strength of the Tories in the English counties reflected the power of the squires over their tenants, while the Whigs ruled the boroughs mainly through the influence of the upper middle class over the remainder of the urban voters. After the establishment of household suffrage in 1867, this influence had, however, to contend against the fact that the material interests of the new working-class voters clashed with those of the middle-class backers of the Liberal party. New methods had to be found for the reconciliation of these divergent tendencies, and the most important and effective of these was the creation of a permanent and all-embracing party organisation.

The 'caucus' of the Liberal party grew out of the nonconformist Education League. This was an organisation founded by the Radicals in order to oppose the Education Bill of 1870 which made elementary education compulsory but consolidated at the same time the position of the denominational schools. Like the Education League, the National Liberal Federation was from the beginning the instrument of the Radical wing of the Liberal party, led by Joseph Chamberlain, and was used by him and his associates as a means of opposing and deposing the aristocratic Whigs. These hereditary champions of the cause of freedom and progress had a practical monopoly of the positions of power and influence on the Liberal side, and Chamberlain and his fellow Radicals used the new organisation as an instrument for organising the strength of the democratic constituencies against this ruling clique. The growth of

modern party organisation was thus part of the struggle for power
between Whig landowners and Radical business men; it was, therefore, a replica on a smaller scale of the similar struggle within
Parliament, and in both cases it was accompanied by a gradual and
limited but none the less very real democratisation of British political
life.

British democracy owed its steady, if slow and prosaic, progress
under Conservative and Liberal governments alike to this subtle
and complex arrangement of social forces, both within Parliament
and within the political parties, for a process similar to the growth
of the National Liberal Federation took place somewhat later even
within the Tory party. A Tory Government enfranchised the urban
workers in 1867. The political hold of the landlords over the rural
masses was first loosened by the Ballot Act of 1872 which abolished
open voting, and ultimately broken by the Reform Bill of 1884
which gave the rural labourers the vote—both measures carried by
Liberal Governments. A Tory Government under Radical pressure
added the extension of popular principles to local government, and
the change-over from the oligarchic rule of the landlords to a more or
less self-governing democracy was almost completed at the time of
the First World War which was followed by the enfranchisement of
women.

Ireland had no important share in the opening move of this great
game, Disraeli's Reform Bill of 1867. But from then onwards Irish
politics played a prominent part in its progress, though rarely in
the way intended by the protagonists. This perversity of Irish
politics was in the last resort due to the savage clash of social
interests in Ireland, and particularly to the explosive force of
economic exploitation coupled with national oppression. The
political outcome of this unstable social situation was the repudiation
by the Irish masses of moderate compromise solutions which would
have been acceptable to the upper and middle classes. Violent
mass discontent could be effectively suppressed by the coercive
power of the State, but the extension of democratic rights to Ireland,
however halting and incomplete, made at least the acquiescence of
the masses in the policy of the privileged classes essential. Irish
politics and the Irish question, which had baffled British statesmanship for generations, thus became completely unmanageable by
the traditional methods during the transition to political democracy.
At the same time it became more urgent than ever to settle this
question, because Ireland, and the English dominion over Ireland,
had become an integral part of the balance of political forces in
Great Britain.

In the struggle between Liberals and Conservatives, Ireland was an obvious field for the stratagems of mines and countermines between the two parties. The Irish landlords had influential friends in both camps, but the bulk of their order were Tories, and the Tory party in both countries was completely identified with the Protestant interest. Thus it was good policy for the Whigs, in the days of Disraeli as in those of Pitt, to keep on good terms with the Irish Catholics, and the mass of English Liberals certainly had no sympathy for the whole race of Irish landlords. At the same time both parties were equally opposed to the Irish revolutionaries who wanted to pull Ireland out of the orbit of British capitalism; respectable people on both sides of the Irish Sea detested Fenianism with its strong roots amongst the Irish residents in Great Britain who formed the bottom layer of the British working class.

Gladstone's first great measures as Prime Minister were mainly concerned with Ireland, because it was only there that the existing social system was seriously menaced. The disestablishment of the Protestant Church of Ireland and the Land Act of 1870 were attempts to wrest the political leadership of the Irish people from the revolutionary separatists and to strengthen the hands of the moderates who believed in the need for closest union with Great Britain. An additional influence may well have been the uncertain political temper of the recently enfranchised British workers: Gladstone's Irish legislation focused attention on undeniably serious grievances which had to be remedied, while leaving conditions in England well alone; in particular, the disestablishment of the Protestant Church in Ireland may have served as a useful lightning conductor for the hostility of British nonconformists against the Church of England.

From a party point of view, the Irish legislation of the first Gladstone Government proved singularly unrewarding. In spite of the Irish Church Act, the Land Act of 1870 and the attempted reform of Irish higher education, the Whigs suffered severely at the next election. In Ireland many Liberal landlords went over to the Tories whom they justly regarded as the most reliable defenders of their privileges. The moderate Irish middle-class politicians found their historic alliance with the Whigs a handicap in their struggle for political leadership against the Fenians, and no other measure of the Liberal Government was more dangerous to the Whigs than the Ballot Act of 1872. Thus the Irish Tories were strengthened by accessions from the Whigs, and the interests of the Irish landlords became consequently more sacred to the Tory party as a whole. Their loss of Irish seats deprived the Liberals of a good deal of their advantage over the Tories in the British parliamentary game; the impending annihilation of the Irish Whigs threatened to wipe out their lead completely and to produce a near-equilibrium between British Liberals and Anglo-Irish Conservatives which promised to constitute the Irish party the master of the parliamentary situation.

The real danger of such a development for the British system of government was due to the fact that Ireland, though formally part of the United Kingdom, was actually a colony in the grip of its foreign masters. As far as Great Britain was concerned, the House of Commons resounded to the loud but friendly wrangles of land-lords and business men whose common interests far outweighed their points of disagreement. 'Much of parliamentary debate', said Lord Morley, 'is dispute between men who in truth and at bottom agree, but invent arguments to disguise agreement and contrive a difference. It is artificial but serves a purpose in justifying two lobbies and a party division.'[67]

As far as the Irish members of Parliament truly represented the majority of the Irish people, the tenant-farmers and labourers, and even the atrophied urban middle class, they were the spokesmen of social interests sharply opposed to those which dominated the House of Commons; and at a time when the British working class was virtually without parliamentary representatives, the Irish members were the only spokesmen for under-privileged majorities in a Parliament ruled by privileged minorities. The extension of democratic rights to Ireland was the inevitable consequence of a policy which treated a colony as an integral part of the 'mother country'; but it introduced into British politics social interests violently opposed to the majority interests in the House of Commons. In England, the progress of democracy was so slow and well contrived that for many years it had the result of bolstering the power of one of the privileged minorities by the votes of the masses; in Ireland even the first few steps on the road revealed almost at once the gulf between the privileged and the exploited, and gave a dangerous outlet to the anti-English feelings of the vast majority of the Irish people.

The effect of this irruption from another world into the aristocratic House of Commons was dramatic. The best club in Europe discovered with shocked surprise that a small number of its members, by refusing to play the game according to the rules, could block the business which had come to be regarded as essential for the government of the world's greatest empire. The task of the obstructionists was made very easy by the archaic and cumbersome procedure of the House which would have prevented the transaction of ordinary business but for the laxity with which it was habitually employed. The policy of obstruction was by no means invented by the Irish members of Disraeli's last Parliament, but their use of the method was so effective that it had all the appearance of a new political discovery. Actually it was preceded by a good deal of Tory obstruction against Gladstone's first Government, and Sir Robert Peel had foreseen the dangers of such a development thirty years before Parnell entered the House of Commons.[68]

The most important innovation in the obstructionist tactics of Biggar, Parnell, O'Donnell and their supporters was the ingenious use they made of the crying defects of the parliamentary system of procedure. These defects were not limited to the formal manner of transacting business but included the neglect of important matters of substance. In particular, Parliament almost completely neglected serious abuses at home and the needs of the overseas colonies. 'If Englishmen', declared Parnell in defence of the new policy, 'insist on the artificial maintenance of an antiquated institution which can only perform a portion of its functions by the "connivance" of those intrusted with its working, in the imperfect and defective perform-ance of much of even that portion . . . I cannot consider it my duty to connive in the imperfect performance of these functions, while I should certainly not think of obstructing any useful, solid or well-performed work.'[69]

Under the pressure of the obstructionists, though very much against their wishes and against those of all parties, the procedure of the House of Commons underwent a complete revolution which brought it more into line with its growing tasks. The rights of indi-vidual members and of minority groups were curtailed in order to allow the passage of essential legislation without undue delay. The indirect result of the obstruction practised by the small but well-knit group of Irish members was, therefore, a great increase in the power of the party machines at the expense of the independent member. Thus it formed an integral part in the much-lamented but inevitable transformation of the House of Commons from a kind of club for the self-governing aristocracy into the ruling and con-trolling body of a modern democracy. The irritant of Irish obstruc-tion did a good deal to overcome the weight of conservative opposi-tion to these changes, and made them much more thorough-going than would otherwise have been the case. As John Redmond put it, 'in order to suspend the Constitution in Ireland, England was obliged to destroy the most cherished tradition and most precious possession of her Parliament, the freedom of speech of its members'.[70]

Even more important than its effect on the mechanism of parlia-mentary life was the influence of the Irish party as the only com-pact representation of unprivileged classes and subject nations in the British Empire. Even before the franchise reform of 1884, the average Irish 'householder' belonged to a different class from his typical British counterpart; he was not only much poorer but also less influenced by the upper classes. The 'natural leaders' of Irish society were either members of a ruling nation or an alien faith, or they were at least suspect to the masses of Irishmen as friends of the English connection. The radical section of Irish representatives in the Tory Parliament of 1874 made good use of this social cleavage in their struggle for the political leadership of Ireland. They knew very well that the British Government was 'a plutocratic oligarchy disguised from the people by the formularies of what is called popular election, but guarded from the people by all kinds of limitations, expenses, and qualifications',[71] and Parnell was particularly successful in enlisting the support of the British Radicals in his struggle against many crying social abuses in England, like flogging in the army, and against the excesses of English imperialism in other parts of the world.

The potential threat and the potential promise of the Irish party in the House of Commons far exceeded the implications of its official nationalist programme. It was a threat to the power of the middle-class Radicals over their working-class followers in England and its very existence held out a promise of an alliance of Irish nationalism, supported by the labouring masses in Ireland, and British working-class aims for the purpose of wresting power from the classical British parties. The forging of such an alliance was regarded as the indispensable condition of success by so penetrating an observer as Karl Marx, who came to the conclusion that the British working class would never achieve anything before it had got rid of Ireland: 'The lever must be applied in Ireland.'[72] The most important practical spokesman of this policy was Michael Davitt, the advocate of land nationalisation in Ireland and founder of the Land League. But the difficulties were insuperable on both sides. Above all, the leadership of Irish nationalism was in the hands of the middle class. Parnell needed the revolutionary energy of the masses, without which he would have been powerless, but he was determined from the first to use it for his own purposes which were centred on the establishment of a middle-class Irish Government. As long as these purposes could only be gained through conflict with the great English parties, he was quite willing to increase the difficulties of his opponents by appealing to the English masses over the heads of their political leaders, but this was merely a tactical device to be dropped when its usefulness had been exhausted.

At the height of the Land League struggle, Parnell issued a long manifesto appealing 'against territorialism and shopocracy which dominate in Parliament, to working men and agricultural labourers of Britain who surely have no interest in the misgovernment and persecution of Ireland. . . . The starting of a working-man or agricultural labourer candidate in every British constituency would soon bring the House of Commons and Radicalism to its senses. A junction between English democracy and Irish Nationalism upon a basis of Ireland's right to make her own laws, the overthrow of territorialism in both countries, and enfranchisement of labour from crushing taxes for the maintenance of standing armies and navies, would prove irresistible. It would terminate the strife of centuries and secure lasting friendship, based on mutual interests and confidence, between the two nations.'[73]

This admirable programme remained a dead letter, and nobody was more responsible for this than its author. After the Kilmainham Treaty Parnell discovered the possibility, and indeed the need, of a compromise with Gladstone, and he was genuinely eager to abandon the uncongenial task of 'agitation' in England as well as in Ireland. His inclination to attack his English opponents by an appeal to the forces of the Left in both countries disappeared with the need for consolidating his position, and that of the Irish middle class, against attacks from the Left.

The explosive character of the Home Rule crisis was due to a combination of national and social causes. The clash between the interests of the stunted Irish middle class and the powerful business interests of Great Britain (and Ulster) would not by itself have been sufficient to convulse British politics but for the parliamentary balance of power which gave the weak Irish bourgeoisie the backing of a colonial people in revolt against its masters. But this apparently irresistible trump card in the hand of the Irish rebel members of parliament was in fact their greatest weakness, for it could be played only if the middle-class leaders of the nationalist movement were ready to sink their particular interests in favour of a truly national policy which, in the conditions of the Irish people, would have been revolutionary in character. Such a policy would not have succeeded without the close alliance with the British workers which Davitt advocated in and out of season; conversely, the vigorous championship of working-class interests would have been the simplest way of removing the strong anti-Irish prejudices of many British workers. At the same time, such a policy would have greatly strengthened the hands of the radical wing in Ireland which demanded Land Nationalisation instead of the Land Act of 1881—and it would have been fatal to the hope of striking a bargain with either of the great British parties.

Parnell's choice between these rival policies was never in doubt. At the very moment when the enfranchisement of the Irish rural labourers gave him the practical monopoly of speaking for Ireland, he roundly condemned Davitt's land nationalisation plans and advised

his followers not to rely 'even upon the great English democracy'
but only upon the devotion of the sea-divided Gael and the people
in Ireland. The classical example of Parnell's strategic blindness,
which contrasted so strongly with his tactical genius, was his later
decision to support the Tories at the important General Election of
1885. The crucial factor in this decision was the apparent willingness of the Tories to grant not only Home Rule but also industrial
protection through fiscal autonomy, but Parnell would never have
been trapped by the Tories, if the narrow social basis of his policy
had not made him obtuse to the social significance of English political
events. That Lord Salisbury never intended to grant Home Rule
may be taken for certain, although this did not prevent him from
making a Home Ruler Viceroy of Ireland as a bid for the Irish vote.
Parnell showed little of his earlier political hard-headedness in his
dealings with the Tory Viceroy, Lord Carnarvon, and still less in
his decision to throw the Irish vote in England into the Tory scale.
This last step not only doomed the first Home Rule Bill but exerted
an unforeseen influence on the British party system as a whole.

In Ireland, the Home Rule crisis completed the extermination of
the Liberals which had been proceeding since the Reform Bill of
1867. The advance of nationalist agitation and its appeasement by
the Liberal leaders drove the Ulster middle-class Liberals with their
strong nonconformist tradition into the camp of the anti-national-
ists. The Irish demand for a protective wall against British competition reinforced the existing social and religious antagonism by the
solid influence of economic self-interests and made any true reconciliation between Ulster and the South impossible. The maintenance of the Union thus became a matter of life and death for Ulster
and created the condition for an organised and well-disciplined
Ulster resistance movement under the leadership of the wealthy
business men of Belfast. The genius of Tory demagogy, Lord
Randolph Churchill, was amongst the first to appreciate the
political advantage of this turn of events, just as he had been the
first to lure Parnell into his sham alliance with the Tories in the
summer of 1885. His slogan 'Ulster will fight and Ulster will be
right' preserved its topical force up to the outbreak of the First
World War.

The effect of the Home Rule crisis on British politics was in
some respects similar but in others very different from its effect on
Ulster. In both countries it was the occasion for a change of party
allegiance for the business classes, and this process was, indeed, more
sweeping in England than in Ireland, because the proportion of
Liberals amongst the business men had been very much higher in
the homeland of modern capitalism. But in England, unlike Ulster,

this development did not strengthen the hold of the middle classes on the workers. On the contrary, while the mass of English business men followed Chamberlain and Bright in their repudiation of Gladstonian Home Rule, and in due course changed from Radicals into Liberal Unionists, simple Unionists and Imperialists, the majority of the English working men steadfastly refused to follow them into the opposite camp.

The Liberal Party of the eighteen-eighties was an uneasy coalition of Whigs and Radicals, representing roughly a minority of the great landed houses (and important financial interests), on the one hand, and the great majority of the manufacturers (with certain significant exceptions, like brewers and cotton masters), on the other. The weight of the Whigs was not due to their numerical strength but to their proximity to the source of political power which made them, in fact, a highly influential well-connected clique. The Radicals tried to wrest power from them by a disciplined mass organisation of the local party workers, manned by artisans and shopkeepers and officered by business men like Joseph Chamberlain and intellectuals like John Morley. The Whigs were on the defensive all along the line, and their days as an independent political force were nearly over. The Radicals were in all essentials robust business men, and their championship of the working class was limited to measures designed to rivet the votes of the newly enfranchised masses to policies which in their wider implications were neither progressive nor democratic. In Chamberlain's revealing phrase, these measures were a 'ransom' demanded from the privileged classes in exchange for the consent of the British people to the perpetuation of their privileges in a formally democratic society.

The undemocratic side of Radicalism was shown from the beginning of its career in imperial and foreign affairs. Although W. E. Forster, the author of the Education Act of 1870 and dictator in Ireland during the Land League crisis, was not accepted as a genuine Radical by Joseph Chamberlain and his friends, he was quite in line with the younger Radical leader in his enthusiasm for Empire Federation, and only a little ahead of him in his preference for coercion in Ireland. Imperialism was not an aberration from the aims of English Radicalism, as preached by Chamberlain and Dilke, and, from the opposite camp, by Lord Randolph Churchill, but its inevitable culmination. It revealed the ultimate purpose behind the progressive home policy of the Radical leaders which was simply a bait for the unprivileged masses whose votes were to be won for a policy of imperialist expansion.

Such a policy had a good deal to recommend itself to some sections of the British working class, and Chamberlain's plan of sharing

some of the material results of Britain's dominant imperial position
with the masses was well designed to convince them of the palpable
advantages of imperialism. Yet this policy ran counter to all the
basic tenets of democracy, and its acceptance would have completed the subordination of the workers to the interests of British
capitalism both at home and abroad. The struggle for power within
the Liberal party was, therefore, a conflict pregnant with political
consequences of the first order, and it was the Home Rule crisis which
brought it to a head.

The supreme surprise of this crisis was the simultaneous defection
of Whigs *and* Radicals from the main body of the Liberal party and
its conversion to Home Rule for Ireland by the influence of Gladstone's personality. The bewildering sequence of events, particularly the famous Hawarden Kite which in its day was a great
political sensation, was influenced not a little by the dramatic
struggle behind the scenes of official politics which had the Liberal
party organisation as its prize. Chamberlain did his utmost to oust
Gladstone from the leadership by committing the party unequi-
vocally against Home Rule, and the conversion of some hard-
boiled Liberal politicians to the Home Rule cause was just as much
due to their fear and hatred of Chamberlain as to their enthusiasm
for 'justice for Ireland'. Gladstone himself finally made up his
mind that Chamberlain was a dangerous enemy in his camp,
though he hardly realised the full mettle of his future opponent, and
when the breach came it was Gladstone himself who took the
initiative in driving Chamberlain out of the Cabinet.[74] Through
his management of the party machine, Chamberlain seems to have
come very near to success in capturing the organisation, but Gladstone's direct appeal to the party proved irresistible and carried the
National Liberal Federation by storm. Only in Birmingham
Chamberlain managed, by careful and somewhat shady methods,
to retain the confidence of the local Liberal organisation, and even
there he was compelled after a short time to destroy his old party
with the help of the Tories, and to replace it by a personal machine
which dominated local politics long after his death and made
Birmingham a Tory stronghold until the end of the Second World
War.

After 1886 the Liberal party (rather like the Democratic party
in the United States after 1896) was only in exceptional circumstances a reliable alternative to the Tories from the point of view of
the business interests, and was invariably regarded as an open
enemy by the landlords. The shift in its social composition was
curiously reflected in the transfer of its geographical centre of
gravity. Neither London nor the English boroughs (and still less

the English counties) but the Celtic fringe furnished the parliamentary battalions of the Liberals, and it took a split within the Tory
ranks on the question of tariffs to produce a Liberal majority in
England, as distinct from Scotland and Wales. The withdrawal of
the business classes from the Liberal fold prevented the relapse of the
British political system into a combination of two complementary
party machines which had been its character before the onrush of
democracy. This transfer in the allegiance of the business interests
paved the way for the peculiar growth of the Labour party within
the bowels of British politics, through the gradual attraction of the
working-class elements of the Liberal party to the new gospel but
without the violent split which would have been inevitable if
Chamberlain's political machine had won the day against Gladstone in the crisis of 1886.

According to a well-worn *cliché*, the Irish question greatly ham-
pered the advance of the democratic forces in British public life by
diverting the attention of the people from the crying need for social
reform in England to the real or imaginary wrongs of Ireland.
Nothing could be farther from the truth than this plausible fallacy.
It is quite true that Gladstone much preferred the settlement of a
great imperial question to the satisfaction of 'socialistic' demands for
which he had little sympathy. On the other hand, it is by no means
correct to identify social reforms unreservedly with the progress of
democracy. Chamberlain and his Radicals, no less than Lord
Randolph Churchill and his Tory Democrats, offered social reforms
not as an earnest of genuine democracy but as an alternative to it.
They acted from similar motives to Bismarck in Germany who
introduced the most 'progressive' system of social insurance of his
time in order to wean the people by the contemplation of sickness
benefits and old age pensions from thoughts of social reorganisation.

Nor is it correct to say that the Irish question seriously interrupted the policy of social reform which was increasingly adopted
by both parties within the limits set by the dominant social interests. Chamberlain's influence in the Unionist counsels was strong
enough to ensure a policy reasonably close to that of other 'middle-
of-the-road' governments, and thereby weakened the resistance to
social reform measures in the Tory camp. The Liberal party, on
the other hand, was steadily pushed to the Left by the pressure of
its working-class elements whose influence was strengthened by the
secession of the Liberal Unionist business men. The Newcastle
Programme, however limited in its practical application, reflected
the awareness of the situation shown by the Liberal leaders, as did
Sir William Harcourt's famous *dictum* 'we are all Socialists now'.

As far as its effect on social reforms was concerned, the Irish

13

question did not retard and may have hastened their acceptance
by all political forces. But the advance of democracy depended
much more on the relations between the organised political forces
than on social reforms which, however desirable in themselves,
were quite compatible with an authoritarian régime like that of
Bismarck in Germany. In its influence on the British party system,
the Irish Question was like a powerful chemical solvent attacking
composite bodies and helping to reduce them to their elements.
The modern Conservative party remembers in its very name of
'Unionist' the service rendered it by the Home Rule crisis; it was
in their common resistance to Irish nationalist demands that landowners and capitalists learnt to sink their differences and to form a
united front of property owners in defence of England's imperial
position which was a vital part of their privileges. In a period when
foreign policy was the naked instrument of organised greed which
demanded the annexation of ever new territories in deference to
strong vested interests, no greater service could be rendered to
British democracy than to make the conduct of imperial and foreign
policy a party question. The influence of the Irish problem, both
positive and negative, made itself felt in countries as far apart as
South Africa and India, in Campbell-Bannerman's policy of reconciliation with the Boers and in the Morley-Minto reforms which
were the first halting step on the path which led to the handing over
of political power in India to the Indians themselves.

While the influence of the Irish question on the progress of democracy in Great Britain and on the Empire was thus mainly beneficial,
its reactions on the destinies of the powerful Liberal party were
wholly deplorable. Gladstone's mission of pacifying Ireland was a
task which his party could not fulfil without losing its distinct character and its peculiar social function. The effect of his early reform
measures, including the disestablishment of the Irish Church and
the first Irish Land Act, had been the demise of the Irish Whigs and
their replacement by an independent Irish Party with interests which
clashed with those behind the Liberal party of Great Britain.
Gladstone's conversion to Home Rule all but destroyed the Liberal
party by alienating both Whig aristocrats and Radical business men
by driving them into the camp of the Tories. His final break with
Parnell weaned the strong Irish element amongst the Irish workers
from their Liberal sympathies, and thereby made an indirect but
important contribution to the growth of an independent Labour
movement.

In this development the Irish residents in Great Britain played a
much bigger part than their numerical strength would have suggested. The extreme poverty and insecurity of their position at the

bottom of the scale made the Irish workers the vanguard of the New Unionism which preceded the formation of the Independent Labour Party in 1893 and the Labour Representation Committee in 1900. Dock labour, where much of the unrest occurred, was traditionally recruited from amongst Irishmen, just because it was one of the worst paid and least secure occupations. The two most characteristic leaders of the dockers, Ben Tillett in London and James Sexton in Liverpool, were both products of the Anglo-Irish slums.

Sexton's career is, indeed, one of the most interesting illustrations of the close link between Irish nationalism and the British Labour movement. An Irishman born on Tyneside and growing up amongst the Irish in Lancashire, Sexton first heard of 'politics' in connection with the Fenians and the shipwreck of their 'physical force' movement. His active political career started with the Parnell movement which organised the Irish in Great Britain in the influential Home Rule Confederation consisting almost entirely of Irish working men. Sexton's bitter personal experiences made him at the same time an 'agitator' amongst the Liverpool dockers, most of whom were Irishmen, both from Ulster and from the rest of Ireland, who worked for little pay and fewer thanks and who quarrelled violently amongst themselves.

The abuse of their common Irish nationalism by middle-class wire-pullers behind the movement weakened the hold of official nationalism over him, as over many other Irish workers, but it was only the break between Parnell and Gladstone and the struggle between Parnellites and anti-Parnellites amongst the Irish which alienated him completely from Irish politics and made him concentrate on Labour and Trade Union affairs. Neither Sexton nor his union—which was one of the constituent bodies of the later Transport and General Workers' Union—was by any means on the left wing of the British Labour movement. The officials of the Dockers' Union were less subject to democratic control by its members than the officials of the older craft unions with their steady membership of intelligent skilled workmen; and the traditional machine methods of Irish politics, inherited from organisations which used the masses in the interests of the middle class, may have contributed to the growth of despotic union bureaucracies with autocratic bosses and devoted henchmen.

An additional, and within certain limits very powerful, factor was the religious bond between the Catholic leaders and the Catholic, i.e. mainly Irish, section of their followers which introduced a new and sometimes disturbing loyalty into the Labour movement. A striking instance of this influence was Cardinal Manning's intervention in the London dock strike, which was not only a first-rate advertisement for the Catholic Church but also an illuminating episode in the relations between the New Unionism and the Irish element amongst its members: when Manning found the dockers set against the acceptance of his compromise solution he threatened that 'he would call on the Irish Catholics in the docks, and they would hear his voice'.[75] On a lower level, James Sexton was again fairly typical of this new and characteristically Irish element in the growing Labour movement where he was one of the leading opponents of secular education in connection with the Education Act of 1902.

The growing estrangement between the official Nationalist movement and the Irish in Great Britain was the inevitable alternative to Michael Davitt's policy of allying Irish nationalism and British working-class democracy, of which the Irish residents in Great Britain formed an integral part. This estrangement did not lead to any hostility between the growing Labour movement and the Irish claim for self-government; on the contrary, the spokesmen of the Labour party in and out of Parliament gave ungrudging support to the Home Rule programme, without any of the reservations which marred the Irish policy of the Liberals during their last lease of power. But the temporary victory of the middle-class leaders over the revolutionary left wing of the Irish nationalist movement destroyed the organic unity between British and Irish democracy. The Irish question continued to influence British politics, and its most spectacular effect on the development of the British constitution and the British Empire was still to come; but as far as the development of the British party system is concerned, the Home Rule crisis and the resulting split within the Irish party marks the climax and almost the end of Irish influence.

Book 4. Compromise or Revolution?

CHAPTER XX

THE DIMINISHING RETURNS OF IMPERIALISM

ALTHOUGH the Irish question continued to serve as a shibboleth in the British party struggle up to the outbreak of the First World War, the years between the first Home Rule Bill in 1886 and the third Home Rule Bill in 1912 witnessed a loosening of the economic ties between Great Britain and Ireland everywhere except in the industrial area of north-east Ulster.

Gladstone's Land Acts recognised the need for protecting the tenants against their landlords, and the judicial fixing of rents not only reduced their level throughout the country, but also provided for periodical revision at future dates—a clause of evil omen for the Irish landlords. At the same time Ireland's virtual monopoly of the English market in dairy and livestock products, which had received its first blow during the depression of the eighteen-seventies, crumbled for ever as a result of steadily increasing competition by overseas farmers. 'In 1896 the supply of fresh beef and mutton, of butter and eggs from Ireland was almost a necessary of life to the English consumer. The importation of Australian, Siberian and Argentine butter, of frozen mutton and chilled beef, was still in its infancy. Denmark has in the interval become a formidable rival of Ireland in the supply of bacon and butter. Refrigerating chambers in the ocean steamers and cold stores at the ports have rendered the English consumer independent of the Irish supplier.'[1] Whatever hopes the Irish landlords may have had for the restoration of their rents after Gladstone's fall and the return to power of a sound Unionist government were dashed for good by this change in the economic relations between Ireland and England. As Ireland's importance as a market for British goods depended on the value of Irish exports to Great Britain, English interest in Ireland, both as a supplier and as a market, slackened and economic considerations for the maintenance of the Union lost weight proportionately, while the Irish question was rapidly becoming an intolerable nuisance in British politics.

As the Anglo-Irish landlords were almost to a man in the Unionist camp, their withdrawal from Ireland was organised and carried through under Conservative leadership and with full consideration for their material interests. The first successful Land Purchase Act was the work of the Tory Lord Ashbourne, Irish Lord Chancellor in the short-lived Conservative Government of 1885. Although the Tories had no love for the 1881 Land Act with its judicially fixed rents and its system of 'dual ownership' which was simply a half-way house towards the complete elimination of the landlords, they were forced in 1887 to extend its operation to the leaseholders, i.e. the class of more substantial tenants who were previously omitted from it in order to maintain inviolate the sacredness of written contracts. In later years the Conservatives enacted three major land purchase laws—in 1891, 1896 and 1903 under the personal guidance of A. J. Balfour as Irish Chief Secretary, Leader of the House of Commons and Prime Minister. Although only the last of these measures, the Wyndham Act of 1903, came within striking distance of solving the problem, this was mainly due to the financial intricacies of the situation and not to any unwillingness on the part of the Government.

The Irish land problem confronted a British Government for the first time with the question of compensation for expropriating private property on a significant scale. Before the time of troubles which broke over the heads of the Irish landlords with the great agricultural depression of 1877, Irish land had generally been regarded as a six per cent investment:[2] how could it be replaced by three per cent public bonds without either halving the income of the landlords or doubling their capital? No amount of ingenuity could have solved the problem, if the landlords had really enjoyed their whole income previous to the introduction of land purchase; in fact it had been mortgaged so heavily that a comparatively small appreciation in capital values compensated them for their apparently much heavier loss of income. To George Wyndham, who was one of the most promising rising young men in the Tory camp before his career was broken by his very success in Ireland, belongs the credit of having worked out a reasonable compromise: he gave the landlords a twelve per cent cash bonus at the expense of the tax-payer and allowed them to convert their mortgages with the help of the Treasury. At the same time he forced them to sell their estates as a whole, and spread the repayments by the purchaser over 68½ years instead of the 43 years under the Balfour Acts. The measure was naturally very popular with the landlords and was supported by the majority of the tenants' leaders; it came very near to complete success but in the end its momentum was exhausted prematurely for the same reason as that of the earlier land purchase acts: the fall in government securities on the London Stock Exchange which made the bargain intolerably expensive for the British taxpayer.

In spite of this setback, land purchase had produced a profound change in the ownership of Irish land before the First World War temporarily put an end to its operation. The Bright clause of the 1870 Land Act and its counterpart in Gladstone's bolder Land Act of 1881 had remained quite ineffective because they could be used only by tenants with substantial capital of their own. Under the Tory land purchase laws, on the other hand, great progress was made towards an Irish 'property-owning democracy'.

LAND PURCHASE SUMMARISED[3]

Acts	No. of Estates	No. of Holdings	Acreage (acres)	Advances	Purchase money (in £) Paid by Purchaser	Total
1870	—	877	52,906	514,536	344,986	859,522
1881	—	731	30,657	240,801	114,793	355,594
1885–8	—	25,367	942,625	9,992,536	170,298	10,162,834
1891–6	—	46,834	1,482,749	13,146,892	254,334	13,401,226
Total	—	73,809	2,508,937	23,894,765	884,411	24,779,176
1903–9	9,459	270,396	9,037,392	84,822,857	1,072,772	85,895,629
Pending Sales	1,248	46,621	1,492,243	10,653,198	65,205	10,718,403
Grand Total	10,707	390,826	13,038,572	119,370,820	2,022,388	121,393,208

As the movement achieved these mass dimensions, its social character changed, and with it the social structure of the Irish village. In 1917, the total number of agricultural holdings in Ireland was 572,574. Of these, 112,787 were less than one acre and belonged to the category of allotments, potato gardens, etc. Of the remainder, 33,357 were over 100 acres each and may be regarded as outside the scope of ordinary land purchase (demesne lands, large grazing farms, etc.).[4] At the same time the number of holdings owned by their occupiers amounted to 367,058—a figure almost equal to the total number of holdings between 5 and 100 acres in size. The total number of tenanted holdings was 205,516 which must have included the bulk of the 112,787 allotments smaller than one acre each, and perhaps half the number of holdings exceeding 100 acres in size, leaving only approximately 75,000 small tenant holdings to be dealt with, a high proportion of them in Ulster.[5]

The policy of controlled and subsidised land purchase had momentous social, economic and psychological results. As early as 1910, John Dillon, who was Redmond's most powerful lieutenant in the leadership of the official Irish party, remarked that the Wyndham Act 'had the effect of changing the whole character of the peasantry. Instead of being careless, idle and improvident, they have become like the French peasantry, industrious and economical, even penurious. Marriages are now contracted later, though the limitation of families had not yet begun owing to Catholic influences.'⁶ Although the influence of the Catholic Church on Irish morals has not waned since, the fall in the Irish birthrate has been particularly severe even in comparison with other West European countries, mainly due to the continuing increase in the average age at marriage.

The economic withdrawal of the Anglo-Irish landlords was nearing completion at the time of the First World War; their political fall from power was already an accomplished fact at the beginning of the new century. During the first seventy years of the nineteenth century the landlords had enjoyed a virtual monopoly of parliamentary representation; this was gradually weakened after the Reform Bill of 1867 and the Ballot Act of 1872, and finally overthrown by the enfranchisement of the rural labourers in 1884. Local government, however, remained firmly in the hands of the landlords until the legislation of 1898, which transferred local administrative power to the Irish middle class in town and village. This law, like the great land purchase measures, was enacted by a Tory Government, and like them it combined a sweeping radicalism in principle with great tenderness for the landlords in matters of finance. Under the old Grand Jury system, the landlords had been obliged to pay out of their own pockets at least one-half of the poor rates. Such an undemocratic practice was indefensible in an enlightened age, and from 1898 onwards all rates and levies struck by the local authorities had to be paid by the occupiers. As this change would have borne hard on the tenants, the Government came to the rescue with an Agricultural Grant of almost £750,000 a year in aid of the Irish County Councils which was, in fact, a gift to the Irish landlords.

This expedient, and still more its much bigger successor, the Cash Bonus of the Wyndham Act, gave an important financial meaning to the policy of killing Home Rule by kindness, which the Tories tried to put into practice. In 1896, the Tory Government of Lord Salisbury received the report of a Financial Relations Commission which had been set up by Gladstone during his last administration under the chairmanship of one of his oldest lieutenants. This Commission submitted evidence of the over-taxation from which Ireland had suffered ever since the Union, based on authoritative private and official calculations. At the time of the report, Ireland paid in full for the excessive cost of administering the country as an English dependency against the wishes of the majority—complete with Viceroy, an inflated judiciary, an expensive and inefficient bureaucracy, a large army and, above all, a police which a high Irish official aptly described as 'an army of occupation rather than a police force'.[7] Although the costs of this overgrown machine of government were more than an impoverished peasant country could have been expected to raise, Ireland contributed in addition more than two million pounds a year towards the cost of running the British Empire. From a purely fiscal point of view, the Union had been clearly successful for Great Britain, mainly because Victorian finance pressed hardest on the poor of whom Ireland had more than her proportionate share.

In 1896, when this report was made, the forces were already at work which were to change this relationship within a few years. The main impetus came from the progress of democracy on both sides of the Irish Sea which was accompanied by a steep rise in social expenditure by the Government; an additional, and for the moment even more urgent, motive force was the need of bribing the Irish people into acquiescence in the existing régime. This was the meaning of the phrase 'killing Home Rule by kindness', which became the declared policy of the Tories and which in the last resort was only a special application of the general principles which underlay the attitude of the privileged minorities towards the masses in a time of growing democratic tendencies. Between 1895 and 1910 public expenditure on 'local' Irish purposes rose by more than £5,420,000 a year, or by more than 90 per cent. This stupendous increase was largely due to the cost of services which materially benefited some substantial class of Irishmen, like the work of the Department of Agriculture, the Land Commission or the increased expenditure on education. Large as the sums required for these purposes were according to the standards of the time, their importance was soon overshadowed by the financial burden of the Old Age Pensions.

As early as 1910 expenditure for Irish Old Age Pensions reached the large total of £2,400,000—and it was bound to increase still further.[8] The huge cost of this new service, although the pension amounted only to five shillings per week for persons of more than seventy years of age, was indirectly due to generations of Irish misgovernment which had seriously reduced the proportion of young people and made Ireland a land of the ageing or aged. It was one of the minor ironies of history that Ireland benefited out of all proportion from the first great measure of social improvement designed primarily to 'kill Socialism by kindness' by strengthening the loyalty of the British working class to the Liberal party.

The exploitation of Ireland by Great Britain took different forms in different ages: in the eighteenth century it consisted mainly in the extraction of rents and raw materials; under the Union in the extraction of rents, labour and taxes. In 1913 all these sources of material exploitation had dried up or dwindled, and calculated in terms of hard cash Ireland had, indeed, become a liability for the British Empire. The Liberals greatly reduced the bonus payable to landlords under the Wyndham Act, though they were to pay a heavy political price for this economy which interfered with the completion of the land purchase scheme. On the other hand, the logic of their position compelled them at the same time to present the aged Irish poor with an annual pension worth almost two and a half million pound sterling which threatened to become still more expensive with every passing year. In order to complete their discomfiture, the Irish consumers refused to respond in the traditional manner to the increase in spirit duties which was to supply the revenue for this additional expenditure. In the financial year 1910–11, the first year under the new dispensation, Irish 'local' expenditure exceeded 'true' Irish revenue by more than one million pounds, with much larger deficits looming ahead.

The radical change in the economic and financial relations between Great Britain and Ireland was not without its effects in the political sphere. Everywhere except in north-east Ulster, the leaders of the Unionist minority consisted mainly of the landlords and the officials of Dublin Castle. The former had lost their political power and, since the great success of land purchase, their economic interest in the maintenance of the existing régime declined, because it was no longer needed as a safeguard for their privileged position.

Irish Land Stock was guaranteed by the British Treasury and its value was independent of the payment of rents in County Leitrim or County Mayo—or, indeed, of the payment of their annuities by the tenant-purchasers. Land Stock was far from stable in value, but its fluctuations were due to the rise and fall of British funds at the Stock Exchange in London, and not to the changing fortunes of war between agitators and police in Ireland. This change produced a complete reversal in the Unionist attitude towards the South of Ireland: formerly it had been governed by the need for a British garrison in control of conquered territory; now the main consideration was the safety of the loyal, i.e. Unionist minority.

The deficit in the balance of Irish public income and expenditure removed at the same time one of the oldest and most intractable obstacles to any real Home Rule settlement. Gladstone's famous first Home Rule Bill might have come to grief on its finance clauses if it had not been thrown out altogether on second reading, and the financial question raised endless and insoluble constitutional difficulties. If Ireland was to be taxed for Imperial purposes, she had to continue to be represented at Westminster, for taxation without representation could not be reconciled with democratic principles, and the endless problems of combining Home Rule in Ireland with an Irish party in the British House of Commons could never be settled. On the other hand, Home Rule without financial self-determination was a mockery—and how could financial autonomy be reconciled with the use of Irish revenue for British purposes? The disappearance of the Irish revenue surplus through the cost of remedial legislation and Old Age Pensions removed this difficulty once and for all.

Far from supplying money for Imperial purposes, an Irish Home Rule Government would have had to be subsidised in order to give it a fair start. The Primrose Committee, set up to consider financial arrangements under the Third Home Rule Bill, suggested that the British Treasury should bear the cost of Old Age Pensions in Ireland which had already been granted before the coming into force of Home Rule, and that the new Irish Government would have to cut down future Old Age Pensions, and in general to show its spirit of national independence by rejecting schemes 'that are sure to be framed with reference to the needs of Great Britain with its vast preponderance of industrial population and which, if applied to Ireland without adaptation, must inevitably lead to grievous waste of public money, if not also to serious demoralisation of Irish life. . . .'[9] In other words, in an era of democratic remedial legislation Ireland, as the poorest part of the United Kingdom, had become an unwelcome luxury for Great Britain. It is, therefore, not surprising that the same Committee found no difficulty in suggesting a simple solution to the vexed problem which had defied Gladstone's matchless ingenuity and resource: 'There is only one way in which all the requirements of the situation can satisfactorily be met, and that is by conferring on the Irish Government full powers over the raising of revenue, as well as over expenditure in Ireland'[10]—subject only to free trade between Great Britain and Ireland and a balanced budget at the start. Although fiscal autonomy, which was thereby suggested in essence if not in form, was not fully equivalent to Dominion status, its recognition as a sound, or indeed as the only possible, solution removed the biggest single obstacle to the ultimate achievement of Dominion Home Rule which had blocked any real progress in the past.

The link of material interests which previously fastened Ireland tightly to England through the medium of rents and taxes had become very weak indeed by the time of the First World War. The same development produced results in Irish economic life which were hardly less significant. The policy of killing Home Rule by kindness involved a substantial scaling down of the rents paid by Irish tenants; positive measures of economic assistance to the particularly poor and backward 'congested districts' on the Atlantic seaboard, and particularly the grant of Old Age Pensions to the mass of half-starved humanity which had been previously left to die as quickly as possible, all had the effect of increasing Irish home consumption of foodstuffs and reducing the economic importance of exports which had been the ultimate purpose of Irish economy from the point of view of its colonial rulers. Another influence which worked in the same direction was the steadily swelling stream of overseas remittances, mainly from the United States, to the relatives of emigrants which later on was to play such an important part in Ireland's international balance of payments.

The progress of land purchase and the incessant agitation of the western peasants encroached more and more on the preserves of the great graziers in the South-west, with their vital interest in the British market and the British connection, while it strengthened the position of the small farmers whose main interests and energies were devoted to subsistence-farming for their own needs. A large part of Irish food exports to Great Britain was no genuine surplus available in excess of the full demands of the Irish people: these exports were partly due to the imperative need of selling food in order to pay extravagant rents and taxes, and partly to the clearance of population in favour of cattle and sheep during the generation after the famine.

The reduction in the burden of Irish rents through the combined agencies of agitation and legislation was striking indeed. As late as 1885 the rental of the country amounted to £11 millions.[11] Under Gladstone's 1881 Land Act, 379,348 tenants had their rents reduced by an average of 20·7 per cent, and more than one-third of their number obtained a further reduction of 19·5 per cent when their 'second term' rents were fixed.[12]

The 344,000 tenants who bought their holdings under the various land purchase Acts, paid annuities of not more than £3,750,000 for their 11½ million acres. They began to accumulate money, and it is reasonable to assume that their domestic food consumption increased at the same time. The two and a half million pounds sterling which the Government disbursed every year since 1910 in the form of Old Age Pensions raised the purchasing power of the most undernourished section of the Irish people whose moral standards must, of course, have seriously suffered from their newly gained ability to obtain the necessaries of life otherwise than by begging. Although Ireland was an exporter of bacon and ham on a large scale, substantial quantities of cheaper cuts were imported at the same time for home consumption, because the pig population was affected by the decline in tillage. Ireland imported not only practically her entire wheat supply but even some butter and eggs— clear indications of the backwardness of Irish agriculture and the increased demands of the home market.

The external pressure which in the past had squeezed large amounts of food out of an underfed people slackened, while at the same time the sale of surplus foodstuffs in the English market encountered steadily growing obstacles. The increase in Irish livestock was almost entirely confined to store cattle for fattening in England, which is notoriously one of the least profitable forms of agriculture. Butter exports actually declined as a result of Danish competition. The output of Irish butter was almost entirely seasonal, due to the absence of proper winter feeding, while Danish butter was not only of very high quality but could be supplied much more regularly than the Irish product.

The most striking feature of this new state of affairs was its contrast to the previous trends of Irish economic life. Ireland's integration in the British economic system showed signs of rapid reversal as soon as the hands of the landlords and the tax collectors were removed from the pockets of the Irish people. There still remained, even outside Ulster, influential sections whose position and well-being was largely dependent on the English connection, like the graziers of Munster and the few large capitalists of Dublin and Cork—bankers, merchants, brewers, distillers and biscuit manufacturers. But the large majority of the small farmers and local business men in control of official Irish politics were decidedly anti-British in their economic attitude not less than in their political sympathies. They tried to invest their money in Irish securities and were far more concerned with their parochial affairs than with the problems of Britain's position in a changing world. The subordination of Irish economic life to the needs of British capitalism, which had been so complete in the past as to be regarded almost as a fact of nature, had not been based on the firm foundation of mutual interest but only on exploitation. As soon as the growth of democracy and the shift in Britain's economic position made imperialist rule over Ireland more difficult and less profitable, the economic bonds between the two countries weakened from year to year.

CHAPTER XXI

THE ERA OF CLERICALISM

CLERICALISM denotes a state of affairs where the needs of society at large are subordinated to the interests of the dominant Church. Although the word it usually connected with the predominance of the Roman Catholic Church, this connection is by no means invariably correct, but Irish clericalism certainly illustrates the easy growth of clericalism in a country where the power of the Catholic Church over the faithful was as great as anywhere in Europe.

At first sight, clericalism seems to express a straightforward relation of power between society and Church which enables the one to dominate the other. Closer observation shows, however, that this relationship is a very complex result of social strains and stresses: the obvious and undeniable power of the Church is usually due to its peculiar position in society as arbitrator between groups with conflicting interests, and not to its absolute superiority over the combined forces of society. In such a situation, alliance with the organised and disciplined Church organisation may be the necessary condition of success for one or the other of the opposed social groups. When this stage of development has been reached, the Church and its special interests seem to take precedence over all other considerations, but these interests are themselves bound up with a certain state of society, and their apparent or real predominance expresses, in the last resort, a certain balance of social forces.

This is a very rough outline of the shape of events in Ireland during the nineteenth century. The alliance of the Catholic Church with Daniel O'Connell and its hostility towards Young Ireland, its indifference towards the Irish Tenant League and its benignity towards the disreputable Pope's Brass Band, its friendship with the Whigs and its mortal feud with the Fenians were part of a consistent policy. By and large the Church was ready to lend its support to every attempt at improving the position of the Roman Catholics within the existing social order, while steadfastly opposing every revolutionary or rebellious movement which tended to endanger the existence of this order. Parnell's political achievement, the combination of the bulk of ex-Fenian rebels and radicals with agrarian reformers and middle-class Catholics in a single movement of redoubtable striking force, took the Church by surprise and for the moment almost eliminated it as a political power. Instead of impressing their peculiar clerical interests on the movement of the laity, the clergy were themselves rent by the hardly veiled conflict between conservatives like Archbishop MacHale (the toothless 'lion of the fold of Judah') and middle-class radicals like Archbishop Croke of Cashel—a clear test of the great powers of attraction which the Parnell movement in its prime had for the Irish people as a whole, including even the Catholic priesthood. It was only Parnell's decisive move to the Right, under the negative impact of agrarian 'anarchy' in Ireland and the positive influence of Mrs. O'Shea in England, which enabled the Church to come into its own again as a political agency. Parnell himself encouraged the priests to take part in the Irish National League in order to counterbalance the still dangerous influence of the revolutionaries. During the following years of Parnell's supremacy, the leaders of the Church were increasingly attracted by Parnell's policy of moderation in Ireland and aggressive demands at Westminster—very much to the displeasure of the Catholic hierarchy in England and in Rome which was openly hostile to the policy of Gladstonian Home Rule.

However, the attraction of Parnell's policy did not by any means imply affection for its author, and no sooner had Parnell tamed the extremists in his camp with the help of the Church than he was himself struck down by a combination of the forces which benefited most from the eclipse of the revolutionists: the Irish middle class and the English Liberals—supported, and to some extent, even guided, by the leader of the Catholic hierarchy in England.

Cardinal Manning was the undisputed master mind among the English Catholics and the most influential adviser of the Pope on English and Irish affairs. Manning had been a somewhat lukewarm supporter of the original Home Rule League under Butt's leadership which had the great merit of splitting, and thereby neutralising the Fenians whom he abhorred. But in spite of a lifelong friendship with the veteran Liberal leader, he was a decided opponent of Gladstone's first Home Rule Bill which he denounced as equivalent to separation.[13] Manning agreed with Michael Davitt on the effects of removing fifty Catholic members of Parliament from Westminster, and opposed it as a 'Catholic and a world-wide danger'.[14] Cardinal Manning was not so closely influenced by the parochial politics of Ireland as the Irish bishops. The latter may well have intrigued against Parnell's dominant position, but they needed him for the same reason for which he needed them: Parnell entered into a close political alliance with the Catholic Church, although he distrusted the Irish prelates, because only thus could he break the power of his own left wing; the Irish bishops feared him as a successful rival in the race for the allegiance of the Irish people, but they regarded him as a safe bulwark against the revolutionary wing of the peasants in alliance with the stirring Labour movement.

Cardinal Manning looked at the situation in a different light; he was just as hostile to the Irish revolutionaries as his Irish brethren, but this fear did not dominate him in his politics. His twin allegiance was to the British Empire and to the Catholic Church, and from both points of view he came to hate Parnellism as 'Tudorism', for the reason that Parnell, like the Tudors, turned the priests out of their due influence and left the laity in command—in this case for the criminal purpose of breaking up the British Empire. The wrong-headedness of his attitude does not reduce its political importance. Parnell's Home Rule policy, however moderate it was against the background of Irish society, was to Manning little better than that of Michael Davitt, and he made the demolition of the incomplete union between moderates and extremists under Parnell's leadership the main object of his policy. The long-term policy which he pursued may well have been inconsistent, but in the short run it certainly benefited the British Empire as he understood it and increased the political power of the Catholic Church in Ireland.

The O'Shea divorce, which was handled and engineered by the same men who had just failed to discredit Parnell by the forgeries published by *The Times*, gave Manning a golden opportunity to impress his policy on the Irish bishops and on his old friend, Mr. Gladstone. On 21st November 1890, immediately after the bomb-shell of the divorce court proceedings, Manning emphasised to Gladstone the crucial strength of his position in seductive terms: 'If you say, do not fetter my freedom of action and take away my strength by putting the cause of Ireland in opposition to the public feeling and instinct of England and my chief supporters (the 'non-conformist conscience'), Mr. Parnell would retire from leadership and still give all aid, as before, to the Irish cause';[15] and after Gladstone's fatal letter of 23rd November 1890 had faithfully reproduced this line of argument, Cardinal Manning had every reason to congratulate him on one of the most important errors of his career: 'Your letter has saved your Party, shut the mouth of the lions and saved Home Rule.'[16]

With the exception of Cardinal Manning, none of the antagonists outside the Unionist camp acted with reasonable consistency during this crisis. Gladstone began by advising Parnell's temporary retirement as a means of placating English public opinion and ended by employing his formidable powers of pressure and persuasion to crush his ally of yesterday out of existence: 'Mr. Gladstone was overwhelmed with telegrams and letters and glorifications from all over England. Still these men ignore that they violate the essence of

Home Rule. They wish to dictate to Irishmen whom they shall not employ as their leader. What greater interference with liberty?'[17] The Irish clergy seem to have been quite willing to overlook Parnell's fall from grace, while he appeared to weather the storm successfully; but when they rallied to the defence of outraged morality under the influence of Manning's imploring letters and Gladstone's demands, their hold on the official nationalist organisation made their change of attitude devastatingly effective. The Irish parliamentarians hastened to assure Parnell of their undying loyalty; but when they realised that this policy brought them into conflict with the priests at home and the Liberals in England, they reversed their position without undue regard to principle and dignity. Parnell himself, who made his political fortune by taming the extremists of Irish politics and by pushing them off the political scene, tried in vain to undo his life's work and to evoke the political ghosts of the Fenians whom he had so successfully exorcised before.

When the smoke of battle cleared, Parnell was in his grave after a struggle of dramatic intensity which was only marred by the ruthless subordination of political to personal considerations, the grand alliance which he had kept together with so much skill was broken to pieces, and the chances of a Home Rule settlement by consent were gone—certainly for a generation and, as it happened, for ever. The positive result of the crisis was the elimination of the left wing of Irish politics from the official nationalist movement. This implied the subordination of the Irish party in the House of Commons to the Liberals and its subordination at home in Ireland to the Catholic Church.

The Irish split put an end to 'Tudorism' in Cardinal Manning's phrase and made the Catholic Church for twenty-five years the dominant political power outside north-east Ulster. Parnell's fall not only compromised the strategy which he had skilfully pursued throughout his career, but it also revealed the pitiful weakness of the middle class which occupied the vantage-point in his political structure. In its own right, it was nothing but an agglomeration of second-rate vested interests which had established themselves on the basis of the semi-colonial order maintained by British arms. Parnell had managed to mould the forces of agrarian discontent and the anti-English radicalism of the ex-Fenian urban lower classes into an organised movement which he had used and abused for his middle-class policy of Home Rule. Now the middle class fell back into its isolated position, without influence over the masses and dependent on the support of the Church for its contact with the Irish people.

The new era fittingly expressed itself in a great increase in the

14

material power of the Church. Contemporary observers noted the phenomenal increase in church-building after the Parnell split. At the same time the numerical strength of the Catholic priesthood grew with every passing decade. During the half-century 1861 to 1911 the number of priests, monks and nuns rose from 5,955 to 15,397, or by 158 per cent, while their flocks decreased from 4,505,000 to 3,243,000, or by 28 per cent.[18] In 1861, one Irish Catholic in 755 was a whole-time servant of the Church, in 1911 one in 210. The steel frame of this impressive edifice consisted of about three thousand parish priests whose influence over their congregations was everywhere very great, and in most rural areas practically supreme. The regular clergy acted as support of the organisation for special purposes, particularly in the fields of nursing and education.

With a tenacity which did great honour to its common sense and its grasp of fundamentals, the Church employed all its power in order to obtain a virtual monopoly over Irish higher education. Its position in the field of elementary education was fully safeguarded under the prevailing system, for out of 1,325 'school managers' in control of Catholic 'national' schools no fewer than 1,184 were priests[19] who ruled the teachers with a rod of iron. Secondary schools and training colleges for elementary school teachers were almost invariably run by Church organisations.

The special interests of the Catholic Church in educational matters cut across the political alliance between the Irish party and the Liberals in the House of Commons. In its educational policy, the hierarchy was in many respects on the side of the Tories and vehemently opposed to the Liberal policy, particularly to that of the powerful nonconformist wing of the Liberal party. The most reliable political allies of the Irish party were the most determined enemies of denominational education. The Tories, on the other hand, in whose programme the maintenance of the Union remained a prominent item, regarded concessions to the Church on educational matters as reasonable and, indeed, as their strongest card in Irish policy.

Lord Randolph Churchill was in this respect, as in so many others, the precursor of policies which were later on adopted by his party. Shortly before the first Home Rule crisis he proposed an informal alliance with the hierarchy as the only practicable method of spiking the guns of the Home Rulers: 'It is the Bishops entirely to whom I look in the future to turn, to mitigate or to postpone the Home Rule onslaught. Let us only be enabled to occupy a year with the Education Question. By that time, I am certain, Parnell's party will have become seriously disintegrated . . . and the Bishops, who in their hearts hate Parnell and don't care a scrap for Home Rule, having safely acquired control of Irish education will, according to my calculation, complete the rout. That is my policy, and I know that it is sound and good, and the only possible Tory policy. It hinges on acquiring the confidence and friendship of the Bishops.'[20] And in spite of the political eclipse of its champion, this was the policy actually pursued with a substantial measure of success by Lord Salisbury and his nephew, A. J. Balfour.

The weakness of this 'sound and good' policy lay in its basic assumption that clerical domination was the fundamental fact of Irish life. But even at the time of its greatest political influence, the power of the Church was by no means unlimited. The clergy were certainly prominent in their opposition to Parnell after the split, but their power on this occasion was mainly due to the policy pursued by Parnell himself in the past. The priests were largely responsible for the complete rout of the Parnellites at the General Election of 1892, but not even then did their political ascendancy go unchallenged even in Catholic Ireland. The West was ardently Catholic in its religion, but the position of the farmers in their small and uneconomic holdings was so unsatisfactory that this area remained a stronghold of Parnellism, and 'Parnellite was anti-priest'.[21]

It was, therefore, particularly important that it was from the West that the new political organisation of the Irish party drew the moderate dose of vitality which it ever possessed. In order to rally the dwarf tenants of the West in support of the existing system, from which they suffered more than any other class of peasants, the religious appeal was not strong enough. County Mayo, which had been the birthplace of the semi-revolutionary Land League, also was the cradle of William O'Brien's United Irish League (1898), which originated in the same spontaneous and irrepressible conflict between the small tenants and their exploiters; with its slogan of dividing grazing estates into peasant holdings it soon set the whole land-hungry West alight and spread to all other parts of the country.

As happens usually in such cases, the true beneficiaries of this development were not at all pleased with it: 'Redmond discouraged it; Healy stabbed it, the priests fought it at the election. It won "hands down". Redmond acquiesces, the Bishop of Raphoe, Father O'Hara and a few more of the abler priests are sailing with it in the hope of getting a hand on the tiller.'[22] This half-baked rehash of earlier political and agrarian movements was sufficiently strong to heal the breach between the two respectable sections of the parliamentary party which were afraid of being by-passed by the new movement, but it was not nearly powerful enough to re-create the political situation of the Land League period when the middle class, all sections of rural Ireland with the exception of the landlords, and the urban masses had been welded into a single political weapon. The clearest symptom of this difference was the position of the priests in the new organisation which soon became as strong as it had been in the Irish National League before. The local clergy selected its candidates for political office, packed its conventions and managed its finances. The latter point was, indeed, an important consideration in the reunion of Parnellites and anti-Parnellites, both of whom suffered badly from the fall in overseas donations to the disunited Irish cause.

A parallel and not less important event than the reconquest of the West for the official organisation was the growth of the Ancient Order of Hibernians (Board of Erin), which began in Protestant Ulster. The position of the Catholic minority in Belfast and industrial north-east Ulster had never been very happy, and after the first Home Rule crisis it grew rapidly worse. The British Tories and the Belfast employers played the Orange card so successfully that the defeat of Gladstone's first Home Rule Bill was followed in Belfast by fierce anti-Catholic riots which lasted for many weeks. As long as Balfour ruled Catholic Ireland with an iron hand, the Orangemen had little reason for dissatisfaction, but tension rose again to dangerous heights with the second Home Rule Bill (1893). Belfast Catholics never had much chance of getting any but the heaviest and lowest paid work, and the combination of religious persecution and economic discrimination bred lasting resentment amongst them which found expression in the growth of the Ancient Order of Hibernians as a Catholic secret society.

The A.O.H. seems to have originated in the old St. Patrick's Fraternal organisation which was in its turn an offshoot of the Ribbonmen of Daniel O'Connell's day. It travelled over the Atlantic to the United States, where it assumed its more famous name and became a secret society of great influence amongst the Irish workers. There was sore need for some such Catholic freemasonry amongst the uprooted Irishmen who badly wanted a centre of support in the wilderness of the American industrial towns and mining settlements. Not all the activities of the Order were of the friendly-society type, and the Molly Maguires in particular won for themselves a terrifying reputation as violent precursors of modern trade unionism. Like all groups of exiled Irishmen, the Ancient Order of Hibernians was virulently anti-British and in close union with the Fenian Clan-na-Gael, quite apart from its obvious usefulness in American domestic politics as a means of delivering the Irish vote in the interests of one or the other American party machine.

The Board of Erin was a branch of the American society which found its way back to the country whence it had originally come. It managed to obtain a strong foothold in Ulster for the same reason which had been responsible for its growth in the United States. It served a genuine need of the Ulster Catholics who were treated as pariahs by the dominant classes of north-east Ulster, just as the Irish immigrants used to be treated by their American masters, and even by their more fortunate fellow workmen. This split between Catholic and Protestant workmen may well have been the critical factor in the growth of bigoted Catholicism in Ulster. In Great Britain, where the common hostility of the workers as a whole towards their employers outweighed the antagonism between Irishmen and Englishmen, the Ancient Order of Hibernians made but little progress, while Irish Catholics played a big part in the development of an independent labour movement which was remarkably free from the taint of racial or religious intolerance.

After some hesitation the more forward-looking Catholic prelates, with Bishop O'Donnell of Raphoe at their head, woke up to the great promise of this new departure for the Roman Catholic Church which in Ulster, unlike the rest of Ireland, was not a triumphant monopolist but the militant defender of a hard-pressed minority. A society of professed Catholics which supplemented the spiritual control of the priesthood over their congregations by the social and political control of a secret order over its members was a real asset for the Church in its struggle for survival against powerful and ruthless enemies.

The rise of the A.O.H. was of much more than parochial importance for Irish politics. Home Rule had a much more emphatic meaning for the Ulster Catholics than for the rest of the Irish people which knew that in the long run its political claims were irresistible and which had been put in control of local government by a Unionist Government. The Ulster Catholics looked to Home Rule as the only chance of deliverance from their pariah position in the land of their birth, and the urgency of their Home Rule sentiments soon made the Ulster Catholics prominent in the United Irish League, with the Ancient Order of Hibernians as the framework for their conquest of the official nationalist organisation.

The United Irish League sprang from the elemental radicalism of the poverty-stricken West, but it was almost at once taken over by the forces which dominated Irish politics after the Parnell split —the rural middle class of 'strong' farmers and shopkeepers, together with their urban opposite numbers, tradesmen and small employers. When it had been in existence for a few years, the Wyndham Act of 1903 put Land Purchase on the map by its cash bonus for landlords willing to sell out, and thereby gave powerful support to the growth of a class of farmers with a stake in the country far out-weighing their traditional sense of grievance. The Wyndham Act owed not a little to the influence of William O'Brien, the founder of the United Irish League and by far the most interesting figure in respectable Irish politics after the death of Parnell. Although O'Brien later on forfeited his position in the Irish party through his undis-guised championship of the interests of the urban bourgeoisie, even where they clashed with those of the farmers, the United Irish League fulfilled its original purpose of extending the political influence of the middle class over the whole country.

The strong farmers of this generation, free from the gnawing anxiety of their previous state of existence as tenants, buying their holdings by easy instalments and supported in their money-making efforts by the co-operative movement inspired by Horace Plunkett and George Russell, had very little in common with the poverty-stricken peasants of the West. In its new social environment the United Irish League soon lost its original driving force and became a political machine, i.e. an organisation which no longer spon-taneously expressed the social purpose which had been responsible for its creation. The first symptom of this change was the assumption of political control by the clergy; its completion came with the conquest of the official organisation by the Ancient Order of Hibernians which occupied the political and organisational no-man's-land between the parliamentary and clerical leadership and the mass of the voters who were partly too much preoccupied with their material interests and partly too well regimented by their clergy to interfere with the process. Joe Devlin, the leader of the Order and at the same time the full-time secretary of the Belfast branch of the United Irish League, made good use of his double position and quickly put reliable Hibernians into the key positions of the nationalist party.

Perhaps the most spectacular political event brought about by the direct political intervention of the clergy was the rejection of the Irish Council Bill of 1907. This Bill was the first-fruit of Campbell-Bannerman's step-by-step policy, and the creation of an all-Irish administrative council, though far from revolutionary, might have been an important step forward in handing over Irish affairs to the Irish middle classes. It was fully supported by the official leadership but rejected out of hand at a Dublin Convention specially convoked for its approval—mainly because its educational provisions were unacceptable to the Church. The coalition between the priests and the A.O.H., which supplied the vocal popular support to the policy of the Church, forced Redmond to eat his own words, and to move the rejection of a measure in which he actually believed, thereby acknowledging his impotence as a leader in the face of the combined hostility of the Church and the party machine.

The clericalism of official Irish politics during the generation before the Easter Rebellion was thus the superficial expression of complicated social strains and stresses. It was the common denominator for the alliance of the rural middle class of the South—strong farmers, publicans, pawnbrokers, etc.—with the land-hungry West and the Catholic pariah population of industrial Ulster which gave it a political sounding-board. The growing success of Land Purchase transformed the social face of rural Ireland over a wide area, reduced the pressure of politically articulate social discontent, which to the Catholic Church had always been suspect as akin to conspiracy and rebellion, and enabled the hierarchy to give open expression to its social conservatism without losing its political influence over the masses. While the 'congested districts' of western Ireland remained a potential danger-spot from which new radical movements might erupt from time to time, rural Ireland as a whole was passing under the sway of the new middle class of small freeholders who were quite willing to take their chance with the existing order of things. Their tribute to England in the shape of the land annuities was not only much smaller than their rents had been but also limited in time, and their economy was still sufficiently tied to that of their British customers to give them a proper sense of the importance of a friendly settlement of their outstanding political claims.

The forces which in the end prevented such a commonplace and common-sense solution of the Irish question originated not in the countryside but in the towns—in the modern industrial centre of Belfast and in the backward and stagnant towns of Southern Ireland.

CHAPTER XXII

THE CLASH BETWEEN TOWN AND COUNTRY

THE rural character of the official Home Rule party expressed the most important facet of the Irish situation. But the countryside, even when its social weight is so overwhelming as it was in Southern Ireland during the early years of the century, generates political power only when it is affected by the pressure of serious material grievances. The series of Land Acts, which reduced the force of these grievances, lowered the energy behind the nationalist party, transformed it into a political machine and disposed its leaders to the acceptance of any kind of Home Rule which would have allowed them to maintain themselves in their position in charge of the political destinies of Ireland. The opposition to this development came from the towns. It was inevitably disunited, because its elements disagreed both on ends and means, but in the long run it became surprisingly effective, and took the leadership of Irish politics completely out of the hands of the Irish parliamentary party.

With the exception of a part of the urban middle class, none of the trends of opinion which stood for the interests of some section of the urban population of Southern Ireland managed to find a permanent place within the official nationalist party. This was inevitable in the case of the weak Unionist element which consisted mainly of a thin layer of town bourgeoisie with close English connections, although some of its leaders tried to come to a working agreement with the Irish party on the basis of a common policy of mutually advantageous economic measures. Sir Horace Plunkett, whose name is mainly connected with agricultural co-operation, belonged to this group. In his case, political and religious differences made success unlikely from the start, but none of these handicaps were present in the case of William O'Brien, the leader of a small group which later on had the support of T. M. Healy and which was known under the pathetic title of the *All for Ireland League*. The group was confined to Cork, the second largest city of Southern Ireland, which had a substantial volume of trade and a fairly numerous Protestant population, where O'Brien was always sure of a devoted following.

In his youth O'Brien had been the ultra-radical editor of Parnell's newspaper *United Ireland*, but at the time of the split he joined Parnell's enemies after some vacillation and was one of the most

prominent Nationalist leaders during the interregnum. In particular, it was he who founded the United Irish League which brought
the West again under the influence of the official movement and
thus prepared the way for its unification under Redmond's nominal
leadership. O'Brien was largely responsible for the success of the
Land Conference between progressive landlords and moderate
nationalists which paved the way for the Wyndham Act and he
had a prominent share in the Act itself which was accepted by the
Irish party at his instance and against the determined opposition
of a strong section of the party under John Dillon.

The social driving forces and the economic motives behind the
policy of reconciliation advocated by O'Brien were clearly revealed
in the Open Letter by John Shawe-Taylor which broached the plan
of a Land Conference for the settlement of the agrarian problem:
'For the last two hundred years the land war in this country has
raged fiercely and continuously, bearing in its train stagnation of
trade, paralysis of commercial business and enterprise, and producing
hatred and bitterness between the various sections and classes of
the community.'[23] It is reasonable to assume that the supporters
of the land purchase policy intended to reverse this state of things
and to promote a union of classes for the furtherance of trade and
enterprise. In O'Brien's opinion, the settlement of the land question
was the necessary condition of Ireland's growth as a modern nation,
and for the practical consummation of his ideal he looked to an
alliance between Belfast and Cork, the Protestant bourgeoisie of
the North and the Catholic middle class of the South. Tim Healy,
for many years O'Brien's chief rival and later on his independent
associate, was still more closely allied with the small clique which
constituted the capitalist element of Southern Ireland and which
rallied around William Martin Murphy, perhaps the most sinister
Irish figure of his generation. Healy acted as Murphy's intimate
adviser and, indeed, as his confidential agent in and out of Parliament, and for many years his brilliant pen and bitter tongue
lacerated the official Irish party which writhed under his mordant,
if frequently unfair, criticism.

The policy of putting Ireland's national cause under the tutelage
of the strong business class of Belfast and its weak Southern counterpart had, of course, no chance of acceptance by the Irish party,
where the influence of the Catholic Church and of the rural gombeen
men was paramount and which came with every passing year more
under the influence of the Ulster Catholics and Joe Devlin. This
political will-o'-the-wisp had, however, a strong attraction for other
and far more extremist political movements of the urban middle
and lower middle classes which in every other respect stood as far

to the left of the official nationalist party as the All for Ireland League stood to its right. The most important political representatives of the unprivileged town population were Sinn Fein, the Irish Revolutionary Brotherhood and the Irish Volunteers and, last but not least, the socialist movement.

Arthur Griffith, the founder of Sinn Fein, had been in his youth a supporter of Parnell and after the split a member of the Parnellite Organisation Committee. For a time he even belonged to the I.R.B., but this cannot be regarded as more than a passing stage in his development. Sinn Fein, as conceived by him, was a new departure in its methods but not more than a consistent continuation of the ideas which had been nearest to Parnell's own heart. Griffith, like his dead leader, was never a revolutionary separatist but an autonomist, but unlike Parnell he opposed parliamentary 'action' at Westminster and advocated the withdrawal of the Irish members from the House of Commons. This apparently illogical demand was not so much the fruit of Griffith's study of the conflict between Hungarian autonomists and the Austrian Royal-Imperial Government during the eighteen-sixties but an expression of the changes which had occurred in Irish politics since Parnell's fall from power. The Sinn Fein programme took shape in the period of troubles after the dissolution of Parnell's grand coalition of all Irish political forces under the leadership, and largely in the interests, of the middle class. When the nationalist party recovered from the disastrous consequences of the split, the interests of the urban middle class were inadequately represented in the new party with its predominantly agrarian and clerical character. Furthermore, in the democratic era which had already begun, the only hope of winning Home Rule at Westminster lay in an alliance between the Irish representatives and British democracy. In such an alliance the Irish middle class would have played a very subordinate part owing to its numerical weakness in an agricultural country. Griffith was entirely in the genuine Parnell tradition in his distrust of British radicals and particularly of the growing Labour movement. He displayed a sound political instinct in advocating a national strategy where the social and economic influence of the middle class could make itself far more effectively felt than in a system which gave full recognition to the numerical superiority of the country population. Although Griffith had to wait twenty years for the success of his patiently planned policy, he lived long enough to witness and manage its complete practical triumph.

Though Parnell, whose utterances were comparatively few and guarded, never developed a complete programme of future action, the economic interests which lay behind his political tactics were those of the urban middle class. He staked the whole success of his agitation on the issue of protective duties against British competition, he expected that under Home Rule Irishmen 'who had made money abroad would come home when things were settled and would start industries'[24]—although he regarded Ireland as the worst country to live in, and England as the best. Finally, Parnell plainly told Michael Davitt that, as head of an Irish Government, he would not tolerate such bodies as trades unions—and thereby showed how completely he carried on the political tradition of Daniel O'Connell. In all these matters, Griffith was the faithful executor of his dead leader's will and his policy was a perfectly straightforward pro-gramme for the economic rehabilitation of the Irish urban middle class on progressive capitalist lines. His programme was first put before an indifferent public in the early years of the century, and again confirmed at the 1917 Convention of Sinn Fein, when events at last promised to catch up with Griffith's plans. It proclaimed the protectionist ideal advocated by Parnell in an extreme form, involving protective duties on imports, an Irish consular service abroad, the creation of an Irish merchant marine, the development of native mineral resources and even the establishment of a Dublin Stock Exchange.[25]

With these aims in mind, Griffith naturally looked to Ulster with a special affection and regarded the scornful rejection of the ideal of Irish self-government by the Belfast business men as an aberration which did not in any way lessen the essential part which Ulster, the only industrial area of the country, would play in the capitalist Ireland of the future. In other words, his ideal Gaelic Manchester could not exist without the well-established Orange Manchester in the north-east. Far from being regarded as a milch cow for taxation in the interests of the poverty-stricken agrarian South, Ulster was in Griffith's eyes a precious plant to be nourished by protective duties at the expense of the rest of the country.

Sinn Fein's tenderness for industrial Ulster was balanced by its steady and instinctive hostility to the growing Labour movement which sprang from the same attitude towards the basic realities of Irish society. Not even Daniel O'Connell's vitriolic denunciations of trade unionism were more bitter and determined than Griffith's attacks on Jim Larkin and the strikers in the great Dublin struggles of 1913. It was one of the peculiar ironies of Irish history that Griffith, the evangelist of Irish capitalism, was during the greater part of his career equally rejected by the business men of Ulster and by the small-town traders and merchants of the South. Only the convulsion of Irish society which tore Ireland from Great Britain after the First World War gave him the opportunity to champion in practice the cause whose genuine advocate he had been for almost a generation.

The lack of success from which Sinn Fein suffered until the First World War is particularly curious in view of the fact that its programme was simply a catalogue of the measures required for putting the urban middle class of Southern Ireland economically on its feet. During the century after the Union all shoots of independent growth had been crushed out of this class by superior competition from the other side of the Channel, and the Irish bourgeoisie existed only as a collection of minor vested interests within the framework of British capitalism. The handful of undertakings which had survived or grown within this cage were so closely connected with the British market and dependent on British interests that their owners were almost to a man staunch Unionists; the rest made no claim to independent economic existence and found their niche in society as middlemen between British (or Ulster) manufacturers and the agrarian consumers.

Sinn Fein was thus the political champion of a class which in Southern Ireland was little more than a memory and a promise (or a threat). However moderate and respectable in its ultimate aims, its main appeal was to social groups which shared these aims without sharing the inhibitions of the actually existing Irish middle class, because the latter was completely identified with a social order which had stunted not only its growth but even its ambitions. Sinn Fein found its adherents mainly amongst the Irish intelligentsia, and particularly amongst the school teachers, who played a similar part in Ireland as in France, and partly for the same reasons. At the same time Sinn Fein rendered an invaluable, though for the time being unrewarded, service to the middle class by connecting it with the extreme wing of the nationalist movement which before the First World War was shunned by all respectable people, but which was to hold the fate of the Irish nation in its hands before that war had come to an end.

The traditional representatives of this extreme nationalist movement were the men of the Irish Revolutionary Brotherhood, the linear descendants of the Fenians of 1867. Unlike Arthur Griffith and Sinn Fein, the Fenians did not stand in the same line of unbroken succession from Parnell. They had formed the extreme wing of the Land League whose downfall made Parnell's political fortune and they had watched with grudging admiration Parnell's later efforts to squeeze Home Rule out of Tories and Liberals. They lent him every assistance in their power when he fought his last desperate fight with English Liberals and Irish prelates: at the Kilkenny election they raised the town mob in his support without being able to avert defeat, and Dublin, the citadel of Fenian influence, remained stubbornly loyal to the baffled leader and later on to his memory.

After Parnell's fall and death the extremists found themselves completely cut off from any influence on the legal political organisation. (The destruction of their influence was, indeed, one of the aims of Parnell's more calculating opponents.) When the I.R.B. began to recover from the stunning blow of this experience, particularly after Tom Clarke's return from penal servitude and exile, it had to free itself from the relics of defeat by a split within its own ranks.[26] The new leadership resolutely set itself the apparently hopeless task of organising a secretly drilled army, or at least the framework of a legal military organisation. These efforts soon achieved success beyond the wildest dreams of their promoters when the growth of the Ulster Volunteers led to a powerful reaction among the nationalists in favour of answering the threat of force by similar methods.

However, not even the purged I.R.B. was a homogeneous group, although its internal differences remained for some time hidden beneath the surface. It was a miniature model of those sections of the unprivileged classes which were left outside the official nationalist party organisation. Their strength was greatest in the towns, particularly in Dublin. Journalists like Bulmer Hobson, solicitors' clerks and junior civil servants like Austin Stack and Michael Collins, small business men like Cathal Brugha and Tom Clarke, with a sprinkling of workers, like the printer MacKee. In the provinces the Fenians could count on the sympathy of most Sinn Feiners, particularly among the school teachers, and their appeal extended to many small tenants, farmers' sons and labourers whose loyalty to the Irish party was largely based on their subjection to clerical discipline.

The right wing of the I.R.B. was in many respects almost indistinguishable from the Sinn Feiners under Griffith, while its left wing approached the position of the militant labour movement. The right wing was represented by Bulmer Hobson, the editor of the separatist *Irish Freedom*, while the left was led by Thomas J. Clarke and, later on, by Patrick Pearse, the first 'President of the Irish Republic'. Bulmer Hobson and his friends did not share Griffith's pious hope of achieving the purpose of Sinn Fein by passive resistance and withdrawal from the House of Commons, but they accepted that purpose as their own. Tom Clarke and Patrick Pearse gravitated more and more into the opposite social direction, towards the nationalist socialism of James Connolly. Although all the Republicans were more sympathetic to the aspirations of the working class than Griffith's Sinn Fein, they were generally suspicious of a movement which did not lend itself to their technique of secret permeation and which had even its own military formation, on however small a scale, and thereby actually anticipated the deeply laid plans of the I.R.B. leaders. But the more resolute heads amongst the Fenians who took their preparations for armed rebellion seriously, soon rediscovered the truth which had been found half a century previously by John O'Leary and his fellow Fenians, and earlier still by their secular patron saint Wolfe Tone, that the men of no property were the only reliable friends and allies on whom genuine revolutionists were able to count.

Unlike Griffith's Sinn Fein, which tried to fight the Irish party in the traditional manner of rival candidatures and which almost perished from its inevitable defeat, the I.R.B. assumed the role of an independent political force with the creation of the Irish Volunteers, the nationalist answer to the Ulster Volunteers. The Irish Volunteers must be regarded as the most important 'open' movement under the control of a secret society which has appeared in Irish history. Though ineffective as a vote-getting machine, they successfully challenged the monopoly of political organisation claimed by the Irish party.

The growth of the new movement was most rapid among the Ulster Catholics, and Ulstermen like the Catholic Professor MacNeill and the Protestant Sir Roger Casement, played a prominent part in it. The I.R.B. thus entered into direct competition with the Ancient Order of Hibernians in its strongest but most vulnerable position. The fortunes of the third Home Rule Bill in the House of Commons with the almost certain prospect of—temporary or permanent—exclusion of Ulster from the scope of Home Rule Ireland weakened the power of the A.O.H. in its Ulster stronghold and made it particularly sensitive to rivalry for the allegiance of the Ulster Catholics. On the other hand, the growth of the Protestant Ulster Volunteers provided ideal conditions for the creation of a counter-movement on the part of the directly threatened Ulster Catholics, and the I.R.B. took full advantage of this opportunity.

It was Joseph Devlin, the 'boss' of the Hibernians and the United Irish League, who first gave the alarm to Redmond early in 1914, only a few months after the establishment of the Irish Volunteers.[27] Redmond appreciated the potential threat of the new development to his party and took steps to neutralise it, first by negotiations with the titular heads of the Volunteers, Professor MacNeill and Colonel Moore, and soon afterwards by an ultimatum which confronted the Volunteer leaders with the choice between surrender to the Irish party or a split. On this occasion the differences within the Republican camp became apparent for the first time. Only nine out of the original twenty-five committee members (amongst them seven I.R.B. men[28]) voted against submission to Redmond's ultimatum, and for a few months the Volunteers were subordinated to the official leadership, very much to the disgust of the American Fenians under John Devoy who angrily opposed the surrender. However, Redmond's support of recruiting for the British army after the outbreak of war in 1914 rallied even the right wing of the Republicans against his leadership and made the split in the Volunteer ranks inevitable. The passive majority followed the party machine and became known as National Volunteers, while the active minority retained the original title, although their popular name was generally that of Sinn Fein Volunteers.

The socialist labour movement in Ireland was no less a child of the national struggle against England than of the social struggle for tolerable living conditions. If the Sinn Fein programme was a more self-conscious and articulate version of 'Parnellism', Connolly's ideal of a socialist Irish republic was an up-to-date form of the aims for which Michael Davitt had striven and suffered. Amongst the fragments of the all-Irish coalition, which came to an end with Parnell's downfall, the Irish working class was the first to achieve independent political consciousness in the work of James Connolly (1870–1916). When Connolly founded the Irish Socialist Republican party in 1896, the I.R.B. was moribund and Sinn Fein had not been heard of. From its inception, it bore witness to its nationalist inspiration by taking a prominent part in some of the most spectacular anti-English demonstrations of the time, the 'Jubilee Protest' of 1897 and the pro-Boer meetings during the South African War. But as a socialist party the little group suffered from inability to contact and move the working class, and in 1903 Connolly temporarily abandoned the struggle in Ireland and emigrated to the United States in search of a livelihood.

An industrial working class in the modern sense of the term existed in Ireland only in the Belfast industrial area and, perhaps, in and around Londonderry. In the towns of the South, where modern industry had never taken root, the working class consisted of a small number of old-fashioned craftsmen and a majority of unskilled hands engaged on the simple work of handling imports and exports on their way from and to the ports. This class was far from unimportant in Belfast with its modern port, but there it was outnumbered by shipyard workers and mill hands. In Dublin, Cork and Limerick, on the other hand, transport workers constituted the main strength of the urban working class. Like the unskilled dock labourers in British ports (who were, indeed, as often as not Irish immigrants or their descendants), the Irish transport workers stood outside the old craft unions and were completely at the mercy of their employers. Thus they were the natural raw material for the architects of the new unionism which began with the dockers' and gas-workers' strikes in London in the late eighteen-eighties, and soon afterwards led to the formation of the Liverpool dockers' union under the leadership of James Sexton. It was as an organiser of this union, which by that time had been sobered into respectability by the successful creation of a stable trade union organisation, that Jim Larkin began his stormy career in Ireland.

Larkin's Irish trade unionism, like Horace Plunkett's much more respectable agricultural co-operation societies, was nurtured in the British labour movement to which both owed a considerable debt of gratitude. At least in Larkin's case this debt remained unpaid, not only owing to Larkin's tempestuous personal hatreds but mainly because trade unionism on Irish soil differed in some important respects from its British prototype. The organisation of the unskilled masses in Great Britain took place within a comparatively stable social framework; it was accompanied by strong growing pains, but its immediate effect was an invigoration of the labour movement and the preparation for a politically independent and self-reliant Labour Party. Although spiritually akin to the syndicalist tendencies which about the same time affected the working classes of Europe and America, the new unionism was kept within fairly narrow social and political limits. The rebellious instincts of the masses were steadily tamed until they had become subordinated to a complicated balance of social forces in which they were allowed to play only a limited part. The *method* by which this transformation was accomplished consisted, in the main, in the amalgamation of the small independent and reasonably democratic unions into large trade union 'empires' with intricate administrative arrangements under whole-time officials who controlled their members rather than they led them and who were in their turn controlled by genuine bosses like James Sexton and his successors in the Transport and General Workers' Union.

The most complete and considered criticism of the new shape and content of British trade unionism at the eve of the First World War came from an Irish socialist. The material basis of the consolidation of British unionism into a powerful vested interest was the steady, though by no means automatic, improvement in the living standards of the masses as a result of union activity which was grudgingly conceded by the employers as a lesser evil than a permanent state of industrial war which would have hurt their interests much more deeply. Conditions in Ireland were very different, and from this vantage-point James Connolly, the strongest and most thorough-going advocate of revolutionary socialism in the British Isles, observed and criticised these crucial changes in the structure and the spirit of the labour movement. Connolly warned the workers that 'the most theoretically perfect organisation may, because of its very perfection and vastness, be of the greatest possible danger to the revolutionary movement, if it tends, or is used, to repress and curb the fighting spirit of comradeship in the rank and file'. He pointed out to them that 'the amalgamations and federations are being carried out in the main by officials absolutely destitute of the revolutionary spirit, and that as a consequence the methods of what should be militant organisations having the broad working-class outlook are conceived and enforced in the temper and spirit of the sectionalism those organisations were meant to destroy. Into the new bottles of industrial organisation is being poured the old, cold wine of Craft Unionism. . . .'[29]

On the surface, the Irish Labour movement at the time of Larkin's first campaign differed very little from its British opposite number before the rise of the new unionism. Up to 1893, Irish trade unions were simply a very modest part of the British Trade Union Congress, but in 1894 they began to hold their own Irish Trades Congress, elected their own Parliamentary Committee and practically withdrew from their never very intimate co-operation with the British organisation which always regarded them as poor and not very creditable relations. 'Our English and Scottish friends', explained the President of the second Irish Trades Congress (Cork, 1895) in justification of the new departure, '. . . cannot be expected to understand the wants of a community largely agricultural, assisting in reviving the languishing manufactures of Ireland.'[30] Such an attitude was, of course, quite inappropriate when applied to industrial Ulster, but only too natural for the rest of the country.

The withdrawal of the Irish unions from the British Trade Union Congress indicated strong centrifugal tendencies and a preponderance of Southerners over Ulstermen in the movement. This is the more remarkable as one of the strongest elements in Irish unionism consisted of the Irish branches of 'amalgamated' unions, like those of engineers, joiners and carpenters, or railwaymen with members throughout the British Isles and headquarters in Great Britain. These 'international' unions were naturally strongest in Belfast, and the establishment of an independent Irish Trades Congress seems to have reflected a certain shift in the centre of gravity of organised Irish labour from Ulster to the South. This underlying trend affected the actions and resolutions of the new

15

body only very little during the first ten or fifteen years of its existence. It remained highly respectable, moderate and anti-socialistic and, as a result of its domination by the skilled crafts, very exclusive, representing only 40,000–50,000 workers.[31] Its main asset was the co-operation between Ulstermen and Southerners, although the inevitable intrusion of political topics caused a good deal of internal friction. In particular, the Unionist Ulstermen wanted Congress to affiliate with the quickly growing British Labour party, while a strong section among the Southern delegates tried to subordinate the trade union movement to the Irish nationalist party.

Conditions changed with the appearance of the new unionism on Irish soil. In 1907 Larkin started his conquest of Ireland, and the changes wrought by the new movement deeply affected the composition and policy of the Irish trade union organisation. When Larkin began his attempt to organise the Irish dockers for the National Union of Dock Labourers, he naturally chose Belfast as his first battle-field. Belfast was the heart of industrial Ireland and the main source of strength of the Irish branches of other 'amalgamated' unions. Larkin's activities began with the great Belfast strike of 1907 which was a landmark in British as well as in Irish labour history. The first part of the strike ended with a victory for the coal carters and was made memorable by the triumphant defeat of an all too obvious attempt by the employers to exploit the religious bigotry of the workers, as well as by a successful police strike caused by the dismissal of a police constable for refusing to protect a blackleg carter. The next round in the struggle, however, was less successful for the men and ominous in its general implications. It consisted in a strike of the Belfast dockers which lasted six weeks until it was broken off by James Sexton, the national secretary of the Dockers' Union, who acted over the head of his agent Larkin because the conflict cost the parent union £1,000 a week in strike pay.[32]

Partly as a result of this heavy blow, which was followed by his expulsion from the union, Larkin turned south, founded the Irish Transport Workers' Union and began to organise the dockers, carters and general workers in Dublin, Cork, Wexford and other towns. After an initial setback suffered by the employers as a result of Larkin's shock tactics, which gained success for the coal carters in Belfast and Dublin, the masters recovered and reacted with vicious vigour to this new threat to their position. Their insistence on the unlimited subservience of their 'hands' and their stubborn refusal to compromise seemed to be fully justified by the immediate results of their policy. By indiscriminate lock-outs in answer to strikes, or even to the simple accession of their workers to Larkin's union, they broke the resistance of the men at Cork, and in the long-drawn-out struggle in Dublin (1913) they all but destroyed the Irish Transport Workers' Union.

The history of this union is, perhaps, the best illustration of the difference between Irish and English labour conditions. In Great Britain, the steady and highly successful work of organising the unskilled masses at first gave the leaders of the new unions only a modest place amongst the representatives of the skilled crafts. Only after their organisations had lost their original impetus and had become solid trade union machines with huge membership figures, did they achieve prominence in the counsels of British trade unionism. In Ireland, the progress of Larkin's new union was at first disappointingly slow: in 1910 the membership of the Irish Transport and General Workers' Union amounted to only 3,000,[33] and at the time of the Easter Rebellion in 1916 it had only risen to 5,000.[34] But with every lost strike the prestige of the union leaders and their influence over the staid Irish Trades Congress seemed to increase. In spite of the determined resistance of the British Dockers' Union, the Dundalk Congress (1910) accepted the affiliation of the new organisation which soon permeated the whole Irish labour movement with its influence, until after (and in consequence of) the disastrous Dublin strike of 1913 Larkin was chosen President of the next Irish Trade Union Congress.

This curious result was, of course, mainly due to general conditions, but it could hardly have been achieved without the remarkable partnership of Larkin and Connolly. James Larkin combined the qualities of a fearless and highly effective strike leader and agitator with an intense egotism which made him impatient of criticism and difficult to deal with. But his lack of business habits, which infuriated British trade unionists like James Sexton, and his lack of balance, which repelled well-meaning supporters like Captain Jack White, the eccentric founder of the Citizen Army, did not prevent him from recalling James Connolly to Ireland, in order to endow the young movement with all the qualities in which Larkin himself was patently lacking. It was Connolly who undertook the forlorn hope of weaning the workers of Belfast from their allegiance to their Protestant employers, and who, though unsuccessful in his immediate purpose, steadily permeated the whole union with the sense of his mission. It was mainly through his influence that the Irish Trades Congress, in the past a timid and colourless imitator of its British model, came out in full support of the principles of industrial unionism and later on transformed itself into the Irish Labour party.

This development, while remarkable from many points of view, had one inevitable but none the less fateful result: it strained the all-Irish alliance within the labour movement beyond breaking-point. The parting of the ways between the Protestant craftsmen of Belfast unionism and the small group of craft unionists in the South may or may not have been inevitable during the Home Rule crisis; but the conquest of Irish unionism by the unskilled and rebellious transport workers under Larkin and Connolly made the break inevitable by weakening the bond of palpable interests common to both groups and increasing the causes of political friction. The failure of the new unionism and, still more, of Irish socialism to conquer Ulster and to detach the workers of Belfast and Derry from the unionist leading-strings, had a critical influence on the Irish labour movement and on Irish history as a whole.

The urban working class of the South was in a hopeless minority. Its struggle against intolerable living conditions and industrial slavery took place on the fringe of Irish society, while the very backwardness of the country increased the bitterness and violence of the conflict. In alliance with the potentially much stronger working class of Ulster, it might have concentrated on social and economic aims within the existing framework, until the needs of its own independent movement would have driven it beyond the boundaries of the social and political system. In the absence of such an alliance, they had to look for other allies and partly even for other ideals. They found both, at least for a time, in a junction between the socialists in quest of social justice and the rebels in pursuit of national liberty which led straight to the Easter Rising.

CHAPTER XXIII

THE RED HAND OF ULSTER

WITHOUT any effort on its part, Protestant Ulster gained and kept a powerful hold on the affections of all the urban movements in the South, from William O'Brien's All for Ireland League to Connolly's Socialist Republican Party. The cause of this strange, and totally one-sided attraction was the fact that in widely different ways Ulster, in all its drab and forbidding reality, was indispensable to the town population of the South as an ally or as an ideal.

For the Unionists in the rest of Ireland, numerically a hopeless minority and socially the impotent remnant of once omnipotent classes, Ulster's determined resistance to Home Rule meant, above all, the torpedoing of any Home Rule settlement at all. For the Southern bourgeoisie, on the other hand, the proud strength of Ulster big business was perhaps the most promising feature of Irish Home Rule: far from looking to Ulster for the prevention of Home Rule, the urban middle class of the South regarded Ulster's participation in Home Rule in Ireland as essential, for it would have permitted the Southern middle-class elements, in spite of their intrinsic weakness and isolation, to establish themselves firmly in the saddle as auxiliaries of their cousins in the North.

On the opposite end of the social scale the strategic importance of industrial Ulster was just as clearly realised. In a backward agrarian country like Southern Ireland, the socialist labour movement had a good chance of making its influence felt in the towns, once it evolved the proper technique for the organisation of the downtrodden labourers, but no hope of achieving independent political leadership. Only an alliance between the rebellious and determined slum-dwellers of the southern towns and the skilled artisans of industrial Ulster might give the labour movement a real chance of victory, not through its own numerical strength but through its social importance and its superior political strategy.

The tenderness both of the extreme urban Right and Left for Ulster was, therefore, based on very real social and political interests; the no less persistent affection of Sinn Fein and of the non-socialist Republicans for the North was less solidly based. For Arthur Griffith, Ulster was the embodiment of the ideal to which his own policy aspired to lead the backward South—a modern industrial community on Irish soil. For the Irish Revolutionary Brotherhood, Ulster was at all times an essential part of the future Irish Republic,

while after the establishment of the Ulster Volunteers it became
a reincarnation of the proud and self-reliant Irish patriots of 1782,
who forced Grattan's Constitution on England at the point of the
cannon. Both Sinn Fein and the I.R.B. were utterly, and almost
ridiculously, wrong in their judgment. Griffith's inability to understand the aversion of the Ulster business men towards his policy
of protection which was designed to benefit the industrial community at the expense of the rest of the people was matched by
Patrick Pearse's welcome to the Ulster Volunteer movement because
it put an end to the myth of Ulster's loyalty to Great Britain.

In contrast to these minority groups, the official Irish Party always
approached Unionist Ulster with well-deserved hostility and ill-
judged contempt. A party dominated by the Catholic Church and
by the Ancient Order of Hibernians was bound to oppose the
bigoted and exclusive Protestantism of the North. The party of the
Southern tenantfarmers was no less naturally opposed to the political
standard-bearers of the Irish landlords. Sir Edward Carson, in later
years the leader of Ulster, quarrelled even with the Tory party
when its defence of Irish landlord interests was at times tempered
by a sense of wider realities. For the first time in his career he
opposed his patron A. J. Balfour in connection with the Land
Purchase Act of 1896, which was not so favourable to the landlords
as he had wished. 'Carson saw in the landlords a small and faithful
garrison of Unionists, persistent in their loyalty to Great Britain . . .
who were now being despoiled by those upon whom they had relied
as their friends.'[35]

The hostility of the official Irish leaders towards 'loyal' Ulster
was, therefore, only natural and inevitable. Their great mistake,
however, was the uncritical identification of Ulster with the Southern
landlords, whom they had learnt to despise, and their failure to
understand the firm social basis of Unionism in the four north-
east Ulster counties. Their self-confident, or at least self-
comforting, denunciation of the Ulster 'bluff' revealed the machine
character of the official party: it completely ignored the hard fact
of industrial Ulster's special material interests, while it did nothing
to allay Ulster's religious scruples and sectarian prejudices.

As long as rural Ireland had been powerless to protest against
its forcible incorporation into the British system, there had been
no Ulster problem. Although the Tories always regarded Protestant
Ulster as their political stronghold, the Liberals maintained a
respectable following in the province until Gladstone's policy of
conciliation towards Catholic Ireland. From 1886 onwards, Ulster
was politically divided between the Unionists in undisputed control
of the Protestant majority areas, and the Irish Nationalists, whose

main support came from the Catholic parts of the province and from the Catholic proletariat of the industrial towns, chiefly Belfast and Derry. The resurrection of the Orange Order during the struggle against Gladstone's first Home Rule Bill was a symbol of the new era which was inaugurated shortly after the defeat of the measure by a series of anti-Catholic riots in Belfast.

In colonial Ireland, which suffered from the cumulative pressure of economic exploitation and national oppression, the Ulster business class represented the exception which proves the rule. In industrial Ulster, the forecasts of the optimistic supporters of the Union had come to life. Although the Union swept away the rudiments of industries which might have competed with those of the mother country, it enabled the Ulster business interests to participate in the triumphal progress of British industry as a sturdy, if modest, auxiliary. At first mainly in the textile industries, later on as an integral part of the shipbuilding and manufacturing empire of north-west England and south-west Scotland, the Belfast area became one of the major industrial centres of the United Kingdom; even Londonderry established itself as the home of a secondary industry, the manufacture of shirts, which used the large reserves of cheap labour in its *hinterland* as the foundation of an industry which was a byword for reckless exploitation.

The integration of industrial Ulster into the system of British trade and industry was as complete as was the economic decay of the Southern Irish towns, with the partial exception of Dublin and Cork. The interests of the Ulster middle class completely fused with those of the British business classes of which it formed an integral part. The opposition of this influential group to Home Rule was from the start more resolute than that of the British middle class as a whole. For the Unionist followers of Joseph Chamberlain in Great Britain, Irish Home Rule, with the possibility of anti-British protective duties in the background, would have been highly objectionable in principle because it clashed with the wider conception of economic policy which soon afterwards became connected with the policy of Empire Free Trade and protection against foreign competition. (For the Gladstonian Liberals the problem of protection in Ireland simply did not arise, for the maintenance of free trade between the two countries was for them one of the fundamental conditions of a Home Rule settlement.) In practice, the adverse economic effects of Home Rule, even in conjunction with anti-British duties, would probably have been very small for Great Britain.

Things were very different for the Ulster business men: the possibility of economic barriers between Ireland and the rest of the world, and particularly between Ireland and Great Britain, was a mortal threat to their material interests. Belfast was not in any sense, as was frequently stated, the 'industrial capital of Ireland', and its economy did not form a genuine part of that of the country in which it was situated. Its credit was governed by the City of London, its raw materials came from the same sources and its output was sold in the same markets as that of other British manufacturing centres, perhaps with a still greater reliance on overseas trade. For this reason, Ulster business men backed Chamberlain's tariff reform policy with great enthusiasm, to the confusion of the Sinn Fein advocates of protective tariffs who found it difficult to understand that Ulster preferred the Englishman Chamberlain's policy to their own carefully laid plans for the furtherance of Irish industries. The explanation of this apparent paradox was very simple. Chamberlain wanted to use Britain's dominant position as the world's biggest importer as a lever for prizing or keeping all doors open for British exports in which Ulster was vitally interested. To exchange their share in British trade for a prospective monopoly of the home trade of an impoverished agrarian island must have appeared as inconceivable madness to the Ulster business men. It would have been the sale of their proud birthright for the mere promise of a mess of very inferior pottage, and every attempt to force such a policy on them was bound to be resisted tooth and nail.

At the same time a new financial danger seemed to threaten Ulster with the adoption of Home Rule. At the time of the third Home Rule Bill, Ireland's prospective Budget showed a deficit of more than two million pounds a year. Even without Home Rule, Ulster claimed to be paying much more than its fair share of taxation, and however doubtful the validity of such a claim, it was pressed home with considerable emphasis. Under a Home Rule régime, and with a permanent agrarian majority ranged against the industrial interests, would not Protestant Ulster have to pay excessive taxes in the interests of the backward Catholic provinces? 'If you want Ulster,' Sir Edward Carson challenged the Home Rulers, 'go and take her, or go and win her. You never wanted her affections. You wanted her taxes.'[36]

Between the first Home Rule Bill of 1886 and the third Home Rule Bill of 1912 the centre of opposition, which had lain at first in the House of Lords and the British middle class, thus shifted to Ulster. In 1912, Ulster was no longer simply the Orange card to be played or withheld at will by the English Tories according to the state of the game. While the English forces of opposition to Home Rule lost a good deal of their strength and cohesion, the opposition in Ulster hardened with every passing year. The remnants of the Unionist side in the rest of Ireland saw themselves condemned to permanent impotence under Home Rule, and their only hope was its defeat through the victory of Ulster. In their opinion, and not only in theirs, Ulster's resistance was a complete guarantee against Home Rule anywhere in Ireland, for the rest of the country would never be able to pay its way without the taxable resources of Ulster. 'If Ulster succeeds,' Carson assured the Southern Unionists, 'Home Rule is dead. Home Rule is impossible for Ireland without Belfast and the surrounding part as a portion of the scheme.'[37]

All the forces most intimately concerned in preventing the emancipation of the Irish people from English rule met in Ulster which thus became the cockpit of the final Home Rule crisis. Belfast big business was the backbone of the resistance movement, because it regarded Home Rule as a mortal threat to its monopoly of power and even to its economic survival. But the business men of Northern Ireland, however respectable their material resources and however steadfast their resolution, were a mere handful of people. In the old oligarchic days their numerical inferiority need not have daunted them, but in 1911 democracy had sufficiently advanced in Great Britain and Ireland to make mass support for their policy imperative. In a life-and-death struggle against the powerful alliance of Irish Nationalists and British Liberals, Ulster needed not only the money of a few rich subscribers and the support of the British Tories, but also the unflinching devotion of the masses. For popular support going to the length of armed resistance to the law of the land, the Ulster leaders had to look to their own workmen and to the tenant farmers.

The adherence of the Protestant farmers to the Unionist policy of the Belfast leaders was given almost without question. The Protestant tenants, however harsh their treatment by modern standards, had always been in a privileged position compared with the mass of the Southern peasants. This difference, and particularly their violent hostility to the neighbouring Catholic peasants in South Ulster, had made them reliable supporters of the ruling powers. Only during the second half of the nineteenth century, when the increase in rents threatened to upset the effects of the 'Ulster custom', had there been any danger of a political revolt of the Protestant tenants. With the alleviation of their economic grievances, the Ulster farmers became resolutely hostile towards the nationalist movement which by then had become mainly concerned with Home Rule and dominated by the Catholic Church. In particular, the farmers of the border counties, like the Ulster business men, regarded Home Rule much more as a social than as a purely political matter: the distribution of Catholic and Protestant holdings was often more vertical than horizontal, Catholics cultivating the poor hilly land and Protestants occupying the more fertile plains. In these conditions, any radical political change involved the danger and, indeed, the likelihood of social revolution, and resistance to Home Rule thus became an article of faith for the Protestant farmers.

The Protestant workers of industrial Ulster had their full measure of the hardships and grievances common to the industrial working class of Great Britain. In addition, miserably paid out-work was common in the textile industries where a living wage was unknown and earnings were only just enough to enable the whole family to make ends meet. Strikes, even in the shipyards which were Belfast's pride, were by no means uncommon, and trade unionism made slow but steady progress. In 1899, Belfast contained fully one-half of the total number of Irish trade unionists, and the Belfast Trades Council spoke for 19,000 organised workers. But even the genuine working-class movement of Belfast reflected the close connection between industrial Ulster and Great Britain: more than half the trade unionists of Belfast, amongst them 'shipwrights and most of the metal trades, workers in wood and leather, printers, tailors and others had joined cross-channel unions'[38] with their headquarters in Great Britain. Of the rest, 5,000 belonged to the linen trade which lived by export. The organic union between the working class of Ulster and Great Britain was not confined to common interests and ideals but was to a large extent a matter of physical identity: to all intents and purposes, Belfast forms one corner of an industrial triangle based on Lancashire in England and Lanarkshire in Scotland, and an unceasing ebb and flow of workers moving to and from Belfast, the Mersey and the Clyde, was the necessary result of this set-up. The economic interests of the shipyard engineers and linen workers of Belfast were naturally identified with the system of which they formed a part, though not with the distribution of power and material benefits within the system.

Ireland's colonial heritage was not without effects on the thinking and the attitude of the Protestant working class of Ulster. Although they were not better treated by their masters than the Protestant workers of Great Britain by theirs, Ulster Protestant workers were in a privileged position compared with their Catholic competitors. This modest share in the fruits of colonial conquest was, perhaps, the strongest tie between them and their masters. With few exceptions, the Protestants supplied industrial Ulster with its skilled workers, while the Catholics had often to be satisfied with jobs for which no Protestant applicants could be found. The fact of an aristocracy of labour which dominated British trade union life before the rise of the New Unionism, became in Ulster part and parcel of the conflict between the 'ascendancy class' and the forces of nationalism. The conflict between Protestants and Catholics, like that between white and coloured workers in the United States, acted as a brake on the growth of a social consciousness and rallied the privileged section of the workers to the side of their employers. The anti-Catholic riots which disgraced Belfast's civic life were, in the main, the work of men belonging to the same social class as their victims, though to its higher strata. The grim outbreak which followed the rejection of the first Home Rule Bill in 1886 started with a quarrel between the Protestant shipwrights of Harland and Wolff and Catholic navvies, who naturally got the worst of it.[39] Whenever the Liberal party was in power, the tension between Protestants and Catholics increased, and the danger of Home Rule with its implied threat to the *status quo* was invariably answered by ugly scenes of mob violence and religious persecution.

The rise of the Ancient Order of Hibernians, though probably an inevitable reaction by the Catholic pariah population to their intolerable position, far from improving matters only added fuel to the flames of sectarian conflict. For a large section of the downtrodden Catholics the existence of this secret society may have been a source of hope and strength in an almost desperate situation, and the growing influence of the Order on the nationalist organisation gave them the full backing of the Irish party which, they fondly hoped, was soon to supply the legitimate Government of Ireland. At the same time, the irritant of a secret society run on strictly Roman Catholic lines only confirmed the worst sectarian prejudices of the Ulster Protestants, while the identification of Home Rule with Rome Rule made it easy for the Ulster leaders to stamp out the remnants of sympathy for nationalist aspirations amongst their Protestant workmen.

In their endeavour to keep the allegiance of the Protestant masses, the Ulster business men had no need to be afraid of Devlin and Redmond. Their real antagonists were Larkin and Connolly, who professed the same religious faith as the official Nationalist leaders, but who preached a very different gospel. The success of their propaganda of militant trade unionism and socialism would have undermined the very foundation on which the Ulster leaders had built. The defection of its mass support through Connolly's socialist propaganda, and Larkin's appeal to the common social and economic interests of Protestant and Catholic workers, who in the past had been separated by petty privileges and discrimination under the influence of sectarian prejudices, would have been an irreparable loss for the business class of Northern Ireland. How, then, did it escape this danger and why did Larkin's challenge fail?

The propaganda of the New Unionism was the only serious challenge to the rule of the Belfast oligarchy. It might well have become the decisive quantity in the political equation, if it had been given sufficient time to fight the ingrained prejudices of centuries. But this was not to be. The first check to its progress came, interestingly enough, from Larkin's own union, the National Union of Dock Labourers, which broke the Belfast strike of 1907 over Larkin's head because it did not want to shoulder the cost of the dispute. This blow might have frightened off any man less self-willed and contemptuous of opposition than James Larkin, but even for him it was a grave matter, and the demoralisation caused by this action was by no means healed by Larkin's desperate, though ultimately successful, venture in founding a breakaway organisation in the Irish Transport Workers' Union. But the break with the British parent organisation, which may have been a recommendation for the new Union amongst many Southern workers, gravely affected its growth in Belfast, where the only permanent foothold gained by the new Union was amongst the Catholic workers in the deep-sea docks, while Connolly's devoted efforts among the Protestant cross-channel dockers remained fruitless.

It is a matter for speculation how far this handicap could have been overcome in the course of time. But time was of the essence of the matter, and time was running out. Larkin's Irish Transport Workers' Union had barely found its feet, Connolly had only just taken up his post as its Belfast organiser, when Ulster was convulsed by the Home Rule struggle of 1911–14. But it was a striking recognition of the reality of this threat to the conception of a united Unionist Ulster that Sir Edward Carson and J. M. Andrews, the actual and one of the future leaders of Northern Ireland, founded in April 1914 an Ulster Unionist Labour Association for the purpose of countering the dangerous spread of 'disloyal' thoughts amongst the workers.

Sure of the political support of their fellow-Protestants of all classes and of the British Tories, the Belfast business men were ready to stake everything on the success of their resistance to the Liberal Government and the Irish Nationalists. They were still sufficiently imbued with the garrison spirit of a ruling colonial minority in the midst of a subject population to take personally the lead in the organisation of resistance, instead of directing the movement of their political puppets from the background. The thousand Ulster business men who presented an address of protest to the great Craigavon demonstration in September 1911 were resolved to put up more than a mere paper resistance to the threatening economic disaster of their separation from Great Britain. In the practical running of the Ulster Volunteers the numerous Irish officers in British service, most of whom were connected with the landowning squirearchy, played an important part as commanders and staff officers. But the local officers 'were mostly business men with much to do in the daytime but who, nevertheless, invariably put in many extra hours of work in carrying out their volunteer duties';[40] and the eight or ten most hard-bitten Carsonite leaders whom Asquith met on his Irish visit after the Rising in 1916 were, as a matter of course, all of them big employers of labour.[41]

The threat of Ulster's armed resistance to Home Rule followed immediately on the self-assertion of the democratic element in the British Constitution through the Parliament Act of 1911; it was, indeed, the direct sequel to this measure which was regarded by friend and foe as the opening move in the impending struggle for Home Rule. Just as Ireland had been the crucial influence in the most determined step towards the democratisation of British politics so far undertaken by legal enactment, Ireland was also the decisive force in the most serious challenge to constitutional government in the British Isles thrown out in modern times. The fight against the relics of feudalism and the undemocratic powers of privileged minorities in England was a necessary by-product of the Irish nationalist struggle for self-determination, for it was the same semi-feudal ruling minority which barred the way towards national self-government in Ireland. For the same reason, the reaction against the nationalist movement by the leaders of industrial Ulster was not only directed against Southern Ireland but also against the democratic element in the British constitution.

Under the leadership of the determined Belfast employers, the Home Rule conflict was transferred from the floor of the House of Commons to the country. For the first time in generations, the supremacy of Parliament was challenged by a section of the governing classes, and this challenge was the more dangerous because it had the full support of the British Tory party. Although at that stage the Tory leaders were no longer the wire-pullers and the Protestant Ulstermen their political puppets, this alliance was of the greatest possible value to the Ulster 'rebels'. For the British Tories, whose political power had been gravely weakened by their dissensions on Free Trade and Protectionism, the Ulster question was a godsend, because on it all the warring factions within the Conservative party were united, while the Liberals were confronted by the awkward dilemma of antagonising their Irish allies or of coercing Ulster out of the Union. The leader of the Tory party was no longer the sceptic A. J. Balfour, but the *homo novus* Bonar Law, who owed his elevation to this rank entirely to the need for a compromise appointment somewhere half-way between Walter Long and Austen Chamberlain, and who felt it necessary to cover the intrinsic weakness of his position by the use of language which in the circumstances could have only one meaning. Bonar Law told an astonished world that in their struggle against Home Rule the Conservatives would not be restrained by the bonds which would influence them 'in an ordinary political struggle' and reminded his Blenheim audience that there were 'things stronger than parliamentary majorities'.[42]

The potential effect of the violent and unconstitutional reaction of the Tory leaders in Ulster and Great Britain to the enactment of a tame and half-hearted Home Rule Bill was very grave indeed. The actual course of the Home Rule struggle was such that a violent solution was by far the most likely outcome. This climax was cut short by the outbreak of the First World War which allowed the Liberal Government to surrender to Ulster and the Conservatives without endangering their immediate position, and British politics and the British Constitution were, therefore, spared the full consequences of the crisis.

Irish historians have laid great stress on the international consequences of the Ulster crisis, and particularly the Curragh incident, which deprived the British Government of their authority over the army in case of an Ulster rebellion. If the Liberal Government had been resolved to crush Ulster's resistance by force, this event would, indeed, have been of crucial political importance, but there is no reason to believe that this policy would really have been pursued. Similarly, it is reasonable to believe that the acute embarrassment of the British Government over the Irish question suited the German war leaders well enough, but in the complicated and confused pattern of events which led up to the First World War Ulster can have played only a very subordinate part. This is shown not only by the known history of these events but also by the hesitation with which the German Government accepted the overtures made by Sir Roger Casement on behalf of the Irish revolutionaries when war had already broken out.

As far as Ireland was concerned, Ulster's successful challenge to the parliamentary institutions of Great Britain was certainly the end of one era and the beginning of another. The hard core of Ulster's unconstitutional resistance to the parliamentary majority of the Liberal Government and its Irish allies was the fear of social revolution lurking in the shadow of Home Rule. The relations between Protestant Ulster and the South reproduced on a smaller scale, and therefore with intensified dramatic power, the relations between imperialist rulers and colonial subjects. To this extent, Home Rule was a symbol of a much greater and more significant development. Was it possible for an imperialist nation to divest itself voluntarily of its privileges and of its power? The pressure of the democratic forces on both sides of the Irish Sea had moved England a long way along this path—manhood franchise and local government reform in politics, land purchase and remedial social legislation in the economic sphere were milestones which indicated how near the ultimate goal of national self-determination had been approached. The alliance between the local vested interests in Ulster and the upholders of privilege in Great Britain effectively prevented the consummation of this policy.

The secret of British democracy was its carefully timed progress which reflected the clearly understood need of preventing social revolution by judicious concessions. Every step on this path had been denounced by the diehards in both parties as a surrender to the forces of revolution; actually it was only thus that dangerous revolutionary situations had been prevented. The material benefits accruing to England from its imperial rule over a host of colonial subject nations contributed to the smoothness and continuity of this process: it encouraged the upper classes to yield a small part of their privileges in order to keep the rest, and it induced the lower classes to accept concessions with the hope of favours to come. Irish politics showed the colonial reverse of Britain's imperial progress towards a democracy, where even the masses looked at the world with the eyes of their governing classes; they were harsh, uncompromising and tainted with the secret futility, and not a little of the heroism, of a country whose every effort was doomed to failure through the overwhelming power of its rulers.

Ireland's political representation in the British House of Commons under the Union made Irish politics a part of the complex social and political balance of forces in Great Britain. With the progress of democracy and the nationalist aspirations inseparable from it, it became impossible to apply special legislation to Ireland, at least in constitutional matters, while maintaining the Union. Democratic advances in Great Britain, therefore, implied the need for similar advances in Ireland. But the Irish masses had none of the inducements which made their British counterpart patient and expectant onlookers at the feast of Britain's world power and prosperity, to be rewarded by increasingly larger morsels from the tables of their betters. If they were to be prevented from making a dangerous use of their democratic rights, they had to be disciplined, coerced or satisfied. In practice, the British Government found a judicious mixture of all three elements necessary. The machinery of coercion was maintained in full strength; for the rest, concessions were made to the 'moderate' elements which induced them to leave the ranks of the malcontents and to neutralise their pressure.

When Gladstone tried to push this policy to its logical conclusion by handing the government of Ireland to the Irish middle classes, the power of the vested interests proved too much for him. Twenty-five years later, the attempt could no longer be safely delayed and Gladstone's successors had the parliamentary means of carrying it through. They and their Irish allies made at first the crass blunder of ignoring the separate interests of industrial Ulster, and afterwards surrendered to the show of force, backed by the undoubted intention of using force, of the Ulster leaders. Ulster's victory over Home Rule was, therefore, a crushing defeat for the Irish parliamentarians who advocated co-operation with England and self-government within the British Empire.

Sir Edward Carson was thus more justified than he knew, and cared to know, when he asserted that Ulster's success would kill Home Rule. This is precisely what happened. Ulster's refusal to play the game of democracy to the extent of subordinating the vital interests of its rulers to the decisions of a hostile parliamentary majority wrecked the whole scheme of government of which the conception of Home Rule formed a part, and it was not the fault of the Tories in Ulster and Great Britain that British parliamentary government survived the challenge unscathed. But the ardent upholders of vested interests and ancient privileges were totally ignorant of the crucial fact that they were killing Home Rule only in order to clear the way for revolution. If they had only insisted on maintaining their own independence, compromise might still have been possible on the basis of excluding the four counties where Protestants were in the majority. But in their spirit of colonial arrogance, they insisted on extending the limits of their claim to the largest area which would give an over-all Protestant majority over the largest possible nationalist minority. Thus they not only sapped the power of the Irish moderate parliamentarians in favour of the revolutionists, but they did all they could to make any settlement which included partition unacceptable to the nationalists and a bar to complete friendship between Ireland and Great Britain.

CHAPTER XXIV

IRELAND AND THE BRITISH CONSTITUTION

IN the years between 1890 and 1914, the Irish party never again approached the single-minded resolution of its heroic age, the Parnell era; yet it was in those years of internal decay and beginning disintegration that it made a startling contribution to the greatest visible change in the political constitution of the country of which Ireland formed an unwilling part.

After the extension of the franchise to the rural labourers in 1884, the electoral system of Great Britain (though still stopping short of complete manhood suffrage and still ignoring the claims of women to political equality) reflected reasonably closely the social structure of the British people. Although Britain was not yet a fully fledged democracy, no government could maintain itself in power without the support or acquiescence of a large cross-section of the people. The democratisation of the electoral system was accompanied by radical changes within the classical parties and followed by a dramatic realignment of social forces between Liberals and Conservatives in which the Irish problem played a very important part.

While the extension of the franchise expressed the democratic aspirations of the British people, the actual government of the country remained in the hands of a small minority of privileged persons. In the past the inherent conflict between these opposed tendencies had been usually disguised, though not resolved, by the paradox of an oligarchic democracy within the House of Commons. The entry of genuinely popular representatives into the lower House was very gradual; on a significant scale it was first effected by the Irish party under Parnell's leadership which was justly regarded as a portent presaging the end of the aristocratic era in British politics. The conquest of the House of Commons by the representatives of the English working men, though a much slower process than hoped for by its champions and feared by its enemies was, nevertheless, only a matter of time. The impending clash between the democratic forces and the real rulers of English society was the storm cloud hovering over the future of British politics, and no other single factor contributed so much to its ultimate precipitation as the Irish Question.

The visible embodiment of the opposing forces in the sphere of politics was the inevitable conflict between a Liberal House of Commons and the Conservative House of Lords. The predominance of the Tories in the upper House had never been in question since the days of William Pitt, and the well-nigh complete break of the Whig grandees with Gladstone on the question of Home Rule in 1886 transformed the House of Lords to all intents and purposes into an annexe of the Conservative party. Although the conflict between the Lords and the interests of the masses was not confined to any single subject, Ireland provided one of the most important controversial issues between the two Houses. The perennial irritant of the Irish Question gave the Peers ample opportunity for frustrating the wishes of the Liberal Government, particularly because in this case they had the support of a majority of the English voters on their side. They were, therefore, only too prone to exploit this question to the utmost, because it permitted them to combine the business of defending the material interests of their order with the pleasure of a party political offensive against an almost helpless enemy.

Amongst the statesmen of the period, Gladstone was the only one who saw and consistently tried to prevent this threatening polarisation of British politics. Far from being an enemy of the existing social and political order, his main purpose was its perpetuation in the circumstances created by the progress of democracy. He never wavered in his conviction that his most controversial measure, the Home Rule Bill of 1886, was 'eminently conservative in the highest sense of the term, as tending to the union of the three Countries . . . and to the stability of the Imperial throne and institutions'.[43] At the same time, and from the same motives, he deprecated 'the prolongation and intensity of the Irish controversy' because it tended to extend 'the widening gap, or chasm, in opinion which more largely than heretofore separates the upper, and more powerful, from the more numerous classes of the community'.[44] It was only on the surface paradoxical that a statesman of such professedly conservative stamp should have been amongst the first men of the highest rank in politics to advocate a reform of the House of Lords which would have put an end to its insensate resistance to any but a Tory Government on all major questions. Gladstone intended to answer the rejection of his second Home Rule Bill in 1893 by the Peers with an instant dissolution on the issue of the rights of the hereditary chamber. But at eighty-three he was too far advanced for his time, or at least for the mediocrities of his own last Cabinet. His failure to carry his colleagues with him not only put an end to his political career but kept the Liberals for a decade in impotent opposition until they were lifted back into office without any fault of theirs by the happy chance of the tariff reform struggle within the Tory party.

The traditional conflict within the Liberal party between Whigs and Radicals was continued during these ten years in the form of a struggle for Gladstone's succession. The neo-Whigs, now appropriately styled Liberal Imperialists, counted amongst them many of the party's best brains and in due course they managed to free themselves from the handicap of Lord Rosebery's temperamental leadership. The latter was, indeed, a liability for his friends through his open hostility towards Home Rule which he regarded as incompatible with the unity of the Empire and wanted removed from the party programme. Lord Rosebery's final break with the Liberal party was caused by his insistence on this point, which was met with a blank refusal by Sir Henry Campbell-Bannerman, the compromise leader of the party. Asquith and his friends, while too prudent for similar suicidal tactics, managed to keep Home Rule completely out of the elections which swept the Liberals back into office. Campbell-Bannerman was a Radical of sorts, but in his attitude towards colonial peoples he was a genuine heir of Gladstone's tradition. His championship of the Boers at the time of the South African War was of infinitely greater service to the British Empire than the sabre-rattling and drum-beating of the professional imperialists who denounced him as a traitor; as far as Ireland was concerned, he had to be satisfied with a policy of preparing 'step by step' for the larger measure, although he was a convinced Home Ruler of old standing, and his early withdrawal from the scene put the right wing of the Liberals firmly in the saddle.

Asquith and his friends were prevented by their fundamental political beliefs from offering Ireland more than a subordinate assembly which would have relieved the Imperial Parliament of unnecessary details of administration without in any way reducing its political sovereignty. This policy of semi-Home Rule by instalments was, however, doomed from the start by the sharpening of social and political conflicts both in Great Britain and in Ireland. Redmond and his followers might have been willing to accept a policy of gradualness, if they did not actually prefer it to a sudden change-over. But the Irish Council Bill of 1907, which proceeded on these lines, was stillborn: the opposition of the Irish Left, at that time not in itself decisive, was strengthened by the hostility of the Catholic Church to a measure which would have weakened its hold on the education of the Irish people. However much the nationalist leaders might have fancied the chance of consolidating their position by gaining control of a good slice of executive power, in view of the strong opposition to the Bill they did not dare to encourage their enemies by openly advocating such a policy.

In England, the political lesson of these years was the demonstration of the political impotence of a Liberal Government with a vast majority in the House of Commons in the face of the determined hostility of the Peers. The Tory leaders were acutely conscious of the painful fact that their defeat at the polls had been their own fault and they behaved as if they had been somehow cheated of their legitimate spoils of office. Thus they felt under no obligation to moderate the recklessness of the Lords who frustrated the legislation of the Liberal Government by the ample use of their veto power.

The nemesis of this attempt to put the clock of British democracy back by a hundred years came with the famous Budget of 1909, which gave the Radicals in the Liberal party their chance of turning the tables on the Lords. By rejecting the Budget, the Peers reached the utmost limits of their constitutional rights in their most extravagant interpretation, broke the old-established customs of the Constitution and put themselves into open conflict with the House of Commons and the electors. The conflict which Gladstone, guided by his true conservative instinct, had wished to resolve in 1893 when it was in practice limited to the Irish question, had grown by suppression until it assumed the dangerous dimension of a first-rate constitutional struggle which threatened the whole fabric of British parliamentary democracy.

The policy of the Tory leaders was short-sighted to an almost unbelievable extent. It was completely based on the false hope of a sweeping victory at the elections which the House of Lords forced on the Liberal Government. This hope was frustrated by Lloyd George's tactical genius and by the suicidal mania of the Peers who fastened on the Budget for the supreme trial of strength. The partial success of the Tories at the first election of 1910 was, indeed, worse than complete failure. They managed to gain parity with the Liberals, and thereby put the Irish party back into a key position such as it had never enjoyed since 1885. This dramatic change in the parliamentary balance of power determined the Irish policy of the second Asquith Government and had an important bearing on the constitutional settlement of the Parliament Act of 1911.

Ever since the failure of the Irish Council Bill of 1907, which gave him a clear idea of the strength of the Irish opposition to a policy of piecemeal reform, Redmond urged on the Government the imperative need of a genuine Home Rule Bill—and the fear of such a Bill may well have contributed to the premature challenge to the Government by the House of Lords. Asquith, who was at best a lukewarm Home Ruler, although he had first come into prominence during the notorious Parnell Commission of 1888, sheltered behind the Liberal election programme of 1906 which had kept a discreet silence on this delicate matter. At that time the Irish party had fallen so low in fortunes and expectations that it actually welcomed Campbell-Bannerman's 'step by step' policy as a reaffirmation of the almost forgotten battle-cry of Gladstone's last heroic years. Meanwhile the official nationalists grew restive under the attacks from their own left wing and demanded an unequivocal undertaking from Asquith to put Home Rule back into the Liberal programme for the impending elections. 'We cannot', wrote Redmond to Lord Morley in November 1909, when the issue with the Lords was clearly joined, 'acquiesce in the present position being continued. There is a large majority in the Government and in the House of Commons in favour of Home Rule, and yet their hands are tied by reason of the fact that the Home Rule issue was deliberately withdrawn from the consideration of the electors at the last election. We must therefore press for an official declaration which will show clearly that the Home Rule issue is involved in the issue of the House of Lords. . . .'[45]

How deeply the Home Rule issue was involved in that of the House of Lords was to appear clearly during the ensuing crisis. Meanwhile Asquith made the requested declaration during a speech in the Albert Hall, and at the elections the Tories failed to turn the Government out, although they succeeded in making it completely dependent on Irish support. The political situation was grotesquely complicated by the fact that Lloyd George's 'People's Budget', with its increased taxation of drink, was highly unpopular with the Irish party, due to the political pressure of the powerful Irish brewers and distillers and to the financial pressure of such taxation on the Irish public. But the real struggle behind the scenes centred on a deeper and more fundamental disagreement between these uneasy political allies.

Redmond had every reason to believe that Asquith and the imperialists within the Liberal party were not genuine Home Rulers in Gladstone's sense at all, and the course of the crisis makes it clear that he expected the Government to shelter behind the power of the House of Lords in order to wriggle out of the fulfilment of their election promises. His main endeavour was, therefore, to frustrate such a manœuvre by compelling the Government to deal with the veto power of the Lords in a manner which would make their opposition to Home Rule ineffective. The tactical opportunity for putting pressure on the Government was the passage of the Budget. The Conservative failure to oust the Government made the acceptance of the hateful People's Budget by the Peers a foregone conclusion, provided it passed the House of Commons, where the Irish party had it in its power to throw it out—and with it the Asquith Government. Should Redmond and his followers, their hearts sick with hope deferred and their position assailed by the propaganda of more militant movements in the Irish towns, obediently vote for the Budget, perhaps only to be rewarded by a compromise between Liberals and Tories on the constitutional issue which might have left the veto power of the House of Lords over Home Rule unaltered? It did not take Parnell's tactical genius to reject this solution and to use this unique opportunity in order to compromise the Liberal leaders beyond the possibility of a double-cross.

'I say plainly', Redmond declared in Dublin on 10th February 1910, 'that if Mr. Asquith . . . proposes to pass the Budget into law and then adjourn . . . the consideration of the House of Lords, that is a policy that I cannot and will not uphold.'[46] On the same day Asquith seems to have made up his mind to maintain his freedom of action towards his awkward allies: 'If the Irish really thought it necessary to push their objection to the spirit duties or their time-honoured grievance against the alleged over-taxation of Ireland to the length of voting against the Budget and ejecting the Government, they must go their own way, and the blood be on their own heads.'[47] The leaders of the allied forces were thus arrayed against one another, and on the outcome of their trial of strength depended the speed and the length of the next step forward in Britain's transformation from an oligarchy into a democracy.

Austen Chamberlain, the leader of the tariff reform wing in the Unionist party and a few months later one of the real powers behind the Diehards in the House of Lords, has left an intimate record of this crucial episode in modern British constitutional history, as it struck a well-informed and unsympathetic observer. On 20th February 1910, ten days after Redmond's public declaration, he was quite sure of the delicate balance of power in the enemy camp: 'In short, Asquith has his own way. Budget first and Veto after. Asquith has beaten his recalcitrant colleagues and now defies Redmond, Barnes (the most prominent Labour representative in Parliament) and Co. who, being beaten, will doubtless come to heel. . . .' Three days later, after Redmond had proved unexpectedly stubborn, Chamberlain was still confident 'that Asquith won't give way in substance and that, if Redmond is to be satisfied, he will have to be satisfied with a shadow concession—not a reality'. Yet another two days later and Chamberlain had to record the disconcerting rumour that Redmond had won the day. However, such news seemed too bad to be true, and a very different *dénouement* now appeared possible: 'At present the best opinion is that Asquith will stand firm; that Redmond will not yield; that therefore the

Government will be beaten on the Budget. . . .' But this was not to be, and before the short month had run its course the Government, through the mouth of Lloyd George, agreed to Redmond's demands, and Chamberlain's bitterness against Asquith and Grey, who had failed to fight the Tories' battle against the Radicals, was unbounded: '. . . the Budget will not be touched till the Veto resolutions have left our House. This is the first surrender to the Irish and other malcontents. Next, the reform of the Constitution of the House of Lords is not to be concurrent with limitation of the veto but is to be postponed to the Greek Calends. Second surrender. Third that the Resolutions are not only to be sent to the House of Lords but that if they are rejected there, the Government will then ask the King for "guarantees" and will resign if they are not granted. Third and most important surrender which makes the real change in the situation. . . . No doubt both sides were bluffing, but in my opinion it was not Redmond's nerve which gave way under the strain. It is Asquith and Grey who have yielded once more. It is Redmond who triumphs, for the time being at least.'[48]

Although the tactical triumph of the nationalist-democratic minority in the House of Commons did not lead to immediate strategic victory, it was nevertheless the turning of the tide. The delays and stratagems of the ensuing months illustrate the dangers to which the cause of democracy would have been exposed but for the parliamentary showdown at the start of the crisis. The resistance of the Lords, supported as it was by the whole weight of the Tory party, could be overcome in the last resort only by the threat of creating Peers on a scale which would have destroyed the House of Lords as an effective part of the parliamentary system. Such a course was repugnant to a large and powerful group among the Liberal leaders, and it would have been impossible without the acquiescence of the Crown in a policy which was positively distasteful to it. As it happened, the death of Edward VII and the accession of King George V caused further delay and uncertainty, because the new monarch naturally tried his best to avoid a political revolution at the commencement of his reign in which he would have had to put himself into personal opposition to the most ardent upholders of royalty. The veto resolutions were, therefore, not followed by open conflict between the two Houses but by a Constitutional Conference between Liberal and Conservative leaders who searched from June to November for a compromise.

This was exactly the situation which the Irish leader had tried to prevent earlier on, but the search proved fruitless after all— mainly because Home Rule remained an obstinate stumbling-block. The differences in constitutional theory between Conservatives and

Liberals might have been settled by give-and-take, but they palled into insignificance compared with the burning question whether such a settlement should include or exclude the enactment of Home Rule by the Liberal Government of the day. The Tories insisted on excluding Home Rule from the scope of such a compromise while the Government, which depended on Irish votes for their daily existence, could not agree to such suicidal terms. The Tory proposal of a referendum on this issue was, of course, prompted by their hope that the British electors would be hostile to the dismemberment of the United Kingdom. But in spite of this opportunism, it is a piquant historical irony that the Irish problem made the party of privilege turn from sovereign Parliament to the sovereignty of the people. The baffled Tory leaders clearly hoped to be able to exploit the prejudices of a ruling nation in its own interests when it was a question of rejecting the democratic claims of a subject people. Their confidence in the narrow-mindedness of the British voters on this issue might have been justified or not, but it is a curious paradox that, in order to back their rejection of Ireland's claim for self-determination, the Conservatives had to try and mobilise the forces of British democracy.

The ultimate outcome of the constitutional crisis was the acceptance by the House of Lords of the Parliament Act of 1911, after a good deal of internal squabbles in the Tory party which ended only after Balfour's withdrawal from the leadership. The surrender of the House of Lords made the creation of hundreds of new Peers unnecessary and settled the shape of the British Constitution for a generation. Balfour and Lord Lansdowne, who advised surrender, showed more political sense than Austen Chamberlain and Lord Halsbury, the leaders of the Diehards, whose stubborn refusal to bow to the inevitable would have meant the end of the House of Lords as an effective part of the British parliamentary system. Under the Parliament Act the House of Lords lost most of its dignity and a good deal of its power, but it remained far from negligible as a last line of defence of the Tory party against a hostile Government.

In spite of its importance as a constitutional landmark, the Parliament Act was not a real settlement of the issues raised by the irrepressible conflict between the political needs of a democracy and the relics of a feudal age which had become the bastion of privilege. In its extent as well as in its limitations it was nothing more than a device enabling a Liberal Government to pass a Home Rule Bill within the lifetime of one Parliament. The influence of the Irish problem on its content was, therefore, not less decisive than the share of the Irish party in forcing it on a Government which was far from being unanimous in its enthusiasm for a radical change in the British Constitution. But such outside pressure, however effective and even indispensable at a time of crisis, was not the ideal motive force for the satisfactory settlement of such a question. Its action was completely one-sided, negative and eccentric in the literal sense of the term. While it was true that the Lords started to toy with the idea of 'reform' only when this was necessary in order to side-track demands for the reduction in their undemocratic veto powers, it is no less true that no curtailment of these powers can make the institution of the House of Lords compatible with democratic principles. While the Irish question was, therefore, one of the forces responsible for the fact that the relations between the hereditary Conservative House of Lords and the Commons became a political problem compelling attention and action by a Government whose democratic wing was far from all-powerful, it must also bear a large share of the responsibility for the incompleteness of the settlement.

The Parliament Act of 1911 was a compromise and not a clear-cut victory of the democratic principle. It did nothing to change the permanently Tory character of the second Chamber. It severely curtailed the freedom of movement of any but a Tory Government, because it made emergency legislation against the wishes of the Lords practically impossible by delaying the enactment of most contentious Bills for at least two years. In particular, it still left any but a Tory Government during the second half of its life-span at the mercy of an unfriendly House of Lords which could embarrass such a Government as it pleased in order to reduce its chances of success at the next election, as long as it managed to deny its victims the dangerous battle-cry of Peers *versus* People. On the other hand, no Government which had any reason to fear the hostility of the House of Lords, because it intended to attack the privileges for which that House stands, or which took the democratic claims of the British political system sufficiently seriously, was and is obliged to live under this threat. The Parliament Act, like any other British statute, can be amended by the normal process of legislation—if necessary under the procedure laid down by the Act itself and against the wishes of the House of Lords, and this was the course of events which led up to the Parliament Act of 1949. The Tory leaders who attacked the settlement of 1911 as a constitutional revolution were, therefore, at least potentially right, however absurd their denunciation of Asquith, Grey, Lloyd George and Churchill as a revolutionary junta.

The intrinsic importance of the principles underlying the Parliament Act has often been underrated because the Act itself was hardly ever applied—and in the rare cases where it was invoked the ultimate settlement differed from the Bills passed under its provisions. Such criticism misses the most important political result of the change, the legal recognition of the supremacy of the House of Commons. This facet of the Act was obscured for a long time by the practical monopoly of power enjoyed by the Conservatives between the two World Wars which automatically prevented conflicts between the two Houses. The legislation of 1911 excluded the repetition of the experiences of 1892–5 and 1906–10, when Governments with a working majority in the House of Commons were stultified by the resistance of the House of Lords, and it paved the way for the acceptance of far-reaching nationalisation measures by the Peers in the first two years of the third Labour Government.

In the intense conflict which preceded the adoption of the Parliament Act John Redmond, not through any deep-seated democratic convictions but through sheer necessity, became the most effective spokesman of British democracy in its hour of crisis, and in opposition to the traditional powers in both political parties. Although the loss of this particular engagement would not have lost the whole campaign for the full democratisation of British politics, speedy victory depended on the action of the Irish party which occupied the tactical key position from which alone victory could be won. Redmond was a conservative in his social outlook and a moderate nationalist in his politics who firmly believed in the necessity of Ireland's close association with Great Britain within the framework of the British Empire. He became a spokesman for British democracy through his position as the parliamentary leader of a dependent country and of a nation in permanent revolt against its colonial status. The British Labour Party, though just as resolutely opposed to any compromise between Liberals and Conservatives at the expense of the democratic development of the British constitution, was as yet not strong enough to take the lead in such a struggle. Its work of detaching the masses from their allegiance to Liberals or Tories was still in its infancy, and its parliamentary influence was limited mainly to labour interests in the most narrow material sense. Redmond and Dillon were hardly more representative of the Irish poor than Asquith and Chamberlain were of the British working man, and this fatal weakness of the parliamentary Irish party was soon to become clear to all the world. Their stand as the most effective advocates of British democracy was entirely based on their position as the leading spokesmen of a subject nation. The Irish struggle for national self-determination involved them inevitably in a conflict with the privileged powers and vested interests of the ruling nation who were incidentally the determined enemies of social progress and political democracy in their native country.

If Asquith appeared, in the considered judgment of a modern historian, in his relations with Redmond 'completely unreliable' and 'at his weakest and worst',[49] Redmond reached his greatest stature as a political leader in this struggle for British democracy. The contrast between his effective leadership on this occasion and his appalling weakness and short-sightedness during the actual Home Rule struggle was due to something more fundamental than his shortcomings as a political tactician. It reflected the difference between his part as the chosen leader of a subject nation fighting for truly national interests and great principles in the attack on the House of Lords, and his attempt to consolidate the petty interests of a privileged section of his countrymen and of a greedy and soulless political machine.

CHAPTER XXV

THE GORDIAN KNOT

THE whirlwind of world history which engulfed Ireland's 'independent' Parliament of 1782 into the struggle between England and France, blew again in 1914 when the crisis of the Home Rule struggle coincided with the outbreak of the First World War. The failure to solve the Irish Question by a compromise which would have been acceptable to the Irish people paralysed the official nationalist party, and the war created the extreme conditions required for the extreme policy of the revolutionists whose main appeal was to the masses of the unprivileged.

War, though not a source of new social forces, powerfully affects them in their action. It reduces social relations to their simplest form of relations of power. It submits individuals, groups and institutions to the radical test of death or survival through involuntary or voluntary connection with powers strong enough to punish opposition by annihilation, and weak enough to carry their allies to perdition with themselves. It is cruel, senseless and unscrupulous, but any attempt to ignore its unrelenting compulsion within its given field of action and destruction is doomed to failure.

The effect of the First World War on Anglo-Irish relations was proportionate to the hostility of the opposed forces, and therefore revolutionary in its consequences. In Britain, the existence of a Liberal Government in 1914 was a piece of rare good fortune for the classes most intimately interested in British entry into the war. Pacifism amongst Liberal supporters was strong enough to be a political danger. A Tory Government would have met the full force of this hostility, and the combination of strong anti-war feelings and the exigencies of party politics might have seriously interfered with the British war effort. The creation of a practically effective, although not by any means complete, united national front in support of the war could only be ensured by the Liberal party.

With the unfolding prospect of a long and bitter war for sheer survival, the balance of forces in British politics shifted significantly to the Tories. The same qualities which helped the Liberals to lead the British people into the war reduced their ability to concentrate on its prosecution with the single-mindedness which the interests at stake demanded. Although the Liberal Government survived until the early summer of 1915, the influence of the Tories grew with every mistake, setback and disappointment—Mons, Ypres, Gallipoli and the 'shell scandal'. With the first coalition the Liberal leadership of the common people of Great Britain came to a formal close.

Nowhere did the role of the Liberal party in reconciling potential opponents to the war find more striking expression than in the attitude of the official Irish party in August 1914. Generations of Irishmen had been taught to regard England's difficulty as Ireland's opportunity, but Redmond's unconditional support for the war seemed to transform Ireland from a threatening stormcloud into the one bright spot on an horizon which was otherwise black with thunder and torn by lightning. Redmond and his party had learned so well to regard their own fate as bound up with that of the Liberal Government and the liberalised Empire that they offered full co-operation in the war without any other consideration than the formal passage of the Home Rule Bill. Such behaviour could only be justified by the conviction that the common interests at stake in the war outweighed all their mutual differences—and, as far as the Irish middle class was concerned, there was some substance in this belief.

The increasing power of the Tories showed the Irish representatives the precariousness of their new position. Since the Curragh incident the true centre of political gravity was no longer in the House of Commons, because the Liberal Government had lost its power of coercing Ulster, even if it had been willing to do so. But Redmond and Dillon had not yet realised the change, and their parliamentary key position still enabled them to put strong pressure on the Government whose parliamentary existence depended on Irish support. The war blunted the edge of party divisions between Tories and Liberals and produced a close political *entente* between the two Front Benches. Their difference over Ireland was settled by the formal enactment of the Home Rule Bill, together with its suspension for the duration of the war and the solemn pledge that Ulster would never be coerced out of the United Kingdom. The Asquith Government thus became independent of the Irish party, which lost its only effective lever for keeping the Liberal leaders to their promises.

The growing influence of the Tories was bound to affect the Irish policy of the Government. On Liberal principles, Ireland's participation in the war should have been the result of the deliberate resolution of the Irish people itself. From the Tory point of view, no such question could arise. Not only was the self-interest of the 'predominant partner' the decisive factor in such an emergency as the war, but all the forces of habit, tradition and party interest encouraged the Tories to suppress all disloyal, i.e. anti-British movements and to re-establish the supremacy of the loyal, i.e. unionist elements throughout Ireland. When the first Coalition Government was formed in 1915, Redmond and his party were not even consulted on the matter, although they had been Asquith's more or less loyal allies for a decade, and were simply confronted with the accomplished fact. Amongst the Tories who joined the Government was Sir Edward Carson, the Ulster leader, whose influence was much greater than his short tenure of office as Attorney-General indicates. Redmond had to exert himself to the full in order to prevent, or rather delay, the appointment of James Campbell, one of Carson's lieutenants in the Ulster movement, as Irish Lord Chancellor, and his influence on the policy and practice of the Irish administration suffered a blow from which it never recovered.

The practical results of Redmond's support of the war were, therefore, singularly meagre. Far from securing Home Rule, Redmond had to accept its suspension for an indefinite period. Far from strengthening his hold on the government of Ireland, he had to witness the conquest of the Irish administration by his worst enemies. Another source of weakness for Redmond and his policy was the rejection of his patriotic endeavours to put the Irish party on the map in the British war effort which only brought him an unending series of rebuffs. Kitchener, himself born in Ireland, had a very low opinion of the loyalty of Irish nationalists and would not trust 'one single Irishman with a rifle in his hand one single yard'.[50] This sweeping declaration applied, however, only to Southern Irishmen, for at the same time he 'had already taken steps deliberately to gather round him in the War Office some of the most important Ulstermen who had been concerned in the Carsonite gun-running at Larne'.[51] Thus it was not surprising that T. P. O'Connor, after Redmond and Dillon the most prominent man in the Irish party, called Kitchener 'an Irish Orangeman who is determined in every way to strengthen the forces against and weaken the forces for us'.[52]

The hostility of the British War Office towards armed Irishmen did not imply any unwillingness to use Irish soldiers in the British army; on the contrary, the eagerness to recruit young Irishmen increased with the stupendous growth of casualty lists, and the insufficient response to voluntary recruitment campaigns soon led to inspired rumours about impending conscription. The issue of conscription was to contribute more than anything else to the crisis in Anglo-Irish relations and the decline in the prestige of the official Irish party.

Although this decline began quite early in the war, it did not at first seem to matter much, because the war pushed most purely political questions, including the holding of elections, into the background. In addition, the early war period was a time of great prosperity for the farmers, and political life in the Irish countryside was, therefore, deprived of most of the spur of discontent which previously had goaded the official party machine into action. What there was of politics, had become concentrated in the towns in what the official leaders had come to regard as the lunatic fringe of Irish politics—the I.R.B. and the Labour movement.

Sinn Fein as an organised force practically ceased to exist with the formation of the Irish Volunteers late in 1913. The latter absorbed most of the Sinn Fein sympathisers, while the hard core of the new open movement consisted of members of the I.R.B. The swamping of the Volunteers by Redmond's adherents just before the outbreak of the war was a heavy blow to the secret leaders of the movement who only bowed to this *coup* in order to avoid a split. But Redmond's recruiting speeches after the outbreak of war made the split inevitable, and only a few thousands of Volunteers sided against the Irish party and remained with 'MacNeill's' Irish Volunteers. Thus in Cork the Volunteer organisation started in December 1913 with a membership of 200–500 in the city. 'By June 1914 it had spread to the country districts with a membership of 2,921. In July 1914 the Volunteers in the City and East Riding numbered 3,460',[53] but after the split no more than thirty 'MacNeill' Volunteers were said to have remained faithful to the old standard. During the following months they began to rally their supporters again, and at the time of the Easter Rising the Cork Volunteers again numbered 653.

In spirit as well as in social composition, the Sinn Fein Volunteers were in the direct Fenian tradition. Their leadership, not unlike that of the original Brotherhood, still consisted of two sections with very different aims. As before the war, the two wings were represented by MacNeill, Bulmer Hobson and Sir Roger Casement, on the one side, and Tom Clarke, Patrick Pearse and John MacDermott on the other. Both sides looked forward to a time of active warfare against Britain, but the former conceived military action in a much narrower sense than the latter, who regarded it as the opening move in a genuine revolutionary struggle. Both groups favoured German help, if it could be procured, but while MacNeill and Casement regarded it as the *sine qua non* of active warfare, Clarke and Pearse were determined to proceed without it, rather than let the hour of 'England's difficulty' pass unused. This internal rift in the leadership of the Volunteer movement had a fatal effect on the

Rising, where it led to a series of last-minute orders and counter-orders which caused a good deal of confusion.

The left wing of the Volunteer leaders found an indispensable, if somewhat too independent, ally in James Connolly and his small Citizen Army who arrived at similar results from very different premisses. For most European socialists the First World War was not only a tragedy but stark catastrophe. The complete surrender of the masses to nationalist hysteria in its early days was followed by conflict between supporters and opponents of the war amongst the socialist leaders, with the latter everywhere in a minority. The official labour movement in most European belligerent states, though its growth had been opposed by the powers that be to the best of their ability, had acquired in most countries sufficiently strong vested interests to make military defeat a serious matter for most national parties. In Ireland, national and social interests, far from conflicting, actually supported one another and counselled resolute opposition to the war, at whatever cost. Instead of the demoralising struggle between conflicting loyalties, the handful of Irish socialists decided wholeheartedly for a policy which was bound to result in head-on collision with the ruling powers, but Connolly and his followers in the Citizen Army were prepared to accept this result.

The peculiar vantage-point of membership of a subject nation gave Connolly's opinion about the war an incisive strength which many better-equipped political leaders failed to achieve. He attacked the war neither on purely nationalist lines, like the I.R.B., nor on pacifist grounds, like the anti-war minority in the British Labour party: 'The war of a subject nation for independence,' he said when the war was less than three weeks old, 'for its right to live its own life in its own way, may and can be justified as holy and righteous: the war of a subject class to free itself from the debasing conditions of economic and political slavery should at all times choose its own weapons . . .; but the war of nation against nation in the interest of royal freebooters and cosmopolitan brigands is a thing accursed.'[54] In this spirit he looked to a national Irish revolution against British rule and the war 'to set the torch to a European conflagration that will not burn out until the last throne and the last capitalist bond and debenture are shrivelled on the funeral pyre of the last war lord'.[55]

With the complete practical failure of European socialism as an active force against the war, Connolly inevitably gravitated more and more towards the I.R.B. leaders who contemplated action, though from reasons partly differing from his own. Just as the left wing of the I.R.B. leaned more and more towards the workers as their most reliable allies, Connolly laid increasing stress on the national aims which he shared with non-socialist republicans. The result was the formal union of the revolutionary groups in the Easter Rising. It was symbolised by Connolly's position as Dublin Commandant of the insurgents, although he was the only non-member of the I.R.B. among the leaders, while the proclamation of the Provisional Government combined a purely national appeal to the 'dead generations' of the Irish people, with the vaguely socialist claim of the 'right of the people of Ireland to the ownership of Ireland and to the unfettered control of Irish destinies'.

The Easter Rising was the consciously planned and prepared work of a secret society; this was both its strength and its weakness. The rebels had ample opportunity for studying the lay of the land, for fixing the ground on which they wanted to make a stand and for choosing their own time. The tactical cleverness of some of their plans has been admitted even by their opponents. To quote only one important case, De Valera's later prominence was partly due to the qualities of leadership which he displayed during Easter Week. On the other hand, the duality of control in the Volunteer movement had catastrophic results at the time of crisis. A revolutionary body whose nominal leaders were blissfully ignorant of the impending outbreak, until they learnt of it just in time to throw all plans into confusion by their refusal to allow it to proceed, was patently absurd.

In a war-torn world, with all-powerful governments bending all the resources of their peoples to the prosecution of the war, the Easter Rising was an event of international significance as the first open act of defiance against the Government of the most powerful amongst the warring nations. In Ireland, it will always retain one of the proudest places in the national calendar and its leaders are among the most cherished heroes and martyrs of the nationalist cause. Their overwhelming posthumous success was not simply due to the half-guilty, half-boastful sympathy of the average man for the victims of the struggle for liberation, but to a large extent also to the very real crisis in Anglo-Irish relations during the second half of the First World War.

The early part of the war was an era of great prosperity for the farmers whose produce fetched excellent prices, while their money outgoings remained unchanged—and it was still too early for them to discover that money had lost a good deal of its value together with its scarcity. All peasants love money, and in Ireland money had always been so rare that the sight of plenty of ready cash gladdened the hearts of big and small farmers alike. However, in due course even they began to feel the excessive rise in the prices

17

of manufactured goods, although their economic position remained very favourable throughout the war. In the towns, on the other hand, the increase in the cost of living far outstripped the rise in wages and salaries. Towards the end of the war, the economic danger of excessive food exports was cleverly exploited by the nationalist propagandists who forecast serious food shortages in Ireland and tried to prevent by force the export of foodstuffs to England.

While Irish producers probably benefited more from the war-time conditions of scarcity than Irish consumers suffered from them, both were unanimous in their opinion about war-time taxation. Before the war, Ireland had become a financial liability for England, but the war-time increase in taxation, particularly on articles of mass consumption, soon put an end to this situation. Instead of costing the British taxpayer two or three million pounds a year, Ireland now contributed comparatively large sums towards the cost of the war. In 1917 this 'Imperial contribution' was estimated at approximately £13 millions.[56] Even patriots are not enthusiastic about their tax assessments, but the Irish people, which vacillated between lukewarm sympathy and active hostility towards the Allied cause, had no reason to welcome this increase in taxation for the prosecution of the war.

But money and even food was of less importance for war purposes than lives. These were sacrificed in endless numbers on the Western Front to the lack of imagination of generals whose ingenuity exhausted itself in the simple process of throwing human bodies against barbed wire, machine-guns and high-explosive shells. With every new cry for manpower, Ireland felt the shadow of conscription creeping nearer. Conscription applied to Ireland was the supreme assertion of England's right over life and death of the Irish people. In Great Britain the resistance to conscription was mainly carried on by men who claimed for themselves the right to decide whether they should serve their country to the extent of taking life (and risking their own in the process). These 'conscientious objectors' did not contest the claim to loyalty of the community to which they belonged—as did the political objectors who opposed the character of the First World War and not the fact of war as such—but they joined issue with the authorities on the moral question of the limits of social power. It was one thing to reject their demands for special treatment and to enforce the will of the majority over the minority within a community, and quite another thing to compel the manhood of another nation, who regarded their interests as distinct from and opposed to those of the ruling power, to take up arms in defence of a system which they did not love and which many of them actively detested.

In its opposition to conscription Ireland was, again, the spearhead of a movement which elsewhere appeared not as a national but as a social tendency. In Great Britain, the ruling minority found it still comparatively easy to induce the masses to follow its lead more or less voluntarily in major questions of national policy. In the other belligerent countries, the semblance of national unity at the outbreak of war soon gave way to a growing rift between the classes actively interested in the prosecution of the war and the masses which had to carry most of its burdens, until the two nations within each country faced one another with almost the same hostility as the British and Irish within the 'United' Kingdom.

The earliest and most primitive Irish reaction towards the threat of conscription was the revival of emigration in 1915. This attempt was stopped by an outcry in the British Press, followed by hostile demonstrations against would-be emigrants at Liverpool and by the refusal of the crews to carry them overseas.[57] These landless young men, somewhat euphemistically called 'farmers' sons', who shared very little in the war-time profits of the established farmers, were to form part of the raw material of the Irish Republican Army of the future.

Even more important was the threat of conscription to the young Irishmen resident in Great Britain who were liable to conscription on the same terms as other residents. They stood traditionally on the extreme left of Irish nationalism and had their Gaelic classes and athletic clubs, their I.R.B. cells and debating clubs. The war presented them vaguely with 'Ireland's opportunity' and soon very forcefully with the danger of being pressed into the army which was to solve 'England's difficulty'. The outstanding representative of this group was Michael Collins, who had left his native West Cork at fifteen for a job in the Post Office Savings Bank in London, joined the I.R.B. when he was nineteen and was its treasurer for London at twenty-four when war broke out. At the end of 1915 he decided to evade conscription by returning to Ireland, and moved to Dublin in order to 'join up'—not in the British army but in the Irish Volunteers. Many of his compatriots from the big towns of industrial Britain took the same step at about the same time and set up camp near Dublin 'where they lived under military conditions, with sentries always on duty, showing their determination to resist with arms any attempt to raid their stronghold'.[58] In British eyes they were all law-breakers, and the Irish struggle against conscription naturally found determined leaders amongst them. Collins himself first rose to prominence as a prisoner in Frongoch concentration camp, where he organised resistance to the attempted identification of potential conscripts by the British authorities.[59] It was in this camp that he re-formed the shattered organisation of the I.R.B. and laid the basis for his future ascendancy over the militant movement.

The struggle against conscription more than anything else revealed the gulf between the official Irish party and the Irish masses. The Irish party opposed conscription for Ireland, because nobody could be under any illusions about the feelings of the Irish people in the matter. But in view of its general support of the war, its attitude was inconsistent and half-hearted and had no chance of success in an extreme emergency where everything was reduced to bare essentials. Hostility towards conscription logically implied hostility towards England and England's war, and the full-blooded nationalists who preached all these things found little difficulty in convincing the Irish people that their leadership held better chances of success in defeating conscription than that of the extinct volcanoes of the Irish party. A realignment of Irish politics was overdue, and during 1917–18 it was carried through with remarkable speed and efficiency.

The starting-point for this political reorientation was the National Aid Association for participants in the Rising and their relatives,[60] which obtained similar importance for the new Sinn Fein movement as the Fenian Amnesty movement possessed in its day for the Home Rule League. It enabled many Sinn Feiners to show in a dignified and constitutional manner their sympathy with the cause for which the rebels had suffered, and served as a rallying-point for the supporters of extreme nationalism. (Michael Collins worked for a short time as its full-time secretary and made excellent use of this position for the development of valuable contacts throughout the country.)

The failure of the Rising deprived the I.R.B. and the Irish socialists of their outstanding leaders and left the stage free for the original supporters of Sinn Fein, the urban lower middle class which now automatically took the lead in the nationalist counter-blow to the rule of the effete official party machine. Although Sinn Fein doubtless benefited a good deal from the popular description of the Easter Rising as the 'Sinn Fein Rebellion' (which was strongly disapproved of by Arthur Griffith and his followers), the main reason for its belated success was its social and political 'availability' at this critical moment.

However, Sinn Fein was not the only force in the field. The imprisoned participants in the rising, strengthened by a much larger number of suspects who had been interned with them and who had thereby come into close contact with the Volunteers and their I.R.B. leaders, returned to Ireland in the winter of 1916–17 and reorganised the Volunteer movement under still closer I.R.B.

control. While the genuine Sinn Feiners were mainly drawn from the middle and lower middle class, the Volunteers, like the Fenians before them, drew their strength from 'shop assistants, clerks, artisans, labourers and in country districts (of) small farmers' sons as well'.[53] They were, therefore, more inclined to radical, i.e. violent methods, and the presence amongst them of numerous fugitives from British conscription reinforced their elemental radicalism. For the moment their political importance lay mainly in their devoted and often reckless activism, but they were soon to become an important factor in respectable politics as well, when the franchise reform of 1918 extended the vote to all men over twenty-one years of age.

Arthur Griffith, the undisputed leader of Sinn Fein, showed great political sagacity as well as sincerity in his dealings with the radical Volunteers. In 1917 the old Sinn Fein movement had an official rebirth through a Convention which confirmed Griffith's original programme. On this occasion Griffith voluntarily withdrew his candidacy as President of Sinn Fein in favour of Eamon De Valera, the most prominent amongst the living heroes of the Rebellion. This action prevented a split within the movement and kept the extremists within the Sinn Fein fold. Griffith and his party thus became a real power in Ireland, and in spite of extremely trying circumstances and many setbacks they survived the era of war and illegality and took a prominent part in the Treaty settlement.

Irish internal politics after the eclipse of the Irish party in 1917–18 were governed by the co-operation and friction between two forces. One of them may be conveniently labelled Sinn Fein, which stood for the middle and lower middle class of the towns, the other took many forms which expressed the innate radicalism of various sections of the unprivileged masses. On both sides, the influence of the urban elements was disproportionately large and at times decisive. On both sides, social interests took the form of differing, and sometimes incompatible, national claims and ideals, and the discrepancy between underlying realities and conscious actions gave to the Irish politics of the period a somnambulistic and almost nightmarish quality.

The most remarkable sign of Sinn Fein's position as the new spokesman of the urban middle class was the conversion of numerous old-time politicians to its previously so unpopular tenets. At the Convention which met under Sir Horace Plunkett's chairmanship during 1917–18 in a hopeless attempt to settle the Irish Question by a last-minute agreement between the Irish party and Orange Ulster, Sinn Fein was not represented, but its shadow dominated the proceedings. The Convention broke to pieces on the question of fiscal autonomy, which included Ireland's right to determine its own tariffs. The dying Redmond would willingly have accepted a compromise suggested by the Southern Unionists, but the majority of his nominal supporters, led by Bishop O'Donnell of Raphoe, refused to follow his lead and thereby foreshadowed the defection of the middle class and the Church from the now useless Irish party to Sinn Fein. Amongst the well-known parliamentary figures those whose championship of the urban middle class had brought them into repeated conflict with the official leadership were amongst the first to show their friendliness towards the new power—principally T. M. Healy and William O'Brien. Their example was followed or anticipated by hosts of others: '. . . what had happened was not that Sinn Fein had captured Ireland but that the politicians in Ireland and those who make them, all the elements which had sniffed at Sinn Fein and libelled it, which had upheld corruption and jobbery, had realised that Sinn Fein was going to win and had come over to it *en masse*'.[61]

Within the Sinn Fein organisation, Griffith's self-effacement showed ample promise of reward. The same Convention which elected De Valera as President returned an Executive with a 'moderate' majority, and at the 1918 Convention the moderates were again generally more successful than the 'Volunteers'. Not for the first time in Irish history, the sacrifices of the extremists seemed to have prepared the way for the victory of the moderates. But Ireland was not an independent country, and at this critical stage the British Government again decided the issue.

The Irish policy of the British Government was completely determined by the British Tories. The defenders of the *status quo* did not want a compromise because they felt strong enough to enforce their own solution, and their measures unwittingly established the leadership of the extremists amongst their opponents. The nation-wide anti-conscription campaign in the spring of 1918 was answered by Lloyd George with a reshuffle at Dublin Castle, which was put in charge of Lord French as Viceroy, and with the imprisonment of 150 leading Sinn Feiners, amongst them Arthur Griffith and De Valera, under the pretext of a German plot. As the moderates amongst the Sinn Fein leaders adhered to antiquated ideas of dignity and therefore refused to run away in time, they were all caught like fish in a net, while Michael Collins, Harry Boland and the other key-men of the I.R.B. made good use of their closely knit organisation and kept out of the clutches of the police. Their deeply laid plot of packing and conquering the Sinn Fein convention had failed, but Dublin Castle obligingly put them in control of the whole organisation.

The results of this change were soon visible. At the elections of December 1918, which in England were fought on the issue of hanging the Kaiser, the enlarged Irish electorate returned no fewer than 73 Sinn Feiners out of a total of 105 members of Parliament —many of whom were in prison at the time of their election and of the meeting of the first Dail in January 1919. The Irish Labour Party had refrained from contesting the election, in order not to weaken the anti-English front, but the enforced absence of the moderates gave the first resolutions of the Dail a social radicalism directly derived from Connolly and Pearse. It outlined an ambitious programme of social reform, with more than a smattering of socialism—and it also went on record with an Oath of Allegiance to the Irish Republic. This step, which was reputedly deplored at the time even by De Valera,[62] later on involved the young Republic in grave consequences and would probably have been impossible but for the complete domination of the proceedings by the left wing.

The Irish War, which began practically at the same time as the first Dail, was to some extent a conscious assertion of leadership by the extremists. In the characteristic expression of one of the local guerrilla leaders at a time when their ascendancy was not yet fully established, 'if this is the state of affairs, we'll have to kill someone and make the bloody enemy organise us'.[63] With the Tories running Lloyd George's Government, the challenge was promptly taken up and events took their fateful course.

This Irish War was, in fact, a revolution with the repressive machine of the Government still in being and unconquerable by the traditional methods of armed insurrection because it was maintained regardless of cost by the British Government. The revolution therefore took the form of guerrilla warfare with swift and often cruel blows against the local exponents of the hostile Government. The painful events of these years have often been described, and the clumsy and ultimately ineffective expedient of governmental frightfulness, connected with the name and the memories of the Black and Tans, has achieved an unenviable notoriety. It would be idle to apportion blame or to defend the indefensible on either side, and it only remains to sum up the results of the unequal struggle.

The expenditure of much blood and treasure finally convinced the British Government that it was not simply fighting a small number of criminals and that it was not simply a matter of getting the murder gang by the throat, as the British Prime Minister assured himself and his countrymen. The complete reconquest of Southern Ireland would not have been a task beyond the power of the British Government, but it would have involved the subjection of the whole country to martial law and its transformation into a giant concentration camp. The realisation of this grim alternative between a fight to the finish and a settlement involving compromise and withdrawal was slow to come, and in the meantime the Government stooped to the employment of methods which have left permanent scars on both sides, but when it came, it led to a sudden and dramatic change of policy through the Treaty of 1921.

On the Irish side, the Sinn Fein Government was faced by problems of even greater difficulty. Although the interference of Dublin Castle with the delicate balance of forces in the nationalist camp weakened the moderates at a critical moment, their influence began to reassert itself again soon after the end of the European war. The social tension within Irish society, which a generation earlier had been so near the surface that only a régime of permanent coercion could prevent it from violent explosion, had been greatly eased by the phenomenal success of land purchase. During the war it was almost completely confined to the lower classes in the towns, to the landless labourers of the South and the land-hungry dwarf tenants and farmers of the West, where land purchase had made least progress—but after the vicissitudes of the war years it reached dangerous force amongst these minority groups.

The extreme nationalists who were so eager to stake their lives on the issue of armed struggle against the British Government and its local agents, belonged largely to the first of these classes, the under-privileged sections of the town population. But their guerrilla warfare could never result in clear-cut victory for the revolutionary forces which numbered only a few thousands of Volunteers. The guerrillas could at best hope to inflict such punishment and such expenditure of arms, money and resources on the ruling power as to make a continuation of the struggle not worth its while. Revolution limited to guerrilla warfare by a small minority was insufficient for victory, though it might produce stalemate followed by compromise. The only alternative to this course would have been the widening of the conflict to the social sphere through the combination of armed guerrilla warfare with the spontaneous rebellion of all the dissatisfied elements in Irish society.

The political crux of these dramatic years was the frustration of such a course of policy by the moderate wing of the Sinn Fein leadership. Griffith strained every nerve to prevent Sinn Fein from getting involved into the social conflict and he used his great prestige for its repression. He insisted that Sinn Fein was not a party at all, but 'a national composition' or, at the least, 'a composite party. No part of that composition may claim its own individual programme until the national ideal of freedom has first been attained.

Then we may press forward our separate ideals. Until then we must sink ourselves that the nation may gain from our unity.'[64] In the midst of guerrilla warfare and Black-and-Tan terror, Griffith managed to keep official Sinn Fein and the Dail Government to this policy. As early as the spring of 1918 agrarian unrest had started again in the land-hungry West, where seizures of land were made—more often than not in the name of Sinn Fein. These were not only promptly disavowed, but the central leadership of the Volunteers forbade their members to take part in them in their official capacity. The agitation spread, and its increasing strength forced the shadow Government of the Republic to embark on its most original venture, the Land Court which became the spearhead of the more elaborate arbitration courts, and succeeded in drawing even the landlords away from the legal courts whose sentences could no longer be enforced. In the first Land Court case, the Republican Minister of Agriculture gave judgment in favour of the landlords, and 'when that judgment was openly defied, the matter was put into the hands of the I.R.A. who one night, a fortnight after the judgment, arrested the offending parties . . . this was startling; and I well remember the shock with which the news was received; for the men who effected the arrest were of the same social order as those who had seized land. . . .'[65] The results of this attitude towards the social needs of the Western smallholders were no less startling: the province which had been the birthplace of the Land League and of the United Irish League remained practically inactive during the Irish war, while the labourers and farmers of the South braved danger and death in their struggle against the British army and the Black and Tans.

Through their refusal to integrate the social movement into the political and military struggle, the Sinn Fein leaders were, in fact, taking sides in the conflict which they pretended to ignore. At the same time, and in the midst of ambushes, outrages and reprisals, they were giving weighty proof to the British Government that they were not dangerous revolutionaries but 'responsible leaders'. While Lloyd George denounced them as a Bolshevist murder gang, some of the less emotional amongst his colleagues—who included some of the most prominent Tory leaders—began to consider the chances of a compromise which would prevent the degeneration of the Irish war into a social revolution and preserve Ireland for the British Empire.

The great obstacle of Ulster's position and separate interests had been removed by the Partition Act of 1920 which established a Home Rule administration for the Protestants of the six counties, the ancient opponents of Home Rule in any shape or form. The path was, therefore, cleared for a realistic settlement satisfying the minimum demands of the Irish nationalists and terminating a struggle which was very costly and damaging to the reputation of Great Britain in the world and, still worse, in the rest of the British Empire. The leaders of the conciliatory section of the Cabinet appear to have been Winston Churchill amongst the Liberals and Lord Birkenhead amongst the Conservatives. Their initiative was powerfully reinforced by the Dominion statesmen who met in London in the spring of 1921, particularly by General Smuts, the spokesman of a nation which had achieved virtual independence within the British Empire after its defeat in armed struggle. The formal overture for an agreed settlement was made in the speech with which King George V opened the Parliament of Ulster in June 1921.

The negotiations which took place during the following five and a half months formed one of the most fascinating political episodes in the crowded aftermath of the First World War.[66] They were conducted by the ablest men on both sides; they were of the greatest consequence not only for the Irish side but also for the British Government, which was threatened by open rebellion amongst a large section of its Tory supporters; and their result was an arrangement which in many important respects turned out very differently in practice from the intentions of either party, but which nevertheless put an end to the Irish Question as it had existed for over a century.

Both sides were substantially in agreement about the necessity of local autonomy for Ireland, for after the Government of Ireland Act (1920) which set up a Home Rule Parliament in Ulster, not even the staunchest Unionist could deny Southern Ireland's right to Home Rule. But Home Rule in the old sense was dead and buried, for the small extremist minority which in 1914 denounced the third Home Rule Bill as utterly insufficient had meanwhile become the overwhelming majority, while Ulster's exclusion from the settlement removed the last remaining reason for moderation of the national demands. Churchill and Birkenhead advocated the sensible method of putting the British maximum offer forward from the very beginning, and with one significant exception this was the line taken by the British negotiators.

England offered the Irish nationalists dominion self-government within the Empire, coupled with certain military and financial guarantees, and excluding the newly formed Northern Ireland territory. The maximum Irish demand which De Valera put forward with considerable boldness and skill was the recognition by Great Britain of an independent all-Irish Republic, in association with the British Empire for specific purposes, like Cuba with the United States. Plainly, settlement could not be reached without a considerable abatement of the Irish demands, and the task of the principal British delegates—Lloyd George, Winston Churchill, Lord Birkenhead and Austen Chamberlain—was the wearing down of Irish opposition by threats and promises.

The Irish delegation to some extent reflected the coalition character of the Irish Government between constitutional Sinn Feiners and fighting activists, though in the course of the negotiations an important realignment of forces became noticeable. Arthur Griffith, the leader of the delegation, had never been a Republican in the fiercely symbolic sense of the left wing, and after more than twenty years in the wilderness he regarded a speedy settlement as essential for Ireland's development on the lines of his social and economic programme. His most prominent colleague, Michael Collins, the youngest and most famous Irish delegate, was the leader of the I.R.B. and chief of the guerrillas who had defied the British army, the Irish police and the Black and Tans for more than two years. He knew better than anybody else the precarious state of his small army and the risks of renewed armed struggle, and in spite of his past role as a guerrilla leader he was a capable administrator who shared Griffith's basic aims. At the last critical moment he actually became the key figure in the negotiations, and his gradual approach to Griffith's point of view turned the scales in favour of acceptance of the British terms.

The representatives of the British Government naturally had the stronger hand, and they played it with great shrewdness, though in Lloyd George's case with more ability than forthrightness. Apart from the background threat of overwhelming force, which was by no means sheer bluff, although the Government intensely disliked the use of so double-edged a weapon, the British negotiators had two bargaining counters of great value to their opponents—Ulster and fiscal autonomy. These had been the twin rocks on which the Convention of 1917-18 had been wrecked, and a real concession on fiscal autonomy, coupled with the elaborate pretence of a concession on Ulster, enabled the British Government to make the Treaty acceptable to the Irish representatives, although it contained an oath of fidelity to the King and Ireland's formal acquiescence in membership in the British Empire.

Ulster's importance for the negotiations was in every way cardinal. Although Lloyd George never budged on the question of Ireland's membership of the Empire as a condition of agreement, the Ulster question made insistence on the Republic untenable for all those Irishmen who laid great stress on the value of Ireland's unity. An independent republic clearly implied the complete loss of Ulster, and Lloyd George made clever use of the great attraction which Ulster had for Griffith and his followers in order to gain their active support for Ireland's participation in the British Empire, because this was their only chance of achieving Ireland's essential unity. It may well be doubted whether Lloyd George ever expected to effect an arrangement between Ulster and the South, but he made first-class use of this possibility and of the alternative of a boundary commission in case of Ulster's persistent refusal. The boundary commission seemed to hold out to the Irish the hope of winning Tyrone and Fermanagh without which they thought that Ulster would become an economic impossibility.

While Lloyd George's success with Griffith on the Ulster question was a genuine diplomatic triumph, his use of the boundary commission, particularly in his decisive interview with Michael Collins,[67] was patently disingenuous. 'The plain truth is', Lord Birkenhead wrote some years after the event, 'that, rightly or wrongly, we offered to the Free State representatives a certain consideration for their signatures. The consideration was that a Commission should be created. . . . We decided upon the appropriate formula for reference to this Commission. Having satisfied ourselves that the words employed were only capable, upon a fair and competent construction, of the meaning which we placed upon them, we assented to the addition of other words at the earnest entreaty of the Irish negotiators. We should not have agreed to the insertion of these words if we had not believed that they were powerless to affect the meaning of the article taken as a whole . . . in other words, we agreed upon a reference to the Commission which many of us knew to be disputable but which we were certain could only be decided in one way.'[68]

Ulster was thus the decoy which secured the voluntary membership of the Irish Free State in the British Empire; but this bait had to be fortified at the last crucial moment by a genuine English concession—full fiscal autonomy which included the right to put tariffs on British goods. As late as the spring of 1921 Lloyd George had confronted the supporters of conciliation in his own Cabinet with the astonished question, 'Would you then allow a Dublin Parliament like any other Dominion to levy a tariff against British goods?'[69] Two months afterwards, on the eve of King George V's Belfast speech, Lord Birkenhead still rejected the claim for full Irish fiscal autonomy, because it would enable Ireland to erect a tariff wall against England and to repudiate her share in the national debt, and permanent free trade between the two islands was one of the conditions attached to Lloyd George's offer of dominion status.

For the British, and particularly the Liberals amongst them, this valued right was thus 'a last sacrifice in the effort to persuade Ireland into voluntary membership of the British Commonwealth of Nations'.[70] On the Irish side it made a deep impression not only on Griffith, for whom it was the realisation of one of his most cherished aims, but also on the convinced Republican Barton and not least on Michael Collins, who regarded it as the most important advance of the final Treaty over the earlier draft.[71]

The real or pretended concessions of the British Government thus concerned questions which the spokesmen of the Irish urban middle class regarded as peculiarly and intimately important for the future growth of their country. On the other hand, the undoing of an independent Republic and the formal membership in the British Empire were categorical conditions of a settlement, and with the oath of fidelity to King and Empire the issue was squarely joined with the extremists who regarded their oath of allegiance to the Irish Republic as the cornerstone of their national faith.

The influence of the British Government on the course of events did not stop at the enforcement of terms which were reasonably favourable to the Irish middle class and unacceptable to the extreme nationalists. During the following months Mr. Winston Churchill employed all his formidable powers of persuasion and pressure in order to widen the rift between pro-Treaty and anti-Treaty elements in Southern Ireland into a chasm. He began with the sound principle of placing the repressive machinery of the Irish colonial state 'as it now stands' with the minimum of alterations into the hands of the new pro-Treaty Government.[72] The ultimate purpose of this State had always been the ruthless suppression of the enemies of the established order, and during the next few months the British Colonial Secretary bombarded Michael Collins with steadily more urgent demands for the use of the State machine in order to crush the extremists by force of ex-British arms: 'Every day that the uncertainty continues must be attended by the progressive impoverishment of Ireland. Nobody can invest or make plans for production while the threat of civil war, or of a Republic followed by a state of war with the British Empire hangs over the country. I trust the end of May or at the very latest the first week in June will see the issue submitted to the Irish people. . . .'[73]

Against this relentless pressure and in a society torn by deep social conflicts which were the more devastating because largely beneath the surface of political consciousness, the most prominent leaders of the earlier struggle tried desperately to prevent the catastrophe of civil war. De Valera, the leader of the opposition to the Treaty, was by no means an extremist, but somewhat 'left of centre' trying to hold the scales even between constitutional Sinn Feiners and 'the old Fenian side'. On the other side of the gap Michael Collins, though a convinced upholder of the treaty and hard-pressed by Churchill's barely veiled threats, hated the thought of civil war against his old comrades, though he showed characteristic fear of the disorderly elements in the country, i.e. of the danger of social unrest. At the Sinn Fein Convention in February 1922 he prevented a breach between adherents and opponents of the Treaty. In spite or perhaps because of the delicate situation created by the anti-Treaty attitude of the majority of the I.R.A., the strange election compact between Collins and De Valera might have delayed or even prevented civil war, but for the resolute counter-offensive undertaken by Griffith and his closest supporters in Ireland—and by the British Government. Churchill bitterly protested against the pact, though he could not undo it, and its practical effect was largely nullified by the right wing of Sinn Fein which opposed the anti-Treaty candidates on the 'panel'—and in many cases successfully.

The crisis came with the murder in London of Field-Marshal Sir Henry Wilson, the military adviser of the Ulster Government. This incident endangered Lloyd George's Government and induced Churchill to order the Irish Government from the Front Bench of the House of Commons to break the resistance of the extremists by force: 'The time has come when it is not unfair, not premature and not impatient for us to make to this strengthened Irish Government and new Irish Parliament a request in express terms that this sort of thing must come to an end. If either from weakness, from want of courage, or for some other even less creditable reasons, it is not brought to an end, and a very speedy end, then it is my duty to say, on behalf of H.M. Government, that we shall regard the Treaty as having been formally violated. . . .'[74] Although the English commander in Ireland disregarded his instructions to start hostilities, which would have reunited the split Irish movement, an uncomfortably large share of the responsibility for the Irish civil war rests on Lloyd George's Government and its Colonial Secretary.

Although the broad lines of division on the Treaty were clearly marked by the previous history of the Irish nationalist movement, the struggle was by no means bound to be so violent and devastating as it actually turned out to be. The difference between De Valera's Document No. 2 and the text of the Treaty, though not entirely a matter of terminology, was far too small to explain the violent explosion of the civil war. In 1922, Cobbett's wise *dictum* concerning an earlier oath still retained its truth—it was 'a mere test of discontent with other things'.[75] The social revolution which

Sinn Fein had kept within the narrow channels of a national struggle against England, was trying to find an outlet now that the English enemy had withdrawn. The paradox that some of the Western districts 'which proved so peaceful under the Black and Tan régime became aggressively warlike after the Treaty was signed',[76] throws a glaring light on the crucial implications of Sinn Fein's conservative social policy on political events. If further evidence of the gulf between the under-privileged sections of the Irish people and their national Government were needed, the widespread attacks on the mansions of landlords and ex-landlords, the revolt of the labourers in Wexford and Waterford, the short-lived 'Soviets' in some urban centres and the occupation of creameries by their workpeople amply supplied it.

The crowded history of the Irish Free State under Michael Collins, Cosgrave, De Valera and Costello lies outside the scope of this study. Although still deeply affected by Ireland's colonial heritage, it was no longer dominated by the all-pervading tension between the subject people and its foreign rulers. Above all, the Treaty suddenly terminated Ireland's political influence on Great Britain, though it contributed largely to the inevitable Tory revolt against Lloyd George's Coalition Government. Yet in its new position the self-governing Dominion played a far from negligible part in the further development of the British Commonwealth.

Book Five: Contrasts and Parallels

CHAPTER XXVI

THE RHYTHM OF MODERN IRISH HISTORY

LOOKING backwards over the tragic course of Irish history, it is difficult to remain undisturbed by the passionate feelings which it still evokes amongst the descendants of its victims—the dead generations which are such a lasting reality to Ireland's best sons. But instead of exalting Ireland's historical significance, such an emotional attitude depresses it. By regarding Irish history as unique in the sufferings of the people, the iniquity of the rulers and the courage of the fighters for freedom and self-determination, the hero-worshipper not only misinterprets Ireland's part in modern history but reduces it to the dimensions of a limited, if colourful, episode.

As a matter of historical fact and appreciation, Ireland's destinies were inseparable from those of the country by which it was dominated from the dawn of modern times to the historical present. Nothing is easier, or more justified, than to denounce the selfishness and stupidity of English rule over Ireland, but it helps very little towards an understanding of the relations between the two countries which show, as under a microscope, the mechanism of colonial rule and exploitation, and the inevitable reaction of the subject people in the shape of an anti-imperialist struggle for national survival and independence. An additional fascination of Anglo-Irish relations lies in their powerful influence on modern Britain and the British Empire, itself one of the most remarkable products of modern social development.

Ireland under British rule was the most important remnant of the old colonial system in the modern world. Even in the heyday of the old British Empire it differed in important respects both from genuine colonies, i.e. settlements by members of the colonising people, and from robber empires *pur sang*, like the American possessions of Spain. It resembled the former in the presence of substantial numbers of British colonists, and the latter in the ruthless exploitation of the native population by the colonists in their own interests and in those of the 'mother country'. The Anglo-Irish, like the American colonists, resented the restrictions put on their development by the grasping policy of the British House of Commons, but unlike the Americans they were prevented from throwing off their English connection by the need of English help for the maintenance of their own privileges.

Ireland's tenacious struggle for national independence was determined by a similar double knot. In self-devotion and romantic incidents at least equal to that of the Poles against three robber empires, it surpasses the latter by far in historical significance and interest: its colonial character made it the prototype of a development which must be counted amongst the most important of the present century—the rise of colonial peoples to independent nationhood. Ireland's colonial position affected the course of Irish and Anglo-Irish history both in fundamentals and in detail. The essentials of this position are the material exploitation of the colony in the interests of the economically more advanced country, or rather of its dominant social groups, the enforcement of this one-sided arrangement by the local agents of the rulers, and the existence or growth of a separate national consciousness of the colonial people. The results of imperialist domination are felt in every sphere of life of the colonial people, and especially in its economy and its politics.

Material exploitation delays the growth and development of the colonial economy. It prevents or reduces the accumulation of wealth in general, and of capital in particular, by burdening it with a tribute to the ruling country. The latter receives the benefit of this relationship, but this is by no means an unmixed blessing for the ruling country as a whole, however pleasant for the immediate recipients. Excessive tributes may be fatal to the receiving country, while even a large single tribute payment need not seriously weaken the defeated country, provided it escapes the shackles of colonial dependence. In the case of Ireland, the tribute was not a single sum, as in the reparations exacted by victorious Prussia from France in 1871, but a continuing heavy drain, large enough to depress the mass of the native population to subsistence level. A substantial part of it was squandered in vulgar extravagance without really benefiting British economy, and all of it helped to bolster up a reactionary and inefficient system which was an obstacle to the free development of England's productive forces.

While the mere Irish were kept in a state of barbarism by the ruthless extraction of their whole economic surplus, and a large slice of their necessaries of life, the leading groups of the Anglo-Irish community were bitterly antagonised by the perversion of their economic life in the supposed interests of the ruling country. The classical grievances of pre-Union Ireland were due to the general principles of British colonial policy, though their application had worse results in Ireland than in the young overseas dependencies. After the Union, Ireland's sufferings were caused mainly by the unnatural integration of its economy into the economic system of a more advanced and infinitely more powerful nation. The Union put an end to Irish industrial development everywhere outside north-east Ulster, and the distance between the two countries widened into an unbridgeable gulf. Instead of following the same road as England, albeit more slowly, Ireland underwent a feverish economic expansion during the Napoleonic Wars and then relapsed completely, degenerating into an economic slum on Britain's doorstep. Finally, when the interests of the British business classes required an expansion of overseas food imports as a means of widening foreign markets for British exports, Ireland lost its economic importance for England, with the exception of the secondary consideration of a market for British goods, and the colonial relationship between Irish peasants and Anglo-Irish landlords and moneylenders became the principal issue between the two countries. At this stage the material foundations of the Union disappeared completely, and the struggle for Irish self-determination entered a decisive phase.

Irish politics were dominated by the social results of this colonial position. The unrelenting pressure of grinding exploitation intensified all social conflicts far beyond the strength which they would otherwise have attained. The load of misery and oppression from which the Irish people suffered for centuries was put on them by the reckless greed of masters who belonged to a different world with very little contact with their victims and correspondingly little reason to fear their revenge. The system was maintained by an overgrown, tyrannical, bureaucratic and inefficient state machine, using the constant threat and the frequent application of physical force as methods of day-by-day government. This outgrowth of a sick society became in the course of time one of the most expensive bureaucracies of its kind which constituted an additional drain on the shrunken resources of the country.

The social effects of preventing Ireland's economic advance on modern capitalist lines were also visible in the political field. The Irish middle class outside north-east Ulster was generally confined to a thin layer of small shopkeepers and usurers in an agrarian country, with a few merchant firms in the ports and an excessive number of lawyers, doctors, journalists and other professional and semi-professional men of frequently doubtful economic standing. The urban middle class was far too weak to contest the social and political monopoly of the landowners by its own efforts like the British bourgeoisie. In normal times it was content to play second fiddle to the landlords and to gather the crumbs which fell from their still very well-spread tables. But the Anglo-Irish gentry was so strongly imbued with the arrogance of the ruling nation and its native imitators that it refused to fulfil the modest ambitions of the Catholic middle class, and times were as a rule far from normal. In periods of crisis the poorer and more enterprising elements of the middle class could not resist the temptation of mobilising the forces of rebellious discontent, which were always at work amongst the peasantry, in support of middle-class claims. The Irish middle class was, therefore, torn between servility towards the landlords and their English backers, because it wanted to share in the exploitation of the peasants, and agitation amongst the peasants in order to blackmail the landlords and the English Government, whom it could not bend to its will by its own strength.

The intrinsic instability of the Irish middle class was further accentuated by the decay of Ireland's material and human resources. Ireland lost in succession most of its budding industries, which were destroyed by English competition, its tillage, which fell a victim to the attractions of the English market for meat producers, and a large part of its population: the Irish middle class participated in the decline of the country, and while its development was stunted by repression from above, its position was also threatened by pressure from below. The dominant social relationship of colonial Ireland was that between the landlords and their auxiliaries and the peasant masses, characterised by complete ruthlessness on the part of the former, and complete docility, alternating with fierce rebellion, on the part of the latter. The middle class did its best to imitate the landlords in its relations with the urban masses, but its means of coercion were far less effective than those of the landlords. Thus it never succeeded in reducing them to complete servility and encountered bitter and not quite unsuccessful opposition in its attempts to solve all its problems by intensified exploitation of the poor.

Within this framework Ireland's political history between the American Revolution and the First World War followed a course full of cross-currents and apparent inconsistencies which was nevertheless eminently logical. The overriding problem which confronted Ireland and the whole Irish people was its colonial dependence on a ruling power which cramped the independent development of every group and class. Nationalism was, therefore, the uniformly valid political creed of every Irish party, and active nationalism invariably involved hostility towards England. But as far as any special group itself enjoyed a privileged position within Irish society which needed the English connection for its maintenance, its professed nationalism was limited and qualified to an extent sufficient to enable this group to combine the advantages of unfettered development for its members with the security which only English support could guarantee.

This basic fact explains the gradual transfer of leadership of the nationalist movement from more to less privileged groups, as each of them in turn was confronted by the choice between the heroic policy of leading a rebellious people at manifest risk to its own privileges, and the prudent resignation to security and stagnation through a compromise with the paramount power.

The Irish landlords had always been an English garrison, and only a small minority of their number were ever on the side of Irish nationalism. After the Union the landlords as a class forswore every thought of genuine political leadership and settled down to the more congenial part of well-paid beneficiaries of British rule.

The Catholic middle class had more substantial grievances and fewer privileges than the progressive landlords, and it was, therefore, more formidable in its opposition to the ruling system. It suffered more than a century of contumely and persecution, and its gradual and incomplete rise to a modest prosperity owed nothing to English favour. In the agitation for Catholic Emancipation and Repeal, Daniel O'Connell achieved a measure of national leadership which was incomparably more real and impressive than the claims of the Grattans and Floods of an earlier generation. Even the most progressive landlords shrunk from contact with the rebellious peasants which would have been fatal to them as landlords, however necessary it might have been for them as Irish patriots. O'Connell, however, discovered that an alliance between the peasants and the middle class could put him on the high road to success, and he resolutely entered upon this policy, using the power of the Church in order to keep the masses in strict discipline.

Although the middle class continued to influence every succeeding nationalist movement, it never again held the same position of undisputed leadership as under O'Connell. From then onwards, periods of middle-class predominance marked the low tide of Irish nationalism, and were invariably repudiated by the next generation of militant nationalists. The next open mass movement of the Irish people, the Land League, was as much a successor of the illegal revolutionary societies as of O'Connell's 'agitation'.

The respectable politics of the privileged or semi-privileged groups had always been paralleled on a lower level but with much greater intensity by the 'criminal conspiracies' amongst the under-privileged. The Whiteboys and Steelboys had been the precursors, and in a sense the cause, of the Irish Volunteers of 1782. The Ribbonmen accompanied O'Connell's movement and supported the shrill claims of the agitators with their threatening murmur. Its attitude towards these underground movements was the acid test for every professedly nationalist party. If it fought shy of an alliance with the peasants, like the original Irish Volunteers, it involved no serious danger to the English connection. If it tried to weld the uncouth and primitive secret societies into a nation-wide organisation, like the United Irishmen or O'Connell's Catholic Association, though the latter with serious qualifications, it was a threat to the existing order and had to be destroyed—either by force or by concessions to the privileged partners as a consideration for dissolving the alliance.

As long as these organisations amongst the under-privileged consisted only of peasants, they never went beyond the stage of loose conspiracies, and their general frame of mind was that of ferocious impotence without active influence on the course of events. These agrarian clubs were upset by the Great Famine, together with the society to which they belonged. From then onwards the leadership of the revolutionary movement was transferred to the towns. The Fenians were mainly recruited from amongst the urban working and lower middle class, and with all their faults they were at least free from the political schizophrenia of the earlier and more respectable 'agitations', because they did not use national slogans as a pretext for the achievement of narrow class purposes. From 1860 until the end of the Union the Fenians served as a cadre, and for some time as the only existing cadre, for the political organisation of the disinherited, until a part of the urban workers began to find their way into the labour movement, which disputed the Fenian claim to national leadership by combining a militant nationalist policy with the resolute advocacy of working-class aims and purposes.

While the leadership of respectable politics fell with every generation a step or two in the social ladder, until during the Land League and Home Rule struggles it rested with the lower middle class, the revolutionary wing of Irish politics grew steadily stronger, until the Fenians contested the claim of the 'moderates' to speak for the Irish nation. In the Land League the Fenians took the initiative and forced the respectable leaders, much against their inclination, to follow their lead. They were ousted from this position by the combined efforts of the middle-class elements and the Catholic Church, but the ineffective Home Rule policy of the moderates finally enabled the heirs of the Fenians to wrest power from the hands of the Irish party and to lead the Irish nation in a revolutionary struggle which ended with the evacuation of Dublin Castle by the British Government.

This development of Irish politics, though in broad outline

corresponding to the general progress of democratic forces in the
transition from feudalism to capitalism, shows certain peculiar and
very important features which are in the last resort due to the
colonial character of Irish life and politics. In the first place, in
colonial Ireland political leadership was by no means the direct
perquisite of economic power. On the contrary, it could be maintained by any social group only as a result of its 'grievances', which
measured the gap between its social aspirations and its actual
position. The rule of the landlords expressed genuine leadership,
if at all, only during the few years immediately before and after
1782. Their economic power remained unimpaired for generations,
but their leading position came to an end even before the Union
of 1800. The middle class led the Irish nation during the Emancipation campaign and in the early stage of the Repeal movement;
its powers of political leadership evaporated during the generation
after the Famine which for a substantial section of the bourgeoisie
offered excellent chances of increasing its wealth at the expense of
the masses. Even the lower middle class of 'strong' farmers and
shopkeepers, the mainstay of the Home Rule movement, declined
as a genuine political force with the gradual abatement of its
grievances, until it was ousted from leadership by the extremists
who had no stake in the country and an all-consuming passion for
its liberation.

In colonial Ireland, genuine political leadership was thus not an
immediate reflection of the economic relations of power. No class
which depended for the maintenance of its position on Ireland's
colonial status could hold the voluntary allegiance of the Irish
people for any length of time. The test for its capacity for leadership
was its participation in the exploitation of the Irish people. The
more deeply it was implicated in this process, the greater the internal
opposition to its leadership, the stronger its need for English support
against its internal enemies, and the less suited was it for the exacting
part of political leaders of a subject people.

Another significant feature of Irish politics was their comparatively plebeian character in an era of aristocratic government. This
was partly due to the impoverishment of the country under British
rule, and partly to the interweaving of social and national dis-
contents which reflected Ireland's reaction to its colonial position.
The masses suffered from the triple burden of economic exploitation,
national oppression and bureaucratic misrule, and their reaction
to this well-nigh unbearable pressure set the tune to the political
beggars' opera of Irish public life. The abuse of mass discontent
for their own purposes by the higher strata of Irish society, and the
nemesis which overtook them in turn as a result of their betrayal,

forms the main content of Irish respectable politics during the
lifetime of the legislative Union.

A peculiarly interesting example of the influence of middle-class
interests and ideas on Irish national policies, and even on the ideals
and aspirations of the whole people, was the tariff question which
bedevilled Anglo-Irish politics ever since the days of Grattan's
Parliament. The Irish demand for protection against British
imports was eminently reasonable in itself and had the full support
of a convinced anti-capitalist like Karl Marx. But it is a matter
of historical notoriety that it prevented an alliance between British
and Irish Radicals during the years of O'Connell's Repeal movement; that it precipitated the break between the British business
classes and the Liberal party at the time of the first Home Rule
Bill and entrapped Parnell into his damning alliance with the
Tories; that it formed an insurmountable obstacle to any compromise between Protestant Ulster and the South, where it figured
prominently in the Sinn Fein programme, and that finally it
turned the scales in the Treaty negotiations, although in this
case opinion may be legitimately divided on the merits of the
issue.

Even more interesting than this subterranean domination of
respectable Irish politics by the tariff question is the gradual substitution of national for social aspirations in the minds of the active
elements of the Irish lower classes which formed the rank and file
of the extreme nationalist movements. In their early stages, these
movements were generally regarded as criminal conspiracies and
nothing else, and the Government was less concerned about their
vague nationalism than about their vigorous reaction to the social
and economic abuses by which they were caused. Later on they
became more and more nationalist, partly as a result of their contact
with the middle-class agitators who needed mass support for their
own purposes and appealed to the masses on religious and national
grounds. This change became particularly striking with the shift
in the centre of political gravity to the towns. Militant nationalism
became the ideology of the politically alert lower middle and
working class, and radiated back into the villages where the new
gospel was eagerly absorbed by the small tenants and landless men.
From then onwards, the struggle between the Irish middle class
and the under-privileged masses assumed the form of competing
national aims—Home Rule on one side, Separation, perhaps in the
form of a socialist republic, on the other, with Sinn Fein as a compromise solution. The victory of Sinn Fein over the Home Rule
party and the struggle between constitutionalists and republicans
within the victorious coalition was the last stage of a development

in which every national victory had been won by the sacrifices of the masses and exploited by the middle class.

Has this fatal law of colonial Irish politics lost its validity with the Treaty and the achievement of independence for Southern Ireland? The Treaty sanctioned the partition of the country, but within these limits this settlement, and the ensuing changes in the character of the British Empire and Eire's constitution, made the Irish people the master of its destiny. But no sooner had the Treaty been accepted than the conflicting social groups within the nationalist camp, no longer held together by the threat of the Black and Tans, were at one another's throats in a deadly but essentially futile war. Irish politics, so efficient and advanced in their methods as long as it was a matter of mobilising the weakness of a subject nation against the resources of a powerful Empire, now seemed to show all the blemishes of the cramped and arrested provincialism which centuries of subjection had forced on the country. Instead of a political line-of-battle reflecting the social dividing lines and the conflicts of first-rate interests, the alignment into opponents and supporters of the Treaty expressed a confusion of purpose in marked contrast with the discreditable ferocity of the methods employed on both sides. The dead hand of the past maintained its stranglehold over the political life of a country which had been deprived for too long of the opportunity of living in the present and of shaping its future by the free will of its people.

CHAPTER XXVII

IRELAND, ENGLAND, AND THE BRITISH EMPIRE

THE history of Ireland's unwilling and unwanted participation in British public life is rich in interesting and even piquant details, and impressive by its dramatic power. Ireland influenced the destinies of the larger and more famous island long before the Union —in the days of the Plantagenets and Richard of Bordeaux, in Tudor times and, most fatefully, during the Great Rebellion. But it was only after the Union that Irish problems became an integral part of British politics, and at more than one decisive point in recent English history they were the crucial facts which made men's minds turn from their accustomed thoughts and follow new lines.

In Britain's history since the beginning of the nineteenth century Ireland's share is out of all proportion to her size, wealth or position. During the first thirty years after the Union, Ireland had few spokesmen and not a single genuine representative of the Irish people at Westminster, but Irish problems acted on each of the historical British parties like solvents on a chemical compound. During the following generation, the passive influence exerted by Ireland on English politics reached a climax in the Free Trade crisis, and an Irish party began to make its influence felt, with greater results for England than for Ireland. Irish votes determined the crucial division on the First Reform Bill, and governments were made and unmade through Irish support and Irish hostility.

From a trial ground and a battlefield for the opposing English parties, Ireland developed with the gradual democratisation of British politics into an outpost of democracy within the United Kingdom. In this process the Irish people found themselves more than once frustrated and betrayed by their 'representatives' who abused their position in their personal interests, until the Irish party under Parnell demonstrated for a few years how these obstacles could be overcome. In the Home Rule crisis of the eighteen-eighties this new force showed the revolutionary effect of a compact modern party on the political structure of Great Britain. Under its pressure the coalition within the Liberal party dissolved into its social elements, thereby establishing the Tories as the authoritative spokesmen of social privilege in every shape, and blazing the trail for the Labour party of the future.

At the same time, Irish opposition and obstruction compelled the modernisation of the House of Commons and its procedure which had become incompatible with effective control over the Government and with the proper dispatch of parliamentary business. Ireland was soon to leave an even more important trace of her influence in the Parliament Act of 1911. In spite of the progress of democracy and the transfer of effective power to the House of Commons, the British Constitution still maintained the feudal tradition of the three Estates—King, Lords and Commons—whose co-ordination was a complete anachronism in an era which claimed the support of democratic principles. Although the immediate occasion of the conflict between the Peers and the Commons was Lloyd George's 'People's Budget' of 1909, there was no issue on which the two Houses clashed more frequently or with greater political effect than that of Ireland, and it was with the help, and even at the insistence, of the Irish party that the Parliament Act of 1911 was put on the Statute Book.

With the First World War, Anglo-Irish relations entered an entirely new phase, and Ireland proved herself again what she had been in most great crises of British history, the test for British imperial relations. The old imperialism had nowhere shown itself more repulsive than in Ireland where its rule was more complete than anywhere else. Its sole content was exploitation at its harshest and with few redeeming features—callous, restrictive, short-sighted and inefficient. It ended in complete bankruptcy amidst a welter of rebellion, bloodshed and the threat of foreign invasion. The Union was intended as a permanent safeguard against the repetition of similar events, but it was not followed by the radical change in the structure of Irish society which alone could have destroyed the permanent causes of anti-British and therefore 'disloyal' sentiments. Apart from north-east Ulster, Ireland remained a backward and exploited colony, and with the advance of democracy the national struggle for self-determination was fed by the sources of social revolt. Repeated attempts to reach a settlement which would have satisfied at least the middle class, and thereby put the responsibility for dealing with Irish unrest on Irish shoulders, were foiled by the resistance of the traditional vested interests. The very success of this resistance defeated its own ends, for it weakened the influence of the Irish middle class to such an extent that the extreme Left could grasp the leadership of the country at the Easter Rising and hold it in the Irish War which ended with the Treaty of December 6, 1921.

Ireland's abnormal position had become an imperial problem in the modern sense some time before the formal recognition of the Irish Free State as a self-governing Dominion. Canada and Australasia contained large numbers of ex-Irishmen whose political sympathies were definitely on the side of the Nationalists, and who expressed the feelings of all their compatriots in their vocal distaste for coercion in Ireland. The new Dominion of South Africa, though less influenced by bonds of racial affinity and common ancestry, had a strong Republican minority and no love for the aggressive imperialism which had been responsible for its incorporation into the British Empire. The great success of Campbell-Bannerman's South African policy, combined with the fear of resentment amongst the other dominions at Ireland's continued colonial status, played some part in reviving the Home Rule issue and in preventing its abandonment by the lukewarm Asquith Government. The war greatly increased the importance of the Dominions for Great Britain, and the Imperial War Conference of 1917 formally recognised them as autonomous nations of the Imperial Commonwealth—in striking contrast to the refusal of self-government to Ireland. The meeting of the Dominion Prime Ministers in the spring of 1921 had a direct bearing on the armistice with the nationalist forces in Ireland. While Sinn Fein's appeal to the Peace Conference had failed completely, the indirect appeal to the Dominions, and particularly to General Smuts, played a considerable part in breaking the deadlock and paving the way for the Treaty.

At that time the grant of Dominion status had ceased to be such a boon as it might still have been a few years earlier. If this policy had been freely chosen in Gladstone's day, or even before the outbreak of the First World War, it would have secured the willing co-operation of the Irish middle class and immeasurably strengthened its hands in dealing with the extreme nationalists at home. The bankruptcy of the traditional Irish policy of the British Government was reflected in the stratagems which were required in order to force the Treaty down the throats of the Irish representatives, in the repercussions of the Treaty issue in Irish internal affairs and in the Anglo-Irish economic war of 1932-8.

The incompleteness of the Treaty settlement was indirectly responsible for Ireland's continued influence on Great Britain in the wider sphere of the British Empire. Under the Union, the Irish representatives had been forced into opposition to the ruling system and, therefore, into a championship of democratic principles against political and social privilege, because Ireland, though nominally an equal part of the United Kingdom, was actually conquered territory ruled by an imperial power against the wishes of the population. The Irish Free State, deprived of part of what its leaders regarded as its due rights, maintained a similar attitude towards the British Empire.

In both cases, the natural reaction of a colonial people was powerfully reinforced by the action of the unprivileged classes within that people whose social radicalism expressed itself for historical reasons as extreme nationalism. Just as the critical reserve of the masses towards the respectable politics of the nineteenth century had goaded good Conservatives like O'Connell, Butt and Parnell into a Radical democratic position in English politics, the strong support for De Valera and the I.R.A. reinforced Cosgrave's similar attitude towards the British imperial system of the early 1920s. In both cases, the Irish attitude was quite in line with the inner trend of development in British and Imperial politics and strengthened the forces which advocated the democratisation of British politics and the transformation of the British Empire into a voluntary association of free nations.

The influence of the Free State on the structure of the British Commonwealth was greater than its intrinsic strength would seem to warrant. In Michael Collins's conception, the British Empire tended to grow into a 'League of free States' (Pakenham), and the Irish Free State was in the van of the movement to make this tendency a reality. The immediate occasion for this policy on the part of the Free State leaders was the imposition of certain limits on their power in the Treaty. Above all, the Treaty confined Irish legislation within its own terms by making repugnant laws *ipso facto* invalid, and the Free State Government naturally did its best to throw off this last vestige of subordination. Its leaders used every opportunity to demonstrate the completeness of their independence, and, as a result of Ireland's membership in the British Empire, their actions strengthened similar tendencies amongst the other dominions, although it would be a mistake to over-estimate Ireland's effective power in the counsels of the British Commonwealth. Thus, at the Imperial Conference of 1926, which laid the foundations of the Statute of Westminster, the Irish representatives were amongst the most outspoken supporters of three measures of first-rate constitutional importance: the legal declaration of complete legislative equality between the United Kingdom and the Dominions, the recognition of independent Dominion action in matters of foreign policy and the abolition of appeals from Dominion courts of law to the British Privy Council.

Impelled by the logic of its own position, the Government of the Irish Free State was thus long before De Valera's advent to power one of the most effective advocates of the 'democratisation' of the British Empire, at least as far as it consisted of self-governing Dominions. De Valera's victory in the elections of February 1932 was nevertheless an event of crucial importance. Ever since the fateful peace negotiations of 1921, De Valera had insisted on the possibility of an arrangement which combined complete internal independence for Ireland with a certain measure of co-operation with Great Britain and the countries of the British Commonwealth. The plan of 'external association' between a sovereign and independent Irish Republic and the British Commonwealth had been De Valera's personal conception, but Lloyd George scornfully rejected it as an idea which seemed to him to strike at the roots of the British Empire as he knew it.

During the stormy first years of his long spell of power, De Valera realised with a remarkable blend of rigidity in principles and elasticity in tactics all the essentials of his original programme by abolishing the oath of allegiance to the King, removing the Governor-General and defining Ireland's attitude towards the Empire in the External Relations Act of 1936. He then consolidated the new position in the Constitution of 1937 and the settlement of the 'economic war' which involved the evacuation of the Treaty Ports by Great Britain; soon afterwards he gave to the world a striking, and until then unsuspected, demonstration of the length to which a British Dominion could go without a formal declaration of independence by maintaining Irish neutrality during the Second World War against pressure from Great Britain and—more difficult to resist—from the United States of America.

The essence of De Valera's policy was the attempt to combine a republican form of government with a certain measure of participation in the British Commonwealth of Nations. Though regarded at first as a policy of squaring the circle and barely worthy of serious consideration, it was easily the most important Irish contribution towards the modern conception of the Commonwealth. In spite of Michael Collins's hopeful speculations about the possible future of the British Empire, De Valera's Fianna Fail, and even Cosgrave's Fine Gael, did not advocate full Irish partnership in the Commonwealth, and De Valera's formula of external association was, therefore, essentially a device for asserting Eire's complete sovereignty without outraging Great Britain beyond the limits of prudence. The Anglo-Irish economic war proved that, even after the Statute of Westminster, the risks of provoking England's anger were very real, although they had to be taken by a party and a leader who had staked their political existence on the establishment of an Irish Republic.

The settlement made by De Valera in the External Relations Act of 1936 and the Constitution of 1937 followed broadly the draft for an Anglo-Irish Treaty proposed by him in 1921 and rejected by the British Government of the day. It maintained a tenuous link between a *de facto* Republic and the self-governing members of the British Commonwealth by section 3 of the External Relations Act which 'authorized' the British King, with the permission of the Irish Government, to act for the purposes of appointing Irish international representatives and to conclude Irish international agreements 'so long as the King recognized by those nations as the symbol of their co-operation continues to act on behalf of those nations (on the advice of the several Governments thereof). . . .'

This ingenious arrangement may never have been intended as anything but a stepping-stone towards Eire's complete separation from the British Commonwealth, but it was nevertheless a remarkable anticipation of the further development of the British Empire into an association of free and independent nations—a process which, though far from complete, has made great strides with the establishment of the three Asiatic member states India, Pakistan and Ceylon. The importance of the Irish Question, both as a model and as a warning, for British Imperial policy in the East is a fascinating problem which cannot be pursued in this place but which has not escaped the attention of students of the British Empire. Ireland's history as a colonial subject country makes the Irish attitude towards the British connection much more similar to that of other colonial nations emerging from British rule than to that of the old dominions, Canada, Australia and New Zealand, with the Union of South Africa occupying an intermediary position. The old dominions tend to regard a representative monarchy, in which the King plays the part of a King of Canada, Australia or New Zealand, as the full expression of their distinct nationhood; as far as Ireland—and India—is concerned, monarchy is inseparable from subjection, the name of the King an unmistakable symbol of British rule and nationhood synonymous with a republic.

De Valera's solution of the problem of squaring the political circle by associating a republic with a group of states united in common allegiance to a monarch foreshadowed in all essentials the Commonwealth Declaration of 27th April 1949 which recognised the membership of an Indian Republic in the Commonwealth. India, like Ireland, did not want to owe allegiance to the British crown and wished to become a sovereign independent Republic. At the same time the Indian Government declared its readiness to accept the King 'as the Head of the Commonwealth and as the symbol of the free association' of its independent member nations which, on their part, accepted an Indian Republic as a full member of their Commonwealth.

Constitutional lawyers may well discover legal differences between this important declaration and the Irish External Relations Act; the underlying conception, however, is clearly the same in both cases. The crucial difference between the two documents is not one of law but of political purpose: India's decision expressed the desire to continue full membership of the Commonwealth, while the conception put forward by the Irish Government intended to weaken the existing links between Ireland and Great Britain. The future may reveal whether the final step of Eire's secession from the Commonwealth on which the Government of Mr. Costello decided in the autumn of 1948 contributed to the Commonwealth Declaration of 1949 by raising the problem of the future of the Commonwealth in a manner which made half-measures impossible, but speculation on this point is at present premature.

It is not a little paradoxical that the final severance of the last link between Eire and the British Commonwealth should have been the work of that Irish party which had always advocated closer relations with Great Britain. Future historians may well come to the conclusion that De Valera's sway over Irish politics was not so great when he appeared to have plenitude of power as when he had been driven from office by a coalition of all his political enemies. It is, therefore, only natural that De Valera did not in any way object to the policy of his successor, even though he refused to share in the celebration of the new Republic because he did not see any reason for rejoicing while partition continued.

If, as seems at least probable, the Irish Government could have chosen to combine the status of a sovereign republic with membership of the Commonwealth on the same terms as India, the practical obstacles to the reunion of North-East Ulster with the rest of the country would have still been formidable but infinitely smaller than they have become since Ireland's complete separation from the Commonwealth. If the Irish Government decided, nevertheless, to cut the last link between Eire and the Commonwealth, it must have known that in doing so it was renouncing the last slender chance of uniting the country by consent. It becomes still more difficult to understand official Irish policy in this matter, when it is remembered that in the Treaty negotiations of 1921 the Ulster Question played a crucial part in the relations between the parties and that it was the promise—or, perhaps, the bait—of essential unity which prevented the Irish delegates from breaking the negotiations on the only point on which they could have been broken off with safety for the 'Irish Republic'. The position is made still more enigmatic when it is considered that it was the leader of Michael Collins's political heirs and successors who made this decision at a time when Michael Collins's vision of the British Empire as a League of Free States was on the point of realisation, at least as far

as the self-governing members of the Commonwealth are concerned.

Although it is still too early to venture on a reasoned explanation
of these paradoxes, it seems highly probable that the effective cause
of the policy pursued by the Irish Government was the internal
political and economic position. However this may be, it is obvious
that this policy has made the problem of partition still more intractable than before. In addition, the immediate effects of Ireland's
separation from the Commonwealth are a curious, if negative,
confirmation of the view that Ireland's involuntary association
with Great Britain was one of the most potent agencies in the
democratisation of British public life.

The political development of north-east Ulster has been stunted
and retarded by decades as a result of the ever-present conflict
between unionists and nationalists. The only serious challenge to
the dominant political conceptions of the area, Larkin's and
Connolly's attempt to organise the working classes of Ulster on a
non-sectarian basis, ended in failure, and neither civil war nor
economic depression seriously weakened the hold of the Belfast
business community over the non-Catholic part of the population.
The dangers and the prosperity of the Second World War, on the
other hand, undoubtedly strengthened the existing links with Great
Britain and widened the gulf between Ulster and the rest of Ireland.
Far-sighted unionists as well as their opponents would probably
agree that the weakness of Ulster's independent labour movement
is an expression of political backwardness—quite irrespective of the
political complexion of the British Government of the day. Any
real change in the political leadership of the North of Ireland could
only come from this source and not from the permanent minority
of Nationalist Ulster Catholics. The political leaders of Ulster have
little to fear from this minority which is, on the contrary, of in-
estimable value to them because it prevents the only re-orientation
in Ulster political life which would be really dangerous to them—
an alliance between the Catholics and the Protestant workers against
the rule of a social minority. It is plain beyond the possibility of a
doubt that Eire's secession from the Commonwealth has made such
an alliance impossible for a long time to come and Labour's resounding defeat in the Ulster elections of February 1949 and the
General Election of February 1950 in Northern Ireland was almost
a foregone conclusion. No taunts against the 'political cowardice'
of a British Labour Government which acts as the protector of the
privileged minority in power at the Stormont can disguise the
crucial fact that reunion by consent is impossible between two
groups of people one of which does not accept membership of the

19

Commonwealth at any price while the other is determined to maintain it.

Partition is thus the most important practical relic of the Irish Question. Partition may be inevitable in certain cases—and Ireland itself is the best example of a country where partition is working reasonably well—but it is at the best an imperfect solution and may be at the worst little better than permanent civil war. Within the framework of competing nationalisms, however, partition has an inescapable logic. By gaining independence at the price of partition, nationalism is pushed to the extreme limits of practical application, where it meets a nationalism of similar intensity and opposite direction. This is a dilemma which cannot be solved by the democratic principle of majority decision, which is valid only within the same community. If it is applied to a group which resolutely refuses to regard itself as part of the community, majority decision becomes sheer tyranny. It is exactly this situation which partition intends to recognise, for the very fact of partition expresses the refusal of one part to accept community with the other.

Is partition then a dead end beyond which no advance is possible? From the nationalist point of view this is undoubtedly the case. In order to overcome partition, the stronger 'part' must either resort to force and thereby violate the faith by which it lives, or offer to the minority terms which would make union more acceptable than independence. Thus nationalism, like patriotism, is not enough. It is a powerful motive force for subject peoples, because it is the ideal form of expression for a host of other grievances as well, but it is not an end in itself. The peculiar importance of partition (where it does not simply re-establish a temporarily obscured state of separation) lies in the fact that it is a permanent memento of the limitations of nationalism and a challenge for its transfiguration into a higher principle of social action.

The Irish Republic still accuses Great Britain of having perpetrated partition against the will of the Irish people. As far as the nationalist majority is concerned, this is correct, and it is in any case impossible to justify the present frontiers of Northern Ireland. But the idea that Great Britain could undo partition against the wishes of the majority in Ulster, and that it is possible to create a united Ireland on such a basis, is itself a curious relic of colonial times not befitting the spokesmen of a free people. As long as the tenets and shibboleths of the colonial era continue to dominate Irish thought and politics on both sides of the border, while new interests are established whose tenacity is equalled only by their parochialism, the chances of Irish reunion must remain remote. These attitudes are nourished by solid interests and deeply rooted in history, and it may be too much to expect any radical change in the near future, but for a nation which has survived centuries of oppression without ever abandoning the life-giving dream of a better future, aims are not less worth striving for because they are difficult of attainment.

NOTES

BOOK I

ENGLAND'S FIRST COLONY

1 Quoted by Moody, 'The New Departure in Irish Politics, 1878–9' (*Essays in British and Irish History in Honour of James Eadie Todd* (1949), p. 315).
2 Spedding, *Letters and Life of Francis Bacon*, IV, 123.
3 Petty, 'Political Arithmetick' (*Economic Writings* (1899), I, 300).
4 Froude, *The English in Ireland in the Eighteenth Century* (1884 ed.), I, 75.
5 Corkery, *The Hidden Ireland* (2nd ed. 1925), p. 23.
6 *Political Anatomy of Ireland*, l.c., I, 187.
7 *A Treatise of Ireland*, l.c., II, 558.
8 Swift, 'Drapier's Letters' (*Works*, (1907), VI, 188).
9 *A Treatise of Ireland*, II, 615.
10 Young, *Tour in Ireland* (1892 ed.), I, 344.
11 *A Treatise of Ireland*, II, 555.
12 Ibid., p. 562.
13 Ibid., p. 577.
14 Ibid., p. 578.
15 Corkery, op. cit., p. 57
16 *Political Anatomy of Ireland*, l.c., I, 164.
17 Hyde, *The Rise of Castlereagh* (1933), p. 380.
18 D. Gwynn, *The Struggle for Catholic Emancipation* (1928), p. 22.
19 Bacon, l.c., IV, 120.
20 Moody, *The Londonderry Plantation, 1609–41* (1939), p. 333.
21 Falls, *The Birth of Ulster* (1936), p. 175.
22 Moody, *Londonderry Plantation*, p. 330
23 *A Treatise of Ireland*, l.c., II, 595–6.
24 Ibid., 577–8.
25 Lecky, *History of England in the Eighteenth Century*, VII, 190 sq.
26 Burke, *Works* (1886 ed.), VI, 58. ('A Second Letter to Sir Hercules Langrishe.')
27 *Drapier's Letters*, l.c., VI, 192.
28 Lecky, op. cit., VI, 373.
29 Murray, *History of Commercial and Financial Relations between England and Ireland* (1903), 171 sq.
30 O'Brien, *Economic History of Ireland in the Eighteenth Century* (1918), p. 316.
31 *Life* (1819), I, 204.
32 Wedgwood, *Strafford* (1935), p. 125.
33 Quoted by Stopford Green, *The Making of Ireland and Its Undoing* (1920 ed.), p. 70.
34 Froude, op. cit., II, 45.
35 Ibid., II, 532.
36 Lecky, op. cit., VII, 47.
37 Parker, *Sir Robert Peel* (2nd ed., 1899), I, 282.
38 Murray, op. cit., p. 181.
39 *Wealth of Nations*, Book IV, ch. 7, p. 2.
40 £1,035,266 in 1781 (O'Brien, op. cit., p. 331).
41 McDowell, *Irish Public Opinion, 1750–1800* (1944), p. 51.
42 Parker, op. cit., I, 176.
43 Hyde, op. cit., p. 214.
44 Wedgwood, op. cit., p. 132.
45 Lecky, op. cit., VII, 430.
46 Froude, op. cit., II, 99.
47 *Speeches* (1822), III, 184 (April, 1795).
48 O'Brien, op. cit., pp. 59 sqq.
49 *Wealth of Nations*, Book IV, ch. 7, p. 2.

50 O'Brien, op. cit., p. 179.
51 Murray, op. cit., pp. 129 sq.
52 Young, op. cit., II, 198 sqq.
53 Quoted by Froude, op. cit., I, 499 (Hely Hutchinson to Lord Harcourt).
54 Rose, *William Pitt and National Revival* (1911), p. 258.
55 Maxwell, *Dublin under the Georges, 1714–1830* (1936), p. 274.
56 E.g. Murray, op. cit., pp. 265 sq.
57 McDowell, op. cit., p. 138.
58 *Castlereagh Correspondence* (1848), I, 361.
59 Ibid., I, 357.
60 Lecky, op. cit., VII, 381.
61 Hayes, *Ireland and Irishmen in the French Revolution* (1932), pp. 61, 206 sq.
62 Lecky, op. cit., VIII, 117.
63 Quoted in *Edinburgh Review*, October, 1834, p. 228.
64 Lecky, op. cit., VI, 323.
65 Ibid., VI, 429.
66 Cf. Dean Tucker's *Reflections on the Present Matters in Dispute between Great Britain and Ireland* (1785).
67 S. Gwynn, *Henry Grattan and His Times* (1939), p. 204.
68 Rose, *William Pitt and the Great War* (1911), p. 389.
69 Lecky, op. cit., VI, 513.
70 *The Creevey Papers* (3rd ed. 1933), p. 521.
71 D. Gwynn, *Struggle for Catholic Emancipation*, p. 145.

BOOK II

THE 'UNITED' KINGDOM, 1801–1846

1 *Castlereagh Correspondence*, III, 252.
2 *Edinburgh Review*, June, 1822, p. 98.
3 Redford, *Labour Migration in England, 1800–1850* (1926), p. 33.
4 *British Parliamentary Papers* (=*B.P.P.*), 1840, XXIII, 773.
5 O'Brien, *Economic History of Ireland from the Union to the Famine* (1921), pp. 302 sqq.
6 O'Connell, *Life* (1846), I, 48.
7 Sel. Comm. on the State of Ireland (Lords), *B.P.P.* 1825, IX, 34–37; Sel. Comm. on Handloom Weavers, *B.P.P.* 1835, XIII, qus. 1251, 1493, etc.; Report on Linen and Cotton Manufacture in Ireland, *B.P.P.* 1840, XXIII, 777 sq.
8 *B.P.P.* 1840, XXIII, 714, 716.
9 *B.P.P.* 1835, XIII, qu. 1206 sqq.
10 *Tour*, II, 294.
11 Pomfret, *The Struggle for Land in Ireland, 1800–1923* (1930), p. 56.
12 *Tour*, I, 402.
13 April, 1809, p. 168.
14 Sel. Comm. on the Corn Trade of the U.K., *B.P.P.* 1812–13, III, 27.
15 Tooke and Newmarch, *A History of Prices* (1928 ed.), II, 2.
16 Connell, *Population of Ireland, 1750–1845* (1950), ch. 4.
17 *B.P.P.* 1825, IX, 59.
18 Sel. Comm. on the State of Ireland, *B.P.P.* 1831–2, XVI, qu. 6736.
19 Pomfret, op. cit., p. 15.
20 Sir Herbert Maxwell, *Life* (1900), II, 241.
21 *B.P.P.* 1831–2, XVI, qu. 6655.
22 Third Rep. on Emigration from the U.K. (1827), quoted in *Edinburgh Review*, Jan., 1828, p. 236.
23 Sel. Comm. on Irish Vagrants, *B.P.P.* 1833, XVI, 31.
24 *B.P.P.* 1825, VIII, 691.
25 Redford, op. cit., p. 137.
26 Ibid., p. 126.
27 O'Brien, op. cit., p. 217.
28 *The Croker Papers* (1884), III, 41.

29 O'Connell, op. cit., II, 361.
30 Fay, *The Corn Laws and Social England* (1932), p. 211.
31 *Croker Papers*, III, 142.
32 Ibid.
33 Walpole, *Life of Lord John Russell* (1889 ed.), I, 445.
34 Greville, *Memoirs*, 3rd May, 1848 (VI, 175).
35 Ibid., 8th February, 1849 (VI, 274).
36 Walpole, op. cit., I, 437.
37 Parker, *Peel*, I, 257.
38 *B.P.P.* 1825, VIII, 210.
39 O'Connell, op. cit., II, 395.
40 Ibid., II, 407.
41 *B.P.P.*, 1831–2, XVI, qu. 2656.
42 Pomfret, op. cit., p. 15.
43 Maccoby, *English Radicalism, 1832–1852* (1935), p. 61.
44 *B.P.P.* 1825, VIII, 81.
45 *Edinburgh Review*, July, 1825, pp. 228–33.
46 *Memoirs* (1858), I, 105, 117.
47 *Croker Papers*, II, 8.
48 *Memoirs*, I, 5.
49 Torrens, *Memoirs of Lord Melbourne* (1890 ed.), p. 234.
50 *Croker Papers*, II, 201.
51 *Mr. Gregory's Letter Box*, edited by Lady Gregory (1898), p. 267.
52 Torrens, op. cit., pp. 263 sq.
53 *B.P.P.* 1831–2, XVI, qu. 1819.
54 In a letter to the Dublin Repealers, 27th October, 1843. (*The Economist*, 4th November, 1843.)
55 O'Brien, op. cit., p. 217.
56 Repeal Meeting, 21st April, 1845.
57 Repeal Meeting, 9th September, 1844.
58 Nassau Senior, *Journals, Conversations and Essays relating to Ireland* (1868), I, 227.
59 *Life of Lord John Russell*, I, 460.
60 H. W. C. Davis, *The Age of Grey and Peel* (1929), p. 215.
61 Aspinall, *Lord Brougham and the Whig Party* (1939), p. 136.
62 March, 1829, p. 219.
63 Butler, *The Passing of the Great Reform Bill* (1914), p. 59.
64 Ibid., p. 211, quoting *Life of Eldon*, IV, 126.
65 Ibid., p. 208.
66 Dod, *Electoral Facts, 1832–1853* (1853), XII.
67 Ibid., p. 156.
68 Maccoby, op. cit., p. 136.
69 *Memoirs*, II, 93.
70 H. W. C. Davis, op. cit., p. 296.
71 *Croker Papers*, III, 47.
72 Peel, *Memoirs*, II, 199.
73 *Croker Papers*, III, 63.
74 *Memoirs*, II, 293.
75 *Edinburgh Review*, July, 1825, p. 228.
76 Lewis, *State of the Irish Poor in Great Britain*, in *B.P.P.* 1836, XXXIV, p. xxx.
77 *B.P.P.* 1833, XVI, 26.
78 Parker, op. cit., II, 117.
79 December, 1826, p. 54.
80 April, 1834, p. 248.
81 *B.P.P.* 1836, XXXIV, pp. xxxvi sq.
82 Ibid., pp. 21, 64.
83 Ibid., p. 28.
84 Ibid., p. 51.
85 Engels, *The condition of the working class in England in 1844* (1936 ed.), p. 90.
86 *B.P.P.* 1836, XXXIV, 84.
87 J. L. and B. Hammond, *The Town Labourer, 1760–1832* (1932 ed.), p. 266.
88 *B.P.P.* 1836, XXXIV, 68.

89 Report on Handloom Weavers, *B.P.P.* 1839, XLII, 55, *B.P.P.* 1840, XXIII, pp. 775 sqq.
90 Welbourne, *The Miners' Union of Northumberland and Durham* (1923), 81.
91 *B.P.P.* 1839, XLII, 19.
92 *B.P.P.* 1836, XXXIV, 62.
93 Sel. Comm. on Combinations of Workmen, *B.P.P.* 1837–8, VIII, qu. 3369.
94 Ibid., qu. 3446.
95 *B.P.P.* 1836, XXXIV, 71.
96 Ibid., p. 108.
97 *B.P.P.* 1837–8, VIII, qu. 2815.
98 Engels, op. cit., p. 124.
99 Hovell and Tout, *The Chartist Movement* (1925 ed.), p. 98.
100 Bronterre O'Brien, *The Rise, Progress and Phases of Human Slavery* (1885 ed.), p. 102.
101 Feargus O'Connor, *A Practical Work on the Management of Small Farms* (7th ed., 1847), p. 51.
102 Ibid., pp. 99 sqq.

BOOK III

REVOLT AND REFORM

1 Marx-Engels, *Briefwechsel* (1930 ed.), III, 457.
2 *Memoirs*, II, Appendix, p. 334.
3 Mulhall, *Dictionary of Statistics* (1909 ed.), p. 13.
4 Ibid., p. 17.
5 *Bessborough Commission*, *B.P.P.* 1881, XVIII, qu. 1627. Sel. Comm. on Tenure (Ireland) Bill, *B.P.P.* 1867, XIV, 219.
6 Lewis in *B.P.P.* 1837, LI, 14.
7 *Greville Memoirs*, 6th April, 1849 (VI, 293–4).
8 Mulhall, op. cit., p. 342.
9 Ibid., p. 341.
10 Pomfret, op. cit., p. 42.
11 Nassau Senior, op. cit., II, 41.
12 Ibid., II, 12.
13 *Briefwechsel*, IV, 228.
14 W. S. Blunt, *The Land War in Ireland* (1912), p. 61.
15 Mulhall, op. cit., p. 427.
16 O'Connor, *The Parnell Movement* (1886), p. 173.
17 Devoy, *Recollections of an Irish Rebel* (1929), p. 17.
18 *Recollections of Fenians and Fenianism* (1896), II, 238.
19 *Bessborough Commission*, *B.P.P.* 1881, XVIII, qus. 4336–54.
20 O'Leary, op. cit., II, 142.
21 Ibid., I, 31.
22 Gavan Duffy, *The League of North and South* (1886), p. 339.
23 O'Leary, op. cit., II, 147.
24 *Briefwechsel*, III, 449.
25 O'Donnell, *A History of the Irish Parliamentary Party* (1910), I, 317.
26 Leslie, *Henry Edward Manning* (1921), p. 197.
27 Ibid., p. 205.
28 Morley, *Life of Gladstone* (1905 ed.), I, 929.
29 *Briefwechsel*, IV, 282.
30 Sir William Gregory, *Autobiography* (1894), p. 244.
31 Morley, op. cit., I, 930.
32 Butt, *Irish Federalism* (1874 ed.), p. 39.
33 Ibid., p. 56.
34 *Briefwechsel*, IV, 251.
35 Leslie, op. cit., p. 207.
36 R. B. O'Brien, *Life of Parnell* (1910 ed.), p. 142.
37 Reid, *Life of W. E. Forster* (1888), I, 237.
38 Davitt, *The Fall of Feudalism in Ireland* (1904), p. 301.
39 O'Shea (Mrs. C. S. Parnell), *Charles Stuart Parnell* (1914), I, 235–6.

40 O'Brien, *Life of Parnell*, p. 278.
41 Davitt, op. cit., pp. 309–10.
42 Quoted by Hammond, *Gladstone and the Irish Nation* (1938), p. 51.
43 Morley, op. cit., i, 808.
44 O'Connor, op. cit., 353.
45 Guedalla, *The Queen and Mr. Gladstone* (1923), ii, 177.
46 Reid, op. cit., ii, 286.
47 O'Brien, op. cit., p. 234.
48 O'Shea, op. cit., i, 207.
49 Lord Morley, *Recollections* (1917), i, 329–30.
50 Reid, op. cit., ii, 413.
51 O'Brien, *Life of Parnell*, p. 316.
52 Thorold, *Life of Labouchère* (1913), p. 169.
53 *The Economist*, 22nd May, 1886.
54 Mulhall, op. cit., 17, Fin. Rel. Comm., 1st Report, *B.P.P.* 1895, xxxvi, 453.
55 Lord Newton, *Life* (1929), p. 47.
56 Marx, *Capital* (1928 ed.), p. 778.
57 *The Economist*, 28th October, 1843.
58 J. L. Garvin, *Life* (1932), i, p. 345.
59 O'Brien, *Life of Parnell*, p. 331.
60 *The Times*, 22nd August, 1885.
61 Ibid., 24th August, 1885.
62 *The Economist*, 29th August, 1885.
63 *Life*, ii, 64.
64 Churchill, *Life of Lord Randolph Churchill* (1907 ed.), pp. 483–4.
65 Davitt, op. cit., p. 478.
66 Morley, *Life of Gladstone*, i, 767.
67 *Recollections*, i, 192.
68 *Memoirs*, ii, 290–1.
69 O'Brien, *Life of Parnell*, p. 98.
70 D. Gwynn, *The Life of John Redmond* (1932), p. 30.
71 O'Donnell, op. cit., i, 187.
72 *Briefwechsel*, iv, 258.
73 Davitt, op. cit., p. 308.
74 Lord Morley, *Recollections*, i, 296.
75 Leslie, op. cit., p. 371.

BOOK IV

COMPROMISE OR REVOLUTION?

1 *Report of the Primrose Committee*, *B.P.P.* 1912–13 (Cd. 6153), xxxiv, 18–19.
2 Pomfret, op. cit., p. 265.
3 Ibid., p. 307.
4 *Agricultural Statistics (Ireland)*, 1917, p. xiv.
5 Ibid., p. 15.
6 Blunt, *My Diaries, 1888–1914* (1932), p. 710.
7 Evidence before the Primrose Committee, *B.P.P.* 1913, xxx, qu. 1178.
8 *Report of the Primrose Committee*, l.c., 5.
9 Ibid., p. 7.
10 Ibid., p. 16.
11 Financial Relations Commission, 1st Report, *B.P.P.* 1895, xxxvi, 455–6.
12 Pomfret, op. cit., p. 201.
13 Leslie, op. cit., p. 403.
14 Ibid., p. 415.
15 Ibid., p. 441.
16 Ibid., p. 437.
17 Lord Esher, *Journals and Letters* (1934), i, 146.
18 Sir James O'Connor, *History of Ireland, 1798–1924* (1925), ii, 219.
19 M. J. F. McCarthy, *Five Years in Ireland, 1895–1900* (1903 ed.), p. 285.
20 Churchill, op. cit., p. 428.

21 Lord Morley, *Recollections*, I, 255.
22 Mackail and Wyndham, *Life and Letters of George Wyndham*, p. 409.
23 Sheehan, *Ireland since Parnell* (1921), p. 88.
24 Lord Morley, *Recollections*, I, 255.
25 Reprinted in Macardle, *The Irish Republic* (1937), p. 951.
26 Béaslaí, *Michael Collins and the Making of a New Ireland* (1926), I, p. 28.
27 Macardle, op. cit., p. 108.
28 Béaslaí, op. cit., I, 37.
29 Fox, *James Connolly, The Forerunner* (1946), pp. 76–7.
30 Clarkson, *Labour and Nationalism in Ireland* (1925), p. 188.
31 Ibid., p. 192.
32 Ibid., p. 219; *Sir James Sexton, Agitator* (An Autobiography) (1936), pp. 201 sqq.
33 Clarkson, op. cit., p. 231.
34 Ibid., p. 324.
35 Marjoribanks, *Life of Lord Carson* (1932), I, 263.
36 Colvin, *Life of Lord Carson* (1934), II, 282.
37 Ibid., II, 104.
38 Clarkson, op. cit., p. 348.
39 M. J. F. McCarthy, *The Irish Revolution* (1912), I, 482.
40 Crozier, *Ireland for Ever* (1932), p. 37.
41 Spender and Asquith, *Life of Asquith* (1932), II, 216.
42 Taylor, *The Strange Case of Bonar Law*, p. 184.
43 Guedalla, op. cit., II, 451.
44 Ibid., II, 447.
45 *Life of Redmond*, p. 167.
46 Ibid., p. 173.
47 *Life of Asquith*, I, 274.
48 Chamberlain, *Politics from Inside* (1936), pp. 201–17.
49 Ensor, *England 1870–1914* (1936), p. 454.
50 White, *Misfit* (1930), p. 335.
51 *Life of Redmond*, p. 368.
52 Fyfe, *T. P. O'Connor* (134), p. 242.
53 Hardinge Commission on the Irish Rebellion (Cd. 8279 and 8311), *B.P.P.*
    1916, XI, 111.
54 W. P. Ryan, *The Irish Labour Movement* (1919), p. 240.
55 Ibid., p. 242.
56 Proceedings of the Irish Convention (Cd. 9019), *B.P.P.* 1918, X, 32.
57 Figgis, *Recollections of the Irish War* (1927), p. 107.
58 Béaslaí, *Michael Collins, Soldier and Statesman* (1937), p. 25.
59 Ibid., p. 40.
60 Macardle, op. cit., p. 208.
61 O'Hegarty, *The Victory of Sinn Fein* (1924), p. 29.
62 W. O'Brien, *The Irish Revolution*, etc. (1923), p. 430.
63 D. Ryan, *Sean Treacey and the 3rd Tipperary Brigade*, p. 56.
64 Figgis, op. cit., p. 259.
65 Ibid., p. 294.
66 Pakenham, *Peace by Ordeal* (1935).
67 Ibid., pp. 274–7.
68 Lord Birkenhead, *Frederick Edwin, Earl of Birkenhead, The Last Phase* (1935),
    p. 239.
69 Churchill, *The World Crisis: The Aftermath* (1929), p. 292.
70 Pakenham, op. cit., p. 296.
71 Béaslaí, *Michael Collins, Soldier and Statesman*, p. 322.
72 Churchill, op. cit., p. 314.
73 Ibid., p. 326.
74 Ibid., p. 342.
75 Cobbett, '13th Letter to the Electors of Westminster' (*Political Register*, April,
    1807).
76 Béaslaí, *Michael Collins and The Making of a New Ireland*, II, 170.

INDEX